D1095743

TWENTY-FIVE
SHORT PLAYS
(INTERNATIONAL)

TWENTY-FIVE SHORT PLAYS

❧ INTERNATIONAL ❧

SELECTED AND EDITED BY

FRANK SHAY

D. APPLETON AND COMPANY
NEW YORK ❧ LONDON ❧ MCMXXV

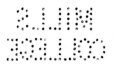

TO
SUSAN GLASPELL

CONTENTS

THE ACCOMPLICE

A Play

By Abigail Marshall

CHARACTERS

Body, *Jay Bragdon*
Brain
Soul
Thomas Brent, *a detective*
A Police Officer
A Bellboy

THE ACCOMPLICE

The scene is a well-furnished bedroom in a large hotel. The bed is set head against the wall, foot reaching almost to center. There is a door leading to a corridor, beside which in back wall is an electric switch. Another door leads to bathroom. There is a table on which are a lamp, writing materials, and a telephone. A coat tree with a lounging coat hanging on it. Chairs each side of table. A window in wall through which streams a white light. This light is focused on SOUL *and follows her all through the play, growing stronger as she speaks and paler when she is prostrated, but never entirely off her. When curtain rises,* SOUL *is seen up right a little above bed. She is fair, ethereal, with quantities of pale hair, and dressed in white flowing robes. She is huddled in dejected attitude, her two arms forward, her head bent, her hair streaming over it, hiding her face. At the same time a key is heard turning and door from corridor opens. From light in corridor* BODY *is seen, with* BRAIN *beside him. He enters and turns on electric switch which lights lamp on table and other light, a long bulb that swings down from ceiling, and which has cord knotted to keep it out of the way.* BODY *is dressed in evening dress, with opera hat and overcoat.* BRAIN, *a tall, commanding, handsome brunette, wears long scarlet flowing garment.* BODY *has a letter in his hand, which he keeps hold of, after taking coat and hat off and hanging them on tree.*

BODY. Brain, Brain, my beloved, my adored!
(*She lets him embrace her.*)
BRAIN. You do care for me—I am your only love?
BODY. I worship you—you are so wonderful, so exquisite, so magnificently formed.
BRAIN (*with arrogance*). I cannot pretend to be unconscious of my worth; I am all you say. But enough, you must read your letter now.
(BODY *sits at right of table and opens letter.* SOUL *half rises and leans toward him.*)
BODY. Come close to me, beloved one, come closer.
(BRAIN *comes to left of table and watches* SOUL, *who rises and comes to* BODY. BODY *passes hand over head as though faint.*)
SOUL. Body—Body—
(BODY *frowns and tries to concentrate attention on letter.*)
BRAIN (*scoffing*). He does not hear you—you do not exist for him.
SOUL. Once he was mine, once he loved me, once he belonged solely to me.

3

BRAIN. That was before he learned to know my worth.

SOUL. Before you grew into a scarlet force.

BRAIN. A force that you must admit has conquered.

SOUL. I do not give up hope.

BRAIN. He loves me—he will never open his house to you again—I am the idol enshrined there.

SOUL. Worthless idols that have held higher places than you now occupy have been shattered and forgotten.

BRAIN. That fate cannot be mine. I am too strong.

SOUL. Yes, you are strong. Together you and I could have worked wonders with this man. But you were envious of my power—

BRAIN (*proudly*). I would reign alone. My power is all-sufficient. I can work wonders without your aid.

BODY (*who has been passing his hand over his eyes and vainly trying to decipher letter*). Brain, Brain, where are you?

BRAIN. Here, beloved Body—here.

BODY. I have been staring at this letter for an hour and cannot decipher a word of it.

BRAIN (*sitting left of table and leaning toward him*). Try again, dear, read.

(BODY *braces up and* SOUL *shrinks back, weakly subsiding until she has resumed her former position.* BODY *glances at letter and rises suddenly.*)

BODY. My God!

BRAIN. What is it?

BODY. It—it's from her.

BRAIN. Well—well—she loves you still, doesn't she?

BODY. Yes, but—but—

BRAIN. Come, come, control this foolish fear and tell me plainly what it is disturbs you. Sit down.

(*She rises and gazes sternly at him.*)

BODY. That name—that name—(*whispering fearfully*) I thought I saw the name of that man.

BRAIN. You are always full of fancies—look again.

BODY (*afraid to look at letter*). What if she—if she has met him?

BRAIN. She loves you, she believes in you—obey me—listen to my counsel and she and her money will be yours within a year.

BODY (*weakly but fiercely turning on* BRAIN). They could be mine right now if you had let me marry her before.

BRAIN. You were not fit to marry her before. You'd have lost everything if I had not preached caution. Why, even now you are full of fear.

BODY. No—not fear—not fear.

BRAIN. What else is it? You are trembling.

(SOUL *half rises, leans forward, and puts a pleading hand on his arm.*)

BODY. I don't seem able to help it.

BRAIN. Throw off that hand of fear that is clutching you now and listen to me.

(BODY *totters into chair*, SOUL *rises, comes nearer, places hand on his shoulder.* BODY *takes dope needle from pocket.*)

BODY. I will—I will—this will calm me.

BRAIN. No, not that! You must do without that instrument, that thing chokes, stifles, paralyzes me! Put it away; put it away at once and promise me never to use it again.

BODY. I haven't strength enough, beloved Brain—just this once—just once more.

BRAIN. No—you have used that more than once too often already.

(SOUL *has put one arm about his shoulder and now is clinging to him.*)

BRAIN (*to* SOUL). You won't get him, you won't get him, you won't get him!

BODY. Don't babble so, Brain, you confuse me.

(SOUL'*s arm curls closer round his neck.*)

BRAIN. Throw away that thing and fling off that hand of fear that is trying now to choke you.

SOUL (*whispering to him*). It is your soul, dearest, not gross fear.

BODY (*to* BRAIN, *always unconscious of* SOUL). I will—I will be strong.

(*Puts instrument in pocket, and with vicious strength throws* SOUL *from him. She staggers and falls in heap at foot of bed.*)

BRAIN. My brave one—my master again.

BODY (*kneeling, passionately imploring, at* BRAIN'*s feet*). Teach me, great wonderful power that you are—counsel me now in this great crisis.

BRAIN (*softening*). You must be calm—otherwise I cannot guide you. (*She helps him rise and places him in chair; he controls himself.*) That is better. Now, relate what I have done for you in the past.

BODY. Is that necessary?

BRAIN. Yes, it will make a firm foundation for you to build your faith upon, your faith in my perpetual, increasing power.

BODY. My faith in you, dear one, can never waver.

BRAIN. It is wavering now.

BODY. No—no; it is more fixed than the stars.

BRAIN. I know better. Do as I bid.

BODY. As you wish. It was by your aid I hid all trace of my crime. It was at your bidding I loved with my hands, my tongue, but kept my heart aloof. By your aid I appeared to adore while I destroyed her to whom I was apparently devoting my life. You alone hold the record of my every step in crime. No scrap of paper exists that can incriminate me. The poison itself was not more subtle than I, thanks to your counsel. No living soul did I take into my confidence, except my own, and she lies dead—(SOUL *moans.*) But does she lie dead, beloved Brain?

BRAIN. So near dead you need never fear her interference. Rely upon me solely if you would succeed again where already you have been so successful.

BODY. But have I—but have I—this letter—?

BRAIN. Ah, yes, the letter. Read the letter through and I'll dispose of that bugaboo also, whatever it may be. (*Telephone rings*, BODY *looks up questioningly*.) Answer it.

BODY (*into 'phone*). Yes?—Yes, this is Mr. Jay Bragdon.—Who?—Oh, how do you do?—Yes, certainly I remember you, Mr. Christie.—Another game of golf?—Why, I've never played a game of golf with you.—No, sir, I'm not joking.—I was beaten?—I could neither have lost nor won as I never even played.—You must be mistaken.—Wait a minute—wait. (*Hangs up*.) He's rung off. Brain—Brain—did I play golf three days ago with Mr. Christie?

BRAIN (*who has risen, very perturbed, walking about, clasping head*). I can't remember—I can't remember.

BODY. You must remember—you must remember—think—think!

BRAIN. I cannot think. (*Suddenly becomes bold.*) This is of no consequence. What does it matter that you played a trivial game and have no recollection of the fact?

BODY. Do not fail me, Brain, you must not fail me!

BRAIN (*scornfully*). You have no faith! Have I failed in any vital matter? I only occupy myself with things of some concern.

BODY (*partly reassured*). Of course, beloved Brain, of course.

BRAIN. A forgotten game of golf is too absurd for you to stir up fears and worry me about.

BODY. I'm sorry—I'm truly penitent, beloved Brain.

BRAIN. I don't want you to be anything but strong; as long as you are healthy I can work. Read that letter and voice those fears that still, I see, possess you.

BODY. No—it is not fear—it's curiosity. If 'tis his name that's written there, why—why—

BRAIN (*angrily*). Who is this man whose power you seem to rank above my own?

BODY. You know who he is—the greatest detective in the country.

BRAIN. What if he is? Haven't we rejoiced together because we have outwitted him? Outwitted him without his even knowing it! Thomas Brent, the hunter of criminals, who doesn't even know that a crime, now six months old, was committed.

BODY. Don't talk so openly about it, I beg of you; it makes me shiver.

BRAIN. Shiver? Is that how you welcome your triumph? Poor weak Body! And I was proud to have you for my devotee, and was ready in return to worship you. I called you master!

BODY. Don't flay me with your scorn, beloved: you are all I have in the world to love.

BRAIN. You have money, friends, the sister of a dead wife worshiping you—

BODY. All of which I owe to you.

BRAIN. The respect of the world you adorn. They call you Jay Bragdon, the devoted husband. Your constant attendance upon your wife is still the theme of society gossip—the admiration of that circle knows no bounds. You could go among them and take your choice of wealthy spinsters if you had not been so foolish as to choose already the sister of your dead wife.

BODY. It was partly a sentiment I could not control.

BRAIN (*searchingly*). But you have it now eliminated?

BODY. Yes. Didn't I tell you my heart was atrophied? She is nothing to me now but a money bag.

BRAIN. Good. You could, if necessary, choose elsewhere then?

BODY. Yes, but would it be wise?

BRAIN. Why not?

BODY. If anything should happen to come to light, she would be silent for her own sake if she were my wife.

BRAIN. It is impossible that anything should become known. I have left not the slightest loophole for a piece of evidence, however slight, to leak through.

BODY. I am sure of that.

BRAIN. But have your way, marry the sister.

BODY (*mechanically taking cocaine needle out again and filling it*). Yes, yes; I want to marry her soon.

BRAIN. Not until you have thrown that in the fire though.

BODY (*looking blankly at instrument*). This—this? I—I didn't know I had it in my hand.

BRAIN (*alarmed*). That won't do—that won't do—throw it away, now—now!

BODY. No, not now—not now—I will—I will throw it away—but not just yet—not now. (*Puts it away.*) We are forgetting the letter.

BRAIN. I forget nothing. Read on. (*Rises and walks about, perturbed.*)

BODY (*with difficulty, trying to read*). "Dear, dearest Jay"—I can't seem to read it, it's all blurred. (*Looking up.*) Don't walk about like that—come here to me—no wonder I can't make it out. (BRAIN *comes to table and stands,* BODY *starts up.*) My God!

BRAIN (*commandingly*). Stop that! What does she say?

BODY. It is his name, the hateful name of Thomas Brent is written there.

BRAIN. What else?

BODY. I don't know—I don't know. Thomas Brent—Thomas Brent—why should his name be in her letter?

BRAIN. Let us lay this ghost at once. Thomas Brent is only a man, with a body like you and a brain not to be compared to me. Let us laugh at Thomas Brent—laugh, I command you. (BODY *tries to laugh, fails, falls weakly into a chair—*SOUL *creeps toward him on her knees, but* BRAIN *dashes across and stands between them, commandingly over* BODY.) Laugh! Laugh at the name of Thomas Brent, the detective we have outwitted. Rise, beloved Body, and be strong—(BODY *staggers to his feet, recovers strength, and* SOUL *shrinks back.*) Laugh! Now laugh! (BODY *laughs, deliriously at first, then more heartily.*) Good, good. Now read the letter slowly through, and be calm.

Body. "Dearest Jay—I am forbidden to tell you something I think you ought to know"—(*Stops, trying to decipher letter.*)

Brain. What is it—what is it?

Body. That half-page is blurred, as though tears had been shed upon it.

Brain. Beware, don't tread upon the thin ice of sentiment again.

Body. 'Tis not my tread, but hers—her sister's name is here.

Brain. But why has Thomas Brent's name been mentioned?

Body (*reading*). "Thomas Brent has been to see her." Been to see her—why?

Brain. Read on—read on.

Body (*reading*). "In response to an anonymous letter received by him, evidently written by the same mysterious party that sent me that telegram two weeks ago, for 'twas signed the same—Accomplice."

Brain. Well?

Body. Who wrote that anonymous letter, Brain? Who calls himself Accomplice?

Brain. Some crazy fool—the world is full of them. Didn't you tell her to burn that telegram and not act on its instructions to call on Thomas Brent?

Body. I did, and she obeyed me. But he—he has called on her. Who could have written that anonymous letter and sent that telegram? Who is Accomplice?

Brain. No—one—you have no accomplice.

(*Knock heard on corridor door.*)

Body. What's that?

Brain. Don't start and shiver at every sound. Change your coat and open the door.

Body (*pulling himself together, quickly gets into lounging coat,* Brain *helping him*). Who is it?

Boy (*without*). Mr. Bragdon?

Body (*opening door as* Brain *pushes him toward it*). What do you want?

Boy (*entering*). Please, sir, Mr. Christie says will you return his fountain pen?

Body. His pen? I haven't got his pen.

Boy. He says to please forgive him for disturbing you so late, but he's been called away and is leaving on the midnight train.

Body. But I haven't got his pen—the man's crazy.

Boy. He said you borrowed it a week ago yesterday, sir.

Body. A week ago—a week ago?

Boy. Yes, you wrote two letters with it in his room, he says, but you went out to look up one of the addresses, and you took his pen away with you.

Body. What did I do a week ago yesterday?

(*Turns to* Brain; *she walks up and down distractedly, head in hands. Boy doesn't see* Brain *or* Soul, *but steps down to table.*)

Brain. I cannot think—I can't remember.

Body. You must remember. What did I do a week ago yesterday?

Boy. The taxi is waiting for Mr. Christie, sir; he hasn't much time.

Body. I don't remember writing two letters last week.

Boy (*picking pen from table*). Why, here it is, sir.

Body. What?

Boy. Yes, sir—see, his initials are on it like he said—F. C.—Frederick Christie. Isn't this it?

Body. Yes, yes—of course—I'd forgotten—please give Mr. Christie my apologies for not returning it before—tell him I've been suffering from a severe nervous headache, and I've been forgetting everything—

Boy. Yes, sir.

Body (*tipping him*). And thank him.

Boy. Yes, sir, he was terribly sorry to have to disturb you—

Body. That's all right—that's all right—(*Hustles boy off and turns to* Brain.) Another! What do you make of that? Another lapse! Brain, Brain, for God's sake don't desert me.

Brain. Don't be a fool. You exaggerate trifles into tragedies. Sit down. Compose yourself. We have the future to think of, new plans, maybe, to make. Go on with that letter.

Body. Yes—yes—but—but—yes—I will—But what did I write two letters for last week, and to whom?

Brain. I remember that quite well; you wrote to your tailor, whose address you had forgotten, and to her.

Body (*with relief*). Yes, yes—that must have been it.

Brain. Of course that was it. Go on now with the letter.

(Body *is trembling so he can't pick up the letter—he takes needle from pocket.*)

Body. I must—I must—the strain is too great.

Brain. Nonsense—rubbish—there is no strain. Put that away—put it away, I command you! (Body *cringes, and at length puts away needle.*) Now take up that letter and continue—take it up—steady your hand—aren't you ashamed to be so weak?

Body. Yes—yes, I am ashamed—I am ashamed—(*Gradually steadies himself and takes up letter—reads.*) "Oh, my love, if you could only read between the lines what I have not dared to write, what I've been wanting to tell you for days—but for the sake of my immortal soul I have been silent—I gave my word of honor not to speak—"

Brain. What folly, what trash! If I could only get control of her for a moment she would speak. Well?

Body (*who has been peering close to letter*). Something's been written and then erased.

Brain. You must decipher it.

Body. I cannot.

Brain. Have you a magnifying glass?

Body. There's writing over it.

Brain. Alcohol and a sponge. (Body *goes off down left a moment, returns*

*with bottle, sponge, and sits and wets letter slightly with sponge and
alcohol.* BRAIN *opens drawer in table at same time and uses magnifying
glass.*) There is nothing to fear, but we may as well know everything. Wise
men listen to the cackle of fools if only to laugh at it and learn more
wisdom.

(BODY *brings down hanging electric bulb close to paper and looks through
magnifying glass which he takes from* BRAIN. *Suddenly scatters glass, paper,
etc., right and left and shrieks, leaping to his feet.*)

BODY. Disinterred! Disinterred!

(BRAIN *claps hand over his mouth.* SOUL *revives, tries to rise, but* BRAIN
stands between her and BODY, *deliberately on guard.*)

BRAIN. Hush! Are you mad?

BODY (*clinging to* BRAIN). Save me—save me—they are going to disinter
the body—perhaps it's really done.

BRAIN. Absurd. She would have written and told you before.

BODY. No—she promised—she wanted to tell me—how long ago did she
say?

BRAIN. What if they do disinter it?

BODY. I should have had it cremated.

BRAIN. I thought of that, you know.

BODY. Yes, I'm not reproaching you. Save me—save me!

BRAIN. But she left strict commands about her burial in her will—you
dared not act against them.

BODY. No—no—but now—now—what's to be done?

BRAIN. The first thing to be done is for you to calm yourself. Then you
will listen to me.

BODY. Yes—yes—I'll be calm.

BRAIN. Control yourself.

BODY. I'll be calm when you can reassure me, counsel me.

BRAIN. Reassure you? Of course I can reassure you. Do you realize that,
thanks to me, there is not a scrap of evidence existing against you?

BODY. Oh, yes, yes—that's right—that's right.

BRAIN. You are not the ordinary murderer who sows blunders with his
crime.

BODY. No, no—that's true. But the letter, telegram, signed "Accomplice"?

BRAIN. You have had no accomplice but me.

BODY. No—that's true—only you. There is no one to betray me?

BRAIN. There is no one, and nothing can betray you. Common murderers
bungle because they do not eliminate emotion. Sentiment, fear, impatience,
overconfidence, passion, befuddles their brain—but I am clean from every such
fog.

BODY. You are wonderful, my adored one, I worship you!

BRAIN. Then trust me—trust me completely.

BODY. I will—I will. Oh, I'm so tired—I must rest now—I must rest.

BRAIN. Rest? Oh, no, there's much to be thought of, much to plan.

BODY (*reeling toward bed*). I can do no more, I am exhausted.

(*Falls on bed.* BRAIN *pulls him up and makes him stand.* SOUL *never abandons hope, but without strength to rise watches for opportunity to approach* BODY.)

BRAIN. Listen. Do you remember how, at the start, when you first met your wife, I said—"Here's your chance, Jay, if you don't let yourself love her—"

BODY. Don't—don't—let me go—let me rest—

(*Tries to push* BRAIN *away, but she clings to him.*)

BRAIN. "You can take advantage of her first spell of sickness—women always have one sometime—"

BODY. Leave me alone now; we've gone over all that before—it's no use reliving it now—

BRAIN. "To administer a tiny dose of our own"—and you carried that plan out under my direction—

BODY. I must get some rest—some sleep—I must.

(*Breaks away and sits on bed.*)

BRAIN (*following him*). And you alone nursed her—you were so devoted she would have no one else.

BODY. Let me sleep, beloved Brain.

BRAIN. The poison you had gathered from different cities in very small quantities; no two visits did you pay in one place, and your information, too, how to administer it safely without arousing suspicion, you secured from libraries all over the country. Not a book on the subject have you ever had in your possession. Not one scrap of paper in your handwriting exists with even one of their titles.

(BODY, *unseen by* BRAIN, *takes out needle and uses it.*)

BODY. I must sleep—I must sleep—I cannot endure the strain.

BRAIN (*suddenly wilting*). I'm tired too—but no—I cannot be—I never grow tired—I—yet something bothers me—I must leave you for a minute—I —I cannot stay —

(*She staggers left and finally falls in a heap on floor.* BODY *draws a long breath and lies down.* SOUL *rises, creeps toward* BODY, *and then leans over him.*)

SOUL. In your weakness I find my strength. Don't shut me out any longer, Beloved—let me live—save me—make me strong again—let me live—let me live. (BODY *stirs.*) Give me back my immortal right to live.

(BODY *rises in stupor and goes to 'phone.*)

BODY. Hello? Send up a boy with a telegraph blank, will you? I want to send a wire.

(*Hangs up.*)

SOUL. You will come back to me?

BODY (*ignoring her*). Where is my beloved Brain, I wonder.

SOUL. She sleeps. Let her rest. She is a scarlet counselor. Hand in hand she and I could work together and perform miracles in the mortal world if she would only listen at times to me. But she is arrogant, proud; she wants to be queen over all and rule alone.

Body. There's a peculiar singing in my ears—if only my beloved Brain were here, she'd tell me what it was.

Soul. It is I, Body; it is I, your long-neglected Soul.

Body. I wish it would go away—I'm so tired. (*Knock at door—he opens it—admits* Boy *with blank and pencil.*) Oh, it's you—come in.

(*Takes pencil and writes.*)

Soul. Dearest Body, I'm growing stronger now.

Body (*to boy*). What?

Boy. I didn't speak, sir.

Body. I thought you did. How soon will that be delivered?

(*Giving boy telegram.*)

Boy (*looking at address*). In an hour, sir, or less, maybe.

Body. Tell them to rush it.

(Soul *puts arms around* Body *and whispers.*)

Boy. Yes, sir.

(*Turns to go.*)

Body. Oh, Boy?

Boy. Yes, sir?

Body. Ask the clerk to send that message by 'phone for me—I'm too tired to do it myself.

Boy. Yes, sir, very well, sir.

(Boy *exits.* Body *comes to table and sits, head in hands, moans.*)

Body. Oh, I'd sell my soul for one hour's dreamless sleep.

Soul (*over him at back*). 'Tis only while you sleep your soul can live.

Body (*rising and going to bed*). Voices, always voices, sleeping or waking.

(*Shows signs of drug's effect wearing off and* Brain *half rises.*)

Brain. Beloved Body, where are you?

Body. I'm tired—I'm tired—I must have rest.

Brain (*rising, sees* Soul). I thought you were gone forever.

Soul. I am stronger now than you.

(*Comes down.*)

Brain. Are you? We shall see. Body, beloved, I am coming to help you.

(*Tries to pass* Soul, *but* Soul *stands so* Brain *cannot see* Body, *who is now seated on the side of the bed using the needle. As he punctures his arm,* Brain *staggers back to former position and lies huddled on floor, moaning.* Body *falls across bed asleep.*)

Brain (*as she is staggering backward*). How can you stand there smiling while our Body is sinning, sinning?

Soul. Material sin cannot touch me—only sin against the Everlasting God can destroy my immortal life.

(Brain *lies moaning in a heap. There is a terrific knock on door.* Body *does not move; it is repeated, then a key is heard and door opens.* Police

OFFICER *enters, stands at door on guard, and* THOMAS BRENT *in plain clothes comes in.* BELLBOY *stands at back.* BRENT *has the telegraph form in his hand.*)

BRENT. You're wanted, Jay Bragdon. (SOUL *places a hand on* BODY'S *shoulder and he stirs.*) Jay Bragdon, wake up, you're wanted.

(BODY *moves, sits up, turns, rubs eyes, and stares.*)

BODY. Who are you?

BRENT. My name's Brent—Thomas Brent.

BODY (*dazed*). Thomas—Thomas Brent?

BRENT. Yes, I think you've heard of me before.

BODY. Oh, my Brain, my Brain, my Brain! (BRAIN *rises, is very weak, staggers across to* BODY. *He clutches her.* BRENT *and the others do not see either* SOUL *or* BRAIN.) What am I to do?

BRENT. Get your coat and hat on; you're wanted.

(BOY *gets coat and hat for* BODY. BODY *lets him help him with coat.*)

BODY. What for—what for—what am I wanted for?

BRENT. For murder. You murdered your wife six months ago.

(BRAIN *whispers to* BODY *who tries to bluster.*)

BODY. You are insane to make such a charge—insane, I tell you. We were the most devoted couple in our set—everybody will laugh at you—(*Clinging convulsively to* BRAIN.) You can have no evidence to warrant such a ridiculous charge.

BRENT. No evidence, man? Do *you* say that?

BODY. Certainly I say that—I repeat, you have no evidence. (BRAIN *still whispering, but weakening while he clings, one arm around her—she is now on his right;* SOUL *creeps to his left side, puts arm around him. He tries to free himself as though he is choking, tries with arm to cling to* BRAIN, *who slips, slips from his grasp, while with his left he grapples with* SOUL. *He talks wildly, frenziedly, without taking his eyes from* BRENT.) Ha-ha— it's too absurd, it's really ridiculous, not to be taken seriously—you will be laughed out of court, hounded out of your profession—(*Suddenly changing from sneering to bravado.*) My man, you'll have to answer for this outrage, do you realize that? You'll have to answer to me, do you hear? And also answer to an indignant world that will not brook an innocent man, whose character has always been above reproach, being impugned, in so brutal a fashion too,—my rest disturbed, my privacy invaded—my—my—my—me—me—(*He babbles incoherently as* BRAIN *slips from his grasp, and finds words as he clutches her again. Now she slips almost lifeless left, and using both hands he tries to strangle* SOUL, *whom he has by this time got down to her knees.*) I will fight for my freedom—fight—fight—what is fight?—evidence—evidence—no—no evidence—what is evidence?—

BRENT (*taking letters from pocket and showing them to* BODY, *who stares at them wildly.* SOUL, *with extreme effort, recovers and rises,* BRAIN *moans*). This is evidence enough, I think—every record of your crime, step by step, from the moment of its inception in your brain—the drug stores patronized, the libraries visited, the books consulted and thumbed by you—all signed Accomplice. Do you recognize the handwriting, Mr. Bragdon?

(BRAIN *rises on her elbow*—BODY *stares at paper, then shrieks.*)

BODY. It is my own, my own—my own! (BRAIN *falls back lifeless*—BODY *makes a dash with clawlike fingers at* BRENT'S *throat.* SOUL *rises straight and stands between them.* BODY *staggers back over foot of bed.* BRENT *signs to* OFFICER, *who comes forward and pulls* BODY *to his feet, standing at* BODY'S *right.*) Something is gone—something is gone—I am so tired and weak. (*Totters.*)

SOUL (*tenderly*). Lean on me.

BODY. Who are you? Why, you are beautiful! I never saw you before, did I? Who are you?

SOUL. I am your immortal soul.

BODY. My soul—my soul—I didn't know—I have something beautiful left—my soul—I'm so tired.

SOUL. With me you will find peace and rest. Lean on me now.

BRENT. Poor devil, no wonder he was wiring to me—(*Reading telegraph form.*) "For God's sake come and take me." Go ahead, Officer, I guess he can walk.

(SOUL *places* BODY'S *arm about her neck and supports him.*)

OFFICER (*picking up* BODY'S *hat and taking his other arm*). He seems stronger now.

(*They start up-stage,* BRENT *following.*)

SOUL. Oh, yes, he's stronger now.

CURTAIN

THE FESTIVAL OF BACCHUS

A Comedy of Words

By Arthur Schnitzler

Translated from the German by Pierre Loving

CHARACTERS

FELIX STAUFNER, *writer*
AGNES, *his wife*
DR. GUIDO WERNIG
RAILWAY GUARD
WAITER
CASHIER (*a woman*)
Passengers and Station Employees
The action takes place in the railroad waiting room of a large Austrian city in the mountains.

Reprinted from *Comedies of Words* by Arthur Schnitzler; translated by Pierre Loving.

THE FESTIVAL OF BACCHUS

SCENE: *Station and restaurant. In the rear glass doors giving onto the platform. Right a stairway conducting downstairs. On the left is a buffet, with a clock above it. A number of tables, covered and uncovered, with chairs. A blackboard near the middle platform door, right. On the wall are time-tables, maps, posters. The cashier is busy behind the buffet. Several people are seated at the tables. The guard stands by the middle platform door, which is open. As the curtain rises the train has just come in. Passengers enter from the platform and pass through the dining room on the right, using the steps. On the left* AGNES *and* GUIDO *are standing, almost motionless, with their eyes fixed intently on the door as if expecting someone. When the last of the passengers has passed through the waiting room,* GUIDO *steps up to the door and peers out on the platform. He makes a step as if to go out but is intercepted by the guard.* AGNES *in the meantime has also loitered up to the door.*

GUIDO. There's no one else.

AGNES. Strange!

GUIDO. Was that the Innsbruck train?

(*The* GUARD *locks the door.*)

GUARD. No, sir.

GUIDO. No?

GUARD. That was the Bavarian express. The Innsbruck train is scheduled to arrive at 5.20.

GUIDO. Why do you say "is scheduled to arrive"?

GUARD. Because it's almost always late. However, there has been no report yet.

GUIDO. You mean that it will arrive on time?

GUARD. No, that it will be late. (*Goes off left by the steps.*)

GUIDO (*glancing at the clock*). We have fully eight minutes before us. (*Lights a cigarette.*)

AGNES. Eight minutes. (*Comes down and seats herself at one of the tables.*)

(*The* WAITER *approaches and hovers about.*)

GUIDO (*after a brief pause to* AGNES, *standing behind her chair*). Agnes—

AGNES. Guido—?

GUIDO (*seating himself beside her*). Wouldn't it be a better idea to—

WAITER. Your order, sir?

GUIDO. Thank you. We have just had something here.

17

(WAITER, *slightly piqued, shrugs his shoulders and goes off left.*)

GUIDO. Wouldn't it be better, I mean, if I waited for him alone?

AGNES. Why this sudden change of mind? Have you completely lost faith in my determination? Do you think that I shrink from meeting him face to face—

GUIDO. No, no. I have the greatest confidence in you. But I repeat: it's quite impossible to foretell how he'll take the news. And that's why—

AGNES (*rising fervently*). No. We've made up our minds. We'll wait for him together. In this way the situation will at once be made clear to him. And that in itself is a big advantage. No superfluous words will be necessary. It's only fair to us—and to him. We owe him that much. Or, if you like, I at least owe it to him. (*The whistle of a locomotive is heard.* AGNES *starts but does not turn.* GUIDO *rises. A railway employee comes from the platform, meticulously locks the door after him, and writes on the blackboard: "Express No. 57 from Innsbruck—44 minutes late." He intercepts a woman with two children at the door and closes it again behind him.* GUIDO *and* AGNES *have not turned around. The whistle of the locomotive dies away.*)

GUIDO (*close to her*). Agnes, do you love me?

AGNES. I adore you. And you?

GUIDO. You know. (*Hastily.*) And in one hour all will be over. Bear that in mind. To-morrow we will be far away. Think of that when you face him. Together—forever!

AGNES (*somewhat mechanically*). Forever—(*without looking round*). Hasn't it come in yet?

GUIDO (*turning round*). The eight minutes are up. (*The* GUARD *reënters.*)

GUIDO (*noticing the writing on the board*). Oh!

AGNES (*following his glance*). What is it?

GUIDO. Delay; forty-four minutes' delay.

GUARD. More likely an hour.

GUIDO. Here it is very plain, forty-four minutes. Forty-four! I dare say that's calculated to the dot.

GUARD (*coldly*). Oh, she may make it in less.

(*He goes over to the buffet, exchanges a few words with the cashier, and then goes off.* GUIDO *and* AGNES *stare at one another.*)

GUIDO. That's so.

AGNES. One hour—

GUIDO. Let's go outside a bit.

AGNES. But it hasn't stopped raining. But if you want to take a walk— I'll wait for you here. I prefer to look at the illustrated papers. (*Sits, taking up a newspaper.*)

(GUIDO *approaches the buffet and sets his watch by the clock.*)

AGNES (*gazing at him with a smile*). He must be pretty impatient, too, in his compartment.

GUIDO (*returning to her*). How—do you mean, Agnes?

AGNES. As you know, he telegraphed that he was coming from Stubai on the five-twenty train. I fancy he's under the impression that I'm waiting for him after these six weeks of separation, and that together we'll take the train back to Seewalchen, to our villa. Well, I am waiting for him—only it isn't quite as he imagined it.

GUIDO. It would be more agreeable to me if you'd refrain from going off on a sentimental jag this way.

AGNES. Sentimental—? I? Would I be here, if I were sentimental? (*Brief pause.*)

GUIDO (*making conversation*). You've missed the six o'clock train anyway.

AGNES. There's another at seven.

GUIDO. Do you think he'll take it?

AGNES. Why not? I'll beg him to— And if you know him at all, he's the sort of man— (*Breaking off.*) He'll find everything at home as he left it. I've ordered Therese to prepare everything as if—

GUIDO. That wasn't quite necessary. If he ever loved you, he will never put foot into a house in which he lived with you for five summers—(*bitterly*) and happily at that.

AGNES. Yes, he will. He's awfully fond of the little cottage and the landscape. At any rate, they haven't changed.

GUIDO. I'm sure he won't go back to it this year any more.

AGNES. If he's wise, he'll go right home and sleep there to-night.

GUIDO. In a house—alive with such memories?

AGNES (*staring straight ahead of her*). Let's hope that he's already started to forget me on the return trip.

GUIDO. Do you imagine that he will?

AGNES. Well, isn't it the best thing we can wish him?

(*She takes a newspaper again and pretends to be absorbed in it.*)

GUIDO (*eyeing Agnes, paces up and down, adjusts his watch again, then stepping up to her*). We might take something. (*Taps on the table, then takes a newspaper and flutters the leaves nervously, glancing all the while at AGNES, who seems quite absorbed in reading; calling petulantly.*) Waiter.

WAITER (*appearing, still slightly piqued*). Yes, sir.

GUIDO. Bring me— (*To AGNES.*) What'll you have?

AGNES. It's immaterial to me.

GUIDO. Well, bring two lemon sodas.

AGNES. I prefer raspberry.

(*WAITER moves away. Pause. GUIDO fixes his eyes on AGNES.*)

AGNES (*continuing to read; smiling*). Here's something about you.

GUIDO. About me?

AGNES. Yes. "Regatta at Attersee. First prize, Baron Ramming, yacht *Storm;* second prize, Dr. Guido Wernig, yacht *Watersprite.*"

GUIDO. Quite right. You see, such insignificant nobodies like myself do get into the papers sometimes. Of course, only on correspondingly insignificant occasions—and then they capture only second prize.

AGNES. Next time it will be the first—on another See.

GUIDO. You're very optimistic. But—isn't it the hand of destiny?

AGNES (*with an inquiring glance*). The second prize?

GUIDO. The delay, I mean. Once again you have enough time to think it over. (*She beckons him to draw nearer.*) Perhaps it isn't so simple a thing as you imagine. When you've once been the helpmate of a great man, to become the wife of a quite ordinary doctor of chemistry—

AGNES (*interrupting him quickly*). In the first place, Guido, your factory in your particular line is quite as well known as the collected works of my husband.

GUIDO. What have I to do with the factory? My father founded it—managed it—I am only his son.

AGNES. Besides, I didn't fall in love with Felix because he was a great man, as you put it. Whoever heard of him when we were married?

GUIDO. But you foresaw it—

AGNES. Foresaw it—yes.

(WAITER *comes with sodas. He places the glasses on the table.* AGNES *and* GUIDO *are silent. The* WAITER *moves away. Pause.*)

GUIDO. Why are you silent, Agnes?

AGNES (*staring straight ahead*). How mysterious life is! Six weeks ago, no more than six weeks ago, I crossed the lake with him in the small steamboat—six weeks. I said good-by to him almost on this very spot. And how the world has changed in this short time! If he—if he had guessed that bright summer day—

GUIDO. Do you regret it, Agnes? If so, there is still time.

AGNES (*as if waking from a trance*). I regret nothing—nothing. All that has happened was destined to happen. Don't you know I realize that, Guido? And all that has happened points to our happiness together—and also to his.

GUIDO. His?

AGNES. I have no doubt he'll thank me right off, seeing I've given him back his freedom. People of his sort—

GUIDO "People of his sort—"

AGNES. Everything in life has its deeper meaning. It is well, it is perhaps profoundly necessary that he should from now on dwell in solitude.

GUIDO. In solitude—? What do you call solitude?

AGNES (*looking up*). What do you mean by that?

GUIDO. Nothing, but what you imagine yourself.

AGNES. Don't try to evade my question. You did the same once before in a similar circumstance.

GUIDO. How so? When?

AGNES. On the train.

GUIDO. I'm sure my allusion is not beyond your surmise. The suspicion that not his play alone kept him in Stubaital six weeks, instead of the projected three, surely is not new to you to-day. You smile?

AGNES. It's a bit amusing to me the way you're trying, very obviously, to make me jealous.

GUIDO. Far from it. But, if you'll pardon my saying it, I don't see any sense in your seeking to surround your—your former husband with a kind of halo. He is every bit of a human being. In certain respects he's not a whit better than I and —

AGNES (*laughing*). And you—you wished to say. Very kind of you, I'm sure.

GUIDO. Don't misunderstand me.

AGNES. Oh, I understand you perfectly. You want me to believe that Mademoiselle X—

GUIDO. Bianca Walter—

AGNES. Whose postscript is on the picture post card, has contrived somehow to detain my husband—

GUIDO. Your husband that was—Herr Felix Staufner.

AGNES. Felix—

GUIDO. I'm not trying to convince you, I merely make the statement.

AGNES. Without evidence you can prove nothing. Besides the truth will soon out.

GUIDO. How do you make that out?

AGNES. He will tell the truth.

GUIDO. In all probability you won't have to hear it. Aside from the fact that it is immaterial to you and that the moment my conjectures are confirmed you will be pleased.

AGNES. I shall be quite happy over it. Need I tell you that? Nothing more desirable could happen to me than if he stepped off the train with Fräulein Bianca or somebody else.

GUIDO. I'm afraid, Agnes, that you conceive life as too simple a thing. Mademoiselle X—

AGNES. Bianca.

GUIDO. Will not accompany him. She will remain in Stubai for the present.

AGNES. With her mother?

GUIDO. Why with her mother? Why bother about her mother?

AGNES. Because her name, too, is on the picture post card. However, I think we are doing the young lady an injustice and celebrating a little prematurely. Doubtless she is a respectable girl of good family. An admirer of my—my Felix Staufner, just like her mother. (*She takes a card out of her purse and reads.*) "Isabella Walter and her daughter cannot omit the opportunity of gratefully sending their heartfelt greetings to the wife of the master—"

GUIDO. A bit wordy.

AGNES. But very unsuspicious.

GUIDO. You carry the card about with you?

AGNES. I had no time to put it away.

GUIDO. You have answered it, then?

AGNES. Why not? It's the last. It arrived four days ago. And it's positively the last he's written as my husband.

(GUIDO *makes as if to take the card; she makes a gesture of refusal, and he seems hurt.*)

AGNES. Just one word.

GUIDO. What sort of word, if I may ask?

AGNES. *Auf wiedersehen.*

(GUIDO *bites his lip.*)

AGNES. Well, doesn't it seem proper? I didn't write *"Auf gutes wiedersehen,"* or *"Auf glückliches wiedersehen,"* simply *"Auf wiedersehen."*

GUIDO. And did you write him letters, too, during this time?

AGNES. Only one.

GUIDO. Well—well!

AGNES. That was before there was anything between you and me; before that evening—when you suddenly appeared in my garden under my window—and called my name in the dark. Yes, in this way one sometimes writes a farewell letter without suspecting it! How mysterious life—

(GUIDO *has taken the card in his hand and seems bent on crumpling it.*)

AGNES. What are you doing, Guido?

GUIDO. You love him still.

AGNES (*earnestly*). No, Guido, I love no one but you. I have never loved anybody—not even Felix—as much as I love you. (*Grasping his hand.*) But I shall never cease (*letting his hand go*) to admire and to respect Felix Staufner; to be spiritually akin to Felix Staufner, the writer. In a certain sense relations such as existed between Felix and myself can never alter—never. The fact that we were married is of least importance. Even if I should never see him again, if we should remain miles and miles apart—

GUIDO (*interrupting*). Yes, if you would only remain miles and miles apart! Well and good. Then everything would be all right; then I'd have nothing to oppose to your spiritual relations. But, unfortunately, I can't spend my life taking endless trips. I must be back in harness in the damned—

AGNES. Certainly; I'd never permit you to give up your profession. You must work, even if it isn't absolutely necessary. I don't propose to take up with an idler.

GUIDO. I don't intend to give up my profession. But what's to prevent my practicing it elsewhere? I'll speak to the governor. As it is, he's been planning for sometime to establish a branch office in Germany or America.

AGNES. Or Australia.

GUIDO. The farther the better.

AGNES. Guido!

GUIDO. I simply can't bear to have you meet your former husband again.

AGNES (*determined*). I shan't permit you at the eleventh hour to violate all our stipulations. You know that Felix is not like other men—

GUIDO. Do you really believe that he won't find another—friend very soon?

AGNES. A friend? No. Never. A mistress—certainly. And whether her name be Bianca or something else—I only hope that I'll be able to approve of his choice.

GUIDO. Why do you hope so? Do you intend to be friendly with the future mistress of your husband?

AGNES. If things should fall out so—

GUIDO. They will not fall out so. I wish to make clear to you that I desire to keep our home—as soon as our affairs are in order, and that will be soon, I trust—respectable. And I warn you that this—mind you, I don't say uninteresting—partly dubious crowd of artists and actor-folk of both sexes who used to frequent your house, will not be welcome under my roof.

AGNES. As regards dubious affairs, you ought to—

GUIDO. That's another matter entirely. A real passion explains, condones everything. And besides, your husband deserves his fate.

AGNES. Oh!

GUIDO. A woman, I hold, must be guarded jealously like a priceless gem. One should never leave a young woman alone, wholly alone among a crowd of young people in summer—near a lake—

AGNES. In spite of his doubts he trusted me. It's all part and parcel of the paradox in his makeup.

GUIDO. A man doesn't trust a woman whom he loves. He trembles for her. He fights for her. I shall never trust you. Even after we've lived together for years. Even if we should have children—and we will have children. I will always be concerned about you. To make sure of a woman one must keep on insulting her.

AGNES. But he never resorted to that. He was jealous oftener than you think. He was jealous even of you.

GUIDO. Of me! Well, I thought—

AGNES. That was before he had the slightest grounds. Even then— How mysterious—

GUIDO. Life is.

AGNES. We had scarcely spoken three times together. Naturally he said nothing, but I noticed that it was so. For the life of me, I couldn't make it out. You were out sailing on the lake all day long—at the outset. Only in the evening did you venture to sit beside us on the hotel terrace and chatter all manner of nonsense which, to tell the truth, didn't interest me the least bit.

GUIDO. Nonsense—why—

AGNES. I only mean to say that everything was quite harmless in those early days. Admit that you didn't trouble at all about me. The little Baroness Fellah meant more to you—and the Lord knows who else? But he saw it coming. I observed it in his glances. He suspected immediately that you—that you only—

GUIDO. And still he left you to your own devices. Saw it coming and went away on a trip.

AGNES. It's a way with him when he's greatly absorbed in a piece of work. Everything else is put aside.

GUIDO. And he fled (*pointedly*) to solitude.

AGNES (*ignoring his innuendo*). At all events he stopped caring about people—that is, about people whom he loved.

GUIDO. Did he leave you alone often?

AGNES. Sometimes. But that was not the worst. It was much more uncomfortable when he stayed at home and left me alone. When my voice had lost its caress, when I became, in a measure, paler, more shadowy than any being he ever created; when I felt myself snuffed out—for him—

GUIDO. For me—you will never be snuffed out—never, Agnes.

AGNES (*as if waking from a trance*). Never, Guido! You will never leave me alone. You will never repair to solitude and forget me for days, weeks, at a stretch, as he's done. It isn't good to leave us women alone. You are right, Guido. It's quite perilous—it's—

(*For several minutes past there has been a commotion in the waiting room. Passengers come up the steps. The* GUARD *enters from the right and goes to the platform door.*)

GUIDO. What's the matter? (*Glancing at the clock above the buffet.*) There's still twelve minutes. (GUARD *opens the door.*)

AGNES. It seems as if—

GUIDO (*quickly to the* GUARD). The Innsbruck train?

GUARD. Yes, sir.

GUIDO. I thought you said it wouldn't arrive before ten minutes yet—?

GUARD. She's made up a bit for lost time.

GUIDO (*to* AGNES). You are pale. Don't you care to—

(*Passengers go through the waiting room to the platform outside.*)

AGNES (*passionately shaking her head*). Let us go out, don't you think?

GUIDO. On the platform?

AGNES. Yes. It's better than waiting out here. I wish him to see us directly from the car window.

GUIDO. I don't know.

AGNES. Come. (*They start to go out on the platform.*)

GUARD. Platform tickets, please.

GUIDO. Good Lord! (*Searching in his purse.*) Here. (*Offers the* GUARD *money.*)

GUARD. Over there, at the ticket machine.

GUIDO. But the train will be in by that time.

GUARD. There's lots of time yet.

GUIDO (*goes to the ticket machine, deposits a few coins and yanks the lever in vain*). It doesn't work.

GUARD (*going over to the machine, tries to manipulate the lever, fails, then shakes his head*). Don't work sometimes.

GUIDO. But we'll—

GUARD. Ah, there you are. It's all right now. (*Hands two tickets to*

Guido (*Back to the door which he has previously closed and now re-opens.*)
Here she comes now. (*Noise of an incoming train.*)

Agnes. Your hand, Guido.

(*Hand in hand they go through the doorway onto the platform. As they pass out* Felix *appears on the right, mounting the steps. He spies* Agnes, *makes as if to follow, observes almost simultaneously that she is not alone, and is just in time to see her disappear hand in hand with* Guido *on the platform. He remains standing a moment. Then makes a step towards them. At the platform door he pauses again. Then he strides to the other platform door and seems to be following with his eyes the pair of them as they go to meet the incoming train. He steps back, passes his hand over his forehead and peers through the glass door. The pair vanish out of sight. The train has already stopped and the passengers pour in from the platform. Most of them pass through the waiting room to the steps on the right. Several take seats at the tables; several step up to the buffet and order refreshments.* Felix *advances to the center of the stage. The stream of passengers rushes by him. He feels he must get out of their path, so he steps back again to the open platform door. He looks for* Agnes *and* Guido. *Gazing intently out, he watches them. Then, as if fearing to be observed, he drops back. On his face there is depicted complete understanding of the situation. Answering a sudden impulse to escape, he hurries to the steps on the right. He remains standing there a moment, shakes his head and hastens again to the closed platform door, peering out. The last of the passengers are leaving the platform. Moving away from the door* Felix *comes to the front in an attitude of suspense, with his face contorted into a smile. Then, growing serious again, he seats himself at a table on the right, the same, in fact, at which* Agnes *and* Guido *had sat before. Mechanically he picks up a newspaper and glances above it in the direction of the platform door. The* Guard *has already shut the door. He opens it again. First there enters a belated woman with a multiplicity of hand bags, then a station official, and lastly* Guido *and* Agnes. *They do not at first discover* Felix, *who is intrenched behind his newspaper.*)

Guido. Amazing—

Agnes. Is there another train to-day?

Guido. Let's have a look at the time-table. (*They go to the time-table on the wall next to the steps.* Guido *studies it carefully.*) Nine—twelve—no, that's not from Innsbruck. If we could only find out somehow. Just wait—

Felix (*putting the newspaper aside, rises and strides quickly toward* Agnes *and* Guido, *who are studying the time-table. For a space he stands motionless behind her. He speaks suddenly in an unsuspecting, joyous tone.*) Well, here you are, Agnes.

(Agnes *turns around, likewise* Guido, *but they utter no word.*)

Felix (*overlooking the awkwardness of the situation very quickly*). You see, I came up on the earlier train, at noon. Unfortunately I couldn't telegraph you in time. It was a sudden whim of mine. I awoke somewhat earlier this morning. My things were all packed. So I said to myself: "Suppose you take the first train and loaf about Salzburg for several hours." I'm glad to see you, Agnes—glad to see you. (*Wrings her hand.*) How d'ye do, doctor? What are you doing here? En route for Vienna? (*Extends his hand.*) Your vacation's over, I suppose.

GUIDO (*hesitatingly taking the proffered hand*). No, I'm not going to Vienna. I was glad to escort your—your wife permitted me to—and, really—

(AGNES *casts an anxious glance at him, which is not lost on* FELIX.)

FELIX (*quickly interrupting*). Very good of you, doctor. My wife loves to chat. Very kind of you, doctor, to keep her company. When one has taken the trip thirty or forty times the beauties of nature grow banal. (*Suddenly.*) But Agnes, let me look at you. We haven't seen each other for such an age. Six weeks! I don't recollect our ever having been parted so long during the five years we've been married. Isn't that so?

AGNES. You're looking very well, Felix.

FELIX. Am I? Well, I hope so. And you, too. Why, you seem to have grown a little stouter. And you're sunburnt, quite sunburnt. You were out in the open a good deal, weren't you? And then the weather was simply glorious. But to-day—of course. It was very nice of you to come to meet me.

AGNES. But you asked me to.

FELIX. I simply wanted to let you know. I didn't reckon on it for a moment. Besides, it's two and a half hours from Seewalchen to here. And you had to change, too. Take it any way you like, it's a trip—even with the doctor's pleasant company.

GUIDO. As regards my accompanying your wife, allow me—

AGNES (*interrupting, suddenly to* FELIX). You were here, then, at twelve? What have you done until now?

FELIX. I'll tell you presently. (*Indicating the table.*) Won't you join me—I've a tremendous hankering for a cup of coffee. And you? Or have you already had some? Waiter! Waiter! What was that you asked a moment ago? How I passed the time? Well, as it was dinner time, I dined in town, of course—very well, too—at the Nurnberg. (*Sits.*) Well, doctor, won't you join us? (AGNES *sits.*)

GUIDO (*with a meaningful glance at* AGNES). I don't really know whether— You see, I have—

FELIX (*quickly*). No ceremony, doctor. Please. (*To* WAITER *who approaches.*) Let us have some—(*to* AGNES)—coffee, eh? And what'll you have, doctor?

GUIDO (*who has taken a seat in response to a wink of* AGNES). I have just—

AGNES (*quickly to* WAITER). Three mélanges, please. (WAITER *is about to go.*)

FELIX. I'll have mine a bit strong. And, by the way, have you still got that coffee cake you had six weeks ago? It was delicious.

AGNES. You remember it still?

FELIX. You liked it, too. (*To the* WAITER.) Well, bring us some coffee cake with the coffee. (WAITER *goes.*)

FELIX. Now—what were we talking about? Oh, yes. I dined at the Nurnberg, and then I loafed about town—

AGNES. In the rain?

FELIX. Ah, I didn't mind it the least bit. Coming upon the sultriness of the morning it was a veritable godsend. Then, you see, I called on Sebastian Schwartz for half an hour.

AGNES (*by way of explanation to* GUIDO). That's the antique dealer, you know.

FELIX. You aren't interested in antiques, I presume, doctor?

GUIDO. I don't understand enough about them. But—

FELIX (*quickly to* AGNES). He has lots of beautiful things. Some of them quite expensive.

AGNES. And I suppose you untied your purse-strings liberally again.

FELIX. Not much. I've already had several things sent on to Seewalchen to the villa. A nampulla such as we've wanted for a long time.

AGNES. For the dining room?

FELIX. Yes, of course. Certainly you can hang it in the dining room if you wish. And then I bought a lovely amulet. Baroque. Genuine. Aqua marine with a little silver chain—wait until you see it. I have it here in my purse. But, tell me, when did you arrive? At four, I take it?

AGNES. No, I dined in town, too.

GUIDO. We had dinner here, too.

AGNES (*resuming*). We ate at the station and—

FELIX (*quickly*). And loafed about town until now. Curious, isn't it, that we didn't meet?

GUIDO. We took a drive.

AGNES. Considering the bad weather—the doctor was very kind—

(WAITER *brings coffee, etc.* FELIX, *moving back his chair, causes the table and glasses to tremble.* WAITER *is somewhat taken aback.* GUIDO *seems to hesitate a moment, then, with nervous haste, he does likewise.* FELIX *stirs his coffee. The* WAITER *goes off with the newspapers.*)

GUIDO (*with sudden determination*). Mr. Staufner, I must ask—

FELIX (*quickly*). But drink your coffee, old man. And let me enjoy mine while I may. Then, if it suits you, you may ask my indulgence to whatever you please. I find tiffin the nicest refreshment of the day. I can do without my dinner, but never without my afternoon coffee.

GUIDO. Mr. Staufner, you asked me a moment ago whether I was going to Vienna. Well—

FELIX (*quickly*). Excuse my having asked. I noticed the effect on you was painful. I don't want to have appeared indiscreet. What you have decided to do with the rest of your vacation is clearly a personal matter. Enjoy life as long—and so on. Aren't you going to take over the management of the Hollenstein factory when your father is ready to retire—

GUIDO. My father is quite robust. He has no intention of retiring from business.

(*He endeavors to exchange glances with* AGNES *who, however, avoids his look.*)

FELIX. How old is he, if I may ask?

GUIDO. Sixty-two. But as I said—

FELIX. In any case, the main burden will soon fall to your shoulders. So enjoy life as long as you may. And above all things else, travel.

AGNES. The doctor has traveled considerable. He's already been to America.

GUIDO. Yes, I've been to South America.

FELIX. Indeed. To South America. And do you know Japan at all?

GUIDO. No, I don't know Japan.

FELIX. Japan has lured me for ever so long. Don't you feel like going there too, Agnes?

AGNES. There are many places not so far.

FELIX. What of that? Do you expect to travel round the world inch by inch? It can't be done. What kind of a hat are you wearing, Agnes?

AGNES. You know it.

FELIX. The red band is kind of new to me.

AGNES. Yes, it is new.

FELIX. Quite a summer hue. It glows and sparkles. (*He repeats the phrase, but almost in an uncontrollable threatening tone of voice.*) It glows and sparkles.

(AGNES *gazes at him in terror and shoots a sudden glance at* GUIDO. GUIDO *involuntarily assumes a dignified posture.*)

FELIX (*glancing up, in a gentler tone*). You are not interested in women's hats, I presume, doctor?

GUIDO (*as if perceiving an opportunity to fasten his fangs*). Not generally. But I am interested in this one, Mr. Staufner. And not only—

(AGNES *looks at him frightened.*)

FELIX. Not only in the hat, but also, the wearer. That *goes* without saying. I am too, doctor. Naturally the hat would be a matter of indifference to both of us, if say, it hung over there on that hook.

GUARD (*entering and calling out*). Passenger train to Schmannemarkt, Bocklabruck, Atnang, Linz, Vienna.

GUIDO (*pushing back his chair as if to rise*). Mr. Staufner—

FELIX. Oh, yes. That's your train. If you intend going back to Seewalchen, you'll have to make a connection. (*To* AGNES, *who looks at him quite confused.*) You thought it was ours, too? No, it is not ours, Agnes. I understand fully, doctor—this attraction to the field of your triumph. Yes, your triumph—(*laughing loudly*). My cordial wishes are perhaps a little tardy at this moment.

GUIDO (*taken aback*). How—?

(AGNES *gazes at* FELIX, *not understanding.*)

FELIX. You—(*pause*)—won—at the Regatta, didn't you?

GUIDO (*involuntarily heaving a sigh of relief*). Oh, thank you. It was only the second prize.

AGNES (*likewise relieved*). How do you come to know about it?

FELIX. Why, it's in the newspaper.

AGNES. You read the sporting page nowadays? Since when?

FELIX. Not all of it. But news about Seewalchen, for obvious reasons, interested me. Moreover, it was on the train, where one reads everything, even one's railway ticket. (*To* GUIDO.) Have you been interested in yachting very long?

GUIDO. Quite a number of years. On Ostersee mostly in the past.

FELIX. On Binnensee, I imagine, it's more difficult.

GUIDO. Not necessarily.

FELIX. Unfortunately, I know nothing about it.

GUIDO. I suppose you haven't taken up sport, Mr. Staufner?

FELIX. Oh, yes—yes. Mostly of a tourist character. I climb a good deal. In Stubai I negotiated several trails.

AGNES. Alone?

FELIX. The big ones, yes. On the little ones I had a party along. Two ladies—mother and daughter. The young lady kept up very nicely on foot.

AGNES. Miss Bianca Walter—?

FELIX. How do you—? Why, yes.

AGNES. I hazard the guess she's blonde. That's your favorite color.

FELIX. Of course, she's blonde. Would you care to know more about her? She's a young actress just beginning her career. She played something for me once—The Jungfrau von Orleans.

AGNES. Very nice.

FELIX. It was indeed. By the bye, I should have her picture somewhere about me.

AGNES. Her picture? You have her picture about you—?

FELIX. Yes. (*He takes it out of his breast pocket.*) She gave it to me before I left. The first chance I get I'd like to show it to a manager. She wants ever so much to get a position in Vienna. She imagines it only needs a word from me. These women certainly are naïve! The mother wasn't bad-looking, either.

AGNES. Isabella.

FELIX. Isabella? Why, yes, of course. Isabella was the mother's name.

AGNES. And the daughter's Bianca.

FELIX. Isabella was the mother's name and the daughter's Bianca. Sounds like a ballad almost. (*To* GUIDO.) Don't you think so?

GUIDO (*icily*). I'm no judge.

AGNES. But I thought you had no intention of making any acquaintances there, and that you were going to devote yourself exclusively to your work?

FELIX. Oh, appearances to the contrary, I was quite assiduous. You will be quite satisfied with me, I think.

AGNES (*with an effort*). Have you finished?

FELIX. Finished? Not quite.

AGNES. Under the circumstances little else was to be expected.

FELIX. How malevolent you can be, Agnes! No reason for it—at all. When luck's on my side, as you know, I can get through in three or four days. Only I need your advice.

AGNES (*joyful in spite of herself*). My—advice?

FELIX. Yes, without equivocation. First, I'd like to talk it over with you. I'll also read you as much as I have. So let's not take the train back to Seewalchen for the present. Until I have cleared up everything I don't care to go back. And here in Salzberg, I know from previous experience I can work extraordinarily well. That's why we'll stay here for a few days.

AGNES. We're going to stay here? That's rather new to me.

FELIX. To me, also. I simply mean that the idea struck me on the train. You're with me in this, aren't you? We've only got to telegraph to good old Therese, asking her to send you whatever you need—absolute necessities. Of course, some superfluous things, too. And whatever for the present you're urgently in want of we can purchase to-day. Or have you, by chance, in response to some secret presentiment, brought your little crocodile purse with you?

GUIDO (*as if sensing the underlying meaning. Externally unruffled, but without malice*). I put the crocodile purse in my suitcase, thinking it safer there.

FELIX. Indeed? Capital! Then everything is in shipshape. And you're glad to stay on, aren't you, Agnes? The three days, I promise you, will pass quickly. All difficulties will be surmounted—and before we return to our little country house I shall put the finishing touch to—(*he hesitates*)—"The Festival of Bacchus."

AGNES (*taken by surprise*). "The Festival of Bacchus"?

FELIX. Yes; why these wide eyes of wonderment?

AGNES. You're writing "The Festival of Bacchus"?

FELIX. Yes.

AGNES. But you started out with quite a different purpose.

FELIX. Quite right. But, soon after, on the way to Stubaital, it flashed upon me, before anything else, I must do "The Festival of Bacchus." There are good and sufficient reasons for this change. It was conditioned by mysterious laws.

GUIDO. Yes, life is very mysterious.

FELIX. Life—no. Not more than ordinarily so. But art is. Yes, art is most— A thing of this sort is leavened within. It matures deep in the recesses of self. (*Indicating his forehead.*) Here one knows nothing about it. So it is. (*Breaking off in another tone.*) Two acts, as I said, are finished. Only in the third act I find I'm up against it, and no thoroughfare. Well, you'll hear it and, I have no doubt, something suggestive will occur to you.

AGNES. If you think so— (*The* WAITER *has appeared.*)

FELIX (*noticing him*). Oh, yes. Well—?

GUIDO. Mine was a mélange—

FELIX. What a notion, doctor! (*The* WAITER.) Three mélanges and three portions of coffee cake.

GUIDO. Four—I had two.

FELIX (*laughing*). Ah, yes; four then.

WAITER. Five.

FELIX. Five?

AGNES. You crumbled one.

FELIX. Oh, did I? Really? Well, then, five.

WAITER. Two crowns, 40 pfennig.

FELIX (*counting*). Very well.

WAITER (*discreetly to* GUIDO). And then there were two lemon sodas.

GUIDO. Ah, yes. (*Is about to pay.*)

FELIX (*noticing* GUIDO's *attempt.*) What is that? Ah, yes? (*Gayly.*) Please, please. (*Is about to pay.*)

GUIDO. I insist—

FELIX—Please let me. Two sodas. Here you are.

(*Pays.* WAITER *goes.* FELIX *extracts a cigarette case from his pocket and offers* GUIDO *a cigarette.*)

GUIDO (*falteringly helping himself to a cigarette*). Thanks.

(FELIX *offers him a light and then proceeds to light his own.*)

GUIDO. And now, if you'll excuse me, I must be going.

FELIX. Good day, doctor, and a pleasant journey to you—whatever route you decide to take.

GUIDO. Thanks. Good-by, my dear Mrs. Staufner. (*Not yet does he dare to extend his hand.*) I trust soon—(*overjoyed at the sudden idea*)—perhaps I shall have the pleasure of seeing you again at the première of your husband's new play—

AGNES. I shall be pleased—

FELIX. You're in no way bound to attend, doctor.

GUIDO. No trouble at all. You see, I've never missed one of your first nights yet. So, naturally, I shall not fail to be present at the opening of "The Festival of Bax—"

FELIX. Bacchus, doctor.

GUIDO. I beg your pardon.

FELIX. It's not a mythological play, as appears from the title, neither is it in verse, if such things scare you away.

GUIDO. Not at all.

FELIX. The title is only used metaphorically, of course. If I attempted to put on a real Festival of Bacchus, I'd have no end of trouble with the censor, as you can imagine.

GUIDO. I'm ashamed to confess that I don't know what a Festival of Bacchus is.

FELIX. Really? The Festival of Bacchus was a quaint custom of the ancient Greeks—a religious custom, you might say.

GUIDO. A—religious custom?

FELIX (*with marginal lilt and brevity*). Yes. A night was set aside once a year at the season of the vintage, if I err not, when men and women were granted unlimited freedom after a fashion—

GUIDO. Unlimited freedom—

FELIX (*very cool, merely informative*). After a fashion. On this night of nights all family ties, all prescriptive laws were dissolved. Men, women, and girls departed from their homes at sundown—homes whose peace they had surrounded and protected—and repaired to a sacred grove (there were many such groves in the land) to celebrate under the sheltering wing of night the divine festival—

GUIDO. The divine festival—

FELIX. The divine festival.

GUIDO. Under the wing of night.

FELIX. Yes.

GUIDO. And supposing the moon shone?

FELIX. That did not matter. At daybreak—the festival was over, and every participant was pledged to forget with whom he celebrated his share of the divine festival. Pledged in all honor. That was a part of the religious custom—just as the celebration itself. To recognize one another afterward would have been considered in bad taste, as being, indeed, frivolous. And, as the saying runs, the votaries of the gods, somewhat tired and yet refreshed, in a measure even purified, wended their way home.

GUIDO. And at home one had an exciting theme for discussion ready to hand—until the next festival.

FELIX. At home nothing was allowed to be said about the festival. There'd be no sense in that. There was as little individual responsibility for the experiences of that night—as there is for dreams.

GUIDO. But didn't it sometimes happen that a couple who had found themselves together in a sacred grove, had no desire to escape from one another's sight so soon—and neither of them showed up at home?

FELIX. That was impossible. The penalty for that was death.

AGNES. Death—?

FELIX. Yes, death. They had to part when the sun rose. The ritual in this respect was very strict.

GUIDO. You say the penalty was death—?

FELIX. To be exact, there was an extenuating circumstance.

GUIDO. Ah!

FELIX (*with emphasis*). When two people who had found themselves together under the wing of night yearned for one another still on the following night—this happened less frequently than one imagines—no one was allowed, either husband nor wife nor father nor mother, to stand in their way. And these two met again on the same spot where they had parted in the morning.

But from the second night—and here we must really marvel at the wisdom of the priests—from this second night, which was no longer a festival to the god there was no asylum. Their former home was closed to them and they were for the remainder of their days dependent on one another. That is why so very few cared to leave their homes on the second night. (*Pause.*)

GUIDO. You've looked up the mythology of it pretty thoroughly for your comedy, Mr. Staufner.

FELIX. It wasn't necessary. If you were to investigate you would discover that my version doesn't correspond exactly. For, as I said, the Festival of Bacchus is but a symbol suitable to my purpose. My play is set in the present, and the present lacks several things which makes the revival of such a beautiful, simple and pure celebration as the ancient Festival of Bacchus, impossible. People have grown too irreligious. Instead of experiencing the natural naturally, they befog things with their pedantic psychology. Nowadays Festivals of Bacchus are no longer possible because our love-life is murky, yes, poisoned by lies and self-deception, by jealousy and fear, by insolence and remorse. Only occasionally—and this but in pious souls—there is kindled a faint or still more brilliant reflection of the marvelous magic which once pervaded the Festival of Bacchus. And this magic is perhaps of a higher order than the other. But who of us can glory in his own piety? Who of us—?

GUARD (*entering*). Express to Freilassing, Rosenheim, Munich, Paris—

FELIX (*in an altered tone of voice*). Isn't that your train, doctor?

GUIDO (*surprised*). My train—?

AGNES. For Paris. Of course it's your train, doctor.

GUIDO. Well let it be— And now I must see about my baggage. Dear Mrs. Staufner—

(AGNES *gives him her hand.* GUIDO *hesitates a moment, then kisses it. He bows to* FELIX. FELIX *extends his hand.* GUIDO *takes it hurriedly, then goes down the steps. Pause. Commotion. Passengers pass out to the platform with porters, etc.*)

AGNES (*looking at him, after a long pause*). And what kind of a reflection is that?

(FELIX *looks at her as if he did not quite follow her meaning.*)

AGNES. The reflection in pious souls which you just mentioned, which to you signifies a loftier magic than the marvelous festival itself—this festival which according to you is no longer celebrated nowadays?

FELIX (*almost crudely*). This magic is called—forgetting. But we don't believe in that, you and I.

AGNES. You may be right. There may, however, be another which is easier to believe in.

(FELIX *gives her a questioning look.*)

AGNES. Understanding.

(*She has the picture in her hand and crushes it.* FELIX *laughs curtly.*)

GUIDO (*entering from the right with two handbags. He steps up to the table*). Pardon me, since it was most convenient to check both bags on one ticket—I—

AGNES (*anxiously*). Thank you, very much. Please put it here.

GUIDO. Don't mention it.

(*He places* AGNES' *handbag on the chair which he previously occupied.*)

FELIX (*rising suddenly*). Dr. Wernig—

GUIDO (*comprehending, with great dignity*). If it is your pleasure, Mr. Staufner, I can likewise put off my departure.

AGNES (*quickly, with determination*). You will depart on this train, Guido.

(FELIX *looks at her.* GUIDO *stands irresolute. Pause.*)

FELIX. You may go! (GUIDO *bows and goes out on the platform.*)

(FELIX *sits. His face is contorted. Then he rises again, as if to follow* GUIDO. AGNES *restrains him by grasping his arm.* FELIX *reseats himself.* AGNES *tears Bianca's picture into small bits.*)

FELIX (*bitterly*). If this were all!

AGNES (*with a ghost of a smile*). We must be pious, both of us.

FELIX (*in a sudden hollow tone of voice*). I hate you!

AGNES. And I hate you a thousand times more bitterly—(*with a new expression of tenderness*)—my lover!

CURTAIN

INTERIOR

A Play

By Maurice Maeterlinck

Translated by William Archer

CHARACTERS

In the Garden—

THE OLD MAN
THE STRANGER
MARTHA } *Granddaughters of the Old Man*
MARY
A PEASANT
THE CROWD

In the House—

THE FATHER
THE MOTHER
THE TWO DAUGHTERS } *Silent personages*
THE CHILD

INTERIOR

*The interval that elapses between the occurrence of a disaster and the break-
ing of the news to the bereaved is one full of tragedy; and here the pathetic
ignorance of the drowned girl's family and the painful knowledge of the
reluctant bearers of the evil tidings provide material for a touching little
play—slight material to all appearance, but in the hands of M. Maeterlinck
sufficient for the display of a wealth of kindly wisdom and sympathetic knowledge of human nature.*

An old garden planted with willows.
At the back, a house, with three of the ground-floor windows lighted up.
*Through them a family is pretty distinctly visible, gathered for the evening
round the lamp. The* FATHER *is seated at the chimney corner. The* MOTHER,
*resting one elbow on the table, is gazing into vacancy. Two young girls,
dressed in white, sit at their embroidery, dreaming and smiling in the
tranquillity of the room. A child is asleep, his head resting on his mother's
left arm. When one of them rises, walks, or makes a gesture, the movements
appear grave, slow, apart, and as though spiritualized by the distance, the
light, and the transparent film of the window-panes.*
THE OLD MAN *and* THE STRANGER *enter the garden cautiously.*

THE OLD MAN. Here we are in the part of the garden that lies behind the
house. They never come here. The doors are on the other side. They are
closed and the shutters shut. But there are no shutters on this side of the
house, and I saw the light . . . Yes, they are still sitting up in the lamplight. It is well that they have not heard us; the mother or the girls would
perhaps have come out, and then what should we have done?
THE STRANGER. What are we going to do?
THE OLD MAN. I want first to see if they are all in the room. Yes, I see
the father seated at the chimney corner. He is doing nothing, his hands
resting on his knees. The mother is leaning her elbow on the table . . .
THE STRANGER. She is looking at us.
THE OLD MAN. No, she is looking at nothing; her eyes are fixed. She
cannot see us; we are in the shadow of the great trees. But do not go any
nearer . . . There, too, are the dead girl's two sisters; they are embroidering
slowly. And the little child has fallen asleep. It is nine on the clock in the
corner . . . They divine no evil, and they do not speak.
THE STRANGER. If we were to attract the father's attention, and make
some sign to him? He has turned his head this way. Shall I knock at one
of the windows? One of them will have to hear of it before the others . . .

THE OLD MAN. I do not know which to choose . . . We must be very careful. The father is old and ailing—the mother too—and the sisters are too young . . . And they all loved her as they will never love again. I have never seen a happier household . . . No, no! do not go up to the window; that would be the worst thing we could do. It is better that we should tell them of it as simply as we can, as though it were a commonplace occurrence; and we must not appear too sad, else they will feel that their sorrow must exceed ours, and they will not know what to do . . . Let us go round to the other side of the garden. We will knock at the door, and go in as if nothing had happened. I will go in first: they will not be surprised to see me; I sometimes look in of an evening, to bring them some flowers or fruit, and to pass an hour or two with them.

THE STRANGER. Why do you want me to go with you? Go alone; I will wait until you call me. They have never seen me—I am only a passerby, a stranger . . .

THE OLD MAN. It is better that I should not be alone. A misfortune announced by a single voice seems more definite and crushing. I thought of that as I came along . . . If I go in alone, I shall have to speak at the very first moment; they will know all in a few words; I shall have nothing more to say; and I dread the silence which follows the last words that tell of a misfortune. It is then that the heart is torn. If we enter together, I shall go roundabout to work; I shall tell them, for example: "They found her thus, or thus . . . She was floating on the stream, and her hands were clasped . . ."

THE STRANGER. Her hands were not clasped; her arms were floating at her sides.

THE OLD MAN. You see, in spite of ourselves we begin to talk—and the misfortune is shrouded in its details. Otherwise, if I go in alone, I know them well enough to be sure that the very first words would produce a terrible effect, and God knows what would happen. But if we speak to them in turns, they will listen to us, and will forget to look the evil tidings in the face. Do not forget that the mother will be there, and that her life hangs by a thread . . . It is well that the first wave of sorrow should waste its strength in unnecessary words. It is wisest to let people gather round the unfortunate and talk as they will. Even the most indifferent carry off, without knowing it, some portion of the sorrow. It is dispersed without effort and without noise, like air or light . . .

THE STRANGER. Your clothes are soaked and are dripping on the flagstones.

THE OLD MAN. It is only the skirt of my mantle that has trailed a little in the water. You seem to be cold. Your coat is all muddy . . . I did not notice it on the way, it was so dark.

THE STRANGER. I went into the water up to my waist.

THE OLD MAN.—Had you found her long when I came up?

THE STRANGER. Only a few moments. I was going towards the village; it was already late, and the dusk was falling on the river bank. I was walking along with my eyes fixed on the river, because it was lighter than the road, when I saw something strange close by a tuft of reeds . . . I drew nearer, and I saw her hair, which had floated up almost into a circle round her head, and was swaying hither and thither with the current . . . (*In the room the two young girls turn their heads towards the window.*)

THE OLD MAN. Did you see her two sisters' hair trembling on their shoulders?

THE STRANGER. They turned their heads in our direction—they simply turned their heads. Perhaps I was speaking too loudly. (*The two girls resume their former position.*) They have turned away again already . . . I went into the water up to my waist, and then I managed to grasp her hand and easily drew her to the bank. She was as beautiful as her sisters . . .

THE OLD MAN. I think she was more beautiful . . . I do not know why I have lost all my courage . . .

THE STRANGER. What courage do you mean? We did all that man could do. She had been dead for more than an hour.

THE OLD MAN. She was living this morning! I met her coming out of the church. She told me that she was going away; she was going to see her grandmother on the other side of the river in which you found her. She did not know when I should see her again . . . She seemed to be on the point of asking me something; then I suppose she did not dare, and she left me abruptly. But now that I think of it—and I noticed nothing at the time!—she smiled as people smile who want to be silent, or who fear that they will not be understood . . . Even hope seemed like a pain to her; her eyes were veiled, and she scarcely looked at me.

THE STRANGER. Some peasants told me that they saw her wandering all the afternoon on the bank. They thought she was looking for flowers . . . It is possible that her death . . .

THE OLD MAN. No one can tell . . . What can any one know? She was perhaps one of those who shrink from speech, and everyone bears in his breast more than one reason for ceasing to live. You cannot see into the soul as you see into that room. They are all like that—they say nothing but trivial things, and no one dreams that there is aught amiss. You live for months by the side of one who is no longer of this world, and whose soul cannot stoop to it; you answer her unthinkingly; and you see what happens. They look like lifeless puppets, and all the time so many things are passing in their souls. They do not themselves know what they are. She might have lived as the others live. She might have said to the day of her death: "Sir, or Madam, it will rain this morning," or, "We are going to lunch; we shall be thirteen at table," or "The fruit is not yet ripe." They speak smilingly of the flowers that have fallen, and they weep in the darkness. An angel from heaven would not see what ought to be seen; and men understand nothing until after all is over . . . Yesterday evening she was there, sitting in the lamplight like her sisters; and you would not see them now as they ought to be seen if this had not happened . . . I seem to see her for the first time . . . Something new must come into our ordinary life before we can understand it. They are at your side day and night; and you do not really see them until the moment when they depart forever. And yet, what a strange little soul she must have had—what a poor little, artless, unfathomable soul she must have had—to have said what she must have said, and done what she must have done!

THE STRANGER. See, they are smiling in the silence of the room . . .

THE OLD MAN. They are not at all anxious—they did not expect her this evening.

THE STRANGER. They sit motionless and smiling. But see, the father puts his fingers to his lips . . .

THE OLD MAN. He points to the child asleep on its mother's breast . . .

THE STRANGER. She dares not raise her head for fear of disturbing it . . .

THE OLD MAN. They are not sewing any more. There is a dead silence . . .

THE STRANGER. They have let fall their skein of white silk . . .

THE OLD MAN. They are looking at the child . . .

THE STRANGER. They do not know that others are looking at them . . .

THE OLD MAN. We, too, are watched . . .

THE STRANGER. They have raised their eyes . . .

THE OLD MAN. And yet they can see nothing . . .

THE STRANGER. They seem to be happy, and yet there is something—I cannot tell what . . .

THE OLD MAN. They think themselves beyond the reach of danger. They have closed the doors, and the windows are barred with iron. They have strengthened the walls of the old house; they have shot the bolts of the three oaken doors. They have foreseen everything that can be foreseen . . .

THE STRANGER. Sooner or later we must tell them. Some one might come in and blurt it out abruptly. There was a crowd of peasants in the meadow where we left the dead girl—if one of them were to come and knock at the door . . .

THE OLD MAN. Martha and Mary are watching the little body. The peasants were going to make a litter of branches, and I told my eldest granddaughter to hurry on and let us know the moment they made a start. Let us wait till she comes; she will go with me. . . . I wish we had not been able to watch them in this way. I thought there was nothing to do but to knock at the door, to enter quite simply, and to tell all in a few phrases. . . . But I have watched them too long, living in the lamplight. . . . (*Enter* MARY.)

MARY. They are coming, grandfather.

THE OLD MAN. Is that you? Where are they?

MARY. They are at the foot of the last slope.

THE OLD MAN. They are coming silently.

MARY. I told them to pray in a low voice. Martha is with them.

THE OLD MAN. Are there many of them?

MARY. The whole village is around the bier. They had brought lanterns; I bade them put them out.

THE OLD MAN. What way are they coming?

MARY. They are coming by the little path. They are moving slowly.

THE OLD MAN. It is time . . .

MARY. Have you told them, grandfather?

THE OLD MAN. You can see that we have told them nothing. There they are, still sitting in the lamplight. Look, my child, look: you will see what life is . . .

MARY. Oh! how peaceful they seem! I feel as though I were seeing them in a dream.

THE STRANGER. Look there—I saw the two sisters give a start.

THE OLD MAN. They are rising . . .

THE STRANGER. I believe they are coming to the windows.

(*At this moment one of the two sisters comes up to the first window, the other to the third; and resting their hands against the panes they stand gazing into the darkness.*)

THE OLD MAN. No one comes to the middle window.

MARY. They are looking out; they are listening . . .

THE OLD MAN. The elder is smiling at what she does not see.

THE STRANGER. The eyes of the second are full of fear.

THE OLD MAN. Take care: who knows how far the soul may extend around the body. . . . (*A long silence.* MARY *nestles close to* THE OLD MAN'S *breast and kisses him.*)

MARY. Grandfather!

THE OLD MAN. Do not weep, my child; our turn will come. (*A pause.*)

THE STRANGER. They are looking long. . . .

THE OLD MAN. Poor things, they would see nothing though they looked for a hundred thousand years—the night is too dark. They are looking this way; and it is from the other side that misfortune is coming.

THE STRANGER. It is well that they are looking this way. Something, I do not know what, is approaching by way of the meadows.

MARY. I think it is the crowd; they are too far off for us to see clearly.

THE STRANGER. They are following the windings of the path—there they come in sight again on that moonlit slope.

MARY. Oh! how many they seem to be. Even when I left, people were coming up from the outskirts of the town. They are taking a very round-about way. . . .

THE OLD MAN. They will arrive at last, none the less. I see them, too— they are crossing the meadows—they look so small that one can scarcely distinguish them among the herbage. You might think them children playing in the moonlight; if the girls saw them, they would not understand. Turn their backs to it as they may, misfortune is approaching step by step, and has been looming larger for more than two hours past. They cannot bid it stay; and those who are bringing it are powerless to stop it. It has mastered them, too, and they must needs serve it. It knows its goal, and it takes its course. It is unwearying, and it has but one idea. They have to lend it their strength.

They are sad, but they draw nearer. Their hearts are full of pity, but they must advance. . . .

MARY. The elder has ceased to smile, grandfather.

THE STRANGER. They are leaving the windows. . . .

MARY. They are kissing their mother. . . .

THE STRANGER. The elder is stroking the child's curls without wakening it.

MARY. Ah! the father wants them to kiss him, too. . . .

THE STRANGER. Now there is silence. . . .

MARY. They have returned to their mother's side.

THE STRANGER. And the father keeps his eyes fixed on the great pendulum of the clock . . .

MARY. They seem to be praying without knowing what they do. . . .

THE STRANGER. They seem to be listening to their own souls. . . . (*A pause.*)

MARY. Grandfather, do not tell them this evening!

THE OLD MAN. You see, you are losing courage, too. I knew you ought not to look at them. I am nearly eighty-three years old, and this is the first time that the reality of life has come home to me. I do not know why all they do appears to me so strange and solemn. There they sit awaiting the night, simply, under their lamp, as we should under our own; and yet I seem to see them from the altitude of another world, because I know a little fact which as yet they do not know . . . Is it so, my children? Tell me, why are you, too, pale? Perhaps there is something else that we cannot put in words, and that makes us weep? I did not know that there was anything so sad in life, or that it could strike such terror to those who look on at it. And even if nothing had happened, it would frighten me to see them sit there so peacefully. They have too much confidence in this world. There they sit, separated from the enemy by only a few poor panes of glass. They think that nothing will happen because they have closed their doors, and they do not know that it is in the soul that things always happen, and that the world does not end at their house-door. They are so secure of their little life, and do not dream that so many others know more of it than they, and that I, poor old man, at two steps from their door, hold all their little happiness, like a wounded bird, in the hollow of my old hands, and dare not open them . . .

MARY. Have pity on them, grandfather. . . .

THE OLD MAN. We have pity on them, my child, but no one has pity on us.

MARY. Tell them to-morrow, grandfather; tell them when it is light, then they will not be so sad.

THE OLD MAN. Perhaps you are right, my child. . . . It would be better to leave all this in the night. And the daylight is sweet to sorrow. . . . But what would they say to us to-morrow? Misfortune makes people jealous; those upon whom it has fallen want to know of it before strangers—they do not like to leave it in unknown hands. We should seem to have robbed them of something.

THE STRANGER. Besides, it is too late now; already I can hear the murmur of prayers.

MARY. They are here—they are passing behind the hedges. (*Enter* MARTHA.)

MARTHA. Here I am. I have guided them hither—I told them to wait in the road. (*Cries of children are heard.*) Ah! the children are still crying. I forbade them to come, but they want to see, too, and the mothers would not obey me. I will go and tell them—no, they have stopped crying. Is everything ready? I have brought the little ring that was found upon her. I have some fruit, too, for the child. I laid her to rest myself upon the bier. She looks as though she were sleeping. I had a great deal of trouble with her hair—I could not arrange it properly. I made them gather marguerites—it is a pity there were no other flowers. What are you doing here? Why are you not with them? (*She looks in at the windows.*) They are not weeping! They—you have not told them!

THE OLD MAN. Martha, Martha, there is too much life in your soul; you cannot understand. . . .

MARTHA. Why should I not understand? (*After a silence, and in a tone of grave reproach.*) You really ought not to have done that, grandfather. . . .

THE OLD MAN. Martha, you do not know. . . .

MARTHA. I will go and tell them.

THE OLD MAN. Remain here, my child, and look for a moment.

MARTHA. Oh, how I pity them! They must wait no longer. . . .

THE OLD MAN. Why not?

MARTHA. I do not know, but it is not possible!

THE OLD MAN. Come here, my child. . . .

MARTHA. How patient they are!

THE OLD MAN. Come here, my child. . . .

MARTHA (*turning*). Where are you, grandfather? I am so unhappy, I cannot see you any more. I do not myself know now what to do. . . .

THE OLD MAN. Do not look any more; until they know all. . . .

MARTHA. I want to go with you. . . .

THE OLD MAN. No, Martha, stay here. Sit beside your sister on this old stone bench against the wall of the house, and do not look. You are too young, you would never be able to forget it. You cannot know what a face looks like at the moment when Death is passing into its eyes. Perhaps they will cry out, too . . . Do not turn round. Perhaps there will be no sound at all. Above all things, if there is no sound, be sure you do not turn and look. One can never foresee the course that sorrow will take. A few little sobs wrung from the depths, and generally that is all. I do not know myself what I shall do when I hear them—they do not belong to this life. Kiss me, my child, before I go. (*The murmur of prayers has gradually drawn nearer. A portion of the crowd forces its way into the garden. There is a sound of deadened footfalls and of whispering.*)

THE STRANGER (*to the crowd*). Stop here—do not go near the window. Where is she?

A PEASANT. Who?

THE STRANGER. The others—the bearers.

A PEASANT. They are coming by the avenue that leads up to the door. (THE OLD MAN *goes out.* MARTHA *and* MARY *have seated themselves on the bench, their backs to the windows. Low murmurings are heard among the crowd.*)

THE STRANGER. Hush! Do not speak. (*In the room the taller of the two sisters rises, goes to the door, and shoots the bolts.*)

MARTHA. She is opening the door!

THE STRANGER. On the contrary, she is fastening it. (*A pause.*)

MARTHA. Grandfather has not come in?

THE STRANGER. No. She takes her seat again at her mother's side. The others do not move, and the child is still sleeping. (*A pause.*)

MARTHA. My little sister, give me your hands.

MARY. Martha! (*They embrace and kiss each other.*)

THE STRANGER. He must have knocked—they have all raised their heads at the same time—they are looking at each other.

MARTHA. Oh! oh! my poor little sister! I can scarcely help crying out, too. (*She smothers her sobs on her sister's shoulder.*)

THE STRANGER. He must have knocked again. The father is looking at the clock. He rises. . . .

MARTHA. Sister, sister, I must go in too—they cannot be left alone.

MARY. Martha, Martha! (*She holds her back.*)

THE STRANGER. The father is at the door—he is drawing the bolts—he is opening it cautiously.

MARTHA. Oh!—you do not see the . . .

THE STRANGER. What?

MARTHA. The bearers . . .

THE STRANGER. He has only opened it a very little. I see nothing but a corner of the lawn and the fountain. He keeps his hand on the door—he takes a step back—he seems to be saying, "Ah, it is you!" He raises his arms. He carefully closes the door again. Your grandfather has entered the room . . . (*The crowd has come up to the window.* MARTHA *and* MARY *half rise from their seat, then rise altogether and follow the rest towards the windows, pressing close to each other.* THE OLD MAN *is seen advancing into the room. The two* SISTERS *rise; the* MOTHER *also rises, and carefully settles the* CHILD *in the armchair which she has left, so that from outside the little one can be seen sleeping, his head a little bent forward, in the middle of the room. The* MOTHER *advances to meet* THE OLD MAN, *and holds out her hand to him, but draws it back again before he has had time to take it. One of the girls wants to take off the visitor's mantle, and the other pushes forward an armchair for him. But* THE OLD MAN *makes a little gesture of refusal. The* FATHER *smiles with an air of astonishment.* THE OLD MAN *looks toward the windows.*)

THE STRANGER. He dares not tell them. He is looking towards us. (*Murmurs in the crowd.*)

THE STRANGER. Hush! (THE OLD MAN, *seeing faces at the windows, quickly averts his eyes. As one of the girls is still offering him the armchair, he at last sits down and passes his right hand several times over his forehead.*)

THE STRANGER. He is sitting down. . . . (*The others who are in the room also sit down, while the* FATHER *seems to be speaking volubly. At last* THE OLD MAN *opens his mouth, and the sound of his voice seems to arouse their attention. But the* FATHER *interrupts him.* THE OLD MAN *begins to speak again, and little by little the others grow tense with apprehension. All of a sudden the* MOTHER *starts and rises.*)

MARTHA. Oh! the mother begins to understand! (*She turns away and hides her face in her hands. Renewed murmurs among the crowd. They elbow each other. Children cry to be lifted up, so that they may see too. Most of the mothers do as they wish.*)

THE STRANGER. Hush! he has not told them yet. . . . (*The* MOTHER *is seen to be questioning* THE OLD MAN *with anxiety. He says a few more words; then, suddenly, all the others rise, too, and seem to question him. Then he slowly makes an affirmative movement of his head.*)

THE STRANGER. He has told them—he has told them all at once!

VOICES IN THE CROWD. He has told them! he has told them!

THE STRANGER. I can hear nothing. . . . (THE OLD MAN *also rises, and, without turning, makes a gesture indicating the door, which is behind him. The* MOTHER, *the* FATHER, *and the two* DAUGHTERS *rush to this door, which the* FATHER *has difficulty in opening.* THE OLD MAN *tries to prevent the* MOTHER *from going out.*)

VOICES IN THE CROWD. They are going out! they are going out! (*Confusion among the crowd in the garden. All hurry to the other side of the house and disappear, except* THE STRANGER, *who remains at the windows. In the room, the folding door is at last thrown wide open; all go out at the same time. Beyond can be seen the starry sky, the lawn and the fountain in the moonlight; while, left alone in the middle of the room, the* CHILD *continues to sleep peacefully in the armchair. A pause.*)

THE STRANGER. The child has not wakened! (*He also goes out.*)

CURTAIN

CHINTAMANI

A SYMBOLIC DRAMA

By GIRISH C. GHOSE

A Translation and Adaptation from the Original Hindu by Dhan Gopal Mukerji

CHARACTERS

BILLWAMANGAL, *a young Brahmin*
CHINTAMANI, *his mistress*
PUNDIT, *or man of wisdom, mendicant*
Disciple of Pundit
With Chintamani: blind man, poor woman, four ragged and starving children
Householder
Householder's Wife
Three Hermits
Drunken Man
Shepherd, *attendant of Billwamangal*
The "Vision"

CHINTAMANI

ACT ONE

Scene I

To the left, outer door of house. In the foreground, front yard of the house. The house has a thatched roof, white walls. Eaves overhang wall. From one of the projecting beams hangs a dead black snake, looking like a thick black rope. There is an open space between roof and wall, passage enough for a man to creep in. At back of stage the Ganges is visible, dark and stormy. Flashes of lightning, low rumble of thunder throughout the scene. Wash of waves also audible.

Curtain rises on empty stage, all is still except for storm. Suddenly voices are heard from within the house. BILLWAMANGAL and CHINTAMANI come out through the door. She has a lamp in her hand. His clothes and hair are wet and dripping. She has long, black curls, loosely falling on her back. Her large, dark eyes are remarkable. She wears silk "saree."

BILLWAMANGAL. Come, see! Here is the rope you hung for me. That is how I came to you.

CHINTAMANI (*mystified*). But I tell you I hung no rope. Why should I? I knew you would not come to-night because of your father's funeral. Does not the law forbid it? Are you not afraid of God?

BILLWAMANGAL (*passionately*). God—I have no God but you—

CHINTAMANI. But the funeral rites?

BILLWAMANGAL. What did I care for that? It is only you I think of, you, you, you,—Chintamani. (*Goes toward her, arms outstretched.*)

CHINTAMANI (*shrieking, as she sees how wet and disheveled he is*). What —you are dripping,—and there is a smell of dead things about you. You have swum the river? (*Wonder in her tones, turns and looks at dark river, shudders.*) A night like this. (*Waves her arm toward the river, gesture of amazement.*) How did you do it?

BILLWAMANGAL (*contemptuously*). The river? I swam it. Why not? You were here. I swam for more than two hours. Had it not been for the log that I clung to, I would be at the bottom of the river by this time.

CHINTAMANI (*as he sways with exhaustion*). You are faint. You must rest.

BILLWAMANGAL. I want no rest. Only you. Come to me, Chintamani. (*Approaches her.*)

49

CHINTAMANI (*distracting his attention*). But why do you not tell me how you got into the room? The door was locked.

BILLWAMANGAL. Locked? Love knows no lock. (*Looks at the door.*) If it were iron, I would break it open to come to you. (*With sudden revulsion of feeling.*) How I love that door because it keeps my treasure secure! (*Goes to the door and kisses it.*)

CHINTAMANI. Be reasonable. I locked the door because I did not suppose you would come. (*As BILLWAMANGAL walks past looking at the wall.*) What are you looking for?

BILLWAMANGAL (*dazedly looking at the hanging snake*). I thought it was a rope.

CHINTAMANI. What— (*Looks at him and then at snake.*) Oh, what is that? (*Draws away in fear.*)

BILLWAMANGAL. Oh, Father! Do not fear it. It is dead.

CHINTAMANI (*in horror*). A dead snake—why?

BILLWAMANGAL. Don't you see? How blind love is! I scaled the wall with that rope, that black rope whose sting would have me lie here—*dead.* In the morning you would have found me dead at your door. You see how I love you. Look at me. With those beautiful large eyes. (*Gazing at her face adoringly.*)

CHINTAMANI (*steps closer to the house, holds lamp near the snake*). Billwa, you are insane. In the dark of night, when the clouds dart down the rain like arrows. The swollen river—the surf in frenzy. How could you do this? And what a sin! Seeking the couch of your mistress on the night of your father's funeral. Have you no fear of sin?

BILLWAMANGAL (*with his eyes fixed on her*). Sin, there is no sin in that face. Those lips with each kiss will wipe away the sins of ages from my mouth. Come—let me kiss you.

CHINTAMANI (*recoiling*). No—I do not believe you. Did you go home at all? Did you perform the ceremonies? Are you not afraid of what—awaits those who neglect the funeral of a father?

BILLWAMANGAL. Father? What is a father? What is anything beside you? When the priest was chanting his Montra, I was hearing the melody of your voice. He asked me to recall my father's face. Yours beamed in the mist of the smoke. In the perfume of the incense I felt your breath. I tried to say many things, but my lips whispered, Chintamani. Come to me, Chintamani; come to me, Chintamani; do not talk of the dead. The only thing about them is that they remain dead. I don't want them to come to life for that will come between you and me. Let us go in. I am cold. (*Comes closer to her.*)

CHINTAMANI. There is the smell of dead things clinging to your clothes. No, I will not go in. (*With sudden whimsical gesture.*) I want to see your log that helped you to swim to me.

BILLWAMANGAL. It may be another snake.

CHINTAMANI. I want to see it just the same.

BILLWAMANGAL. Can't you wait till morning?

CHINTAMANI (*petulantly*). I want to see the piece of wood. (BILLWAMANGAL *shrugs his shoulders and gives in, and they walk toward the river bank, she still holding the light.*)

CURTAIN

SCENE II

(*At river bank; at a distance, to the left, lies a dead body.*)

CHINTAMANI. Where is it?

BILLWAMANGAL. I do not remember where I left it. Let us go back now; we will come in the morning.

CHINTAMANI. But that horrible smell that hangs about you! It must have been something other than wood.

BILLWAMANGAL. If it is, what difference does it make? I love you. Isn't that snake testimony enough? I might have clung to a crocodile when I swam. Oh, Chintamani, come home. I know it is a log.

CHINTAMANI. I will not go back. You are insane. Look! See if you can find the place where you came out of the water.

BILLWAMANGAL (*bending with her*). It is hard to tell. The rain has washed away the footprints. Oh! Here is one. Let us follow it.

CHINTAMANI. There is another! (*They go nearer the hidden body on the left.*)

CHINTAMANI (*starting*). You smell so horrible. (*The light falls on the rotting corpse; she shrieks.*) "Dead!" (*Drops the lamp.*)

BILLWAMANGAL (*catches lamp as it strikes ground, horror-stricken as light falls on corpse*). Oh!

CHINTAMANI (*in awed voice*). Billwa, you clung to a corpse!

BILLWAMANGAL. How I love you!

CHINTAMANI. You are insane. You have no abhorrence of dead things.

BILLWAMANGAL. Even death brings me to you! Chintamani, how I love, love you! (*Comes near her.*)

CHINTAMANI. Don't touch me! (*The lamplight falling on her face, shows her pale and more attractive than before.*)

BILLWAMANGAL (*gazing at her face. As he speaks, she stays in deep thought*). How beautiful!

CHINTAMANI. If you gave this love to God instead of to a harlot; what could you not become? A snake, a corpse, only to kiss a girl's painted lips.

BILLWAMANGAL. All my gods are in your face. All my passions, all my emotions are in your eyes, Chintamani! Your eyes charm my heart from me.

CHINTAMANI. Don't talk to me. Oh, leave me!

BILLWAMANGAL. What are you saying, Lila? Can a man leave his soul? Only Death can take it away from our body. And (*pointing to corpse*) I have conquered Death.

CHINTAMANI. Billwamana, you are a god.

BILLWAMANGAL. Your slave. For you I will be a god. My wealth, my name, my fame, all I have has been given up for you. When other men would have been sorrowing for a dead parent, I was rejoicing over your living beauty. Beauty is eternal. Chintamani, you shall live, live for ages, and each age I will be with you! Chintamani. (*Draws closer to her.*)

CHINTAMANI (*withdrawing*). I am beautiful. But how long will that last? A few more years. All these black curls will be white; this forehead will be furrowed; these brows, shaped like bows whence love hurls his arrows, will droop, and (*choking with her emotion*) these eyes, what will they be? Dim, hollow—

BILLWAMANGAL. Don't! I love you. You must remain young.

CHINTAMANI (*with a sardonic laugh*). Young to satisfy your lust. Your love will not let me grow old. Then I must die. What then?

BILLWAMANGAL. No. (*Looks at corpse.*) Yes.

CHINTAMANI. Death will take me. Will my memory then stay with you? No, you will seek out another Chintamani.

BILLWAMANGAL. You are my only Chintamani!

CHINTAMANI. Death, Billwamana—

BILLWAMANGAL. Death—what is death!

CHINTAMANI. What have we done that can make us scorn death? Have we any noble work that would have to be completed after we die? Is there one aspiration that will go beyond the funeral pyre? Our life! How hollow! It will end with death! (*Throws up her arms despairingly.*) It cannot go beyond.

BILLWAMANGAL. My God, stop—

CHINTAMANI. I will not stop. God, yes, isn't he watching us? Billwa, think! Isn't it written in his book that he who seeks his mistress' couch on the night of the funeral ceremony of his parent, for him heaven will hold no room? How we are throwing away our youth! Bilwa, you are a Brahmin—

BILLWAMANGAL. Don't. I am not a Brahmin. The day I saw you I gave up my caste and creed. All that I know, Chintamani, is that I am yours!

CHINTAMANI. You will have to know much more. When you see God, what will you say to him?

BILLWAMANGAL. I will say to Him, that you are my God! While I have you, I don't want God! (*Tries to embrace her.*)

CHINTAMANI (*with such awed majesty that his arms drop*). I—keeping you from God! Billwa, love God as you love me. Why not? You can do it. Look (*points at the snake*), you can do the impossible. Go, do that for God! He is the true Chintamani. Look for Him! (*Gesture.*)

BILLWAMANGAL. You are my only Chintamani!

CHINTAMANI (*paying no attention to him*). Look!

BILLWAMANGAL. I will but look at you.

CHINTAMANI (*pointing to corpse*). That is the end of such lives as ours. (*They look at it silently. Even* BILLWAMANGAL *is awed for a moment.*)

CHINTAMANI. Look to God! (*Gesturing upward again.*)
BILLWAMANGAL (*forgetting all but her beauty*). How fair you are,
Chintamani!
CHINTAMANI (*stepping back*). Not me, but God alone!
BILLWAMANGAL. All my God is in your face!
CHINTAMANI (*dashing the lamp to the ground from his hand; nothing can
be seen in the dark*). God alone! (*There is a moment's silence. Then, with
a sob,* CHINTAMANI *runs back to her house, goes in and shuts the door.*)
BILLWAMANGAL (*turning quickly round as he hears the door shut*). Chin-
tamani! (*In heartbroken tones.*) Chintamani! (*Takes a few steps toward
the house, realizes the futility of such an attempt, comes back to center of
the stage, still in darkness.*) Dark clouds follow dark clouds. What darkness!
I cannot see far or near. Come back, Chintamani! (*Lightning and thunder.*)
Why does not lightning strike me? Roar, thunder, I fear you not! Waves,
rise, I care not. Life—what is life—without Chintamani? I will never see
her again! How can I find her? Chintamani! (*Waits and listens.*) Chintamani! (*Pale glimpse of dawn, shows corpse and* BILLWAMANGAL. *He is
standing in an attitude of despair. He sees corpse, shudders, turns to the
dawn.*) Gone—mother, father, one by one, have floated on the stormy breast
of the Ganges. None to call mine. Who is mine? Yet, am I alone? (*Looks
up at the dawn, raises hands to it.*) From birth, who has been mine? I seem
to know someone! Who is he? Is he that Chintamani, the Most High?
Where is he? (*Goes toward the right almost in a spell.*) Where is the light
that will lead me to him?

CURTAIN

ACT TWO

SCENE I

*A street paved with red macadam, like other Indian towns. In the back-
ground is a row of white houses with black iron-plated doors.
The crimson rays of the setting sun fall along the street; the purple shadows
of the white houses slightly touch the pavement. People are passing—a
stray beggar leaning on his stick; a girl barefoot, with silver anklets and
pale yellow face. Two men enter. One old and the other young. The old
man is a "pundit," and the young man is his disciple. The* PUNDIT *wears a
white tunic, yellow toga; the young man wears a plain white cotton garment. They talk a little.*

(*Enter* BILLWAMANGAL *dressed in the yellow tunic of a mendicant. He
listens to them attentively; he leans on his staff.*)
PUNDIT. What do you wish, my son?

BILLWAMANGAL. I have heard of your fame,—I have come to learn wisdom of you.

PUNDIT. What are you seeking, my son?

BILLWAMANGAL. I am looking for Chintamani.

PUNDIT. Oh, great man, I make my obeisance to you. Blessed art thou, seeker after truth!

BILLWAMANGAL. I am a humble pilgrim looking for the light.

DISCIPLE. I am glad to see your humility, my friend. Our master possesses all the wisdom of the world; he will impart all the knowledge you want.

PUNDIT (*looking vaguely at* BILLWAMANGAL, *then in the direction of the sunset*). Do you see the hermits bathing in the Ganges? (*Turning to* DISCIPLE.) Wouldn't you like to lead an existence like that? They are purifying their bodies and their souls in the holy waters; for the evening worship is at hand. Those great souls know too well that to cling to passion, love and emotion is to cling to a dream. They have realized that the soul is the only reality. Having realized, they are spending each day of this brief existence in search of truth. Aren't they blessed?

DISCIPLE. I know that, master. They inspire me for the highest, it is true. But their lives do not fascinate me.

BILLWAMANGAL. And I who live their life know it is hollow.

DISCIPLE. There is an uncouthness about it. (*Looking to the right.*) Look how beautiful the sunset is. The slanting rays, what magnificent mesh work they have wrought on the river. Look at the birds,—they are soaring high in the air, then they fly for their nests. (*To* BILLWAMANGAL.) Do you not like a life like that? Bird life is what existence ought to be.

PUNDIT. Ah, poor mortal, you see not the higher charms that are more enchanting than this mortal existence?

BILLWAMANGAL. What is the higher charm? How do you know of it?

PUNDIT. You remind me of what I learned once at my master's feet. It was a story about a certain righteous man. His life was spotless. He was famed to have possessed wisdom. Once the god of death came to him and took him to pay a visit to a saint. After they had reached the river bank, they found a tall man, covered with long white hair, standing there and looking at the sun. At his feet lay a pile of such white hair, which he was supposed to have shed in course of time. At the arrival of the god of death, he said, "Why are you here? The time of your arrival is not yet at hand." Death asked when the hour should come. The saint replied, "Ere long,—I have only a few million more hairs left—each of which I will shed in every ten years. When I shall have shed the last one, that will be the signal of your coming. Please don't disturb me now. I must apply this brief period to work out my salvation." The god of death then asked him a question—that is—What is the most astonishing thing in life? The saint replied, "From day to day, so many are dying, yet, those that live are contented and happy as if they did not have to die." My son, this story made me realize my ignorance.

DISCIPLE (*to* BILLWAMANGAL). What do you think of it?

BILLWAMANGAL. That tells me nothing of Chintamani.

DISCIPLE. The master's wisdom will tell you all that you want to know, for he knows everything.

PUNDIT. No, I know very little. I am only one of those who have been able to count a few waves of the ocean of wisdom.

BILLWAMANGAL. I am pleased to hear your remarks, sir. But have you been able to know where Chintamani is?

PUNDIT. Yes. No—I do not know how to answer your question. My knowledge of him is like this evening hour. The sky yonder is illumined with the fragments of light that are still lingering after the sun. Above from the hollow of the blue, peers a single star. I feel like saying that I know the star for I see it, yet, that ever increasing darkness that is rising from the darker surface of the river makes me say, "Perhaps it is all dark." I yet seem to know—though I don't feel so, yes—my knowledge is like this evening hour. Light here, dark there, day here, night there. Perhaps it is all a dream.

BILLWAMANGAL. Then you haven't found it yet? Chintamani could surely be seen, if seen could be expressed without difficulty.

DISCIPLE. You speak aright, venerable stranger. But you should bear in mind that God cannot be known in a short time, for he is the whole universe.

PUNDIT. He is unknowable.

BILLWAMANGAL. Words, words, words, words.

DISCIPLE. Word is God.

BILLWAMANGAL. No, God is love.

PUNDIT (*bell rings at a distance; restrains the* DISCIPLE, *who was trying to answer* BILLWAMANGAL). Come, let us go to the evening worship. The hour has struck. (*Exit.*)

BILLWAMANGAL. You vain beings, how could you know of Chintamani? I know—I possessed Chintamani once. (*A woman enters, she goes to the door of the first house from the right. Her anklets jingle. She enters. The door closes behind her,* BILLWAMANGAL *observing her.*) How she resembles Chintamani! She has her eyes. Ah, God, you are merciful at last. (*Goes slowly toward the door.*)

CURTAIN

SCENE II

Setting same as Scene I. BILLWAMANGAL'S *staff leaning on the wall of the house. The street is darker and deserted. Enter* CHINTAMANI *leading a blind man by the hand. They are followed by two ragged children; behind them another woman, holding a child in her arms.*)

CHINTAMANI (*stopping*). Let us rest here for a few minutes.

BLIND MAN (*feeling the ground with his hands*). I am so tired. (*Sits down.*) How far from here is the place, Mother Chintamani?

CHINTAMANI (*looking at the other woman, who makes the two children sit by her, and tries to put the baby to sleep*). How far is it, sister?

THE WOMAN. Not very far. About half an hour's journey from here. (*Looking at the sky.*) It is the new moon. Look at the yellow horns of the crescent. (*Ring of gong from a distance.*)

THE WOMAN (*to* CHINTAMANI). They have commenced the evening worship.

CHINTAMANI. Ah, God, how long should we have to repent?

OTHER WOMAN. Please, Chintamani, don't grow sad. You do not know yet what suffering is. You were born rich. Had many luxuries—but look at these who are born poor. (*Pointing at the children.*) You had wealth, you had love. To these even mother's love has been denied.

CHINTAMANI (*aside*). Ah, what a blessing we had no child!

BLIND MAN. Do you know how I lost my eyes, it was mid-summer, about thirty years ago—I was very young then. I was passing through the town, Bajara, on my way to Benares. At an inn in Bajara, one night, as I lay on my back staring at the dark roof, something fell into my eyes.

CHINTAMANI. Oh—do not say any more. Always some misfortune befalls each one of us. Life without misfortune is impossible. Look at the setting crescent.

BLIND MAN. I cannot see. Is it red?

OTHER WOMAN. Chintamani! (*Who had hid her face in her hands.*) One of the boys has fallen asleep. It is getting dark. Let us go before the other one gets sleepy.

CHINTAMANI. Shall I wake him up?

OTHER WOMAN. No, carry him in your arms.

BLIND MAN. But who will lead me in the dark? (*A light is lighted on the doorpost of the house, on whose wall the staff is leaning. The gong sounds again.*)

CHINTAMANI. Let us go—they are ringing.

OTHER WOMAN (*looking at the staff leaning against the wall*). There is a staff. God is always with us. Brother, couldn't you lean on that staff and walk behind us?

BLIND MAN. Yes, I will. Give it to me. Is it very, very dark now? They are ringing.

OTHER WOMAN (*taking the staff in her hand, looking at it*). Oh, Chintamani, who has written your name on it? This must be a hermit's staff. He has written God's name on it. For that is his only support. Wherever we go we find your name. How kind God is—He is always with us.

CHINTAMANI (*looking at the staff, aside*). He is here,—Billwa, where are you? (*Aloud.*) Let us go, somebody may come.

OTHER WOMAN. What is that to us? We are beggars. (*Hands staff to blind man.*) Come on, brother, let us go. (*Exit. Gong rings.*)

BLIND MAN (*rising*). They ring, is it for the last time?

Scene III

(*In a room inside the house.*)

(Billwamangal *seated on the floor with the householder, the latter's wife making a bed in the inner room, to the right.*)

Householder. Have you visited Juggernaut, too?

Billwamangal. Yes, I was there for a week.

Householder. Is it a very beautiful place?

Billwamangal. The city of the protector of the world is not only beautiful but full of love, too. Love rules supreme in Juggernaut. None goes hungry in that city. One and all, from the hermit to the householder, each has plenty to eat. Fasting, too, is prohibited there. People believe that in the city of the supreme protector, starvation of any kind should remain unknown. There they feed every one—because they love one another.

Householder. They have the sea there, I hear. How does the sea look? I have never seen it.

Billwamangal (*paying very little attention*). At evening, like this, you go to the beach, you hear the roar of waves wax louder. The sea looks dark blue. The stars rise up from the abyss one by one; the lights carried by the incoming pilgrims from afar look like so many stars. About you sitting on the beach are hundreds at their evening meal. It is all love and harmony there. It is the city of Chintamani. (*Noise outside.*)

Householder. Excuse me for a moment. (*Exit to the left.*)

Billwamangal (*peeps at the inner room at the right, aside*). How—(*As he hears the approaching footsteps, collects himself.*)

Householder (*entering*). Some beggars passed by.

Billwamangal. Didn't you ask them in?

Householder. Yes, but they had already found shelter somewhere else.

Billwamangal. This is a generous town.

Householder. Yes, we are not very poor, by the grace of God. (*Gong rings.*)

Billwamangal. Is it late now? They are ringing—is it for the last time?

Householder. No, this is the last but one.

Billwamangal. Does it ring like this always?

Householder. Yes, it tells people how time passes.

Billwamangal. Do you wish me to do anything for you when I arrive in Benares?

Householder. Yes, please pray to Biawanath to give us a child.

Billwamangal. Anything else?

Householder. No, nothing else.

Billwamangal. I must sleep now.

Householder. I will show you where. Do you desire anything else? Everything is at your disposal.

BILLWAMANGAL. Send your wife to me to-night.

HOUSEHOLDER (*staggering*). Such a humor for a hermit!

BILLWAMANGAL. Observe the rule of hospitality. Do what I bid you.

HOUSEHOLDER. If she consents. (*Exit.*)

BILLWAMANGAL. You blinded fool. Can you not see? I am not a saint. There are no saints. What eyes she has! They are so large, so dark—dark like the darkest night. She is fairer than Chintamani. Eh, where is she? At the bottom of the Ganges! Where is she? Dead? For me—she died. Her eyes are there searching for me, Chintamani. (*Gong rings.*) Who rings, wrings my heart away? Chintamani, Chintamani, my love, my soul; I have sinned, sinned against you. Where are you, Chintamani? Forgive. (*Some-body knocks.*) Come in. (*Enter* HOUSEHOLDER'S WIFE.)

SHE. My lord's orders are to obey you to-night as I obey him.

BILLWAMANGAL (*as if dazed*). Bring me a couple of needles.

SHE (*timidly*). They may be here. (*She goes into the inner room, looks in the box under the bedstead.*)

BILLWAMANGAL. What's your name?

SHE (*timidly*). Sarala. (*She comes out again and hands the needles to him.*)

BILLWAMANGAL. Sarala, go fetch your husband here. (*She goes out.* BILLWAMANGAL *turns his back to the audience. Enter* HOUSEHOLDER, *followed by* WIFE.)

HOUSEHOLDER. What more do you want? Shelter, food, bed, and even honor I have given you. What else do you want?

BILLWAMANGAL (*groans, turns round, his eyes bleeding*). My eyes, where are they now? They sinned against Chintamani. How dark it is now! (HOUSEHOLDER *and* WIFE *give out a shriek.*)

BILLWAMANGAL. Don't cry. Sin must be paid with sacrifice. I am punished. My eyes, look now! Can you see her face? Mother Sarala, my mother, give your hand. (SARALA, *weeping, goes forward and gives her hand.*)

BILLWAMANGAL. Do not weep. Shed tears of joy. You have done me the greatest favor of life. Your needles they are my saviors. My mother, forgive your son. Henceforth I will go from door to door and beg my living. My feet will be bruised. And my blind eyes look to heaven and cry to Chinta-mani for light. Don't cry, my mother, your eyes are not to shed tears for a sinner like me. Shed tears of joy, for you have saved me. Let your eyes be two untarnished mirrors of virtue and love for the good to look in. Where are you, my son? Give me your hand. (HOUSEHOLDER, *bewildered, takes his other hand in his.*)

BILLWAMANGAL. You, too, must forgive me. I am always your grateful slave. It is at your house I realized what a sinner I am. Come, put me on the street. There I will find my way to Chintamani. (*They move out slowly.*) Ah, Chintamani, Chintamani!

(*The curtain goes down on the second act before they go off the stage.*)

ACT THREE

A street. CHINTAMANI, *a blind man, a lame man and three or four children seated on the ground. They are all talking.* CHINTAMANI *is distributing some food.*)
(*Time: Afternoon. Enter three hermits in yellow.*)

FIRST HERMIT. How painful a spectacle. Famine is raging everywhere. There are so many hungry and thirsty. Their suffering is as inconceivable as their number. What horror. I wonder what it means,—particularly in a city like this, where people are so generous.

SECOND HERMIT. This is the punishment for sins committed in the past. Who can tell how mysteriously the law works? Who knows, maybe you and I in some previous life gave no alms to the beggar, nor rendered help to the helpless. Probably we gave no shelter, food, nor drink to the homeless, hungry and thirsty. All those accumulated evils are reaping their harvest now.

FIRST HERMIT. Who can tell? You, perhaps, are right. This world is heaven and hell as we deserve it. Yet—why should they, all these human beings, suffer, all at the same time?

THIRD HERMIT (*he is young looking*). It might be the will of him who created them, and— (*Enter a drunken man from the left. He presses his back close to the background, that is, the wall of the house, until he reaches the middle of the stage. Then looks vaguely at hermits.*)

THREE HERMITS (*eyeing him*). What are you doing there?

DRUNKEN MAN (*speechless*).

FIRST HERMIT. What are you?

THIRD HERMIT. Who are you? (HERMITS *come nearer to the right, almost where the beggars are eating.*)

DRUNKEN MAN. You need not come near, don't touch me. I am a picture drawn on the wall. (*The* BEGGAR *smiles and wonders.*)

THIRD HERMIT. What idiocy!

SECOND HERMIT. He is drunk. Leave him alone.

DRUNKEN MAN. Sure, you cannot get me off. I am made of ink. (*The* BEGGARS *laugh.*)

THIRD HERMIT. Are you not ashamed?

DRUNKEN MAN. I am not lazy like you.

FIRST HERMIT. You know, my son, people are dying of hunger while you are wasting your money on drink.

DRUNKEN MAN. That makes no difference. They eat, I drink. Man has got to do something. Especially when wine makes one forget hunger.

SECOND HERMIT. But you must not drink at such a time as this.

DRUNKEN MAN. Why must I not? When I see stars from hunger, and

I can hardly stand up, should I not take a little wine if I can get it? (*Looking to the left.*) There he comes. I am off. (*Exit.*)

(*Enter* SHEPHERD with a bundle.)

FIRST HERMIT (*stopping him*). What have you got, my son?

SHEPHERD (*timidly*). Food.

CHINTAMANI. Won't you give us some?

SHEPHERD. No, my man has not eaten anything these two days.

FIRST HERMIT (*to* SHEPHERD). Wait a minute, my son. (*To* CHINTAMANI.) My daughter, may I ask you what you have been giving them?

CHINTAMANI. My lord, these children, these children have been starving for about a week. It was so little. (*The* HERMITS *wonder.*)

BLIND MAN. For three days I haven't eaten anything. Mother, is there anything left?

HERMITS. Shepherd, give them some. We will bring some to you very soon. If you wait here till we come back, you will get what you have given away. (SHEPHERD *hesitates.*)

BLIND MAN. (*Striking his staff thrice on the ground.*) Ah, God, ah, God, why was I given this existence? (SHEPHERD *gently gives the bundle to* CHINTAMANI. *She distributes the contents of the bundle to her companions.*)

SECOND HERMIT (*to his comrades*). Birth, growth and death are the three laws of life. We travel from birth to death, not knowing what awaits us at the end.

FIRST HERMIT. Suffering and ignorance are the soil where grows the plant of life. Destiny is the axe that hews it, in time.

THIRD HERMIT. Creation, preservation and destruction are the eternal laws of existence.

CHINTAMANI (*coming nearer them*). My lords are you going to bring some more food?

SHEPHERD (*to first hermit*). My man has been waiting all day long. Please give me something to bring to him.

FIRST HERMIT (*to his comrades*). Let us fetch what we can get. (*To* CHINTAMANI *and* SHEPHERD.) We will do our best, our children. Wait here for us. (*Exit.*)

BLIND MAN. Who is coming?

LAME MAN. I have been fasting I know not how long. Give me some grass. (*The deep, crimson blue from the left betokens the sunset.*)

SHEPHERD. He is waiting for me, and crying— (*From a distance, drawing nearer, a voice.*) Chintamani!

(*Enter* BILLWAMANGAL, *leaning on his staff, feeling his way with it.*)

SHEPHERD. Oh, brother, I was coming to you. Why do you come out here?

BILLWAMANGAL. I feel a presence, somebody calls me. What a pain,— Who is here—is anyone weeping? Shepherd, brother, forgive me. Go back to your flock. They are bleating in hunger. Please go. See! Oh—

SHEPHERD. I will go. But I will come back soon. Don't go away anywhere. Wait here for me. (*Exit.*)

BILLWAMANGAL. How happy he is. Each day he— Ah, day! It is dark, so dark, minute for minute, score for score. It is darker and darker and desolate. There is no day for the blind. Somebody is near. Chintamani— (CHINTAMANI *signs to her people to draw aside and keep silent.*)

BILLWAMANGAL (*touching the lame man*). Who are you?

LAME MAN. I am a lame man.

BILLWAMANGAL. Why are you sitting here?

LAME MAN. The lame always sit.

BILLWAMANGAL. Can't you walk at all?

LAME MAN. I can if I have my crutches.

BILLWAMANGAL. You can see, too. You walk, you see, what a blessing. Ah, Chintamani.

A BEGGAR CHILD. Mother!

BILLWAMANGAL. Mother! How sweet. When did I call, mother? How long is it since these eyes had vision, and I looked at her face full of affection. Oh, mother! Holding her hand I used to stand on the bank of the Ganges and watch the rising sun. How the golden God rose from the purifying bath in the Holy Water, and coursed up the sky, higher and higher. What joys He gave me. Now He, too, is merciless. The sun is so hot here. It must be a very red sun. It is so warm. (*To* CHINTAMANI.) Where are you? Each day leaves me feebler and fainter. These legs can hardly support this body. Shall I find you at all—at all in this life? Shall I see you at all? (CHINTAMANI *struggles hard to restrain herself.*)

BLIND MAN. Mother, whence is that cool light?

BILLWAMANGAL. How many dark days have been spent in this vain search. Who can tell? I will not see you again. Ah, my eyes. Ah, my eyes. They sinned against you. (*Strikes his forehead.*) Oh, fate—Chintamani. Can you not see from above? I sinned. But I was ignorant. No pardon for such a sin?

LAME MAN. What do you want?

BILLWAMANGAL (*not heeding*). Oh, Chintamani, come to me, lead me on. Don't leave me to the sun and the wind.

LAME MAN. Who are you?

BILLWAMANGAL. I am Billwamangal, the sinner. Have you ever heard that name? You have eyes. Have you seen Chintamani?

LAME MAN. What is she? Why do you want her?

BILLWAMANGAL. You can ask her about me. Tell her how her Billwa died of hunger. No, no, do not. I do not want her. Tell her nothing. I want him, the ruler, the supreme Chintamani. Where is he? Where is the light that will take me to him? (*A pause as he turns to the right. The moonlight, with distinct three colors: white, blue and yellow, falls on his face, bathes him in its radiance. The light falls from the right. He thrills and shivers; he goes as if hypnotically drawn by the light. Others make movements to follow.*)

CURTAIN

ACT FOUR

From the foreground rise up jagged rocks, tier upon tier, till they meet upon the sky in the background. On the top of the highest tier, in the middle of the background, is a cave whence emanates the three-colored light. A sad melody is almost imperceptibly heard from the cave. Flakes of light shimmer in the eastern sky to the right. It is just before the dawn, though very hard to distinguish.

Enter BILLWAMANGAL *from the left, climbing the rocks. He gropes, yet walks up and on. The morning breeze faintly stirs in the few bushes here and there. At last he reaches the cave where, amid its darkness, is seen the vision of a man in white. His face, except his white beard falling luxuriantly on his breast, is not discernible. As* BILLWAMANGAL'S *groping hand touches the white cloak of* THE VISION, *the light goes out. They are seen like shadows in the slowly progressing light of the dawn.*)

BILLWAMANGAL (*ecstatically*). The Presence!

THE VISION (*touches* BILLWAMANGAL'S *forehead.*) Let thy soul fear not to face the Unknown. (BILLWAMANGAL *shudders and groans.*)

THE VISION. What seest thou?

BILLWAMANGAL. Man. He walks by the ocean—the ocean parts in two. He walks between two oceans. Many follow him. Ah! Ah!

THE VISION (*touching his heart*). What seest thou?

BILLWAMANGAL. A child. The child grows into a man. The Man weeps. Don't, don't! Who are they? They scourge him. Oh, oh!

THE VISION (*puts his hand on* BILLWAMANGAL'S *head*). What seest thou?

BILLWAMANGAL (*slowly, almost in a trance*). A prince. Night; a woman and a child asleep. He leaves them. He climbs the Himalaya. He ascends to the highest. (*As a strong ray of light, pure white light, falls upon him from behind* THE VISION, *the audience sees* BILLWAMANGAL *distinctly, but* THE VISION *remains shadowy as before.*) Don't close it! Open! Open the door! Show me— (*Pauses slightly.*) Now I see you! (*Kisses* THE VISION'S *garment.*) You pilgrim from Sinai, bringing the divine ten laws to man. Child of man, healing hatred with love! Raising the dead to life eternal! Meek, merciful. The waves of the sea are silent at your word. I know you (*reverently*), the Son of Man. You trample the high Himalayan crests, opening the gates of Nirvana!

(THE VISION *touches* BILLWAMANGAL'S *eyes. The other lights have become dim, so that the stage is almost in darkness. At the touch upon his eyes,* BILLWAMANGAL *sees again, and at that instant all the stage flashes into light. This is due to the sudden dawn, the flashes of light upon the horizon having presaged it. The cave and* THE VISION *have vanished.*)

BILLWAMANGAL. I see! I see! (*Raises his arms above his head in joy and thanksgiving.*)

(*Enter* CHINTAMANI *and beggars, from the left. They climb to him and stand before him. As* BILLWAMANGAL *and* CHINTAMANI *face each other there is a hushed pause. They have lost all trace of passion; there is nothing but spiritual feeling between them.*)

CHINTAMANI (*as she and her followers fall on their knees about him*). Glorious being, cast your benign glance upon us, your children. Show us the pathway to Light.

BILLWAMANGAL (*his arms raised in benediction above them*). Come! See! It is the Light! The Light! (*Blesses them.*)

CURTAIN

THE WITNESS

A PLAY

By Jaroslav Vrchlicky

———

Translated from the Czech by Charles Recht

CHARACTERS

IUSTUS KORBER, J. D., *fifty-five years of age, a lawyer.*
THERESA, *his wife, thirty-three years of age*
GUSTAV CERNIK, J. D., *thirty-five years of age, a lawyer, Korber's associate*
JOSEPH VALENTA, *about sixty years of age*
MARY, *a servant*
A plainclothes policeman

THE WITNESS

The dining room in KORBER'S *apartment. The servant is clearing the table at which* KORBER, *buried in a newspaper, is sitting.* THERESA *is taking things down from a buffet. The appearance of the room indicates that the family is about to remove. Most of the pictures are on the floor and are set back against the walls. Near the hearth is a barrel, and a trunk on the left; near the window is a lady's writing table. Atop of it are hat boxes, toilet articles and similar trifles. As the curtain rises, the servant, having placed the dishes on a tray, is taking them out into the kitchen on the right.*

THERESA. You'll have to excuse that poor lunch, dear—the moving upsets everything.

IUSTUS. Oh! don't mention it.

THERESA. And are you not vexed?

IUSTUS. Not about the luncheon; there are plenty of other things.

THERESA (*going over to him*). Poor boy, you are worried.

IUSTUS. Some things just do not succeed, and in others people take advantage of you.

THERESA. But you ought not to worry any more. There's no need of it now.

IUSTUS. Easily said. Well, it will not kill me. (*Pause.*) Will you be through to-day with this (*surveying the disarranged articles*) veritable babel?

THERESA. I hope so. Does it not give you a queer feeling to move after all these fifteen years? It is a big part of our life from which we are forcing ourselves.

IUSTUS. But you insisted yourself on this moving.

THERESA. Of course, I did. We did not have enough space here. (*Going toward the window.*) Across the yard is the insane asylum with its high walls and a row of tiresome windows.

IUSTUS. And it annoys you only now, after these fifteen years. Women! Women!

THERESA (*smiling*). There you go, against women again.

IUSTUS. Do I wrong you then? I was fully contented here for twelve— fifteen years, and you for the last twelve never uttered a word against the neighborhood. All at once—"it's gloomy here." All of a sudden, the "high walls" and "tiresome windows." You know well that I do anything to please you, and so I moved. Had you wanted to remain here, we would have never moved away.

THERESA (*seriously*). Thanks, very much, for catering to my whims.

IUSTUS. You are entirely welcome. (*He reads. Pause.* IUSTUS *continues to read the newspaper.* THERESA *is removing dishes from the buffet into the basket.*) Well, all in all, are you glad to move away from here?

THERESA. Yes, I am longing for a change.

IUSTUS. You know that we can still remain here if you wish it. The flat is not rented. I can stop over at the landlord's and tell him. All you have to do is to hang up your pictures, and things will go on as in the past.

THERESA (*quickly*). Oh, no! no! What would the people say about us? Everybody knows now that we are moving, and besides, you'd forfeit a month's rental in the new house.

IUSTUS. How practical you are.

THERESA. We'll be through with everything before evening. Only let's get away from here.

IUSTUS. For my part! (*He puts away the newspaper, rises and goes into the adjoining room.* THERESA *continues her work. Presently* IUSTUS *returns with hat and overcoat and goes over to the hearth and lights a cigar.*) There's another thing!

THERESA. Yes, dear?

IUSTUS (*taking a paper out of his pocket*). I found this on my desk this morning. Dr. Cernik sends me his immediate resignation.

THERESA (*surprised*). Resignation?

IUSTUS. Yes—stupid fellow—his style and all, is insulting.

THERESA (*suppressing her nervousness*). That's why you lost your appetite this noon.

IUSTUS. Bah! Nonsense. But to leave me after ten years suddenly—without the slightest cause. And he has not enough decency to come straight to me and tell me like a man. He writes it and puts it on my desk and goes.

THERESA. He probably will want to open his own office now.

IUSTUS. Then I could understand his motive, but he does not.

THERESA. Where is he going?

IUSTUS. He says he is going to America.

THERESA (*stops in her work and repeats very slowly*). To America.

IUSTUS. Evidently he is insane. But whatever he does is immaterial to me. It's only that I was so dependent upon him. He was so reliable and, as a rule, he did not talk much. I can't bear a prattling fool. In that way Gustav was perfect—even if he was not a good worker, he did not talk. God knows whom I'll get. Some fellow who'll talk politics, literature, drama and what not, from morning till night.

THERESA. Well, young men must take an interest in life.

IUSTUS. They should be like me. My life is in my law books and cases. The other things are superfluous.

THERESA. Unfortunately so for you.

IUSTUS. Fortunately, you ought to say. If you'd follow my ways, you would not be so nervous. But people who have no cares of their own, make everything their business. And so they get themselves into no end of trouble. Now I have made my little speech, and I can go.

THERESA. When are you coming back?

IUSTUS. I don't know. Hardly to this place. We'll see each other in the new flat.

THERESA. And you say that so indifferently.

IUSTUS (*in the doorway*). Should I cry about it? Some people move every half a year. If they were like you, they'd have no tears left for the regulation family funeral. Good-by.

THERESA. Good-by, dear. (THERESA *remains alone for some time, continuing her work.*) To America—to America. He, the only witness (*going to the window*) except these high mute walls. (*She shivers nervously.*) Away from these witnesses—to America.

(GUSTAV CERNIK *enters. He is dressed for travel.*)

GUSTAV. Good evening.

THERESA (*surprised*). You? (*Collecting herself.*) Yes—Good evening.

GUSTAV. I see that I should not have come here at all. Forgive me, and farewell!

THERESA. Good luck to you, Cernik.

GUSTAV (*looking around*). So you are really going away.

THERESA. It is best to end all at once.

GUSTAV. Just as I am doing.

THERESA. Yes, Korber told me that you are going to America.

GUSTAV. The only solution to our problem, Theresa.

THERESA. Pardon me—our problem——

GUSTAV. At times the solution of a problem is forced upon us before we ourselves expect it. Both of us are solving the problems of our hearts Theresa, though each in his own way. I am leaving the old world, and you at least—the old apartment. It will be a relief to rid ourselves forever of the old witnesses.

THERESA (*sobbing*). How cruel you are!

GUSTAV. What would you have! Let's talk sensibly. You, yourself told me when we first met, that ours is a practical age, that Romance is highly repugnant to our prosaic souls. You told me this at the time when you returned to me the *Letters of Jacob Orthis,* was that not sufficient? Oh Romance, Romance! Alfieri bound himself to his chair so that he couldn't go after his love; that was romantic. I am leaving this country so that I would not have to love you; that is practical. To love! Theresa, I shall never cease to love you. I am leaving; leaving only because I am cowardly. I can no longer stand the daily torture of seeing you and hearing you here and being unable to call you my own and to press you to my heart as I did then.

THERESA. Stop for Heaven's sake!

GUSTAV. Oh, let me recall those moments. Only in that moment did I live. I lived only in that moment when I felt your breath unite with mine, when I felt your heart, even though for a moment, beat upon my heart.

THERESA. Be silent. Please be silent!

GUSTAV. I'm leaving because I see that this shall never occur again.

THERESA (*darkly*). That which should never have happened at all.

GUSTAV. —and that I no longer have the strength to bear this.

THERESA. Please go now. Please go!

GUSTAV. You no longer love me, Theresa!

THERESA. I must not.

GUSTAV. You want to forget even that moment of your happiness.

THERESA. It must be so. I must live on.

GUSTAV. So you are moving. You want to get rid of the last tokens of our joy.

THERESA. Say of our sins.

GUSTAV. Call it what you will. For me it was joy, I, who am the last romantic man in our practical age as your husband calls it. But you are right, it will be better. You are moving to another place and I am moving away. Oh, I have noticed quite well how since that day, you have moved your furniture and you have hung the pictures in different places. You wanted to forget that which was so sweet to me. Finally you persuaded your husband to give notice to the landlord. . . . You cannot reproach me that I am making it any harder for you to forget.

THERESA (*weeping*). For Heaven's sake, what would you have me do? You yourself say that this cannot last. This constant anxiety, this restlessness, these struggles, the sight of this good man here, those sleepless nights of mine since that unhappy moment. I have often felt that I shall not be able to endure it, that I shall fall on my knees and confess everything. But then I am too cowardly—no, I still love you too well.

GUSTAV. Still, but not as you did before, Theresa!

THERESA. No my friend, I am quite constant in my feelings. But I am more strict now in my duty, my honor. I read once in a book which you gave me that honor is the poetry of stern duty. De Vigny wrote it, I think. De Vigny, who writhed under the yoke of duty all his life, but remained honorable to the end. (*Firmly.*) Let us be like him, dear friend. It is the only and the best way, the way from which we should never have departed.

GUSTAV. You are moralizing.

THERESA. Something which neither Orthis nor Werther did. See, that is just the distinction between our practical and their romantic period. We find more poetry in morality than in sin, more in self-denial than in enjoyment.

GUSTAV. Perhaps your morality is another kind of Romanticism. It has at least a practical solution and it is well that it has. Let us abide by it.

THERESA. Yes, I beg it of you.

GUSTAV. It shall be as you say. In your new apartment there will not be a single witness. You shall live for the fulfilment of your duty, for your husband. You shall fill your life with your heroism and your self-denial.

THERESA. Please do not insult me.

GUSTAV. I'll say no more. (*Putting his hand in his breastpocket.*) We exchanged some letters at one time. (*Pulls out a small package.*) Do you still recall those beautiful days? They are of course very brief. They were jotted on pieces of newspaper, discarded envelopes, often there was only a word or two on them. They were abbreviated so that no one else could understand them. I collected all these pieces as though they were rare relics. Here they are. Take even those. Let there be an end to all, altogether, so that you can enjoy your new life freely and fully.

THERESA (*darkly*). I thank you.

GUSTAV. And shall I go now?

THERESA (*placing letters on the mantel*). As you like.

GUSTAV. Good-by, then. Will you not give me your hand?

THERESA (*softly*). Here are both of them. (*She extends both hands. He pulls her to himself. She resists him but weakly.*)

GUSTAV. Just like at that moment which, Theresa, you are now cursing.

THERESA. I have not cursed it.

GUSTAV (*kissing her*). Which you want to forget.

THERESA. Yet, I want to forget— But for God's sake we are not alone in the house.

GUSTAV (*releases her*). I am going presently. This was our last kiss, Theresa. Just like at that time but yet not quite the same.

THERESA. Be silent. Be silent.

GUSTAV. You loved me then wholly and truly.

THERESA. Please go now.

GUSTAV. Do you know that we shall never see each other again?

THERESA. I know. I know everything, but go now please. Have pity on me.

GUSTAV (*steps toward her quickly. Kisses her quickly on her forehead*). Good-by. (*He goes.*)

THERESA (*quickly after him*). Good-by. (*Exit. She staggers to the door of the adjoining room.*)

(*A long pause. Enter JOSEPH VALENTA, a tall, grayish man, poorly dressed. He holds his cap in his hand. VALENTA takes a few steps into the empty room, looks around, goes back again to the door, coughs.*)

THERESA (*entering from adjoining room*). Who's here?

VALENTA. Pardon, Gnädige* Frau, pardon my liberty.

THERESA. Who let you in?

---

* I have used the title of "*Gnädige Frau*" and not "*milostpani,*" its Bohemian equivalent. My reason for it is twofold: in the first place, it is a strictly German custom imported into Kleinstädtliche, Bohemia; and secondarily, because the American readers will more readily understand the meaning of that custom if it is in German. Personally, I should have preferred to use the Bohemian "*milostpani*" in colloquial usage. This flattering title is pronounced "*gnä'ge,*" and it is used in this form by Valenta.

VALENTA. I did not have to ring at all, Gnädige Frau. The door was open, there was no one in the vestibule, so I walked in here.

THERESA. And what do you want?

VALENTA. I wanted to ask you kindly, to—I met Dr. Korber in the street about half an hour ago, when he left the house, and I begged him—I asked for some kind of employment even if it were ever so small. The doctor, he was so kind, he said I should come over here, that he will come back here and we'll talk about it. Some minor clerical work or errands. I would do anything; you'd be satisfied—I am an old man, but I am well preserved, and when the doctor gave me hopes he said he would see—excuse me, Gnädige Frau. I was so bold as to——

THERESA. But my husband will hardly return to-day. And you can see that we are moving. There's no time for it to-day.

VALENTA. That's just why I took the liberty to-day, Gnädige Frau, as long as we are, as it were, still neighbors——

THERESA. Neighbors?

VALENTA. Certainly (*pointing to the windows*), Gnädige Frau does not know me, but I know her very well.

THERESA (*not noticing his motion*). No, I do not know you.

VALENTA. And I know the doctor, very well, too, and also that young gentleman who always sits over the law books—there. When a man sees the same faces every day for fifteen years, he knows them like his own family.

THERESA (*disturbed*). You watched our faces daily for fifteen years. That's terrible! But from where?

VALENTA (*goes to the window and points*). From there, Gnädige Frau.

THERESA (*frightened*). That's the madhouse—man—did you escape from there?

VALENTA (*smiling*). I am not a lunatic. I was the caretaker of the inmates there, Gnädige. But I was unfortunate. Every man has his enemies, and I am the victim of mine. We had a new superintendent and he believed the report that I drugged and mistreated the patients there. So, yesterday, he discharged me. After fifteen years, Gnädige, it is hard, and so in my distress, I wondered if the doctor and you could not assist me with employment of some sort. A person who lives across the way for fifteen years and notices everything that goes on in the opposite apartment, and sees day after day who comes in and who goes out, he feels that they are sort of old acquaintances, Gnädige Frau, begging your pardon.

THERESA. You have spied on us for fifteen years. And you use that as an inducement for me to employ you! That is a strange recommendation.

VALENTA. Good Lord, Gnädige, you cannot blame me. When I had to sit there (*pointing at the windows*) with nothing at all to do. My work was over early. All the windows are on this side, so this was the only interesting place I could look on, as you never did lower your windowshades.

THERESA (*disturbed*). Who could fancy that—you insolent, low fellow——

VALENTA (*smiling*). Really, Gnädige, do not excite yourself—I will not mention a word to a living person—I am a very discreet man, you know—but—our sort gets into all kinds of places and learns of all kinds of secrets—because them fellows across the yard there, they give away many dark things—so our sort, as I say, goes deeper into secrets than the priest or the doctor——

Theresa. Yes—I know it. So here we were spied upon for fifteen years, and you have the brazen boldness to brag about it.

Valenta. But, Gnädige, when I mentioned it to the doctor he was not a bit excited about it. I told him the same that I told you, but he only smiled and told me to call a little later. And I watched him all these years, there in his room at his desk where he sat over his masses of law papers and books, just as I watched the young man, his assistant. They used to sit in there and you used to sit at the window. There was also a couch—it is not here now— You sat alone and sewed and sang. And right here over your head hung a beautiful little canary which sang loudly as though it wanted to compete with you. What became of it—did it die—the poor, dear thing?

Theresa. Keep quiet, man, for heaven's sake, keep quiet.

Valenta. I used to envy you this peaceful, well-regulated life, Gnädige Frau. Right over there in the hall hung a large picture—it's not there any longer either. (*Looks about.*) You have moved and changed it all—and it is a long time since you sang, Gnädige.

Theresa. Why are you torturing me?

Valenta. I—Gnädige—heaven forbid—Good Lord, your simple life,—at least, the way I saw it—(*looking intently at her*) gives you no reason for alarm or reproach.

Theresa. Listen, my man, why then are you telling me all this, and what are you bothering me for? When my husband comes, I'll tell him to have nothing to do with you. I do not want you in my house. A man who spies on his neighbors for fifteen years is a shameless fellow.

Valenta. Especially if he keeps quiet about it.

Theresa. You know nothing at all, nothing.

Valenta. Yes, I saw it.

Theresa. From across there?

Valenta. Yes. One afternoon, the doctor was down town and the servant girl was out of the house. You were alone. You sat here, your sewing in your hands, looking at an open door. Then from the adjoining room the young gentleman came in and looked at you so lovingly. I seem to see it even now. He held a cigar between his fingers and sat down (*does likewise*) on the edge of this table.

Theresa. Why do you remind me of it?

Valenta. So you'd know that I know it, Gnädige Frau. He stood here and talked and talked to you a long while. I was looking at you all the time and was getting tired of it. He had talked to you in that way many a time before, and then quietly went away. But on this particular day when he stood against the table he spoke so vehemently——

Theresa. Be silent!

VALENTA. Well, I am not saying anything, not a word. You resisted him as much as you could. I can't deny that—but in the end——

THERESA. Keep still, you wretch!

VALENTA (*coming nearer to her*). Well, Gnädige Frau, you put in a good word for me with the doctor—and you will see how discreet I can be—an old veteran like myself—believe me, I can't even remember such little trifles—but you reminded me of it with your excitement. Who'd think of it— What's happened, has happened, now we must be good friends and help each other.

THERESA. God, this is dreadful! We must help each other—this man has the audacity to tell me this so quietly because—— You are an evil and dangerous fellow.

VALENTA. No, Gnädige, I am not.

THERESA. Prove it, then, swear that you will never utter a word, and that you will go away and never cross my husband's or my path.

VALENTA. But, Gnädige Frau, I am a poor, miserable man. My enemies have ruined me. I have nothing to eat. I am penniless.

THERESA. So that's the game. (*Goes into adjoining room.*) Wait—— (*Short pause. She returns presently with a roll of bank notes.*) There you are. There's more there than you expected.

VALENTA (*just glances at the bank notes, then quickly puts them into his coat pocket*). God bless you, Gnädige Frau.

THERESA. Now, go quickly—and don't let me hear from you again.

VALENTA. No—no. I'll leave the city to-day, and you shall never see me again.

THERESA. Thank God for that.

VALENTA. You have saved a destitute man, Gnädige Frau. (*He takes her hand and wants to kiss it, she quickly withdraws it and points to the door.*)

THERESA. Go!—and quickly—— (VALENTA *exits.*)

THERESA (*sighs*). That's over, God! Now for a new, clean life. (*Calls.*) Mary! Is there no one here? (*Calls.*) Mary! (*Runs from one door to another excitedly.*) Always alone—always. (*Presses bell button nervously, and continuously.*) God! (*She clenches her hands and brings one to her lips.*)

MARY. You rang, Gnädige Frau?

THERESA. Where have you been all this time? There's no one in the whole house. Nice order! A strange man walks right into this dining room without ringing—and I had my hands full to get rid of him.

MARY. You have forgotten, Gnädige Frau, that you sent me to urge the expressman to come. He is on his way now.

THERESA. Of course, I sent you. But why did you leave the hall door wide open?

MARY. The doctor was the last one to leave, Gnädige Frau, he probably left it open. I am always careful about the hall door.

THERESA. You always have an excuse for everything.

MARY (*going to the window*). We'd better begin to get ready. The van and moving men are out there. (THERESA *goes to the windows and looks.*)

MARY. But, Lord, look, what is that—two men are fighting down there.

THERESA. God Almighty, that's the same man!

MARY. And the other fellow does not want to let him go. Look at the crowd—how they run! Too bad we can't hear what they have to say up here. Here's the doctor, Gnädige Frau. He is taking that man's part—that old man's—he talks to the other fellow—they are quiet now—they are coming up here. (*Turning to* THERESA.) Is that the man who frightened you so badly, Gnädige Frau?

THERESA (*extremely upset*). Yes.

MARY. Here they are. (*Enter* DR. KORBER, *followed by a plainclothes policeman, who holds on to* VALENTA.)

POLICEMAN. Begging your pardon, Gnädige Frau, for intruding, but this fellow (*pointing to* VALENTA) was discharged from the crazyhouse for bribery and drug-selling, and we had him under surveillance. We saw him enter your house, and after a while he re-appeared and was in a great hurry. I stopped him but he acted so suspiciously that I searched him and found in his possession the bank roll (*showing money*), about five hundred crowns. I wanted to take him to the station-house quietly, he protested, so I had to use force. Then your husband came by, and we thought we'd all come up to investigate.

IUSTUS. This man was our neighbor for fifteen years, and he asked me for employment this morning.

VALENTA. Yes, this gentleman told me to call here for a job, but he was not at home.

POLICEMAN. That part of your story is quite right, old chap. But what did you do here when the boss was out?

THERESA. He asked me for work.

POLICEMAN. But the money?

IUSTUS. Money?

POLICEMAN. Yes, that's why I pinched him. A man like he never had that much money in his life. They (*pointing to the window*) don't get that in two years, in salaries. (VALENTA *is silent*.)

POLICEMAN. You people would better look over your things here. If this money does not belong here, it belongs some other place. We'll find out soon enough. We'd better be going. (*Wants to lead* VALENTA *away*.)

THERESA. It was my money, I gave it to him. Let him go, he's innocent. (*The* POLICEMAN, *surprised, looks from* KORBER *to* THERESA, *and then at* KORBER *again. Short pause.*)

IUSTUS. Well, officer, if my wife says so, it must be true. Let him go and please go, too.

POLICEMAN. Begging your pardon, sir, no harm meant, I was just doing my duty.

IUSTUS. I understand—it's all right. I thank you.

POLICEMAN (*to* VALENTA). Now, get yourself away as soon as you can.

IUSTUS (*to* POLICEMAN). You leave him here a while. Good-by, officer.

(OFFICER *leaves. Long pause.* KORBER *is pacing up and down the room, goes over to the mantel and picks up the papers left by* CERNIK. THERESA *is standing by the window, her back to audience and to* KORBER. VALENTA *is nervously fingering his cap. He is standing at the door and is looking at bank roll left on the table.*)

IUSTUS (*to* VALENTA). You were a keeper in the insane asylum over there?

VALENTA. Yes, sir.

IUSTUS. And you were discharged, and came to ask me for employment?

VALENTA. Yes, sir.

IUSTUS. Then you did not find me at home, when you called?

VALENTA. No, sir.

IUSTUS (*to* THERESA). Did you give this man five hundred dollars, Theresa?

THERESA (*still in the same position.*) I did.

IUSTUS. You told me that you watched my house carefully for fifteen years, and you knew what went on there.

VALENTA. Yes, I did.

IUSTUS. Dr. Cernik's boat leaves Hamburg to-morrow morning, Theresa.

THERESA. Does it?

IUSTUS. He was here and told you. (*Pointing to papers on the mantel.*)

THERESA. He was, but he did not say.

IUSTUS (*to* VALENTA). Sit down. (VALENTA *takes a seat at the table.*) What did you say to my wife when you called here to-day, and what did she tell you? Now tell me all you know.

THERESA (*turning to* IUSTUS). Excuse me, Iustus. At what time does the next train leave for Hamburg?

IUSTUS. Seven-twenty. You still have time.

THERESA. I'll get my hat and coat in the meantime. (*Exits. Goes to adjoining room.*)

IUSTUS (*taking seat*). Now you shall tell me just all you said to my wife this morning, and all she said to you. Everything!

VALENTA (*moving about uneasily in the chair*). Well, doctor, it was like this. I am a poor, miserable, penniless fellow. I have a lot of enemies—— (*From the adjoining room a revolver shot is heard.* IUSTUS *rushes into that room.* VALENTA *picks up money on the table, puts his cap on and goes out.*)

CURTAIN

PYENTSA

A Play

Translated from the Burmese by J. Smith

Adapted by Frank Shay

CHARACTERS

THE KING OF PYENTSA
THE KING OF THE CITY OF THE SILVER MOUNTAIN
THOODANOO, *the Prince of Pyentsa*
THE QUEEN OF PYENTSA
MANANHURREE, *daughter of the* KING OF THE SILVER MOUNTAIN *and wife to*
    THOODANOO
A HUNTSMAN
AN ASTROLOGER
BELOO, *the devil*
NOBLEMEN, Generals, Guards, Ladies of the Palace, etc.
THE NINE PRINCESSES

PYENTSA

THE ARGUMENT

*The Nine Princesses of the City of the Silver Mountain, which is separated
from the abode of mortals by a triple barrier (the first being a belt of prickly
cane, the second a stream of liquid copper, and the third a* BELOO, *or devil)
gird on their enchanted belts, which give them the power of traversing the
air with the speed of a bird, and visit a pleasant forest within the limits of
the south island (earth). While bathing in the lake they are surprised by a
huntsman, who snares the youngest with his magic noose, and carries her
to the young prince of Pyentsa, who is so much struck by her surprising
beauty that he makes her his chief queen, though he has but lately been
united to the daughter of the head astrologer of the palace. Being obliged
soon after to take the field against some rebels, the astrologer seizes advantage of the prince's absence to misinterpret a dream, which the king calls
upon him to explain; and declares that the evil spirit, whose influence is
exerting itself against the king's power, is only to be appeased by the sacrifice
of the beautiful* MANANHURREE, *who has supplanted his daughter in the
young prince's affections. The prince's mother hearing of the offering about
to be made, visits the lovely* MANANHURREE *and restores to her the enchanted
belt which had been picked up on the shore-edge of the lake by the huntsman, and presented by him to the old queen. The princess immediately
returns to the Silver Mountain; but on her way thither she stops at the
hermitage of a recluse, who lives on the borders of the delightful forest
before mentioned, and gives to the old man a ring and some drugs, which
confer the power upon the possessor of them of entering the barrier and
passing unharmed through its dangers. The young prince having put an
end to the war, returns to the city of Pyentsa, and finding his favorite
queen gone, he instantly sets forth in quest of her. Having come to the
forest, the appearance of which astonishes and delights him, he dismisses
his followers and visits the hermit, who delivers to him the ring and the
drugs; he then enters the frightful barrier, and after meeting with many
adventures, arrives at the City of the Silver Mountain, and makes known
his presence to his beautiful bride by dropping the ring into a vessel of
water, which one of the palace damsels is conveying into the bath of the
princess.*

SCENE I

(The Palace of Audience, four Noblemen sitting facing the entrance.)

FIRST NOBLE. My lords, let us not be false or neglectful to our royal master, to whom we have so many times sworn allegiance; we bear the weight of government on our shoulders, and constitute the strength of the country,—How shall we conduct affairs, so as to extend his authority, and benefit the state?

SECOND NOBLE. True, my lords; let me explain to you whence our noble monarch sprung. In the distant beginning, after the earth had been destroyed successively by fire, by wind, and by water, the lily which sprung from its bosom blossomed, and produced fine embryo deities, on which account the celestial beings bestowed upon this system the title of Battakat. The various incidents that have occurred from first to last, among the four divisions of the human race, are voluminously recited in the 49,000 volumes of the History of Kings, but I will merely give you a sketch. The nine beings who descended from the visible heavens, having eaten of the fragrant earth, peopled it after the manner of mortals—in process of time the inhabitants began to use deceit towards each other, to pillage, to steal, and to strive amongst themselves continually; and in order to put an end to these calamities by instruction and discipline the embryo deity Mahathamata came, and was hailed by the voice of the whole people. This was the first.

THIRD NOBLE. When the millions of worlds had sunk under the influence of fire, air, and water—when the four grand divisions of the creation had been rent asunder—when the system had been again restored, and set in motion— the emerald-leaved lily sprung up, and gave forth from each of its fine blossoms the eight articles of clerical use; then the beings of the celestial regions understanding the sign regarding the five embryo deities, called this world on which we live Batta (kat). Is it not so, my lords?

FOURTH NOBLE. My friends, in the Palace of Audience, the thirty-three images of superior beings and the images of lions are keeping watch over the throne—the gold, the silver, the emeralds, the flowers, the sapphires, the topazes, and the rubies, are glittering among the other emblems of royalty—the canopy of state is being spread—the noblemen are in attendance in their robes and helmets—the sovereign of the golden palace is arraying himself in his royal habiliments—the procession will soon be formed to the music of the silver gong, the golden bell, and the celestial harp and lute, and issue forth headed by the four grand divisions of the Royal Army, marching to the sound of the martial drums. Let us therefore listen in silence for the warning of the five silver gongs.

(The royal procession enters.)

KING. From the period when the system was destroyed by fire, air, and water, and again renewed, the dynasty which has produced five valorous monarchs has descended unbroken to me, the sovereign of the south island: Are the people happy in the remotest hamlet of my possessions?

NOBLE. Oh, wearer of the jeweled crown, who unfurleth the royal canopy, and sitteth on the throne, guarded by rows of lions! the hundred subject kings are in attendance with their daughters.

KING. Represent to the sun of the world, truly and quickly, what you have to say.

NOBLE. Oh, king of the universe, whose merit is sublime; whose glory is increasing; whose august coronation has been celebrated; whose merchants and rich men go hither and thither under the royal protection; whose markets, rivers, rivulets, and lesser streams are crowded with people, canoes, and boats passing to and fro; whose royal staff being set up is surrounded by thousands of people going and coming; whose officers of customs, guards, and ferrymen keep watch at the landing places—the Governor of the seaward provinces sends a dispatch to the golden city, the contents of which shall be truly conveyed into the royal ear.

CURTAIN

SCENE II

City of the Silver Mountain. The Nine Princesses in the palace with their attendants. To the right may be seen the grove and the royal bathing pool.

PRINCESS. Shory Tsa! Shory Phee! Ye wise waiting women, who live under the shadow of the single pillared abode of royalty, come with me to my bath.

(*They follow* MANANHURREE *down the grove to the pool.*)

PRINCESS:

> Oh, bright are the flowers that carpet this vale,
> And yield their sweet breath to the murmuring gale;
> Bright flowers!—fragrant zephyrs!—how sweet, 'tis to rove,
> In this Eden of pleasure—this garden of love.

(*The* PRINCESSES *having taken off their enchanted belts, enter the pool. Enter the* HUNTSMAN.)

HUNTSMAN. Now, skilful ranger, enter thou the dense forest, and try to discover where the beasts of the chase are most numerous. Let me go quickly, but cautiously. Ah! what abundance of hares, elks, elephants, leopards, tigers, wild cows, bisons, and bears; there are harpies too, and unicorns, swans, *huoungs,* peacocks, and monkeys frisking about from place to place. Well; this is indeed a wonderful place. (*He discovers the* PRINCESSES *bathing.*) Ah! what creatures are these? Mortals, or celestials?—I must instantly entrap one of them with my magic noose, and ascertain what they really are.

(*He casts the noose, and snares* MANANHURREE, *the youngest.*)

MANAN. Oh, my royal sisters! save me, save me.

HUNTSMAN. Tell me, maiden, art thou a mortal, or a being of a superior order? Speak quickly, I pray you, and relieve me from my doubts.

MANAN. I am the daughter of the king whose palace is in the City of the Silver Mountain, and came hither with my companions to play. Release me, for I am afraid.

HUNTSMAN. If so, I shall have my fortune made, for I will carry you this moment to the court of Pyentsa, sweet maiden, and present you to the young prince.

(*He leads her off.*)

CURTAIN

SCENE III

The Palace. Pyentsa. (Same as Scene One.)

(*Enter* HUNTSMAN *leading in the young* MANANHURREE *to the Prince.*)

HUNTSMAN. Oh, prince, the lord of life and wealth; having but just now snared a palace-fostered maiden of a delicate and gentle form, I have brought her without delay to the golden foot.

PRINCE (*to* MANAN.). Be not concerned, sweet palace-born child, I could exist with you forever. Wait; I will hasten to my royal sire and petition him to let me make you my chief queen.

MANAN. Do with me, my lord, as you say.

PRINCE. Come with me.

(*They go off together as the* KING *and his* NOBLES *enter the opposite side.*)

KING. Nobles of the palace!

ALL: Lord!

KING. Why fails the prince Thoodanoo to come into the presence?

FIRST NOBLE. Oh, ruler of a hundred subject kings,—whose light is like the sun of the universe; he has but even now wedded the daughter of the philosopher Naythoda. The governor of Setang, and the chiefs of Siam and Cochin-China, who have heretofore annually brought tribute, and presents of ingots of gold and silver, white and red cloths, velvets, bales of cloths, gold and silver lace, and gold and silver flowers, have now failed in their duty. Nor is this the limit of their folly; they are making encroachments upon the frontier, and in the pride of their hearts are destroying the villages, and oppressing the people. The confusion which they have created is so great that the inhabitants are afraid to remain on the frontier; an ambassador has only now reached from the Tsaubwas.

KING. If this is true, call the lord of the east house and let him appear forthwith!

(*The four* NOBLES *go in opposite directions, calling.*)

FOUR NOBLES. Oh, my lord. The king awaits you. The royal sire desires your presence. Come, my lord!

(*The* PRINCE *re-enters alone.*)

PRINCE. Say what thou hast to say.

FIRST NOBLE. The royal sire has sent to command your presence.

PRINCE. If I am called, I will adjust my turban and come with you to the audience chamber.

(*They enter the palace.*)

PRINCE. My lords, tell me, who am the royal son, whose glory is like the sun of day, who enlightens the four islands; whose renown is universally spread; whether the imperial father—the embryo deity whose white canopy is unfurled—has yet entered the palace of audience; tell me, too, if the royal mother, who reclineth upon the throne of lilies, has yet displayed her golden countenance, and is well?

(PRINCESSES *enter singing.*)

> Wrought o'er with gems, and regal gold,
> And glitt'ring flow'rs in ev'ry fold,
> There stately canopies reveal,
> To kings, who hither come to kneel,
> The boundless riches of our land,
> Whose rocks are rubies—gold its sand.
> In all the southern world beside,
> There is not such a land of bliss;
> Where'er the ocean rolls its tide,
> It comes not to a shore like this;
> Delicious odors fill the air,
> And mirth and love reign everywhere.

(*The* KING *enters.*)

PRINCE. Oh, mighty father, this lion-hearted son, when he received the imperial order, placed it upon his head, and hastened to obey.

KING. My second self, my son Thoodanoo!

PRINCE. Sire!

KING. The people of the whole country, the rebellious wretches, are up like flames of fire—go, and exterminate them.

PRINCE (*bowing*). I have heard that Setang, Siam, and Cochin-China, not fearing the golden sword, are in open rebellion. It is nothing. They seek a quarrel, and the golden son will root up the whole race; without making use of the weapons of war, he will but publish forth the king's glorious title, and they are gone.

KING. Good, my son; go forth and repay to me the favors I have bestowed upon you. Let Cochin-China be your first point of assault, and return not till you come as conqueror.

PRINCE. I will reverently obey the royal command, and make the golden cause conspicuous.

CURTAIN

SCENE IV

(*The* PRINCE'S *Palace.*)

PRINCE *to* MANANHURREE. Delicate creature; silver palace-born beauty; whose charms are so surpassingly wonderful; I must go with the army which marches with to-morrow's dawn.

MANAN. Oh, my lord, why will you thus desert me? You are my only protector here, at once my father and my husband. If indeed you have resolved to abandon me, I must bear the fate that awaits me.

PRINCE. It must not be so, pride of my soul. I must not neglect the duty which a child owes its parent: moreover, consider, I beseech you, that I am nearest the throne, and must yield to the custom of my country, and lead the army against the rebels.

MANAN. Alas! If you possess so little affection for me, as to leave me here alone, I must submit to my evil destiny.

PRINCE (*to his* NOBLE.) Hear you not, my lord? She does not say, stay; nor does she desire me to go!—she weeps!—her tears and smiles are so fascinating, that I shall be vanquished; her tears are like sparkling drops of dew upon the leaf of the lily; whenever I look upon them, I have not resolution enough to go.

NOBLE. Let me explain to your highness. The princess is here without friends; if you desert her, she will be as much alone as the *kynneya* without its mate; she will be confounded with her lot, and will be no more than a waxen image. There is indeed no necessity for your departure, and leaving her here in tears.

PRINCE. Alas! If I avoid this campaign, I shall have my name held up to the scorn and contempt of posterity. The king, my father, will be enraged against me if I do not accompany the army. Oh, I must indeed depart. Then this friendless one, when left alone, will break her heart, and I shall be left destitute. I am in a painful dilemma (like a bamboo between two boards)! I may as well swallow poison, or throw myself into a furnace. If I petition the king to allow me to remain at home, he will order me to do so; but after what I have already promised it will be improper to ask!—then she will not die!—she will only waste away. I *will* join the army; caparison my elephant Mengala, and bring him to the palace, and the lord of the golden universe will depart.

(*As* MANAN. *is about to whisper to the* PRINCE *he departs.*)

MANAN. (*resignedly*). Mala, Menasa! My faithful maidens come hither. Go whisper to the king that I am about to become a mother. Let the priests pray that it may be a son.

TREASURER. I must hasten to the camp and communicate the tidings to the royal ear.

CURTAIN

SCENE V

The Palace of the PRINCE.

PRINCE (*entering*). Gem of my heart, my chancelor tells me that I am blessed with a son. Manan. It is so, my love! It is music to the royal ear.

PRINCE (*to his lord in waiting*). Make known to all the army that the little prince has received the name of Moung Shory Gyew. (*To the* PRINCESS.) Pure leaf of silver, captivating creature, picture of softness and beauty, mother of our babe—stay but for a brief space with your companions, in the palace, and I will again be with you in three months.

MANAN. Pray do not be concerned about me, my lord, I will stay here; commence your journey, and be true to me.

PRINCE. You say well, my rose tree, but it is not my own wish to depart; I must obediently perform my sire's command; of course I must not avoid my duty.

(*The* PRINCE *departs.*)

MANAN. Oh, my maids; the little prince is now seven days old, let us place him in the emerald cradle and rock him (to sleep).

Gently let us rock the swing,
  And hush to sleep the baby king;
Palace maidens—softly sing,
(*Chorus*) And lull to sleep the baby and the king.

Coolly let the palace rose
  In his jewell'd couch repose:—
Persuasive voices, hither bring,
(*Chorus*) And lull to sleep the baby and the king.

CURTAIN

. . . . .

ACT TWO

Scene I

The Palace of Audience.

King. Oh, wise ministers, who continually wait in my presence like the seven mountains which surround the lake Nandat, I have dreamed that the country of Pyentsa was surrounded by my intestines and that the sun and moon descended from the firmament and fell into my lap. Explain quickly what this means.

Noble. Oh, king of the golden palace, whose glory is great, the Brahmin Naythoda, whose place is near the throne, will be able to interpret the royal dream.

King. Call hither the Brahmin Naythoda. (Naythoda *and his disciples enter.*) Oh, learned teacher, I have dreamed that my bowels surrounded the country of Pyentsa, and that the sun and the moon fell at my feet. Show me the interpretation of this thing.

Naythoda. It is well, oh, benefactor!—let me but consult my astrological tables; (*he consults his scheme*) one from one—nothing; nine from one— nothing; two and five.—I have made the calculation—(*The Pawn tumbles in the water.*) Oh! are there nine, or one? (*To his scholar.*) The benefactor dreams propitiously, but I will divine unfavorably. (*To the* King.) The benefactor, the lord of life and property, must sacrifice to the Yeet spirit one hundred fowls, and one hundred hogs, and it will be appeased.

King. Is this all, O teacher?

Naythoda. Lord of the earth, I am afraid to—

King. Say on, learned teacher, without regard to anyone; only let myself and the chief queen be exempt.

Naythoda. Oh! benefactor, cut the throat of that celestial spirit who is like the *kynneya,* and offer up her blood before the Yeet Nat. (*To his disciple.*) Close the doors of the prince's palace on all sides, for so is the king's command.

(*Exit all. Enter* Princess *and* Maidens.)

Manan. Oh, my faithful women, Mala, Maensa, go and take your rest. My doors are closed and my blood is to be poured out before the Yeet spirit . . . must it indeed be so? Oh, my absent lord, our son Moung Shory Gyew is yet an infant.

(*Enter the* Prince's Mother.)

Queen. Oh, daughter of the pleasing countenance, here is your enchanted belt. Take it and escape to the City of the Silver Mountain.

Manan. Thanks, royal madam, thrice I salute you reverently.

(*She fastens the enchanted belt about her and leaves.*)

CURTAIN

Scene II (Scene in one)

(*At the hermitage of a recluse who lives on the boundary which divides the earth from the country of the Silver Mountain.*)

Manan. Holy hermit, should the Prince of Pyentsa come hither, deliver, I pray you, this ring and these drugs into his hand.

CURTAIN

ACT THREE

Scene I

The Prince's *Camp.*

Prince. By the strength of this arm have I made my father's glory great. Cause my elephant Yauoung to be caparisoned, for the princess Dwaynow's lord will return to the city of Pyentsa.

Noble. My lord!

Prince. Let the golden spearsmen, swordsmen, and the golden shield-bearers and armor-bearers be set in order, and the four grand divisions of the imperial army.

Noble. They are so, my lord.

Prince. Good general, the princess Manan., who keeps her court in the north palace, will bend her head in watching for my return like the golden lily shaken by the wind—she will droop with fatigue, let us therefore make long marches.

CURTAIN

Scene II

The Prince's *Palace. Matrons, waiting women.*

First Lady. Our royal mistress upon hearing of the plot against her life, fled to the City of the Silver Mountain—we shall all without exception undergo the royal punishment. Hear you not the voice of the great guns? Let us go forth and meet the returning army.

(*Enter the* Prince.)

Prince. Oh, sweet ladies, Mala, Maensa! the princess Manan., where is she? The charming mother of our infant son—where is she gone?

Matron. I will explain, my lord, about the princess, to whom I gave the same care, as to this hair I daily dress—she who was the celestial spirit of the palace, oh, king of the city of the sun. The royal father having had a dream sent for the astrologer, who cherishing resentment and malice towards your highness, purposed to offer up the mother of Shory Gyew as a sacrifice to the Yeet Nat, upon hearing of which she forsook the palace and returned to her own country.

PRINCE. Oh! The love that is felt for the father should be extended to the child. I was absent; would that I had been present! My little son Moung Shory Gyew has not even quitted his mother's breast!—I have had no regard paid to me in my absence—Manan. and myself are one. I am the head of this royal line, my son Shory Gyew is the king's grandson, and my queen was his daughter-in-law. Let me brood over all this! I swear, by the sacred books, that I will remain here no longer. Oh, attendants! every one of ye! let none be absent!—the lord of the mundane circle will journey towards the Silver Mountain—let the huntsman be called into the presence.

NOBLE. Thy servant, the huntsman, has been called, and is now here.

PRINCE. Oh! quickly show the golden prince, who rules this universe, the land they call the Silver Mount, whence came the mother of my son; and quickly show the rural lake, in which thou did'st thy captive take.

HUNTSMAN. The country of the Silver Mount! I know not where it is, my lord.

PRINCE. Then quickly bring me to the delicious pool in which thou foundest the mother of Shory Gyew—the prince has never yet been there. Oh, huntsman, rise, without delay, and bring the prince upon the way.

HUNTSMAN. My lord, I will be gone.

CURTAIN

SCENE III

(They enter the Haywonta Forest.)

> These plashing colors surely come,
> Reflected from the upper sky,
> Where Tawadyn's celestial dome
> Is hidden from the mortal eye.

PRINCE. Look, my lords, at the delightful bath of the mother of Moung Gyew! how beautiful the flower trees that grow upon its banks, and what a delicious perfume they diffuse through the forest; the woods are dense with leaves, which form a dusky shade in which are sporting butterflies, beetles, and bees. Water-quail, kingfishers, and pheasants nestle beneath the shadow of those golden lilies. How pleasant and exhilarating, my good huntsman.

HUNTSMAN. True, my lord, indeed most pleasant; I dare not venture to number all the beautiful flowers that grow in the lake.

PRINCE. I see by your countenance, that if I demand their names you will be wearied in telling them. You may now make your way back to the city.

(*Exit* HUNTSMAN.)

PRINCE. Oh, my dear lost wife! take me with you, for I am in grief, or in a little time I shall be like one that is dead. I must subdue my longing! Oh, divine beauty, dear to me as this life! Twice has her voice reached my ear, crying, husband, husband! Oh, let my fate like Ramas be, who lost and found his lovely bride; let Manan. be restored to me!

This spot must surely be like the region through which flow the seven celestial rivers; dragons, galongs, and spirits must here abound, as well as devotees and hermits. Spices of all descriptions grow here—the trees are wedged together—and the crowds of aerial spirits who frequent the thickets, pass each other with the uniformity of machinery, without confusion, like the traditions which have been handed down to us, from remote times, upon tables of stone.

(*Arrives at the hermitage.*)

PRINCE. Oh, meek recluse, who findeth pleasure in practising the duties of religion—master of this holy dwelling—pray tell me if you are happy and in health.

HERMIT. Whence does my lord come, who fearlessly enters this enclosure armed with a flying spear?

PRINCE. I will tell you, holy man. The golden ear listened to the misrepresentations of a foolish astrologer concerning the queen of the royal hair, the mother of Moung Gyew, who is a lesser spirit; and as she was near losing her life, she abandoned her little son, and quitted the city of Pyentsa, which is the cause of my coming here armed with bow, spear, and sword.

HERMIT. Hist, Hist! Do not follow her; do you think the road is easily traversed? the way is most frightful. Oh, what a savage road it is, rocks, hills, and precipices; the air is stagnant; thorns and briers lie scattered in the path, and vast creepers entwine themselves among the trees; and beasts of prey abound everywhere. Oh! do not go, my lord, for this is not all; what numbers of enemies you will meet with!—beyond the dense jungle about twelve miles there are speckled monsters which lie in wait across the road to devour you; oh, do not go. Besides these there are other obstacles, there is a stream of copper, which burns to atoms; beyond this about twelve miles there is a frightful devil which will instantly devour you, for there will be no one to help you: if my habitation were near, the monster would respect my presence—oh, my lord, each step of the road is a great grandfather to the last passed over; do not go.

PRINCE. If I do not meet with Maydow of the Silver Mountain, though nine or ten worlds may have passed by, yet I shall not think of returning.

HERMIT. My lord, as sure as that the castanets direct the measure of the song, so surely is your highness leaping into the mouth of the tiger.

PRINCE. If I do not meet with Maydow of the Silver Mountain, I would not think of returning, though hell itself were before me.

HERMIT. There are other Dwaynanhas in the south island besides the one of the Silver Mountain; cannot you search for one here? Give me the magic bow which Your Highness carries, that good may come of the gift, and then depart on your journey back.

PRINCE. If Your Holiness requires the bow, take it.

HERMIT. Astonishing! surprising! wonderful! To look at it, it is but an insignificant thing; but how heavy it is, and what strength it has!—I detained him because I thought he was one of the common order, but I now find he possesses many powers; so many indeed, that he may travel in safety wheresoever he chooses, either on the air or under the earth. Let me see if I can find the ring and the drugs which the benefactress Manan. entrusted to me—I will go and look for them!—Ah! here they are—I bestow them upon Your Highness.

PRINCE. If Your Reverence's hair was more than three cubits in length, my obeisance would be still longer.

(*The* PRINCE *arrives at the haunt of the devil.*)

PRINCE. I will just sit down here, and take some betel leaf to refresh me.

BELOO. My tribe have reigned in this Haywonta forest from the beginning —here have we held uninterrupted dominion, killed whatever we found, and eat it without cooking—our power, I fear, is about to be overturned. (*Sees the* PRINCE.) Oh, what is this? a mortal or a spirit? Didst thou arrive here by the road? You are my victim.

PRINCE. Listen! and I will tell you. I am neither a dragon nor a spirit, Pyentsa is my country; Thoodanoo my name; will you indeed eat me?—look at my sword, foolish devil!

BELOO. Tush! Tush! Your sword is only a hand's breadth—you are unarmed—you are like the flimsy paper which is tough in the sunshine, but which falls to pieces in the rain.

PRINCE. Listen, devil! Your pride is excessive; if you do not retreat, you will be slain.

BELOO. Attend, prince! Whoever enters this forest of Haywonta must acknowledge my power, and become my prey.

PRINCE. Forest king, are we not near the cane barrier and the copper stream? conduct me past them.

(BELOO *conducts the* PRINCE.)

BELOO. Oh, good prince, if anything happens to you, remember to call upon me for aid, I will now return to my post.

(*Exit* BELOO.)

PRINCE. The Silver Mountain towards which my face is now turned is still distant; my good genius is forsaking me, and my bad fate is leaving me a prisoner in this wilderness of dangers.

(*The* PRINCE *arrives at a gigantic thorn tree, upon which are sitting two monstrous birds, with faces like mortals.*)

FEMALE BIRD (*to her mate*). We have satisfied our hunger to-day upon the flesh of lions, elephants, and deer; what I wonder shall we find to-morrow?

MALE BIRD. Beautiful is thy speckled plumage; to-morrow the princess of the Silver Mount will bathe and anoint her head. I smell the food preparing for the feast; there will be more than I can devour—I will keep some in my pouch for you.

PRINCE. Oh, powerful birds, which roost upon this immense thorn tree!—

MALE BIRD. Since I first alighted upon this tree, I have never heard the human voice. What art thou?

PRINCE. Oh, mighty bird, listen, and I will tell—assist me to reach the Silver Mountain, and I will repay your favor.

MALE BIRD. Be not concerned, for I will give you the help you ask, young prince—neither horse nor elephant assisted you to make the journey thus far—only your own perseverance; my mate is sick, but I will take you upon my back.

(*The* BIRD *carries the* PRINCE.)

PRINCE. Oh, Bounmadee! thou mighty bird, alight under the shadow of these banyan trees, and leave me alone.

SCENE IV

City of the Silver Mountain.

KING. Millions of nobles, wearers of the golden chains of nobility, who follow behind me—my daughter Devay Manan. having returned from the country of mortals, will bathe and anoint herself; appoint therefore five hundred beautiful maids with budding breasts, to take each nine golden goblets, and go in procession to the east side of the city, to draw water for the ceremony.

NOBLE. My lord, we attend. Let Maensa be appointed directress of the procession. (*To* MAENSA.) Go forth to the lake without the walls to the east of the city, and draw water for the approaching ceremony.

SCENE V

Procession of Women.

MAENSA. Ladies, under the shade of those banyan trees before us I see a young (NAT) spirit sitting, if he calls answer him not; she that transgresses shall pay a fine of five tecals.

PRINCE. Lovely palace damsels, if you have with you a little betel leaf, I entreat you to give me some.

ONE OF THE LADIES. Do not be concerned, my lord, for betel leaf; if you desire it, I will give myself to you.

PRINCE. Oh, deities, angels, and spirits! let this ring which I drop into the water reach the hand of my beautiful Manan.!

(*He assists a maid to place the vessel of water upon her head and drops the ring into it.*)

(*Enter* MANAN.)

MANAN. (*while washing finds the ring*). Ladies, tell me if anything happened at the lake, when the procession went out to draw water.

MAENSA. Under the shade of these banyan trees we found a young spirit resting himself, and he assisted one of the maids to place the water vessel upon her head.

MANAN. (*seeing the* PRINCE). Oh, my husband, come and take me!

CURTAIN

BROTHERS IN ARMS

A COMEDY

BY MERRILL DENISON

CHARACTERS

J. ALTRUS BROWNE, *a business man*
DOROTHEA BROWNE, *his wife*
SYD WHITE
CHARLIE HENDERSON } *Backwoodsmen*

BROTHERS IN ARMS

Scene. A hunting camp in the backwoods.
Time. Dusk of a November evening, 1919.

A room in an abandoned farmhouse used as a hunting camp during the deer season. There is a door and window in the far wall, a double-tiered wall bunk at the left and at the right a shanty stove. There is a bench beneath the window, a couple of up-ended boxes near the stove. The room is dirty and squalid.

The curtain rises showing DOROTHEA BROWNE, *a romantic young woman, seated on the bench, her chin in her hand, gazing wistfully into the fire. She shifts her pose so that she may watch her husband, who is pacing nervously up and down.*

J. ALTRUS BROWNE *is a business man with a penchant for efficiency. He served as a Major in the Army Service Corps during the late war and spent a most rigorous time at Sandgate. He looks forward to the next war.*

DOROTHEA (*pleadingly*). Altrus, dear, won't you sit down? You're so impatient.

BROWNE (*baring his wrist watch with a click*). But, Dorothea! We've been here half an hour and not a sign of this man who owns the car. (*Viciously*) We'll miss that train as sure as . . .

DOROTHEA (*impatiently*). Oh, I know, dear . . . but don't you love it here? (*Rising, with an outflung arm gesture.*) This simple camp, its rustic charm . . . the great big out-of-doors? (*Goes to* BROWNE *and fondles his arm and lays her head on his shoulder.*) I don't want to go back to Toronto, Altrus. (*Emphatically.*) I'd like to live in a place like this forever.

BROWNE (*with a tired indrawn breath*) But, my dear, we must go back.

DOROTHEA. Oh, yes, I know, dear. But this is our first trip together since we've been married. Since you came home from France.

BROWNE (*with controlled impatience*). Dorothea! I've explained to you that we must catch this midnight train. It is most important. If this man who owns the Ford ever turns up.

DOROTHEA. But, dear . . . you can't do any good by walking around like that. Come and sit down beside me on this simple, rough hewn bench.

BROWNE (*growling*). I'm all right, thanks.

DOROTHEA (*her chin on her hand, pensively*). Oh, it's Canada and it's the wilds. Don't you love the wilds?

BROWNE. I do not! Might have known that something like this would happen coming up to a God-forsaken hole twenty miles from a railroad. **And** if that chap doesn't turn up pretty soon . . .

DOROTHEA (*ecstatically*). I do hope he does. I'm just dying to see one of those hunters. They must be such big, fine, simple men, living so close to nature all the time.

BROWNE. I'd like to see the one that drove us up. He'd do me.

DOROTHEA. Why, Altrus, he was only a common taxi-driver. I mean one of those *coureurs-du-bois*. One of those romantic figures we've read of in books about Canada. And we've seen them in the movies.

BROWNE. Taken in California, probably. (*Half to himself.*) If it took us five hours to drive up to the MacDougal's in the daytime it will take us a good six to get down to that station to-night.

DOROTHEA (*half to herself*). I remember the hero in the "Land of Summer Snows." (*To* BROWNE.) It was about Canada. (*To herself.*) A big, strong, silent man. (*To* BROWNE, *ecstatically.*) Oh! Didn't you love him?

BROWNE. Unh?

DOROTHEA. Didn't you love him!

BROWNE (*absently, with puckered brows*). Love who?

DOROTHEA. That big, strong, silent man in the "Land of Summer Snows."

BROWNE (*deliberately*). My dear Dorothea! Can't you realize that if we don't catch that train at Kaladar to-night, I stand to lose twenty-five thousand dollars?

DOROTHEA. I know, dear. But I did hope we'd see a real Canadian frontiersman before we left.

BROWNE. We've got to see one before we leave. One frontiersman with a Ford.

DOROTHEA (*sobbing*). You never think of anything but your old business.

BROWNE (*going rapidly to her*). There, there, dear, there, there. I only worry about the business for your sake, dear.

DOROTHEA (*dabbing her eyes*). It's selfish of me . . . but I can't help being a romantic little fool.

(*Blubbering lustily.*)

BROWNE. You're not a fool, dearest. Tell me you're not a fool.

DOROTHEA. Oh, but I am. (*Wiping her eyes.*) And ever since you met Jim MacDougal on the battlefields and wrote me of him, I've looked forward to coming here. During those horrible days of the war when you were at Sandgate, I've looked forward to coming here, where you would be safe and out of danger and we might find romance . . . romance in the land of Robert Service and Ralph Connor.

BROWNE. Yes, yes, dear.

DOROTHEA. I have wanted to see one of those noble men from whom they drew their characters.

(DOROTHEA *is sitting on the bench, Altrus kneeling beside her. Neither of them see* SYD WHITE *enter.* SYD *is a backwoodsman. He is wearing an old army tunic, a nondescript cap covered with red and his trousers are thrust inside a pair of heavy boots. He observes the pair on the bench, nods toward them and turns to place his gun against the wall. At the sound of the gun falling* DOROTHEA *starts and* BROWNE *rises quickly to his feet.*)

DOROTHEA. Oh!

BROWNE (*importantly to* SYD, *who is going on with his work*). My name is Browne. Major J. Altrus Browne. Mr. MacDougal told me that I'd find the man who drove me up from the station here.

SYD (*mildly interested*). Oh, he did, eh? (*Looks at the stove.*) Fire's kinda low, eh? (*Goes to the corner and gets some wood.*) You couldn't find no wood, I spose, to put on it. We jest rip a board off'n the floor. (*Going to the stove.*) Saves a feller quite a bit of time.

BROWNE (*trying to impress* SYD). I received a very important business communication this morning which makes it imperative that I return to Toronto to-night.

SYD. Oh, got to go back, eh?

DOROTHEA. And I do wish he would stay longer. But the Major is a business man, you know.

(*She is trying to fit* SYD *into innumerable rôles in fiction.*)

SYD. Oh, he is, eh? (*Filling his pipe.*) Kinda dark in here. (*Looks around.*) A feller might have a bit of light. (*Gets up and prowls around.*) They was a lantrun some place around here with the chimley cracked.

BROWNE (*impatiently and imperiously*). Never mind the lantern. We'll only be here a few moments, anyway.

SYD (*still searching under the beds*). Won't do no harm to have a bit of light. (*Finds the lantern and lights it. The globe is so sooty that just a glimmer shows.*) There, kinda helps make the place more cheerful.

BROWNE. Where is the man who drove us up from the station?

SYD (*hanging the lantern and sitting down behind the stove*). Well, that's kinda hard to say. When was it he druv you up?

BROWNE. Last Tuesday.

DOROTHEA (*helpfully*). And it rained the whole way. I loved it.

SYD (*politely*). Kinda wet, eh? (*To* BROWNE.) Last Tuesday? That must a been Charlie druv you up.

BROWNE. It doesn't matter what his name is. What I want to know is when he will be back.

SYD. Charlie it was. Charlie Henderson. That's who it'd be. He ain't here.

BROWNE. Yes! Yes! Yes! But when will he be here?

SYD (*lighting his pipe*). Well, that's kinda hard to say. The lads went over to Wolf Lake this mornin'.

BROWNE. This Charlie is with them?

DOROTHEA (*to* SYD). You know, I think your camp is adorable. It's so simple and direct. So natural.

(*With appropriate gestures.*)

SYD (*to* DOROTHEA). This here place?

DOROTHEA. Yes. Oh! I love it.

BROWNE. Dorothea!

SYD (*observing* BROWNE *walking near the corner by the head of the beds*). That floor ain't none too good since we've been usin' it for the stove.

BROWNE. Never mind about me. (*Exasperated.*) When will these men be back from Wolf Lake?

SYD. Well . . . that's kinda hard to say. It's most ten miles over there and the trail ain't none too good. But I figger they ought to be comin' in most any time now.

BROWNE. And this fellow Henderson will be with them?

SYD. No . . . he won't be with them. That is, it ain't likely.

BROWNE. Can't you understand that I have only five hours to catch that midnight train at Kaladar? And I must find this fellow Henderson to take me down.

DOROTHEA (*to* SYD). And I simply hate to think of going back so soon.

SYD. Shame you can't stay till the end of the huntin' season. He might kill a deer.

BROWNE. Dorothea! Will you please try and keep quiet? Now (*to* SYD) when will Henderson be back? Answer me definitely.

(SYD *is cleaning his gun for several successive speeches. This adds to the hopelessness of* BROWNE'S *position.*)

SYD. Well . . . that's kinda hard to say. He went still huntin' over back of the big rock . . .

BROWNE (*almost frantic*). Yes, but you must know when he'll be here. I've got to have him drive down to that train to-night.

SYD. Oh . . . you want him to drive down to catch the midnight?

BROWNE. Yes, yes, yes. When will he be back?

SYD. Well . . . if he went back of the big rock he'd most likely leave about dark. . . .

BROWNE. It's been dark half an hour. How long would it take him to get back?

SYD. I figger it'd take him about half an hour if he had a boat.

BROWNE. Half an hour, eh? Should be here, then, soon. (*Thinks.*) Did he have a boat?

SYD. No . . . he didn't have no boat.

BROWNE (*infuriated*). What in heaven's name are you talking about a boat for, if he didn't have one?

DOROTHEA. Don't be impatient, dear.

SYD. As I was sayin'. If he had a boat. . . .

BROWNE (*screaming with rage*). But you said he didn't have one.

DOROTHEA (*helpfully*). But, dear, if he did have a boat.

BROWNE. Dorothea! Will you kindly keep quiet and leave this to me? (*To* SYD.) Now, if it's within the range of human possibility, will you tell me when you expect Henderson back here?

SYD (*laying down his gun and doing his best to be explicit*). Well, I figger it this way. If he had a boat . . .

DOROTHEA (*patiently*). He means that if he had a . . .

BROWNE (*disgustedly*). Let's forget about the boat. On foot, how long would it take him to get over here? Don't you realize that he's got to take me to that train? Will he be back in ten minutes? Twenty minutes?

SYD. Well . . . it's kinda hard to say. He mightn't have went back of the big rock at all. He might have picked up a fresh track and followed it west. But that ain't likely because most of the deer's scared off'n this side of the lake.

DOROTHEA. Oh! What scared them?

BROWNE. Dorothea! How many times must I ask you to keep quiet and not interrupt? I must find out when we can get out of here. (*To* SYD.) You feel sure that he went back of the big rock?

SYD. I figger that's most likely where he's went. And if he couldn't have got the loan of a boat. . . .

BROWNE. He might have borrowed a boat then?

DOROTHEA (*helpfully*). Why, yes dear, he might have *borrowed* a boat.

BROWNE. Is there some place that he might have borrowed a boat?

SYD. No. . . . There ain't.

DOROTHEA. You see, dear, he couldn't have got a boat anyway.

BROWNE. Good God!

SYD. Ain't no one's got a boat over here except Levi Weeks and he's got his'n up to Buck Lake.

BROWNE (*striding over to* SYD). Look here, we've established this point. He couldn't have gotten a boat.

SYD. Well . . . I wouldn't go as far as to say that. He might . . .

DOROTHEA. Dear, won't you sit down?

SYD. Yes, you'd best to sit down. That floor ain't none too good.

BROWNE. Never mind about me. I can look out for myself all right.

DOROTHEA. But do be careful, dear.

BROWNE. Dorothea! (*To* SYD.) Now let's find out about your friend Charlie.

SYD. He ain't no particular friend of mine. Kind of a brother-in-law, it seems to me. His halfsister Nellie married my stepbrother Aligan. My father's . . .

DOROTHEA. Why, you're related then.

BROWNE. Dorothea! (*Pleadingly.*) Do keep quiet. (*To* SYD) He could walk back in an hour, couldn't he?

SYD. He might. But it'd depend on whether he got a deer or not. If he got a fawn and it wasn't too much to heft, he'd most likely try and drug it out.

BROWNE. From what I've seen of this country, it's likely he never saw a deer.

DOROTHEA. Why, Altrus, they catch lots of wild things in the wilds.

Syd. Well . . . if he didn't get a deer the chanctes is he'd stay in the bush all night.

Browne. Do you mean to say that there is a possibility of his not returning at all?

Dorothea. We'd have to stay over then, wouldn't we?

Syd (*laughing*). I figger you would. He often stays out all night when he's still huntin'. It ain't likely though. Charlie most often gets his deer. He ought to be here any time now . . . if he's a comin' at all.

Dorothea. I almost hope he doesn't come. You know, this is the first trip we've had together since we've been married. Since Altrus left his battalion.

Syd. You're his woman, eh? Married?

Browne. Dorothea, do shut up. Can't you realize what twenty-five thousand dollars means to us?

(*She pouts.*)

Syd (*seriously*). If you'd really wanted to have gone you should a went this morning.

Browne. I didn't know till four o'clock. (*Angrily.*) I should never have come up into this God-forsaken hole at all.

Syd (*mildly remonstrative*). This place ain't bad. The deer's about scared off what with the Finches runnin' hounds all the year around but they's still some left.

Browne (*disgustedly*). I'm not talking about the hunting. I'm talking about the distance it is from the railroad.

Dorothea. That's why I love it. It's so far from everything.

Syd. Might be another twenty miles and do no harm.

Dorothea (*excitedly*). Oh, Altrus. He loves the wild, virgin country, too. Far, far from civilization . . . and phones . . . and motors.

Browne. I'd give a lot to see one, just one, now.

Syd. It's quite a ways from them things, but I figger it's just as well. Keeps folks out a here in the summer. City folks is a kinda bother.

Dorothea. I know. They encroach on the freedom of your life.

Syd. They's always tryin' to get a feller to work. One way and another they figger they's doin' a feller a favor to let him work for 'em.

Dorothea. I know, you want to be left alone to lead your own simple life.

Browne (*who has been walking like a caged lion and has neared the dangerous corner*). Simple is right. Now look here. I'm going to give Henderson ten minutes more.

Syd. He might be back in ten minutes. If he got a deer and didn't try to drug it out with him. (*Pause.*) And he come by the lower trail, (*Pause*) and he didn't stop down to the MacDougal's to listen to that there phonograph. I'd figger he'd most likely be about . . .

(Dorothea *screams and runs over to* Altrus *who has tripped in a hole and is rubbing his ankle, cursing softly to himself.* Syd *makes no change in position.*)

SYD. I told you to keep out of there.

DOROTHEA. Dearest, what have you done? Did you hurt yourself, dear?

BROWNE. My ankle. (*Hobbles.*) It's only a wrench probably.

SYD (*chuckling*). I kinda figgered you'd do that. You should've sot down. What did you do? Sprained it?

BROWNE (DOROTHEA *has helped him across to the bench where he sits rubbing the ankle*). I didn't do anything to it. (*Explodes.*) It was your infernal floor. Holes all over the place, because you're too damn lazy to chop down a tree for firewood.

SYD (*indignantly*). We h'ain't got no time to split firewood when we're huntin.

DOROTHEA. Did you hurt yourself badly, dear? (BROWNE *winces.*) Oh, do hurry and tear up something clean for a bandage. And get some hot water.

SYD (*laughing*). There ain't no water nearer'n the lake and there ain't nothin' clean here. He ain't hurt bad.

DOROTHEA (*anxiously*). I hope not.

SYD. Why, he was lucky. One day last week one of the hounds fell down that there hole and broke his leg. We had to shoot him. You'd do best to sit quiet for a while. Have a chew? (*Offering* BROWNE *a plug which he refuses with a gesture of repugnance.*) To my way of thinkin' there ain't nothin' side of a good steady chew to quiet a feller's temper.

BROWNE. I'll just sit here and keep my weight off it for a few minutes. If Henderson isn't here in ten minutes we'll go.

SYD. Have a chew?

BROWNE (*white with rage*). By God! I'd like to have had you in my battalion for about six months.

(DOROTHEA *rises.*)

SYD. Yes, you was lucky.

BROWNE. I'd teach you a few things if I had you in the army.

SYD. Was you in the war?

DOROTHEA. Oh, yes. Altrus was in the Army Service Corps for over a year. He was a major.

BROWNE. I'd teach you a few things.

SYD. I suppose you might.

BROWNE. I'd give you ten years if you ever said might again.

SYD. Perhaps you might . . . I was in the army.

DOROTHEA (*with dawning wonderment*). Dear, he, too, fought for his country in the great war. You're brothers in arms.

BROWNE (*silencing her with a gesture*). What outfit were you ever with?

SYD. The 284th Battalion, but I didn't see no sense to it, so I left.

DOROTHEA. How could you leave? Altrus had a lot of trouble getting out. They were awfully mean about it.

BROWNE. Left? Do you mean you deserted?

SYD. No, I didn't desert. The head lads told me to come home. I couldn't get the hang of it like the rest of the lads. They were willin' to walk around doing nothin', but they wasn't no sense to it to my way of thinkin'.

DOROTHEA (*reminiscently*). I felt that sometimes. (*To* BROWNE.) Didn't you, dear?

BROWNE (*explosively*). Certainly not. (*To* SYD) Why, the very thing you need is a few years in the army. Straighten you up, teach you discipline, make a man of you.

DOROTHEA (*to* BROWNE, *brightly*). It helped you a lot, didn't it, dear? (*To* SYD.) It really was wonderful what the army could do.

SYD. To my way of thinkin' it didn't do nothin' except help make a feller lazy. That's what I couldn't see no sense in. If they'd been somethin' useful for a feller to do I'd a stayed and helped them with their war, but they wasn't except in the clink.

DOROTHEA. Well, why didn't you get them to transfer you to the Clink Department, if you liked it and were useful there? Altrus got transferred to the Quartermaster's Branch. One is always so much more useful in work one likes.

BROWNE (*looking helplessly at his wife*). I suppose you spent most of your time in the clink?

SYD. No, not most of it. But a feller was doing somethin' useful there. When I wasn't in jail . . .

DOROTHEA. Oh, who put you in jail?

SYD. One of them head lads. When I wasn't there we done nothin' but drill. One of them head lads'd get us out and walk us. 'Tweren't no sense to that. Walkin' a feller around just for the sake of walkin'.

DOROTHEA. It does sound silly, doesn't it, dear?

BROWNE. Dorothea! You know nothing about this at all. (*To* SYD) Didn't you want to fight for your country?

SYD. To my way of thinkin', that's why I joint the army. But we wasn't doin' no fightin'. We wasn't doin' nothing but follerin' them head lads around, drillin'.

BROWNE. You had to be drilled. You had to learn the rudiments of soldiering.

DOROTHEA. But don't you think they overdid it, now and then, dear?

SYD. To my way of thinkin' they did. Why, them head lads'd make us clean our boots and then walk us around in the dust. Why didn't they keep us inside if they wanted our shoes shiny?

DOROTHEA. I remember all those clean-limbed young fellows at Camp Dix walking along the dusty roads. It did seem a shame. (*To* BROWNE.) You had a horse, didn't you, dear?

BROWNE. Dorothea! (*To* SYD.) But can't you understand that you had to learn the job of soldiering? Your job was to fight Germans and you had to learn how to do it.

SYD (*emphatically*). That's just what I figgered. All them Germans havin' to be licked and us wastin' our time follerin' them head lads around. They even tried to learn me how to use a gun.

DOROTHEA. How absurd! They didn't really, did they? They wouldn't try to teach a frontiersman to use a gun, would they, dear?

BROWNE. Certainly they would. All these things are very necessary from the standpoint of discipline, my dear.

SYD. That's what the head lads used to say. (*Looking at* BROWNE.) Was you a head lad in the war?

BROWNE. I was an officer.

DOROTHEA (*proudly*). Oh, yes, my husband was a major and he was much too valuable to go to the front. They kept him, quite against his own wishes, in Sandgate, all during the war, didn't they, Altrus?

BROWNE. Dorothea! Don't be absurd.

DOROTHEA. But you told me so yourself, dear.

SYD. I kinda figgered you was a head lad.

BROWNE (*sarcastically, evasively*). I suppose you told your officers what you thought of discipline?

SYD. Yes, I says to the head lad, I says, I wasn't goin' to waste my time doin' things they wasn't no sense in.

DOROTHEA. How courageous!

BROWNE (*dumbfounded*). You told one of your officers that?

SYD (*surprised*). Yes, I says to him, I says . . .

BROWNE. You were put under arrest, of course.

DOROTHEA. Would they arrest a man just for saying what he thought?

BROWNE. They generally shot them for that.

DOROTHEA (*with enthusiasm*). But, dear, don't you love his sturdy independence? It's so Canadian.

BROWNE. That's not independence. It's insubordination. What crime did you commit to get you in the guard house?

SYD. 'Tweren't no crime.

BROWNE (*sharply*). But, man alive, you must have done something.

SYD. 'Tweren't no crime. I was out walkin' with my gun outside the tents where the lads slept and one of the head lads come around and ast me a lot of questions which I didn't know the answers for, because they was kinda riddles anyways, and he got mad and says to me I was guardin' the camp from Germans.

BROWNE. Why, you were on sentry duty and he was the officer of the day!

DOROTHEA. But, dear, he said it was at night.

SYD. Yes, it was at night. So I says to him, I says, all right, just to get rid of him, for I seen they wasn't no sense to it. They wasn't a German this side of the ocean and they wasn't no sense hangin' around in the cold. So I went in and went to bed.

BROWNE (*horrified*). You could have been shot for that. On sentry duty and deserted your post!

SYD. That's what the head lad says the next mornin'. Couldn't shoot a feller fer that. Wouldn't be no sense to it. I told the head lad, and he seen I was right. He come near to cryin' and says I could be his batman. But I wasn't goin' to stay up till four in the mornin' to pull anybody's boots off'n them, let alone one of them head lads, so he sent me to jail.

DOROTHEA (*romantically*). How cramping it must have been to a free out-of-doors spirit like yours. What did you do?

SYD. I liked it right well, but the head lads wouldn't let me stay when they found I was kinda enjoyin' it.

BROWNE. My heart bleeds for your officers.

SYD. Them head lads? Why, they didn't do nothin' but think up ways for us to waste our time.

DOROTHEA. You fought in France, of course? (*With a change of mood.*) Altrus always wanted to go to the front and fight, but they wouldn't let him leave England. I don't know what they would have done without him. He's so clever at business, you know.

SYD (*genuinely interested*). He is, eh?

BROWNE (*the conversation is becoming embarrassing*). How about this man Charlie?

SYD. Well . . . he'd been here long ago if he could a got a boat.

BROWNE (*whimpers*). Back to the navy again?

DOROTHEA. But didn't you adore England? Oh, I love London.

SYD. London's quite a place, but to my way of thinkin' a feller can have just as good a time down here to Belleville.

DOROTHEA (*understandingly*). I know. You love the simplicity of this big free land.

BROWNE. Too simple-minded to like anything else. How did they get rid of you? Dishonorable discharge?

SYD. No, they wasn't nothin' dishonorable about it. They had a meetin' one day and I told 'em what they ought to do to my way of thinkin', and one of the old fellers, the head lad hisself, I figger it was, says I was incorr . . . incorr . . . incorr . . .

DOROTHEA. Incorruptible.

BROWNE (*explosively*). Incorruptible nothing. Incorrigible.

SYD. That's it. Says I was goin' home in disgrace. Ain't that just like the army? Why, when I got outside, the rest of the lads says I was a lucky stiff to be gettin' home at all. (*Gets up and listens.*) Someone's comin'.

BROWNE. I can hear no one.

SYD. Perhaps you ain't used to listenin' much in your business. We got a feller up here that got his eyes blew out in France can hear most a mile.

DOROTHEA. Some one is coming, Altrus. I can hear them. Listen! I do hope it's one of those men I've read about.

BROWNE (*peremptorily*). Is that Henderson?

(SYD *nods his head.*)

DOROTHEA. Only the taxi-man. I'm so disappointed.

BROWNE. Well, I'm not. Now we can get something accomplished.

(*He rises, awaiting* CHARLIE'S *entrance, as if all would now be well.* SYD *rises and waits expectantly, showing an entirely new interest in life.* DOROTHEA *pettishly fingers a glove.* CHARLIE *comes in the door, carrying a gun, nods to* BROWNE *and his wife and goes to the stove and warms his hands.*)

CHARLIE. Evenin'. Harye, Syd?

SYD. Any luck?

BROWNE. See here, you're the man who drove us up from the station, aren't you?

CHARLIE. Last Tuesday, wasn't it? (*Turns to* SYD *as if he had no further interest in* BROWNE.) Well, Syd, I got a nice four-year-old buck.

DOROTHEA. Oh, did you catch a buck?

BROWNE. See here, I've got to catch the midnight at Kaladar.

CHARLIE (*politely interested*). Got to catch the midnight, eh? You'd best be startin' soon.

SYD. Where'd you get him?

CHARLIE. In them hard woods north of Dyer Lake.

DOROTHEA (*thrilled*). I'd love to have been there, wouldn't you, dear?

BROWNE. I would not. See here, Henderson!

SYD. How'd you get him, runnin'?

CHARLIE (*sitting down*). It was this way, Syd. About four o'clock I was 'bout a mile north of Dyer Lake, a standin' on top of a little rise, smokin'.

DOROTHEA. Isn't it exciting? I do wish we could have been there, don't you, dear?

BROWNE. Dorothea!

CHARLIE. I thought I seen somethin' move, but you know how you can look at a frozen deer and think it ain't nothin' but a tree.

DOROTHEA. Oh, do they freeze?

SYD. It ain't freezing like ice. They stand still without movin' a hair. Just like that doe I missed yesterday.

BROWNE. Look here, Henderson. I stand to lose twenty-five thousand dollars. . . .

CHARLIE. Twenty-five thousand dollars. Quite a lot of money. Just like that doe, it was, Syd. I looked again and seen him move his head. Why, he wasn't seventy-five feet from me.

DOROTHEA (*excitedly*). Weren't you awfully nervous? I know I would have been. I'm so excited.

SYD (*sucking on his pipe*). Afraid of scarin' him, eh?

CHARLIE. Yes. Well, I started to drug the rifle to me. Slow . . . slow . . . slow.

BROWNE. Drug it faster, in heaven's name. Shoot your blithering deer and listen to me.

SYD. But you got him, eh?

DOROTHEA. You got him?

CHARLIE. Yes, sir, I got him. I waits for him to move a bit so's I could get a sight on his shoulder. Didn't want to shoot him in the head.

DOROTHEA (*breathless*). No, you wouldn't want to do that.

CHARLIE. Well, I waited till his shoulder come across the sights, and then I took a long breath and drug down on the trigger.

DOROTHEA AND SYD. What happened?

CHARLIE. I shot him.

DOROTHEA. Did you kill it?

CHARLIE. Dead.

SYD. What did you do with him? Leave him in the bush?

CHARLIE. Cleaned him out and hung him up on a tree.

SYD. Quite a ways in, I suppose?

CHARLIE. No, he ain't very far from the big lake.

SYD (*nodding his head and sucking his pipe*). He ain't far from the lake, eh? Now, Charlie, if you'd only had a boat . . .

(*The dialogue has worked* BROWNE *into a fine frenzy, and at the mention of the boat his control breaks completely.*)

BROWNE. Oh, God! Let's get out of here. Dorothea, come on.

(*He picks up his coat and stick and marches out the door.* CHARLIE *and* SYD *rise, very surprised, and* SYD *takes down the lantern.*)

SYD (*leaning out the door*). That's a hard trail to foller in the dark. Best take the lantrun.

BROWNE (*outside*). I don't want your damned "lantrun." Come on, Dorothea, we'll go back to the MacDougals.

(DOROTHEA *goes to the door and waits.*)

CHARLIE. What's the matter with the old feller? Seems kinda crabbed.

SYD (*tersely*). He was a head lad in the war.

CHARLIE (*understandingly*). So that's what's the matter with him.

BROWNE (*from some distance*). Dorothea!

DOROTHEA. Yes, dear. (*To* CHARLIE.) Good-by, I'm so sorry I have to go, but I have enjoyed your story so much.

BROWNE. Dorothea!

DOROTHEA (*to* SYD). And I did love your simple, beautiful camp. (*Calling.*) I'm coming, dear.

(DOROTHEA *goes out and* CHARLIE *looks around for wood.*)

CHARLIE. Seems a nice sort of woman?

SYD. About the pure hog's fat, I'd figger. They's some wood over there where Jim ties his hound. (CHARLIE *goes to the corner.*) The old lad fell down the hole a ways back.

(*The two men laugh heartily and* CHARLIE *carries a stick or two over to the stove, puts it in and then turns questioningly to* SYD.)

CHARLIE. He wasn't thinkin of going down to Kaladar, to-night?

SYD. Seemed kinda sot on it. Said he wanted you to take him down.

CHARLIE. I wouldn't go down for twenty dollars. Why don't you take him, you ain't doin' nothin'?

SYD. Talked like he wanted you, all the time.

CHARLIE. Don't see why you shouldn't take him. I'll call him. (*Going to the door.*) HEY! HEY! COME BACK HERE!

BROWNE (*from some distance*). What is it?

CHARLIE. COME ON BACK! (*To* SYD.) The chancetes is he might let you drive him in.

SYD. It's kinda hard to say. He seemed sot on havin' you.

(*The two men smoke, waiting for* BROWNE, *who comes in shortly in a very black mood.*)

BROWNE. Well, what is it now?

CHARLIE. We been thinkin'.

BROWNE (*wheeling*). No! It's impossible.

CHARLIE. No, it ain't impossible. We was wonderin' why you was so all fired anxious for me to drive you down?

BROWNE. Anybody will do. They told me at the MacDougals that you were the only person who owned a car.

CHARLIE. Shucks. Syd owns half as much of the car as I do. Why don't you get him to drive you down?

BROWNE. Syd? Syd? Syd, who?

CHARLIE. Why, Syd, there. You been talking to him for the best part of an hour.

(DOROTHEA *comes in the door.*)

BROWNE. Him?

CHARLIE. Yes, him. Might as well drive the old lad in, Syd. You ain't got nothin' much to do.

SYD (*reaching for his coat*). No, I ain't got nothin' to do. Might just as well a started an hour ago. Been well on the way.

BROWNE. And you stayed here talking when you could have started with us?

SYD. Yes.

(*Stopping with one sleeve on*).

BROWNE (*his temper shot completely*). Why didn't you say you could drive us in? Why didn't you say you owned half the car? Why did you keep us here wasting valuable time?

SYD. I didn't keep you. I'd a taken you in if you'd ast me to.

BROWNE. Well, why in hell didn't you?

SYD. You never ast me.

CHARLIE. No, you never ast him.

DOROTHEA (*helpful to the last*). Why no, dear. You never asked him once.

CURTAIN

THE THRICE PROMISED BRIDE

A MODERN CHINESE PLAY

By CHENG-CHIN HSIUNG

CHARACTERS

WANG TA-MING, *the Magistrate*
TUAN CHAI, *his Secretary*
CHUNG TING, *the Knight*
LI CHE-FU, *the Wealthy Merchant*
WANG MEI-PAO, *the First Match-Maker*
HAN CHU-YIN, *the Bride*
THE BRIDE'S MOTHER
CHIEN-SHOU, *an Old Man*
TO KUANG-YANG, *the Beggar-Scholar*
LIU MA, *the Second Match-Maker*
ATTENDANTS, MUSICIANS, ETC.

THE THRICE PROMISED BRIDE

TIME. *Long ago; many years before China became a republic.*
PLACE. *The Magistrate's Court in an interior district in Ho-Nan Province, China.*

The rise of the curtain, if a proscenium curtain is used, discloses a Chinese stage. There are two doors in the rear wall; the left for entrance, the right for exit. At each door there must be a curtain exquisitely embroidered with threads of gold and bright-colored silk; on the left door curtain the figure of a dragon, and on the right, the figure of a phœnix. In the center there is a table. The audience cannot see the table legs, for the table is curtained with a rich tapestry on which the figure of a unicorn is embroidered. On the table are a pen-rack with Chinese pens; ink-stones, one for red ink, the other for black ink; a wooden block resembling a mallet; a massive wooden official seal; two carved bamboo holders for warrant-sticks; two wooden panels with the representation of a tiger's head and with Chinese inscriptions which signify to the Chinese that the scene is unmistakably in a district court. To the right of the table is a chair where THE SECRETARY *is to sit. Behind the table is the chair for* THE MAGISTRATE. *On the center wall we may have a picture of the God of the Theater. But, lest* THE MAGISTRATE *should duplicate or intercept the picture, we had better have a painting of pear trees instead, under which the first Chinese actors are supposed to have practiced the histrionic arts. There is no other furniture on the stage.*

The American audience is supposed to know the setting from the "write-up," in the newspaper, the "give-outs" of the press agent, from the showy posters, or, even at the last minute, from the printed program. But, lest everything should fail, the American playwright has adapted the traditional Chorus and made him prepare the audience. We will keep the Chinese convention and let the principal character relate the circumstances and establish a close contact between the players and audience.

We shall not introduce the property man, since he is obtrusive to some sophisticated Chinese dramatists and to all the uninitiated Western playgoers.

Music we must have. To avoid the overwhelming din of a Chinese orchestra we will invest the power of music in a single Maker-of-Sound, behind the scene.

With the overture, in which a variety of instruments are used, the left door-curtain is raised, and THE MAGISTRATE *majestically enters with his attend-*

ants, one in front and one behind him. He has more than two attendants,
but we must make imaginary puissance. He pauses before the door for a
moment; then he walks gracefully down stage. He strikes with both hands
his mandarin gauze hat to pay a public homage to the emperor and to wish
secretly for a promotion to higher rank. Slowly he straightens the lateral
appendages of the official bonnet. (These are not in the form of the
Manchurian peacock feather, but in the shape of the wings of a bat,
symbolizing happiness.) Carefully he makes sure of the clasp of his stiff
belt which is beautifully decorated. Augustly he smoothes his imperial
robe displaying the gorgeous colors and designs of his costume.
When the audience has had enough of his front elevation, he turns, and with
pompous strides proceeds to the center of the stage to exhibit his profile.
He waves, sweeps, and shakes his large and long sleeves to show that he has
nothing there. Solemnly he walks up stage to show his gorgeously em-
broidered back to the audience; and then he "ascends" the dedicated chair.
When the applause has abated he tells his story.

The Magistrate. My humble name is Wang Ta-Ming, the magistrate of
this Yen-Ling District of the Province of Ho-Nan. I was born in the Hain-
Kien District of the Province of Kiangsi, of scholarly parents. At the age of
eighteen moons my mother taught me to write with a reed in the sand. When
I was yet wearing my hair like the tentacles of an octopus I studied the
Four Books and the Five Classics. At the age of fifteen years I passed my
first examination and won the degree of Blooming Talent. In my second
decadal anniversary I was honored with the degree of Raised Man. The
next leap year bestowed on me the rank of Entered Scholar. As a reward for
my literary distinction I was appointed the magistrate of this district. I
hastened to this post that I might glorify my family name. I am watched by
a thousand eyes and listened to by a thousand ears, for there is always an
attentive audience within these four walls. It makes me shudder to think of
the important duties I have to perform. Attendants!

(The audience's attention is directed to the attendants who have been
standing on each side of the table. They are dressed alike. They wear thin,
flat-soled shoes but make up in height by their tapering felt hats. Their
costumes are of plain silk painted with the emblem of the district court.
When not employed, each leans on his bamboo stave, a much abused symbol
of justice.)

Attendants. At your service, Your Honor.

The Magistrate. Call Mr. Secretary Tuan Chai!

(The First Attendant goes out and returns immediately with The Secre-
tary, dressed as an old gentleman with a heavy mustache, who is ready to give
the young officer his experience and opinion when needed. He carries a fan.)

The Secretary. What is your honorable wish?

The Magistrate. Have you any invention concerning the case of the
interrupted wedding?

THE SECRETARY. I have found the matchmaker, Sir. It is time the plaintiff Chung Ting and the defendant Li Che-Fu be here.

THE MAGISTRATE. Strike the gong and open the court!

(*The gong sounds behind the stage. The attendants pull open the imaginary doors. The Chinese drama demands that acting create scenery rather than vice versa. The people who are yet to enter must orient themselves first, walk and step to suggest to the mind of the audience, doors and steps. The military man enters briskly with accompaniment of martial music. He is dressed in the costume of an ancient Chinese Knight, beautifully embroidered mantle, plumed bonnet, close-fitting uniform, a sword and trim, embroidered boots. He bows to* THE MAGISTRATE *but does not kneel.*)

THE MAGISTRATE. Are you Chung Ting, the plaintiff?

CHUNG TING. Yes, Sir, newly returned from my military career.

THE MAGISTRATE. What can you do besides disbanding the wedding procession of Li Che-Fu?

CHUNG TING. I can shoot with a 300-pound bow and pierce a half inch willow leaf 100 steps away. I can separate and pacify two fighting bulls. However, I did not expect to win a wife by sheer force, but by a prior claim.

THE MAGISTRATE. Why didn't you claim the maiden's hand until she was carried in the sedan chair to her new home?

CHUNG TING. I had taken my military examination in the capital and was serving His Majesty and our country by defending the northern borders against the barbaric tribes, so I have not been able to plan to establish my own family.

THE MAGISTRATE. You didn't know your fiancée was to be married to Li Che-Fu until the wedding day?

CHUNG TING. Not until I came back with my title and my plumes and my sword.

THE MAGISTRATE. (*He takes a warrant stick and gives it to the* FIRST ATTENDANT.) Bring the defendant Li Che-Fu!

(*The* FIRST ATTENDANT *goes out and returns presently with* THE RICH MERCHANT. *Gay music accompanies the entrance.* THE RICH MERCHANT *is a man of about thirty years. His costume surpasses the magistrate's in richness. Like* TUAN CHAI, *he may not use the design of dragons and clouds, but he may use the bat motif, or better, the ancient-coin motif. He wears jeweled Chinese shoes. He walks pompously into the court. As soon as he sees* THE MAGISTRATE *he kneels. There is no property man to assist him; such privilege is granted only to an important personage or to a famous actor. An ordinary actor is expected to take care of his costume, however cumbersome and costly. The property man is ubiquitously watching to see that the costumes are properly displayed, and not in the actor's way. Handling any property attracts the audience's attention and spurs the audience's imagination, often to the neglect of the actor. The costume is to be admired as it is worn, much like the long train formerly worn by the Western hostess. The wearer would consider any meddling on the part of another as a kind favor,*

or as an insult. Thus, comfortably, and without assistance, THE WEALTHY
MERCHANT *prostrates himself.*)

THE MAGISTRATE. Li Che-Fu, did you know this man Chung Ting?

LI CHE-FU. Not until he collided with my bridal chair, Your Honor.

THE MAGISTRATE. Did you know he was the first betrothed to the maiden
of the Han family?

LI CHE-FU (*hesitating*). N—

THE MAGISTRATE (*warningly*). The truth, or the bamboo.

(THE ATTENDANTS *stand erect and threaten* LI-CHE-FU *by tapping the table
sides alternately with their bamboo staves.*)

LI CHE-FU (*looks at* THE SECRETARY *for advice.* TUAN CHAI, *who has
been bribed, nods his head*). I heard that my bride, Han-Chu-Yin, had been
promised to a person before either was born. The family of the boy moved
away to the region bordering the barbaric tribes and was never heard of for
twice eight years. My marriage was negotiated under the six ceremonies.
All the village was invited to my feast. My matchmaker alone will establish
the evidence.

(TUAN CHAI *nods repeatedly and whispers to* THE MAGISTRATE *behind his
spread fan.*)

THE MAGISTRATE. Bring the matchmaker!

(THE FIRST ATTENDANT *goes out and returns with* THE MATCHMAKER.
THE MATCHMAKER *is often the fool or the clown in the Chinese plays. She
(it might just as well be he) defies conventions, customs, all the reality and
realism in the Empire and all the traditions of the world save that of the
Chinese stage. She may be streak-faced and grotesquely costumed. No
Chinese playwright describes this figure definitely, but grants the character
all the license and the gagging which perfect or spoil the play according to
which way you take it. During the clownish entrance, humorous music.*)

THE MAGISTRATE. Are you Matchmaker Wang Mei-Pao by name?

WANG MEI-PAO. By profession, mister. Are you unmarried? Do you
want me?

THE MAGISTRATE. Neither yourself nor your service, but your account of
the families of these people.

WANG MEI-PAO. My account, to be sure. I can make the ignorant learned;
the ugly beautiful; the blind see; the deaf hear; the shrew tame; in a word
poverty, riches; misery, happiness; and earth, heaven. (THE MAGISTRATE
is nonplussed.) And they all seem to believe me. They drink to my health
and lift the stuff to the level of their eye-brows and live together contentedly,
and harmoniously as the proverbial harp and lyre. (THE MAGISTRATE *murmurs as if not knowing what to do with her.*) Of course, if your first match
is not so supremely perfect as you wish, you can depend upon me for
concubines.

THE MAGISTRATE. Did you try to tie your blind and aimless cords around
this merchant Li and the maiden of the Han family?

WANG MEI-PAO. Yes, Sir, a heaven-made match. Their ingots of gold total the same figure, the gates of the two houses cope with one another. A perfect equation withal!

THE MAGISTRATE. That is enough, you may go home.

WANG MEI-PAO. (*She walks reluctantly to the right, where the retiring character may say the last word.*) I live next door to the house of Everybody. Don't forget to send for me when you want to augment your family; for I know all the superb marriageable maidens in the whole district.

(*She goes out.*)

THE MAGISTRATE. Bring the Han family in!

(THE FIRST ATTENDANT *goes out and returns directly with* HAN CHU-YIN *and her mother. The women walk down stage, between the two flags which are painted on the outside to suggest the wheel of a carriage, and are carried by supernumeraries. The supers withdraw as the women walk to the center of the stage with an accompaniment of slow and soft music, but not with mincing steps, for foot-binding has never been universal in China. It is superfluous to comment on their costumes. They are just beautiful. The designs for the young woman's costume are gay flowers and aquatic grasses of a smaller and more exquisite pattern.*

The young woman is about eighteen years old. The mother is old enough to require the rôle of "Lao-Tan" (the married woman's part). Like the men without a title all women must kneel before the magistrate. In a district court or in a theater there are always enough cushions for that purpose. The women bow down low.)

THE MAGISTRATE. Face toward the north!

(*The women face him. While he is looking at the young beauty, music expressing magnetic enchantment is played. The bashful woman turns her face from* THE MAGISTRATE *toward the audience.*)

THE MAGISTRATE. The looks that destroy cities, the looks that destroy kingdoms! Small wonder you men quarrel with each other. Are you Han-Chu-Yin, formerly promised to Chung Ting and now being borne to the house of Li-Che-Fu?

(*The young woman is so shy that she can hardly hold her head up or make an answer.*)

THE MOTHER. Yes, my Lord, if she is nothing else.

THE MAGISTRATE. And you, her mother?

THE MOTHER. Yes, my Lord, her only living parent.

THE MAGISTRATE. Why did you intend marrying your daughter to the Li family while there was yet an engagement contract standing between the family of Han and the family of Chung?

THE MOTHER. Because we thought the Chung boy sacrificed himself for His Majesty, and my dear little Chu-Yin was past her peach-blooming age.

THE MAGISTRATE. You may not marry your daughter to two men. (*Softly.*) I do pity your daughter. No ceremony has yet been completed. Whom do you prefer?

THE MOTHER. I will marry . . .

LI CHE-FU. I offer you my golden ingots.

CHUNG TING (*advancing*). I have my silvery horses.

LI CHE-FU. I have built my red mansion.

CHUNG TING. I have won my scarlet jacket.

LI CHE-FU. My calculation always bears fruit.

CHUNG TING. My arrows always hit the bull's-eye.

THE MOTHER. What say you to these genteels, my dear Little Chu-Yin?

HAN CHU-YIN. A maiden has no lips, but heart.

THE MOTHER. Well, whom does your heart yearn to choose?

HAN CHU-YIN. I may neither choose whom I like nor refuse whom I dislike. I do as my parent decides.

THE MOTHER. The parent should be wiser, but I am not. (*To* THE MAGISTRATE.) Your honor is the parent of the people. Graciously decide this according to your honorable will.

THE MAGISTRATE. I am not old enough to be the maiden's parent, though my intention toward her is good. (*To the men.*) You deserve—(CHUNG TING *takes a step toward* THE MAGISTRATE; LI CHE-FU *straightens himself from his knees up.* THE SECRETARY, *who you remember has been bribed, whispers to* THE MAGISTRATE *behind his fan.*) Chung Ting, you deserve *not* to wed this maiden after you have neglected her till her full-plum period.

(TUAN CHAI *grins.*)

LI CHE-FU. A Kao-Yao to the judgment!

THE MAGISTRATE. And you, Li Che-Fu, scarcely deserve to wed this maiden who might be claimed by a more worthy and younger man.

(*Both* TUAN CHAI *and* LI CHE-FU *are disappointed and downcast.* TUAN CHAI, *the secretary, again whispers behind his fan.* THE MAGISTRATE *pays no attention.*)

THE MOTHER. But what are we to do with my daughter who is in her prime-plum period?

THE MAGISTRATE. I know what to do with your daughter. You just wait—

(TUAN CHAI *motions with his hands to* LI CHE-FU *and extends his six fingers —meaning the six ceremonies.*)

LI CHE-FU. But the six ceremonies, and the matchmaker!

THE MAGISTRATE. She confessed herself that she could make anything out of nothing. Besides, the maiden has not entered the threshold of your house.

CHUNG TING. Sir, *I* have a reliable witness. He is a very *old* man. He was witness to the verbal agreement between her father and mine. It's time he should be here.

(THE OLD MAN *enters feebly. He is old enough to use a stick—even in a district court. His robes are embroidered with symbols of longevity. He wears a long white beard, not hanging from the chin, but from the upper lip and the jaws. Perhaps the flowing beard has been used to cover up the bad teeth—if there are any—should the character open his mouth to sing. Or maybe it is to save the trouble of make-up in extending the wrinkles to the lower quarter of the face. Anyway it is very convenient to hang up this beard at the last moment so that the player can drink tea, eat refreshments, and smoke a water pipe in the green room until his call. Our* OLD MAN *has to speak through such a heavy beard.*)

THE MAGISTRATE. Who are you?

THE OLD MAN. I am Chien Shou, friend to Huan Chung and Fuan Han.

THE MAGISTRATE. Are you a go-between?

THE OLD MAN. Not exactly.

THE MAGISTRATE. By the hoary locks on your head I conjure you to speak the truth.

THE OLD MAN. Precisely. It was because of *my old age* that my two friends appointed me to be the witness to their gentlemen's agreement. One asked me to be the Fairy-Below-the-Ice, the other the Aged-Person-Under-the-Moon; namely, a formal matchmaker. Said the parents-to-be to one another: "If our children be both girls, sister them; if they be both boys, brother them; if they be of opposite sex, espouse them." And I was the only witness beside the two babes that were yet in their first nine months of infancy and whom you see now here as grown-up children.

THE MAGISTRATE. Was there any document? Were any betrothal gifts exchanged?

THE OLD MAN. Nothing but their word of honor.

THE MAGISTRATE. That is scarcely valid.

THE OLD MAN. But it is negotiable. By my three score and ten years I crave the law.

THE MAGISTRATE. Old man, do you gain anything by this union?

THE OLD MAN. Yes, the fulfilled trust of my deceased friends. The marriage was upon even their dying lips.

THE MAGISTRATE. The law is for the living.

CHUNG TING. Here I am; I, too, crave the law.

THE OLD MAN. And I am still alive, and hail and hearty.

(THE MAGISTRATE *looks inquiringly at the women.*)

THE MOTHER. The old man speaks the gospel truth through that heavy beard.

HAN CHU-YIN. O, Unkind Time, that the vase of my soul be the gossip of the court! I would rather seek the Other World.

TUAN CHAI. Sir, this is a very difficult case. We should see everybody get his just reward according to law.

CHUNG TING. Justice!

LI CHE-FU. The law!

THE MOTHER. Give my daughter of the four virtues a husband. Beget me a grandson!

THE MAGISTRATE. I told you to wait until . . .

(*Just at this moment* THE SCHOLAR *enters. He is not the God of the Machine, but a beggar, half dreaming, half starving. Still he has a princely bearing. His scholarly headwear is awry, his shoes have perfectly lovely tops but only half soles. His gentleman-beggar coat is all patched but made up of the most elegant silks and intricate patterns, like the frostings on a frozen window-pane. There is no hole in any part of the theatrical attire, though the outfit may have lasted the company several generations.* THE SCHOLAR *haughtily walks down stage, surveys the imaginary doors, steps in, goes clear to the right, makes the motion of seizing something, and strikes the imaginary drum on high. The drum sounds behind the stage.*)

THE SECOND ATTENDANT (*who may have retired and be on the job just now. Unlike* THE FIRST ATTENDANT, *he sulks through his duties.*) Hey, you, why do you drum the drum of justice? What wrong have you suffered?

(THE SCHOLAR *does not speak but hands a scroll of paper to* THE SECOND ATTENDANT, *who spreads it from left to right.* THE SCHOLAR *twists the paper so the right side is up.* THE SECOND ATTENDANT *extends his lazy palm to ask for wine-money—an institution, like opium smoking, the Chinese dramatist wishes to slight.* THE SCHOLAR *turns his purse inside out, revealing nothing but an old book. He beats again the imaginary drum, emitting a louder sound.* THE FIRST ATTENDANT *comes to them, pushes away* THE SECOND ATTENDANT, *snatches the paper and takes it to* THE MAGISTRATE, *who reads it in about the same short time.*)

THE MAGISTRATE. Kao-Yao be praised! Still another disputant! (*To* THE SCHOLAR.) Tu Kuang-Yang, do *you* claim the hand of this maiden? (*Everybody is startled except the girl,* HAN CHU-YIN, *who seems to be pleased.* THE SCHOLAR *nods his head.*) Who is your matchmaker?

(THE SCHOLAR *goes out and returns with* THE SECOND MATCHMAKER. *Without a matchmaker a Chinese match does not strike aright. On the Chinese stage,* THE FIRST MATCHMAKER *would also play the part of* THE SECOND MATCHMAKER *without even the outward pretense of different make-up and costumes. To furnish variety, however, we will make* THE SECOND MATCHMAKER *old, old enough to think everything aloud in Chinese maxims. She is dressed in uncouth apparel. Much of her character and her gagging are left to the producer and the player, for even the standard acting version should not be long.*)

THE SECOND MATCHMAKER. I thought some nobler and more affluent person than you would want my service. (*Seeing* THE MAGISTRATE *and imitating his bearing.*) Oh, my Lord is handsome, clever, and young! Are you contemplating furnishing another golden mansion? I know the dwellers of any red chamber.

THE MAGISTRATE. Do you know this young man and this young maiden?

THE SECOND MATCHMAKER. Yes, since they were weaned. They went to the primary school together. They studied the Book of Odes, the Book of Spring and Autumn, The Book of Filial Piety, The Book of Great Learning, Histories of The Three Ancient Celestials and The Five Dynasties, and, well (*gesticulating from the young woman to the young beggar*) the other classics that have made the young ones as they are. They rode on the same bamboo-twig horse, kicked the same shuttle-cock, looked at each other in the same boss mirror, played hide-and-seek until age separated them. (*Euphuis-*

tically.) Then the girl hides herself in the red chamber, and the boy—seeks rice on the street. He has the natural capacity of eight piculs and book learning of five wagon-loads. He can compose the Five Phœnix Verse while pacing only seven steps.—And they were so fond of each other. One day they said to me, "Liu Ma-Ma, we have played groom and bride; when we become man and woman we will be husband and wife, and you will be the match-maker, won't you?" And I promised them even as they promised each other.

THE MAGISTRATE. When was that?

THE SECOND MATCHMAKER. It must have been in the *last* cycle of sixty years. Let me see. The ox-year has occurred twice, so probably it was the year of rats. The common denominator is six times ten. Ten stars form the heavenly system, and twelve creatures rule the animal kingdom. It should be about thirteen years ago.

THE MAGISTRATE. *About* thirteen years ago, Liu Ma?

THE SECOND MATCHMAKER. Yes, and we did have a plague in that year. It was three years before the year of The Great Earthquake when the King Dragon whirled his trunk, six years before the Emperor moved south and made the people sing the song of the Call of the Deer, and nine years before Master Tu was admitted to the Circle of Bamboo Shoot and bestowed the blue-and-purple gown after the Red-Robe-Fairy had nodded his head to the civil examiner.

THE MAGISTRATE. How came he to this?

THE SECOND MATCHMAKER. Because the long travel to the capital wasted and spent him as the chase does the hound. He was reduced to selling even his library, as the elephant disposes of his ivory; but he has induced many a hero to come back and tell his luck and aspirations to me.

THE MOTHER. I never knew anybody aspired after me as a mother-in-law, behind my back.

THE MAGISTRATE. What evidence have you that they were willing to be husband and wife?

THE SECOND MATCHMAKER. Here is a picture of the Great Monad which they painted on a triangular lantern during the Lantern Festival. (*She displays a picture of the Great Monad, a symbol of Chinese cosmogony representing the dualistic principle of man and woman, the male in the female and the female in the male, supposed to be the first Chinese philosophical document.*) The one said to the other, "That black is Yin, that's you; this white is Yang, it's I." And each of us has kept a copy as a testimony.

(TU KUANG-YANG *takes out a similar copy from his book and* HAN CHU-YIN *takes out her copy from her sash. All, including* THE MAGISTRATE, *are surprised.*)

THE MAGISTRATE (*to* THE MOTHER). Do you wish this man as a son-in-law?

THE MOTHER. My Lord, if my humble self be permitted to select a husband—

THE MAGISTRATE. I grant you the right to choose one, for your daughter.

THE MOTHER. I will choose—

THE OLD MAN. Remember the will of your departed husband.

TUAN CHAI. Remember all the gossip of the villagers and the six ceremonies.

CHUNG TING. My silvery horses, my scarlet jacket, and my skilled arrows.

LI CHE-FU. My golden ingots, my red mansion, and my prosperity!

TU KUANG YANG (*speaking earnestly but reservedly for the first time*). My affection for Chu-Yin.

THE MOTHER. I think I will not choose the beggar.

VOICES. No, not the beggar!

LI CHE-FU. Accept my riches!

CHUNG TING. My glory!

THE OLD MAN. My age!

TUAN CHAI. My humble wish!

THE SECOND MATCHMAKER. My word!

THE MOTHER. I declare I never had so many suitors in my bygone days— not even a beggar.

THE MAGISTRATE (*to* HAN CHU-YIN). Well, your mother does not approve of the beggar; what is your wish?

(HAN CHU-YIN *is silent and hides her face in her sash.*)

THE MAGISTRATE. Tell me, what do you choose?

HAN CHU-YIN (*distressedly*). I choose to die!

THE MAGISTRATE. In order to settle the case?

HAN CHU-YIN. Yes, and quickly!

THE MAGISTRATE. Good Maiden, Kao-Yao had no more sagacity in dissolving disputes, but I fear you have made up your mind to deny yourself wealth, happiness, and power which you might find in any of these people.

HAN CHU-YIN. I am denied that which I value most. I wish to end it all.

THE MAGISTRATE. Is that final?

HAN CHU-YIN. Yes, to eternity!

THE MAGISTRATE. May your ancestor bless you! I accord you the potion that brings eternal tranquillity. (*To* THE SECOND ATTENDANT.) Bring forth the potion phial provided by the ancients to impart to the mortal the pleasant sleep.

(THE SECOND ATTENDANT *goes out; this time he makes us wait for some time. Slowly he brings the potion to* HAN CHU-YIN. *She holds it in her trembling hand; life and death struggle within her. She sighs, lingers, and sighs yet again.*)

THE MAGISTRATE. Be courageous, virtuous maiden. One dies only once; the rest is peace. If you cannot lift the phial, I shall have the attendant help you.

(HAN CHU-YIN *lifts the phial to her quivering lips.* THE MOTHER *and* TU KUANG YANG *advance toward the young woman, but are held back by the attendants. She swallows the contents at a gulp, and sinks to the floor.*)

HAN CHU-YIN. I depart. May peace be with all!

(*She lies down unconscious. Everybody is petrified. Solemn music. At length* THE MAGISTRATE *speaks.*)

THE MAGISTRATE. Well, she died a virtuous death. Li Che-Fu, she was almost married to you. Will you bury her in your family grave yard?

LI CHE-FU. I wanted a live housekeeper, not a dead wife. Since she had an early betrothal, the body belongs to the first betrothed.

THE MAGISTRATE. Chung Ting, your stars crossed each other before either of you was born. Now you can accept the will of your parents and your parents' parents, you may have your claim.

CHUNG TING. We never saw each other and were not formally married. Let the legal husband or the true lover take the body.

THE MAGISTRATE. Tu Kuang-Yang, there is the spoils of your love. She was your promised wife. Will you take care of her?

TU KUANG-YANG. Yes, I loved her. A promise is a promise. I will take her, and will follow her soon.

THE MOTHER (*realizing what has happened, she breaks into an hysterical cry*). You beggar! You kill-joy! You will soon pay for it!

SEVERAL VOICES. The beggar! The kill-joy! Hang him! Let him pay for it!

THE MOTHER (*turning to* LI CHE-FU). You yellow dog! (*To* CHUNG TING.) You spotted tiger! (*To* THE OLD MAN.) You white-whiskered monkey! (*To* TUAN CHAI.) You greedy rat! (*To* THE SECOND MATCHMAKER.) You lowly snake!

THE MAGISTRATE (*striking the mallet on the table*). Order! Order!

(THE ATTENDANTS *tap the table sides with their bamboo staves. The people rise to leave.*)

THE MAGISTRATE. Wait a while! The case of the thrice promised bride is not yet finished. Among you three disputants only the beggar, Tu Kuang-Yang, is a true claimant; the other two are as false as shifting sand. I hereby confiscate, Li Che-Fu, your property, and deprive you, Chung Ting, of your degrees and privileges appertaining. On you, Tu Kuang-Yang, the true lover, I bestow the golden ingots of the merchant, the horses of the Knight, and the life service of Liu Ma, so that you can have feasts and rituals. And now I grant you the privilege of administering a potion to revive the unconscious but virtuous maiden from the effects of the sleeping potion I gave the maiden to be known hereafter as your legal wife.

(THE SECOND ATTENDANT *brings the potion to* TU KUANG-YANG *who ceremoniously takes it to the heap of beautiful costumery, stoops over the beautiful face and goes through the motion of administering the potion.* HAN CHU-YIN *comes to consciousness, and is bewildered at seeing* TU KUANG-YANG *bending over her.*)

HAN CHU-YIN. Am I dreaming, or are we meeting in the Other World?

TU KUANG-YANG. No, my beloved, we are under the sky, on the earth, and in the Middle Kingdom.

THE MOTHER. And before all these people! (*Gesticulating.*)

THE MAGISTRATE. Han Chu-Yin, I marry you to Tu Kuang-Yang and give you wealth, happiness and love in one.

(*Successively he applies black ink and red ink with the Chinese brushes and then imprints his official seal to the three copies of The Great Monad.*

The couple kow-tow to THE MAGISTRATE *and then to* THE MOTHER. THE SECOND MATCHMAKER *and* THE MOTHER *help the couple to get up, holding the pictures of The Great Monad over their heads.*)

THE BRIDEGROOM (*facing the audience*). Long live my wife!

CURTAIN

WHEN LOVE DIES

A WORLDLY COMEDY

By JOSÉ ANTONIO RAMOS

Translated from the Spanish by Isaac Goldberg

CHARACTERS

JULIA, *Twenty-one. A flower of modern culture. Very beautiful, aristocratic, and frail as a doll; nervous and impressionable. A deeply feminine soul, recently married (a pure love match) to*

ROBERTO, *Thirty. Handsome, winning, elegant in manner. A clubman and a distinguished sportsman. He bears a noble title.*

FERNANDO, *Twenty-eight. A timorous, moody, passionate sort; likewise a handsome youth of aristocratic family.*

EUGENIA, *Intimate friend of Julia.*

VICENTE, *Twenty-six. Friend of Roberto.*

CARMEN }
LUISA } *Guests.*

RICARDO, *Eugenia's lover.*

A MAID

WHEN LOVE DIES

SCENE: *A small salon, richly furnished. To the left, a fireplace; facing it, an armchair. At the rear, a doorway half draped by a portière, through which one catches a glimpse of a large ballroom, flooded with light and festive animation. To the right, a little stand before a table; a door. On the mantelpiece above the fireplace, an artistic jar brimming with flowers. As the curtain goes up, the strains of a waltz are heard from a piano in the ballroom.*

PLACE: *Anywhere; Madrid, for example.* TIME: *the present.*

(CARMEN *is on the stand beside the table.* THE MAID *is kneeling before her, mending the hem of her gown. Presently, enter* LUISA.)

CARMEN (*impatiently, to the maid*). Aren't you through yet?

THE MAID. In a moment; a moment. Just two seconds. . . .

CARMEN. Heavens. . . . The last waltz. . . .

THE MAID. Only another stitch . . . and it's done. Please wait. (CARMEN *hums the waltz, and sways in time to the tune.*) Ma'mselle! Ma'mselle! I can't sew when you move like that. . . .

CARMEN. Not done yet! Ah! I'm ready now.

LUISA (*outside*). Carmen!

CARMEN. Eh? I'll be with you in a second!

LUISA. Where are you? What are you doing?

CARMEN. Oh, it's you, is it? I thought it was he. Where is he?

LUISA. Here in the doorway. He's waiting for you.

CARMEN. Heavens!

LUISA. Did they rip your gown?

CARMEN. That dragon of a Baroness de Urquijo, no less, with her four hundred and fifty pounds avoirdupois! Horrible! Just look! (*She tugs at her gown.*)

MAID. Ma'mselle! (*She sucks her finger.*)

LUISA. The hem?

CARMEN. What's the matter?

MAID. I've stuck myself.

LUISA. A mere scratch.

CARMEN. Dear me! Have you lost the needle? Where's the needle now? This'll never end.

MAID. Here . . . here it is. Now . . . You mustn't move, ma'mselle.

CARMEN. Very well. Now I'm ready. All done! (*To* LUISA.) Didn't he say anything to you?

LUISA. He asked for you.

CARMEN. He knows that you're a friend of mine. Isn't he just grand? So gallant! He was booked for this waltz with one of the Brinas, and he left her in the lurch to dance with me.

LUISA. So that's it! Now I understand Juanita's glare every time you waltzed by her.

CARMEN. And how ridiculous her cousin is!

LUISA. Who's that?

CARMEN. The one who danced the last waltz with Manolo Riera. It's the first time she's dancing in a distinguished ballroom.

LUISA. Anyone can see that. Now I know whom you mean.

CARMEN. I've seen all sorts here to-night. Don't imagine. . . .

LUISA (*referring to the maid*). Hush! (*They both laugh.*) Julia is awfully good in her way—altogether too good. Sometimes she'd rather allow herself to be imposed upon than hurt anyone's feelings.

MAID. You are right, ma'mselle. Forgive me for daring to speak. My mistress is unlike any I've known. I haven't met her better yet.

LUISA (*looking into the ballroom*). She's having this dance with her husband. Have you noticed how wonderfully they get along?

CARMEN. Yes, indeed! How charming! Like a pair of lovers. I believe they are very happy.

LUISA. As madly in love as on the first day. Julia just bubbles with enthusiasm!

CARMEN. How few can say as much, girlie!

LUISA. Yes, but then there are few who marry as she did. Hers was a marriage for love. Love and nothing else. What a pleasure it was just to look at them. As for me, I've made up my mind never to marry unless I'm madly in love with my husband.

CARMEN. As if we poor creatures had any say in the matter!

LUISA. And why not?

CARMEN. Oh, for no reason at all. When is the choice ever up to us? We're picked out, and we're asked for. And off to the wedding!

LUISA. Well, it won't be that way with me. And you know that I mean what I say.

CARMEN. Then you'll be left an old maid.

LUISA. There's no help for it. When it comes to misfortune . . .

MAID. All done, ma'mselle.

CARMEN. At last! Thanks, ever so much.

MAID. Don't mention it.

CARMEN (*to* LUISA). Does it look all right?

LUISA. You can't notice a thing.

CARMEN. Thanks, thanks! (*She surveys herself in the mirror over the mantelpiece.*) Goodness, what a face! (*To* LUISA.) Am I presentable?

LUISA. Excellent.

CARMEN. Then I'm off. See you later. So long! (*Exit.*)

LUISA. So long. (*Goes toward the door.*)

MAID. Did the ma'mselle need me? (*The music stops.*)

LUISA. No, thank you.

MAID. Then good night, ma'mselle.

LUISA. Good night. (*Exeunt both,* LUISA *by the rear, the maid by the right. Enter* JULIA *with* EUGENIA *on her arm.*)

JULIA. Here. Let's get off here by ourselves.

EUGENIA. I know, I tell you. I know just what you're going to say.

JULIA. Will you dare deny it now? (*Silence.*) Speak!

EUGENIA (*lowering her head*). No. After all, I never did deny it. And you know I didn't.

JULIA. Yes, you did. Remember?

EUGENIA. I asked you to change the subject. That was all.

JULIA. So you're no longer my friend? You don't consider me, as you once did, your closest friend, your confidante?

EUGENIA. Yes I do, Julia, I do. Why not?

JULIA. That's false! You're not sincere. Once upon a time we used to tell each other everything, all our deepest secrets. Now you've forgotten it all.

EUGENIA. Is it as long ago as all that? You were the first to forget.

JULIA. There, there! Don't say that again!

EUGENIA. You had just married and were head over heels in love. Ever since then your poor friends have never heard from you. From that day up to my return to Madrid, only a week ago, I didn't get ten letters in all from you—if that much.

JULIA. You exaggerate!

EUGENIA. Not a jot. Last month made a year since you married.

JULIA. On the tenth.

EUGENIA. I can forgive you the time of the honeymoon; a whole month in Paris with only a solitary letter from you. Remember that: a solitary letter in a month.

JULIA. And four or five post cards.

EUGENIA. In your husband's handwriting.

JULIA. That's the same as myself.

EUGENIA. Let's proceed. Then, a month and a half in Switzerland.

JULIA. Of which I was three weeks in bed.

EUGENIA. And in all that time, only one letter.

JULIA. But a long and intimate one, with full details of the wedding; remember that.

EUGENIA. I remember. Then, Paris again; and Brussels. Another month, and another letter.

JULIA. That's not so! There were two!

EUGENIA. One.

JULIA. I recall positively that there were two, because there was one that I didn't read to Roberto. The one in which I told you about that Swiss who fell in love with me and whom I was sure to find staring at me whenever we walked into the salon of the hotel.

EUGENIA. Very well, then; let's say two. You're right.

JULIA. Then you left Madrid, and the note announcing my return remained at your home.

EUGENIA. That was when my husband was appointed to his post in Gerona. And during my exile I hardly received two letters per month from you.

JULIA. You exaggerate! You exaggerate scandalously! I wrote you every week. It was during just those two months that our correspondence began to cool off.

EUGENIA. On account of you.

JULIA. And it was precisely those two months in which your affair with Ricardo del Cerro began.

EUGENIA. That's not so!

JULIA. So you've lied! Behold yourself confounded and defeated. I've always been the same. You're beaten. What, smiling? A sign of surrender? Do you give up?

EUGENIA. Very well. I surrender, conditionally.

JULIA. Remember that implacable motto: Woe to the conquered! I hold you in my power, and I can demand of you what I will. Judge of my generosity, then, when I sentence you only to be as frank as you were in the good old days. Come, now; I'm listening.

EUGENIA (*taking* JULIA'S *hands*). The same as ever! Do you remember those intimate afternoons in my house? Just now, it seemed to me that you were a girl once again, impatient to know the secrets of marriage, begging me for details, urging me. . . .

JULIA. There, now! That's the way I like to have you. Now I may confess that our meeting struck me as awfully cold, altogether unworthy of the beautiful friendship that linked us. Even at our previous meeting I was worried by the same thought. Now I've abandoned my last doubt. You're the same good friend as ever, aren't you?

EUGENIA. Yes, Julia, I am. (*Somewhat sadly.*) And I need your friendship badly indeed, right now.

JULIA. I knew it. Somehow or other I had the feeling that you weren't happy. (*Pause.*) Have I guessed?

EUGENIA (*shrugging her shoulders*). Frankly, I can't say. I haven't the time to think about it.

JULIA. Then? . . .

EUGENIA (*after a pause*). Why would you have me speak freely? Aren't you afraid that my escapades will cast a shadow over your happiness?

JULIA. Not at all. Speak. (*Pause.*) Why did you say "escapades"?

EUGENIA (*preoccupied*). Are you still in love with your husband, Julia?

JULIA (*growing serious*). Why do you ask me that?

EUGENIA. I'm ashamed to mention my illicit affairs in this house, and to you, who are still faithfully in love with your husband.

JULIA. You don't have to feel any shame before me for anything, Eugenia. Don't say that again. What does it matter if I do still love my husband?

It's only a year since I was married. You've been married for seven. Besides, I married for love, while you simply didn't care to let the chance slip by.

EUGENIA (*dreamily*). How time flies! Already a year since I was at your wedding! And ten months since I first met Ricardo. . . .

JULIA. Ten months, you say.

EUGENIA. I met him while you were in Brussels, on the twelfth of February, at the home of Manuelita Albacete.

JULIA. Eugenia! (*Offended.*)

EUGENIA. From the very first moment he fascinated me so powerfully that I could not confess it to a friend who was in the full glow of her honeymoon. Forgive me.

JULIA (*vexed*). No. . . . I can't forgive you that! And not a word from you! Not even a hint!

EUGENIA. Such a confession was altogether too intimate to write down and sign, Julia. You must understand that.

JULIA. Why? Why? How many times, at your house, haven't we discussed the men that took our fancy? Enrique Martin, for instance, over whom you went wild. "Ah, if I could only kiss his eyes!" you used to rave. . . .

EUGENIA. Quiet, for God's sake!

JULIA (*lowering her voice*). And I, too . . . don't you remember? Don't you remember Abelardo? I was fond of him—awfully fond. . . . That way he had of planting himself right in front of you! And do you remember how gracefully the dear fellow would recline against the back of the chairs? No mannerism, you'll understand; just inborn elegance.

EUGENIA. Have you seen him again lately? (JULIA *nods Yes.*) Here?

JULIA. Every afternoon . . . almost every afternoon my carriage passes within ten paces of his.

EUGENIA. And he?

JULIA. Salutes me politely. My husband suspects nothing.

EUGENIA. Suspect! What?

JULIA. Naturally! It was merely a whim, an innocent intimacy of ours. . . . How about Fernando? Have you seen him to-night?

EUGENIA. Which Fernando?

JULIA. Fernando Aguirre, that platonic lover.

EUGENIA. Oh, yes! I remember now. The fellow who made some sort of declaration to you.

JULIA. And how I did scowl at the poor chap! And how many more are there? How many men we've loved in our way, for a day, for an hour, without their so much as dreaming of the feelings they had aroused!

EUGENIA. It seems to me now that I could never have been in love with any other man.

JULIA. Eugenia!

EUGENIA. Well?

JULIA. That's just what I said to you when I was the sweetheart of the man I'm married to; and you used to laugh at me!

EUGENIA. No. No. This man is different.

JULIA. That's just what I answered to you, too. That "this man is different." They're all "different," and they're all the same; that's what you
answered me.

EUGENIA. I tell you that he's different, Julia. I swear it. I feel that I
never loved so much. . . . (*A long silence.*)

JULIA. And . . . Have you made friends? . . . Do you see him?

EUGENIA. Simpleton!

JULIA. He's known all along, of course. . . . But have you told him?

EUGENIA. What do you mean? I don't understand.

JULIA. Have you told him that you are fond of him,—that you are in love
with him? . . .

EUGENIA. Julia! Does that seem so awful to you?

JULIA. What?

EUGENIA. No. . . . No. . . . Then there's no sense in making me tell you
the story. Your incredulity is itself a subtle accusation, but one that I feel
very deeply. No. No. Don't ask any more. . . . Let's change the subject.
(*Pause.*)

JULIA (*pensively*). Then . . . (*Another pause.*)

EUGENIA (*distrait, engrossed in her thoughts*). A month ago. . . . (*A long
pause; suddenly she grasps Julia's hands.*) Do you forgive me? Do you
pardon me? Do you think as much of me as ever? . . . Speak! Say that you
regard me just as highly as you did before I fell; that you feel the same simple
affection for me as before. . . . At least, that you pity me.

JULIA (*her voice is veiled; dreamily*). And why should I cease loving you?

EUGENIA (*kisses her friend and then dries her eyes*). I'm so unfortunate,
Julia. I appreciate more than anyone else the significance of the step I've
just taken, and yet, I don't know why I've done it—why I didn't stop and
think before I went ahead and did what's now beyond recall! I swear to you
that I did it all blindly, that I'm still under the influence of the selfsame
terrible power. I'm obsessed with the notion that my voice has changed, that
my gestures are no longer the same, that my very look is different! . . . The
day after I gave myself to him I met my husband face to face and I thought
I was lost, discovered. . . . Yet I must have been calm, for my husband asked
no questions, and nobody about me seemed to be aware of my awful agitation.
. . . Up to then I had never realized how able we are to hide our feelings.
I swear to you that I didn't mean to hide anything—that I was seized by a
mad impulse to confess everything at the top of my voice. And yet my
nature, my instinct—whatever it was—got the best of me and I concealed
my feelings wonderfully. I'd never have believed it! You can see for yourself. Now I don't know whether to look upon myself as a terribly perverted
woman, or to see in those I consider as such less perversion than I previously
supposed. (*Pause.*) In the eyes of society, in the eyes of men, I know that
I can plead no excuse; in the eyes of God I hope to deserve some leniency.
I married without knowing what I was about; a good match came along,

my parents accepted him and praised him to the skies; it's the custom to marry, and I neither detested him nor was he such a hateful chap. Then again, he was so plainly wild over me, and they kept telling me that I was the idol of his heart, the sole object of his life; I was surrounded by the thousand attentions showered by sweethearts, my friends' questionings, preparations for the wedding, purchases, plans . . . such a pleasant excitement, to tell the truth! So I married, and belonged to a man for whom I had never felt any violent desire. At first I was happy; I was desired, I inspired love, I was embraced with a passionate fire that finally touched me with its flame and compelled me to sincere response. For a moment I thought that I, too, was in love. My nature, now awakened, in its turn experienced desire—the fires that at first it had not offered. . . . It was then that the awful disillusionment began. I was no longer desired with the ardor and the fascinating brutality of the beginning. I was simply taken, calmly, altogether too calmly. The abandon of desire was succeeded by the satisfaction of the inevitable excitement that life in the same room must bring. Poor me! Satiety had come at last!

JULIA (*eagerly*). Go on. . . . Go on! You describe it so well. Go on!

EUGENIA (*absorbed*). And yet I hadn't lost my good looks; I was still attractive. Everywhere I went I felt glances upon me, filled with desire, just like those my new husband had cast upon me. . . . At times I heard burning words whispered by bated, murmuring voices, such as had first enchanted me coming from my husband's lips. My charms roused desire in those who could not have me; only in him who could honor them they awoke not the slightest response. Good God! You have to admit that all this is humiliating, devastating, simply unbearable. And a person has to be gifted with more than human resignation to bear such a life of unending humiliation without rebelling, while at every moment the sensual suggestions of strangers reminds our self-esteem how precious is our beauty, the most sought-for treasure in woman through all the ages, say what folks will against this truth. (*Pause.*) Then, it isn't only our beauty that is insulted. Our simplest feelings are despised. At first they talk a lot about our talent; then they tremble when we're among distinguished company; our virtue was formerly our most beautiful ornament; afterward, they exhibit a gross jealousy that has nothing to do with love, and very much to do with suspicion and insult. A suspicion that little by little corrupts us, because it gradually familiarizes us with crime and dissimulation. (*Pause. To* JULIA.) What's the matter?

JULIA (*pensive, motionless*). Nothing. . . I'm listening. I'm listening. Go on.

EUGENIA. Why go on? You can guess the rest.

JULIA. Go on. Go on.

EUGENIA. The woman who isn't subject to temptation, who has other things to occupy her mind, or who has children, can forget everything and be content with having been happy for a year. But I'm not allowed to do anything. I've got only a little son whom I hold in my arms surely no more than twice a day. I see men here, men there and everywhere, all in love with me, fascinating talkers, who break down a woman's last scruples. I got acquainted with him, fell in love with him; he knew it; he pursued me, I allowed him a kiss, I wrote him a letter, I made an appointment with him. And now everything's in the mud. I'm simply one of so many. I swear to you that it's horrible; that I deny any charm at all to adultery; that this deceit repels me,—this uncertainty, this feeling that the new man will turn out just the same as the old; that I'm unhappier than before I fell. . . . But it's all inevitable: I'll keep on the downward path with a stoic resolution that's the one thing I've won out of all this. We'll see. There are times when I think of my child, and I suffer and cry. I don't know. I'm chained. Before, my only master was my husband, from whom I had need to hide nothing. Now I belong to a man who holds me in his power; my honor and my future happiness are at his disposal. Tell me now whether I'm not more to be pitied than condemned! (*A long pause. Another waltz begins.*) But Julia! What are you thinking about?

JULIA (*mastering herself*). Nothing, nothing. I was just listening to you.

EUGENIA (*rising, and with deep interest compelling* JULIA *to rise as well*). You, too!

JULIA. What? (*Frightened.*) No!

EUGENIA. I'm sure of that. I know you're a pure woman. . . . But you, too, have begun to suffer. Your disillusionment has begun!

JULIA. I don't know. I don't know. No, no. I'm a fool, that's all it is. (EUGENIA *is rapt in thought.*) No. Don't pay any attention to me. It might come to that, some day, perhaps. But have no fear, no fear at all for the present. Roberto still loves me. Can't you see. (*Sadly.*) To-night he gave me a waltz.

EUGENIA (*tenderly*). Julia! So soon! Good heavens! (RICARDO, *from the doorway outside, to* EUGENIA.)

RICARDO. At last I've found you, dear lady!

EUGENIA (*in confused surprise*). Ah!

JULIA. Who is that? (EUGENIA *gestures her to be silent. Enter* RICARDO.)

RICARDO. Aren't you dancing the last waltz?

EUGENIA (*as before*). Yes . . . yes. . . . Let's be going.

RICARDO (*bowing to* JULIA). Forgive me the interruption.

JULIA. Not at all. Don't mention it.

EUGENIA. Come along. . . . See you later, Julia.

RICARDO (*bowing again*). Madam. . . .

JULIA. See you later. (*The lovers walk off, conversing in low tones and pressed close to each other. For a long while she watches them, as in mechanical manner, she takes a flower from one of the vases, leans an elbow upon the mantelpiece and falls into a deep meditation. During the following dialogue the strains of the waltz keep floating in from the ballroom and from time to time a couple whirls by.* FERNANDO *appears in the doorway, glances in, and then enters guardedly.*)

FERNANDO. Am I intruding?

JULIA (*surprised*). Ah! No, no.

FERNANDO. At the same time, you seem awfully surprised.

JULIA. No, no.

FERNANDO. I must take your word for it, I suppose. But I confess I still feel like a sinner. I can't shake the impression that I've come at a bad time.

JULIA. No, no. Don't imagine that. I was resting here a while. I felt so tired.

FERNANDO. Do you forgive me, then, for having so rudely interrupted your . . . your rest?

JULIA (*trying to smile*). With all my heart. (*Disquieted.*)

FERNANDO. Then let my excuse be that I simply could not help it. That if I happen to be in this salon it's perhaps because I still happen to be in the world; because you are yet in it. . . .

JULIA (*as if she hasn't heard*). Besides, it's not you, but rather I, who should beg forgiveness, for having left the ballroom. (*As if to leave.*) I'm crazy! (*Smiling.*) Until later, Fernando.

FERNANDO. Julia!

JULIA. Do you wish to accompany me?

FERNANDO. No, no. . . . It's so nice here. . . . Just keep on forgetting your guests, I beg you. Grant me the happiness—it's so easy for you—to admire you for but a moment with all the religious fervor, all the mysticism that this delightful nook of your home pours into my soul. . . .

JULIA. Fernando!

FERNANDO. No reproaches now, Julia. My words cannot possibly offend you. I dare not ask you for anything. I'll not sully the respect I owe you. All I beg is a second that means abiding happiness to me and that to you is only the same as any other second. A moment to chat in. You know that I cherish for you a feeling that's fairly religious, a mad veneration. I know how unreasonable my passion is, and that makes my love for you all the sadder, growing daily more despairing, Julia.

JULIA. You must understand, Fernando, that to express such offensive sentiments to me is in itself an offense.

FERNANDO. No, Julia, no. Don't talk to me like that. You're a woman far above the average. Such words don't sound seemly from your lips. Why should it offend you that I love you? Can there be any way of teaching the heart even a single man-made law?

JULIA. The law itself is the way.

FERNANDO. No, that's not so. Laws repress or punish, but they don't convince. I've loved you ever since the first time I laid eyes upon you. I've loved you for a long time, in silence, with almost mystic devotion, hiding my love at the very bottom of my soul, seeking eagerly, unceasingly in you for a smile, for the merest sign of sympathy toward this passion of mine which you have always known. When I made up my mind to ask your hand, you had already promised yourself to a luckier fellow than myself, luckier than all other men in the world. How can it offend you if, in spite of having lost you forever, I continue to love you with the same tenderness, in the same absolute secrecy? (*A long pause.*)

JULIA (*intimately, almost to herself*). Fernando! Why are you men so deceitful? Why do you take pleasure in betrayal, in feigning great passions, in swearing eternal vows, when you know that you're so inconstant, so fickle?

FERNANDO (*surprised*). Julia! (*Pause. She smiles.*) You astound me. I can't imagine the reason for your strange question, really. . . .

JULIA. You asked for a brief space of intimate conversation: I give it to you. Now answer my question. I propose to disarm you; to convince you that you do ill to pursue me. And to-night I feel equal to accomplishing my purpose.

FERNANDO. But . . . Why mention inconstancy in the face of so decidedly opposite a proof? Aren't you convinced by my unchanging affection, which I have preserved despite all your rebuffs?

JULIA. No, I'm not. Stop talking like that; quit exaggerating your love for me, and answer to the point. I know that love, such as you profess for me, is beautiful, loyal, constant and capable of every heroism when it is sincere. But why does love, complete and satisfied love, slay the lover? Why does the longed-for possession bleed and murder the desire for possession? If I weren't as sure of myself as I am, I'd never venture to put a question of this sort to a strange man who pretends to be in love with me; because of the very indifference I feel, however, I hope to obtain a sincere reply to my question. I can't ask my husband; you are the closest friend we have; you inspire me with confidence, and strike me as being sincere and of more than ordinary talent. Answer me! I promise you in return what I have already offered you more than once: my friendship, a simple, sincere friendship. Answer me, Fernando!

FERNANDO (*slowly, as he gazes at her*). I very much doubt, Julia, whether I can give you a satisfactory reply, even though I swear that I would be capable of laying bare to the scalpel the very last fiber of my soul, just to please you; even though I could take with you the poison of truth, though that truth proved to be the poison of the most terrible disillusionment in return for its precious secret. . . . But first let me tell you at least all the sadness that fills my poor heart at this moment. . . . Julia! Why weren't you mine? Why do you love another? Why am I not the master of this precious soul, of which just now I caught a tiny, enchanting glimpse? (*In despair.*) And to think that you might have been my wife, my friend, the companion of all my years! To think that it might have been with this sweet soul of yours, with this deep, beautiful soul, that my own soul—forever tortured with dreams—might have been blended! . . . Can't you see how unhappy I am, Julia, how disheartening it is to find your dearest ideal, your most intimate ideal that can never achieve embodiment, alive in the flesh, in the beautiful flesh . . . and yet more intangible than your very dream! (*A pause. Resuming.*) Yes, life is like that—very bitter, pitilessly bitter.

It may be that Werther would have tired of Charlotte; Romeo and Juliet might have been divorced. I don't know. I hold a very personal, desperate conception of life. It's something I haven't yet managed to understand. We live in perpetual contradiction of ourselves, we call ourselves animals endowed with reason, and our very first principles are word-phantasms that nobody has succeeded in deciphering to this very day. We chase after Truth, and yet Truth is inexorable; it confounds us, it enmeshes us and destroys us without pity. We execrate deceit and trickery and yet they fill our souls with a healing balm, their caresses cradle our lives in an ecstasy of release. If, at the end of each of our disillusions, the truth had not thrust in its horrible visage, we should still be enjoying to-day that happiness which always was and always is expected, and is never enjoyed at the full. (*Pause.*) How can I answer you? At this moment I have been sincere; you can see that. If I had been able to deceive you even to the point of winning you away from all your ideas, perhaps I'd have left in your soul an impression quite distinct from that which these words of mine must leave, just because they are sincere.

JULIA (*after a pause, offering her hand*). Thanks, Fernando! You have given me what I wanted. Thanks! (*He kisses her hand and then pulls himself away. He leans against the mantelpiece, lost in thought.*) At last I've met with a sincere man. Good God! (*To him.*) You are right, Fernando. How sweet it is to live in illusions!

FERNANDO. No, Julia, no. You're wrong. We're both wrong. To seek the bottom of every sensation for its bitter dregs is nothing but useless mortification.

JULIA. How grateful it is to live, cradled in a dream, without a thought of the inevitable awakening!

FERNANDO. Why scorn the little happiness that it is given us to enjoy before the final disillusionment? Why bring on the end before its time? Let us live; let's take life as it comes without accounting to life. To rebel is to suffer in advance.

JULIA (*shaking her head*). No. Let's not run from the truth; let's not be afraid. Make up your mind, Fernando, that you'll have to give up this persistent suit. I'm not going to be yours, above all because I don't love you and because I know too well what all men's love amounts to. I talk to you like this because I esteem you, because I'm silly enough to believe that your affection is sincere. If I had found you to be a commonplace wooer I wouldn't even have taken the trouble to answer you. I'll never be unfaithful to my husband, even though I should cease to love him as I now do, Fernando. I want to preserve the tranquillity of my life, for love is worth less than one's peace of mind. I'm resolved never to stoop to the folly of accepting a lover, or to be deceived by my own heart. Consider, now, whether it's possible to seduce a woman who speaks to an admirer as I'm speaking to you at this moment, without a trace of coquetry, with not a bit of affectation, without a mental reserve of any kind.

FERNANDO (*disconcerted, nervous*). You haven't told me anything new,

Julia. I repeat that I've never dared to imagine you capable of loving me—that I love you without hope, knowing beforehand that my efforts are in vain. I know that these words, spoken as I speak them, with all the clumsiness and nervousness of an adolescent, are shamefully ridiculous. Yet this is not my greatest shame. No. What I can't forgive myself for is the fact that I am unable to flee from you; that I can't rid myself of this passion that makes a child of me, a man devoid of will-power. . . .

JULIA. Remember, Fernando, that I offered you my friendship when I was compelled to ask you not to visit my house again. Please act so as to make me believe that I did not offer too much.

FERNANDO (*in a husky voice*). Forgive me, Julia. (*A long pause.*)

JULIA (*amiably*). Why aren't you dancing?

FERNANDO (*trying to smile*). I don't know! . . .

JULIA. I think it's the last waltz. They must be looking for you in the ballroom.

FERNANDO. No. . . . No. . . . Let me remain here. I feel so well. This little nook is so charming, so inviting to dreams. . . .

JULIA. You dream altogether too easily!

FERNANDO. What would you have? I can't help it.

JULIA. Oh, don't imagine I blame you for it. It's the most natural thing in the world. That's how you all are at first. So dreamy, so romantic, so tender. . . .

FERNANDO. Julia, why do you speak like this to-night?

JULIA. To-night? And why precisely to-night?

FERNANDO. Yes, to-night. Up to now I never knew the pessimistic depths of your soul. One would imagine that you were resenting some very deep, very painful disillusionment. (JULIA *averts her face.*) That you were suffering a very bitter disappointment. (*Passionately.*) And I'd dare more than to say it. I'd dare assert it, for this agitation of yours betrays a recent wound that my words have opened. . . .

JULIA (*composing herself*). No, Fernando, you're mistaken; you're mistaken, I assure you.

FERNANDO. You're suffering some pain, some disappointment. . . . Yes, you are, Julia.

JULIA. I'm nervous—nervous for no reason at all. . . . Perhaps the ball, or memories. . . . No. Leave me. We've been here far too long already. I granted too much. I've been too frank. . . .

FERNANDO. Julia!

JULIA. Yes, yes. I've been imprudent. Believe nothing I've said; forget all our nonsense of this moment.

FERNANDO. Julia, Julia. I beg you. . . .

JULIA (*disconcerted, in her turn*). Cease dreaming, cease hoping, cease harboring the remotest hope that I'll ever listen to you on some distant day. I'll never love, I've been disillusioned, destroyed; I'll devote myself to anything that will bring me distraction. It's by no means certain that one must love . . . one may devote one's life to noble ideals. . . . I want you to take this as my very last word, Fernando. For the last time I ask you to end your hateful persecution. Up to this night I've treated you as a friend. Now I'm resolved to use even indelicacy so as to root out all hope from your heart. Forgive me, but you simply force me to this extreme. . . .

FERNANDO (*calmly*). You do wrong, very wrong, to torture yourself in this way, Julia. I tell you once more that I hope nothing, that I haven't even the remotest hope of ever making you mine. Great God, at what a cost I speak these words. (*Slowly.*) I hope nothing, I ask nothing, I wish nothing! . . . I adore you; I must see you now and then, hear your voice, inhale the perfume that you scatter as you move about. . . . I must repeat my madness to you just as a madman must keep harping on his mania.

JULIA (*hurt*). Fernando!

FERNANDO. Forgive me again. It was a simple reply to your first request. I want to tell you that your resolution never to love will in no case have as great success as mine never to see you again. For a promise of fidelity to a dead love is as fragile as a resolution to forget before forgetfulness comes of itself. How long will it last—this childish, human attempt to make everything everlasting? There is nothing eternal or constant; even the gods are born and die, each in his time; the most beautiful objects likewise perish; form is always transitory. Love alone, Julia, the origin of all created things, is eternal, immanent in Life! . . .

JULIA (*shaking her head*). It's perhaps the thing that dies soonest of all.

FERNANDO. No. A love may die as any other animate thing may die— as this flower that you hold in your hands. But love never dies. . . .

JULIA. Then it alters; it amounts to the same thing. And in the end, it dies.

FERNANDO. And why lament that a love should die? It made us happy for a day, it gave us warmth, life; it scattered its fragrance, while in our eagerness to enjoy it to the full we were all the time crushing it, perhaps without realizing it, just as you've been doing with that poor flower. (*Referring to the flower that she has been fingering since the beginning of the scene.*) Wouldn't it be cruel to reproach it for its loss of freshness and bloom, when it was you who robbed it of them?

JULIA (*sadly*). No. . . . No. I reproach it for nothing. (*Gazing at the flower.*)

FERNANDO. It would be an unpardonable folly, Julia; an ingratitude. . . .

JULIA. I reproach it for nothing.

FERNANDO. Then let us bless it, rather. Let us leave it to die without troubling its agony with bitter recriminations. Why not, as well, love the remembrance of the pleasure which it gave us, if that memory is sweeter, perhaps, than the love itself?

JULIA. Very well. So be it. Let me remain faithful to the recollection of my poor dead flowers.

FERNANDO (*slowly, and with marked symbolic insinuation*). And why, if the rose bush offers us many a flower like the poor dead rose, fragrant and downy, every one of them—why not enjoy them, too? It's so sweet to love, always to love. Julia! It's not true that first love is the best—that a single love makes life more beautiful. Who can assure us that the happiness we find in a single love is all the happiness that love has in store?

JULIA (*rising*). Neither can anyone assure us that the pain we find in a single love is all the pain that love has in store, Fernando.

FERNANDO. Pain!

JULIA. Let's go back to the ballroom, Fernando. Will you give me your arm?

FERNANDO (*after an effort, as if really awakening*). Let us awake. (*Offers his arm*). At your service.

JULIA (*impulsively*). Promise me, Fernando, not to persist in your useless endeavor! Promise that you'll forget me, that you'll go! I'll never be yours. Let's be good friends. I beg you, I entreat you. Heed my words, if you truly love me!

FERNANDO. I promise.

JULIA. And you'll leave me?

FERNANDO. Anything you ask.

JULIA. Are you in earnest? Aren't you jesting?

FERNANDO. It's so sweet to dwell in an illusion, Julia! Be assured that I'll cease loving you—that I'll have to forget you. . . . Life is a dream! . . .

JULIA. Fernando, I beg you!

FERNANDO. Let's deceive ourselves! Truth is so prosaic!

JULIA. Fernando! (*They walk out. Soon* ROBERTO *and* VICENTE *come in.* ROBERTO *strides resolutely toward the right, disappearing for a moment. At the first words, the music stops playing.*)

VICENTE (*settling himself in the armchair before the fireplace*). Do you know, it's mighty comfortable here, Roberto? This little anteroom is a dream, upon my word!

ROBERTO (*returns, with cigars for his friend*). Have a cigar.

VICENTE. Thanks. (*Takes one.*)

ROBERTO. Yes, my boy. You can take my word for it. (*Sits down.*) I'm just wild about that woman. Simply off my head.

VICENTE. I can't say she's bad looking.

ROBERTO. She's got such a confoundedly cute way of talking and laughing, and everything. . . .

VICENTE. You've certainly fallen hard.

ROBERTO. The other day she was telling us . . . (*Interrupting himself.*) But what do you say? I tell you she's my style, I'm daffy over her. Do you think I'm fooling?

VICENTE. No, not at all. I can see.

ROBERTO. The dickens! I give you my word she has me going! When it comes to dancing and singing, she outclasses them all. Don't talk. I know I'm exaggerating. But what do you expect? Others may dance better than she does, but there's no match for her in charm and looks. . . .

VICENTE. As for her voice, you can't deny that every time she opens her mouth she ought to be begged to close it.

ROBERTO. Voice! Voice! What does an artist of her stamp need a voice for? Come, come. It strikes me you've gone crummy.

VICENTE. Out of what? Envy? Do you imagine I'm jealous of your good luck?

ROBERTO (*laughing*). I'll wind up by thinking so!

VICENTE. You're joking. You know that ever since her first appearance I voted against her. I can't stand women of her type on the stage. Too fleshy, my boy, and I tell you so again.

ROBERTO. Quit that, you chump!

VICENTE. Matter of taste.

ROBERTO. You don't know a good-looking dame when you see one, that's what I tell you.

VICENTE. So you think.

ROBERTO. Now you imagine that Dolores is good-looking.

VICENTE. So do you.

ROBERTO. Not so bad! Take my word for it, there haven't been three women on the stage of the Apollo to outdo Maria-Luisa. What arms and what a throat, and what hair . . . and what a woman, my boy! See her and then die!

VICENTE. Do you know who's taken up with Dolores now?

ROBERTO. Felipe. I heard it last night.

VICENTE. She treats him like a dog and kicks him out of the house. But back he comes as meek as a lamb.

ROBERTO. And poor Esperanza! Doesn't she look awful? She wasn't married quite two years at the time of my marriage, was she? A year and a half, about?

VICENTE. Less. Hardly more than a year.

ROBERTO. She was a peach! On the street she made a wonderful appearance.

VICENTE. Poor thing. That's what I say.

ROBERTO. And now she's old, ugly, played out. They say she's going to America. Is that so?

VICENTE. So they say. There's what happens to your fat women such as Maria-Luisa on the stage. They soon wither away and become scarecrows.

ROBERTO. But Esperanza is too fleshy, too coarse, a regular peasant type. Maria-Luisa is elegant, highly distinguished. What magnificent movements, boy! When she plays in *Carceleras* she certainly gets the crowd. Have you seen her in *Carceleras*?

VICENTE. No, I haven't. But they tell me she plays it well. You see, I didn't know who was her favorite then. That's the time they told me it was you. I burst out laughing. What the deuce! I don't think it was yet six months after your marriage.

ROBERTO. See here. You don't imagine that this is anything serious, do you? I fancy the woman; she's good-looking, she likes me, and that's all. I say that I'm crazy about her, that she's got me daffy, simply because we always talk like that, as you know. Do you imagine, for a moment, that I consider Maria-Luisa a woman?

VICENTE. The fact is that you're once again as you used to be.

ROBERTO. What do you mean?

VICENTE. That you're just as if you hadn't married, of course!

ROBERTO. Don't be a child, for heaven's sake. Do you think that I intend to run around, as before, from the club to the theater and from the theater to the café? There's nothing childish about taking a woman that comes one's way. I know what I'm about. Did you think that because a man marries he must become a fool?

VICENTE. After marriage, every slip looks a little pale!

ROBERTO. Bah! You, too! Quit your nonsense, old boy, for marrying is the simplest thing in the world. Everybody marries, and in worse circumstances than myself. Let's see what there is to marriage. What does it keep a fellow from doing? Spending the whole day at the café or the club? Much loss that is! Suppose you do have to take your wife on a visit, or to the theater, or to some place on a certain night? I don't imagine you'd call that a great sacrifice. Then where are its disadvantages? Besides, Vicente, you know my wife; she's an angel! To protest against marriage, with a wife like that, would be the depth of vulgarity. . . .

VICENTE. Now there you're talking sense.

ROBERTO. If it rested with her, we'd still be billing and cooing in every nook and cranny of the house.

VICENTE. Poor women!

ROBERTO. (*A pause*) Poor women? Why? Do you think me capable of making my wife unhappy?

VICENTE. No, not that. I hadn't any such notion.

ROBERTO. Then what made you say it?

VICENTE. You take me too seriously. I was just talking . . . in general. No special reason.

ROBERTO. Out with it!

VICENTE. My word of honor. . . .

ROBERTO. You needn't, then. It's all the same. You've given me to understand, and that's enough.

VICENTE. I swear that I hadn't any intention of reproach.

ROBERTO. Don't try to smooth it over. Why should you? Berate me for forgetting my wife in favor of a dancer! Go on! Call me faithless! That's all you need.

VICENTE. But I'm telling you that I had no intention of the sort!

ROBERTO. Excellent hypocrite! To condemn me for . . . Enough. I'd better say no more. If you were a boy, I'd laugh at you. I don't quite know how to take it from you.

VICENTE. Come, come! Take it as you please. You can't have a very easy conscience if you leap to defense when no one has accused you.

ROBERTO. None of your sophistry. You *did* accuse me, and I *am* defending myself. That's our psychology, however much this night may disturb your tinsel moralism. As long as a man fulfills his duty to his home and maintains it free of scandal, he is free to do as he pleases outside of it. That attitude is legendary, and up to the present no exceptions have been recognized. I love my wife, I respect her, I satisfy everything from her genuine needs to her most frivolous caprice, and I'm incapable of causing her displeasure. You're wrong, then, if you think my conscience is uneasy. I give you my word that there are few husbands as rigorous as myself when it comes to that point. . . .

VICENTE. Except for your chatter about my "tinsel moralism," I quite agree with you. Let me assure you, though, that I had no intention of preaching morality; I was thinking of something altogether different, and you may take my word for it. I was prompted to say what I did out of a sincere compassion for women, and not out of any wish to read you a lecture. I don't believe you can conscientiously deny the injustice of that law which always allows men the freest conduct. . . . There's no woman within hearing. Am I right or not?

ROBERTO. Bah! I don't deny it. At first sight it looks so. . . . But isn't that the psychology of each sex?

VICENTE. Perhaps. . . . I'm not convinced.

ROBERTO. We carry on as we please outside, yet always we can preserve respect in our households and the affection of our wives.

VICENTE. There you take the effect for the cause and go round in a vicious circle.

ROBERTO. I'm very fond of Julia. You know that. Well, does it mean that I've ceased loving her just because I go off for a night with some woman or other who addresses only my senses?

VICENTE. Not exactly that, but . . .

ROBERTO. It's the same old case, repeated endlessly. Have you ever seen a marriage broken up by such trifles as these accomplished with the necessary discretion?

VICENTE. No, no. Because the woman forgives.

ROBERTO. On the other hand, the slightest inclination a woman may feel for another man, the most innocent flirtation, destroys the peace of a home. Say what you will, I don't believe women can dissemble. Even a fellow who's not so clever can't help noticing some betraying sign of the first steps toward adultery.

VICENTE. Just the same, there are strange cases. Take the Marchioness and Pepe Salas.

ROBERTO. But the Marquis knows and has no objections. How does that fit here?

VICENTE. Hush. Your wife is coming. (*Enter* JULIA.)

JULIA. Ah! You're here! Then it's all right!

ROBERTO. What's that?

JULIA. I thought you'd left, or run off to bed. All our guests have gone.

VICENTE. And I'm still here! (*Rises.*)

JULIA. Oh, no . . . no. I didn't mean you.

ROBERTO. Keep your seat.

VICENTE. I wouldn't think of it.

ROBERTO. (*To* JULIA.) Has Fernando left, too?

JULIA (*slightly disturbed*). Yes, he's left, too.

VICENTE. I'm the one who's to blame, madame. I've been keeping Roberto here with my talk.

JULIA. No, no. It's perfectly all right.

ROBERTO. Did you say good night for me to Eugenia and her husband?

JULIA. Yes, to everybody . . . everybody. . . .

ROBERTO. I didn't realize. . . .

VICENTE (*bowing*). Madame. . . . Many thanks for all your kindness.

JULIA. Oh, no. . . . Don't leave yet. I'm afraid I interrupted you. Please sit down.

VICENTE. You never interrupt us, never, my dear lady. I was about to leave, anyway. I had just stopped for a moment.

JULIA. In that case, then, good night.

VICENTE. Your humble servant, madame. (*To* ROBERTO.)   Good-by, Roberto. A thousand thanks for the delightful conversation.

ROBERTO. I'll see you out.

VICENTE. Please don't trouble yourself.

ROBERTO. No ceremony, now. Let's be going.

VICENTE (*from the rear*). Madame! (*Bows.*)

JULIA. Good night. (JULIA, *left alone, leans against the mantelpiece for a while in meditation, inhaling the fragrance of the other flowers of the bouquet. All at once, as if frightened, she changes her mind and turns around, as if looking for something. At last she espies the flower that she left on the armchair and runs forward to seize it.*) No. Ever faithful to you, ever! (*She kisses it. At this moment her husband returns.*) Roberto! Roberto! . . .

ROBERTO (*hastening in*). What is it?

JULIA (*coquettishly, wheedling*). Come.

ROBERTO. Here I am.

JULIA. Throw your arms about me. . . . Love me. . . .

ROBERTO. Silly goose! (*Embraces her.*) There are my arms around you. I love you.

JULIA (*freeing herself*). Did you like me to-night?

ROBERTO. Very much.

JULIA. More than all the other women that you saw here?

ROBERTO. Much more.

JULIA. Story-teller! I saw you eyeing Carmen all night!

ROBERTO. Are you going to begin that all over again?

JULIA. No, no. Forgive me. But is it really true that you like me more than you do all the other women?

ROBERTO. As certain as that I have you in my arms at this moment.

JULIA. I don't believe it! For you would have told me so without my dragging it out of you!

ROBERTO. Don't be stupid.

JULIA. You're not fond of me, you're not so fond of me as you used to be, Roberto. I was watching you to-night while you chatted with Carmen, and I coughed and laughed so as to attract your attention. As far as you were concerned, I might just as well not have been there!

ROBERTO. I must have had my thoughts elsewhere, silly.

JULIA. No, there's no excuse for you. To-night I had my maid dress me as quickly as possible, so that you could see me and tell me how charming I looked, just as you used to before. . . .

ROBERTO. But how's a fellow to guess. . . .

JULIA. Not a word, now! All you did was to tell me that the neck was too low.

ROBERTO. Of course. I think it's altogether too low.

JULIA. This neck too low! Why, you're crazy! How about the ones you used to praise so highly when we sat in the box at the theater?

ROBERTO. There you go again with your "before." Always that "before" . . .

JULIA. Does it bother you?

ROBERTO. It doesn't bother me; don't get angry. All you keep doing is comparing the past with the present. That's nonsense. Each epoch has its own character. As a sweetheart I might have found a low neck attractive; now that I'm your husband . . . it's quite different. You simply won't admit that marriage is anything more than child's play. A fine figure we'd cut billing and cooing in public like a couple of calf-and-puppy lovers. Good heavens! It's high time you woke up and realized things!

JULIA. Enough, Roberto, not a word more! I asked you to embrace me, to show me some affection, to love me. And now see what you've done!

ROBERTO. Well, is it my fault, I ask you?

JULIA. Very well. I'm through. Forgive me. I promise to be as you please, to suit your taste. Are you satisfied?

ROBERTO. There are times when you get too silly for words.

JULIA (*throwing her arms around his neck*). No more. Forgive me. Remember, you didn't use to scold your Julia like that in bygone days. Quite the contrary, in fact. Don't you remember? Look at me; look me in the eyes. So. . . . Now smile. . . . Smile! More. So! Now! (*She embraces him.*) You're mine, mine! I don't want to lose you! Do you hear? I don't want to lose you, for the very idea puts mad thoughts into my head, terribly mad thoughts. I don't want you to be like the rest. I don't want to lose you. I want you always to love me so much, so much, just as I love you.

Do you hear me? You turn your eyes away! You're not listening to what
I say. . . .

Roberto. I'm listening, I hear you. Come, come, don't be so foolish. (*He
kisses her.*) You're very nervous to-night; let's go to bed.

Julia. No, no. . . . Come here. Let's sit down before the fireplace, close
together. Let's recall our youthful dreams. Come. Don't tell me that I'm
nervous. Sit down. (*They sit down.*) To-night I suddenly felt a desire to
be loved as I used to be loved, ardently, passionately. We are still very
young, Roberto. It doesn't matter that marriage is a serious proposition.
Do you remember our nights at the hotel in Paris?

Roberto (*fondling her hands*). I remember them ever so well, little
precious—ever so well.

Julia. We'd be sitting like this, before the fire, until midnight. I'd fall
asleep on your shoulder. So. (*She rests her head against his shoulder. Her
voice grows languid, and she speaks slowly, as if evoking the memories one by
one.*) Outside it was cold, oh, so cold. The poor people who had neither love
nor warmth, as we did, hurried by, rattling their heels on the pavement. The
echo of their footsteps came to our ears, and softly they died away. And that
tiny infantile voice, tremulous, almost weeping—don't you remember—which
used to wheeze the verses of a waltz beneath our balcony? (*She sings in a
very soft voice, which resembles a sigh.*) "When all is o'er." (*She bursts
into tears.*)

Roberto. Julia! What is this? What do you mean by this crying?

Julia. No, no. I'm not crying. See. How happy we were, good God!
And yet, Roberto, those memories make me sad, bring tears to my eyes . . .
they seem so far off, so very far. . . .

Roberto. Come, come, brace up. No more of this.

Julia. What wouldn't I give to be living again in those days. What
wouldn't I give to be kissed as you kissed me then!

Roberto. Why do you complain of the present? Aren't you happy?

Julia. Not so happy as then, Roberto. You no longer love me as you . . .

Roberto. Enough! I don't like to hear you say that. Don't say it again.

Julia (*recalling Fernando's words*). Why this human insistency upon
making everything everlasting? There is nothing eternal! If the truth had
not shattered our dream, we should still be enjoying that sweetest of happiness. . . .

Roberto. You persist in complaining of the present. Have you any fault
to find with me?

Julia. Yes, Roberto, I have. You don't love me as you used to. You
don't love me as you . . .

Roberto. In the name of our peace of mind, I beg you not to repeat those
words. . . .

Julia (*sadly*). I'll be silent.

Roberto (*angered*). "I'll be silent!" Don't say it like that, as if you were
obeying some despotic command. I begged you. (Julia *withdraws from him*

and is silent, her eyes closed.) Do you think I can stand this harping of yours—the past was better, I don't love you any more, I'm different from what I was? Good God! You torture me, and all to no purpose. I'm the same, I love you the same. Do you lack anything? Isn't every whim of yours catered to? What more do you want? Do you imagine that other women have as many comforts as you for making their lives happy? What do you want? What is it you desire? Would you have me trailing after you like a simpleton, kissing you in every corner? Heavens! That's ridiculous. A husband is neither a suitor nor a sweetheart. It seems to me you ought to know that. . . . (JULIA *bursts into silent tears.*) And now! Now she weeps! That's the last straw! That's all that was needed! . . . (*He gets up and paces nervously about.*) I confess I can't understand you, my girl. I can't possibly do a thing more for your happiness. You're bent on turning our married life into a hell. . . . This is terrible! Unendurable! If I were to repeat these scenes to anyone, he'd surely take us for a couple of lunatics! What's behind all this? Why are you crying? Let's see. Answer me. Why these tears? (*He hears a sound outside and walks over to the door.*)

JULIA. It's nothing, Roberto. I'm not crying.

ROBERTO (*speaking harshly to some one outside*). No, you're not wanted. (*Enters angrily.*) There go the servants, spying upon these little scenes of ours. And the scenes grow more and more frequent! No, no! This must have some remedy, and the remedy's got to be found.

JULIA. Enough, Roberto.

ROBERTO. We can't go on like this, for it's impossible, absolutely beyond anyone's understanding. . . .

JULIA. Roberto, enough. I have the remedy. Listen. . . .

ROBERTO. It's the worst possible silliness to spoil our happiness with scenes. . . .

JULIA. Roberto, I'm talking to you.

ROBERTO. Speak, then. I'm listening.

JULIA. I'll never question you again. Never, never. Do you hear?

ROBERTO. I see. We've reached the dramatic finale. "Never."

JULIA. Listen to me. I'll never again ask you whether you love me, or make comparisons between the past and the present. . . .

ROBERTO. Do you see? Didn't I tell you? It's sheer nonsense, a mere phrase. . . .

JULIA. And now, no more. I ask your pardon for having caused you all this annoyance.

ROBERTO. But why this offended tone?

JULIA. I don't feel like laughing now, Roberto; that should be obvious.

ROBERTO. And you'll keep that wry face?

JULIA (*scornfully*). Oh, no. That, too, will go away.

ROBERTO. Again! At it again! No. To-night you're certainly too nervous altogether.

JULIA. That's why we should end it peacefully, Roberto. Please, I beg you, don't scold me any more. I'm much calmer now. Let's have done with this.

ROBERTO. You're right. Let's go to bed. (*He approaches her.*) Shall we kiss and make up?

JULIA. Why not?

ROBERTO. Please shake that manner, Julia. . . .

JULIA. I can't, Roberto. . . .

ROBERTO. Then there's no use . . . Until to-morrow. I'm going into my study for a moment. Good night.

JULIA. Good night. (*Exit* ROBERTO. *She turns to the mantelpiece and leans against it. She looks into the mirror and her eyes fall upon the bouquet. She takes it and inhales the perfume of the flowers. Then, timorously, as if trespassing upon forbidden ground, hesitantly, she takes a flower, breathes in its fragrance, and surrenders herself to deep meditation.*)

SLOW CURTAIN

EPILOGUE

Up to this point the author has observed and transcribed, believing that he could interest you in the comedy.

What scenes follow?

Three or four acts are to-day generally granted the dramatist in which to develop his play.

I have written only one.

The other three are up to you. Fill them in as you please!

But let it not degenerate into a gory drama, a tragedy of blood.

Have these persons pardon one another; let them love one another above their several rivalries and hatreds; let them forget.

In that way you will be creating a noble and elevated Art. And a work of sound Morals, or Humane Morality.

Don't hesitate. Consider that here, as in life, the evil and the good are inextricably intermingled.

Could you tell me which of these persons is in the right?

Let me tell you:

They all are.

Madrid, 1911.

EYES THAT CANNOT SEE

A PLAY

By ALBERT GNUDTZMANN

Translated from the Danish by Arvid Paulson

TO
THE MEMORY OF MY FRIEND
RICHARD MANSFIELD, 2ND,
WHO DIED IN THE SERVICE OF HIS COUNTRY,
I DEDICATE THE ENGLISH VERSION OF THIS PLAY.

A. P.

CHARACTERS

HAMMELEV, *a public school teacher*
MRS. HAMMELEV, *his wife*
ANTON, *their son*
LOUISE THORSEN
KIRSTEN

First produced at the Royal Theatre, Copenhagen, September 10th, 1903.

Reprinted from the Appleton Modern Plays.

EYES THAT CANNOT SEE

The action of the play takes place in the living quarters of the HAMMELEVS' *in a Danish country school.*

A living room at the HAMMELEVS', *with low ceiling and antique furniture. In the background two windows, through which is seen a garden. Between the windows an old-fashioned linen closet. By the windows, on the right, a platform with a sewing table. A bird cage with a canary bird stands on the window sill; white curtains; a number of flower pots. Doors on each side of the stage. To the right a big chiffonier. Nearer the footlights a smoking table, above which, on the wall, hangs a pipe-rack with pipes. On the left a sofa; in front of it stands a table with a rocking-chair and a couple of other chairs. Above the sofa hangs a mirror; on each side of the mirror portraits of Luther and Melanchthon; underneath these, photographs of members of the family. The room has the stamp of cozy homeliness—sunshine outside—the sun rays pour into the room in broad streams through the windows.*

SCENE I

(MRS. HAMMELEV *and* KIRSTEN. *They are drinking coffee at the center table, which is covered with a small tablecloth.*)

KIRSTEN. Yes, Lavst's promised. The carriage will be there, I'm sure. It's all been arranged.

MRS. HAMMELEV. Thank you very much, Kirsten. And remember now, it is the 8:20 train.

KIRSTEN. Oh, yes, yes—

MRS. HAMMELEV (*eagerly*). And the carriage should be at the station in plenty of time. I should say eight o'clock at the latest. So it must leave here at seven.

KIRSTEN. Oh, it don't take no more than a half hour to get there.

MRS. HAMMELEV. I am always so afraid that something may happen. And if we should come late! You must remember, Kirsten, that he is quite helpless. And in a railroad station, especially, in the midst of people who think only of themselves.

KIRSTEN. Yes—I wonder sometimes how he can travel like that, all alone, without gettin' into trouble, the poor boy! How helpless a man is without a pair of eyes to see with!

149

Mrs. Hammelev. Everything is in God's power, Kirsten. And then you must know that by this time he has become accustomed to helping himself. It is now seven years since the misfortune came upon him.

Kirsten. Heavens! Is it really? Yes, time flies—indeed it does! I remember very well the time when you and Mr. Hammelev took him to the doctor, and you was told that poor Anton was goin' to lose his eyesight. Both me and Furst felt awful sorry over it.

Mrs. Hammelev (*painfully touched*). Yes, Kirsten, but—

Kirsten (*without interruption*). It was an awful and terrible thing to think of! Such a nice-lookin' boy as he was! He had that curly hair of his that suited him so fine—and them beautiful eyes of his—oh, what beautiful eyes he had, anyhow! Poor Anton! Yes, we used to always call him "poor little Anton," 'cause he wasn't very strong. But he was a pretty big lad at that time. Wasn't he just goin' to graduate? Let's see—he graduated from high school when—

Mrs. Hammelev. Twice—two years in succession he failed, and he used to be the first one in his class, and then—(*Pauses.*) But, God be praised, he has amounted to something in spite of all. He has turned out to be a very clever boy—although he took up a different profession than we had wanted him to.

Kirsten. Yes, both Mr. Hammelev and you wanted him to study to be a minister, didn't you? And what's a musician! And *you* was a minister's daughter!

Mrs. Hammelev. Musician! But, Kirsten, my son is not an ordinary musician. He is an artist—yes—you know what that means, don't you, Kirsten? He plays in big halls where people gather just to hear music. Have I never read to you what has been said of him in the newspapers?

Kirsten. Yes, thanks, and I must say it was a real pleasure and comfort for me to hear, 'specially when it's a person you have no right to expect too much from; that fate has struck like him and who must bend to the will of our Lord, as long as it's got to be. But it's awful sad to think that His choice should fall on poor Anton. I always thought, when I saw him, that he was made to live in sunshine and light all the time. And to think that he should have to wander in darkness!—as it is written in the Bible.

Mrs. Hammelev (*half to herself*). Yes, Kirsten, there was a time when I thought as you do. Many a night I have lain awake, struggling with God for my child. I wouldn't let Him go until He blessed me. And when I saw that Anton's sight, with every day that passed, grew dimmer and dimmer, there was a moment when I turned against Him, and in my foolishness wanted Him to account for His acts. At times I almost thought it would be best if He would take the child back to Him.

Kirsten (*with sincerity*). Perhaps it would have been best.

Mrs. Hammelev. No, Kirsten, it wouldn't. And I shall never forgive myself that I once in a dark moment let Anton understand that I did think so. Now it has dawned upon me that God nevertheless has heard my prayers.

He has given my son new light; but He has lighted it in the depth of his soul. *There* grow flowers and sparkle springs as pure as neither you nor I have imagination to dream of, Kirsten. (*Noise outside of voices of children, mingled with the clatter of their wooden shoes.*) I suppose school is over.

KIRSTEN (*rising from her chair*). Good heavens! Is it that late? Oh, I got to be goin'!

MRS. HAMMELEV. Oh, no. Stay a while, Kirsten. Mr. Hammelev will be in soon. We'll have another cup of coffee.

SCENE II

(HAMMELEV *enters from the left. An elderly man with a kindly, somewhat tired expression on his face.*)

MRS. HAMMELEV. Kirsten is here, pa!

HAMMELEV. So I see, mother, I see. (*Goes to* KIRSTEN *and shakes hands with her.*) How do you do, Kirsten? I hear that your husband will drive to the station for us to-night. I want to thank you for your kindness.

KIRSTEN. Oh, that's nothin' to thank us for, Mr. Hammelev. It ain't the season of the year when we use our horses much.

HAMMELEV. No, oh, no—now that you've got the hay in, I guess you don't. But it isn't the first time we have had reason to thank you and your husband. Since we haven't any horse and carriage, we ought to be thankful that we have such kind and helpful neighbors. (*Goes to the pipe rack, takes down a pipe, and fills it with tobacco.*) Well, Kirsten, I suppose you know what a great day it was in school to-day?

KIRSTEN. Oh, yes, I can imagine, Mr. Hammelev. It is in a way a day of rejoicin'—we can't say nothin' else. The Lord has dealt severely with you, so we are glad when He helps you along a little and makes it easier for you.

MRS. HAMMELEV (*who has been serving the coffee, interrupting*). You'll take a cup of coffee, too, won't you, pa?

HAMMELEV (*who has lighted his pipe*). Yes, thanks; we can always drink a little coffee. (*Sits, smokes, and drinks his coffee.*) Yes, you see the cross we have to bear, Kirsten—we ought never to complain of that. (*Good-naturedly.*) At your house you don't complain, anyhow, I don't think. Do you, Kirsten?—You haven't anything to complain of.

KIRSTEN (*knocks under the table, from superstition*). I'd better knock on wood before it's too late.

HAMMELEV. Yes, do that, Kirsten. Well, I won't say that we have anything to complain of over here, either. We get our daily bread. And now this great joy when our son comes home. We haven't seen him for four years.

KIRSTEN. Is it as long as that?

MRS. HAMMELEV (*to herself*). Four long years!

HAMMELEV. Yes, it has always been worst for mother, of course. You see,

I have the school and the church singing to think of. But she has to sit alone here in this room day after day. Then, of course, her thoughts go far, far off—we all know how it is. I often say to mother: "Mother, I have a hundred little children to take care of every day." That means a hundred little hearts and a hundred little brains that I must keep watch over. And so I say to mother, it seems to me as if she ought to be able at least to keep track of herself. But it is easy enough to find fault. Sorrow is a weed that it is not so easy to pull up by the roots.

KIRSTEN. Yes, if I'd had such a misfortune to think of, I don't know what I'd have done.

HAMMELEV. But now mother will get her reward for all she has gone through, poor mother. To-night he'll be here in this room, he whom she is always thinking of. She hasn't even slept during the last half-dozen nights.

MRS. HAMMELEV (*smiling*). Now you are exaggerating again, pa!

HAMMELEV. Well, well—you haven't had very much sleep. A little with one eye is about all, if we should sum it up. And there has been such a housecleaning and scrubbing and frying and baking, as if the vicar himself was expected. The boy's room is fixed for him; it is just as it was when he was at home last, excepting, of course, that everything is newly washed and cleaned and polished.

KIRSTEN. But when he ain't able to see it—

HAMMELEV. No, he can't see it. But the blind instinctively feel what we others see. They can, for instance, enjoy a beautiful landscape. The color rays work on their skin, you understand, Kirsten. It is just as if they were taking a sort of bath in all the beauty. And then, of course, they have the sense of smell. Well, now—and there are twelve new shirts and twelve pairs of socks for him on his bed. Those he can get a great deal of pleasure from. Would you like to see them, Kirsten?

MRS. HAMMELEV (*somewhat impatiently*). Oh, that's nothing—

HAMMELEV. Yes, Kirsten, just to make mother feel ashamed, I'll show you how diligent she has been. She knows how to do these things. She has a linen closet that would make many a woman envious.

KIRSTEN. Yes, we sure have to have clothes on our body.

HAMMELEV. Yes, Kirsten; but you and your husband no doubt have more than we. Come along now; I'll show you what mother has made for our boy.

KIRSTEN (*puts away her coffee cup, rises, shakes hands with both*). Yes, all right. Well—thank you ever so much for the coffee.

(*All three go out, right. At the same moment are seen, through the windows in the background,* ANTON HAMMELEV *and* LOUISE THORSEN, *approaching by the roadway outside.*)

SCENE III

(ANTON HAMMELEV *and* LOUISE THORSEN *enter from the left.* ANTON *is a young man in his twenties. He has the appearance of an artist—face smooth-shaven and hair rather long. In spite of his blindness he moves about in the room without any apparent difficulty.* Louise *is in her thirties —a weary and somewhat faded and passée woman. It is apparent that she is trying to improve her appearance with the use of powder and paint. She is quite well dressed. She gives the impression of being of an amiable though timid disposition, and she has a sad look in her eyes.*)

Anton (*merrily*). You never thought, Louise, that *I* should ever lead *you.* Did you notice how well I knew the way? And I know where every piece of furniture stands in this room. (*Points.*) There stands mother's sewing-table —and there are father's pipes. Am I not right? You may ask me about every little thing if you wish. I can tell you where every picture hangs on the wall. Do you want to try?

Louise (*pleadingly*). No, Anton, not now.

Anton. Why not? You haven't lost your courage, have you?

Louise. We shouldn't have done this, I think. If you had come alone, you could have explained to your parents much better.

Anton (*somewhat impatiently*). If I could ever get you to understand why I have arranged it as I have! What do you think my parents are, anyhow? Do you think they'll assault me? Assault a defenseless woman —eh?

Louise. No, of course not. But—I don't know—when I look about in this room it seems to me as if I had entered it to steal something that doesn't belong to me.

Anton. Oh, is it that way? Listen now, Louise. Who do you suppose knows the old folks best—you or I?

Louise. Why—you, of course, but—

Anton. Well, then let it be so. Now, don't you think it would be best to let me do as I think fit? (*More quietly.*) I'll tell you, Louise, my parents have hitherto not been used to see anything but a child in me! "Poor little Anton," they always used to call me, even after I had gone through the conservatory. Four years ago, when last I was at home, father couldn't get it into his head that I, like other men, had to shave and get my hair cut. And I was at that time a big chap—nineteen years old. (*In a temper.*) Good God! Am I then but a child! A helpless, unfortunate, poor being, and can I never grow to be like other human beings!

Louise. You who know so much—you are not as badly off as that! And you know it, too, Anton.

Anton. Yes, God help me, Louise! When one is lacking in one of the senses one is a child, an incomplete specimen, three-fourths of a man or hardly that. But let that be as it may! The fact remains that neither father nor mother in their wildest moments of imagination would think that I might become engaged. And I don't think it would be of any use for me to begin to explain how the whole thing has happened. Even if I should describe you as an angel of God, they would say I was the most foolish being in the world.

Just for that very reason they ought to have the chance of seeing for themselves.

LOUISE. If only we hadn't met, Anton! It would have been so much better for you.

ANTON. What nonsense! When once they see you! That's why I wanted you to come with me and surprise them.

LOUISE. Oh, God! I only wish I was twenty miles from here. I don't even know what to say to them.

ANTON. You don't need to say anything at all. I'll talk for you; you'll see. I'll say: "Look here, father and mother, this is Louise. She is the woman to whom I owe everything. If it hadn't been for her I wouldn't be a human being with a cheery outlook on life—I wouldn't care to live. I myself have never seen her, but I know so well how she looks. She is fair as the day, and she has a dimple in either cheek—they are just like a couple of little rills where the sunbeams play hide-and-seek. She has also a little bent-up nose—quite a resolute little nose—that always points in the right direction, just like a compass needle. But what is most beautiful about her are her eyes; they are so deep, and yet so clear; one feels so sure there is something beyond their depth—but one can't see it. And the other little things about her—can't you see for yourself how fine and nice and good she is?"

LOUISE (*pained*). Oh, Anton, but I don't look like that!

ANTON. Yes, that is how you do look. I know it. (*Takes hold of both her hands.*) And yet I can't show them your warm, faithful heart; they'll have to learn to know that little by little.

LOUISE. If you would only not make so much of me, Anton! If one of us has anything to be grateful for, it is I. And you know I haven't hidden anything from you.

ANTON (*drops her hands; seriously*). You had nothing to hide, Louise. I know you have had a hard time. But pure metal can't be spoiled, and you have come out of it all unstained—with your beautiful eyes and your good heart. Perhaps you have cried a great deal. Perhaps others can see the traces in your face—if so, it is an advantage to me to be blind. (*Listens.*) But listen! I can hear the old folks upstairs. I think, perhaps it would be best, if you went out for a second; you need only go outside till I call you. You see—I think I ought to be alone with them the very first moments.

LOUISE (*close to him; entreating him*). Anton—don't you want me to leave you now? Shan't I—

ANTON (*impatiently*). You must do as I say. Be a sensible girl—don't be hysterical. Now go, please.

LOUISE (*going out to the left*). I'll do as you wish me to. But if you regret it, remember I told you you shouldn't do it.

(ANTON *stands for a moment listening to the steps of his parents overhead. Then he hides himself behind the door to the right, which opens at the same moment.*)

Scene IV

(Kirsten, Mrs. Hammelev, *and* Hammelev *enter from the right.*)

Kirsten. Yes, Lavst will be there in plenty of time to-night, I promise.

Mrs. Hammelev. Thank you, Kirsten. You understand, we are a little nervous. But what is—

Anton (*coming forward with open arms*). Mother!

Mrs. Hammelev (*overwhelmed; sobbing*). Anton! (*She throws herself on his bosom and kisses him passionately.*) Oh, Anton, Anton—

Hammelev (*who, in his excitement, has taken the pipe from his mouth*). But, Anton, dear—we didn't expect you until to-night!

Anton. Yes, but "poor little Anton" had a notion to surprise you. So we took—so I took an earlier train. (*He feels with one hand in the air, while holding his mother tightly pressed to his bosom with the other.*) How do you do, father!

Hammelev (*pressing his hand*). How are you, dear boy?

Kirsten. Well, I guess I ought to say how do you do, too. I am Kirsten, Lavst's wife.

Anton (*lets go his mother's hand and presses Kirsten's hand in a faltering manner*). How do you do, Kirsten. I suppose everything is the same with you as ever?

Kirsten. Yes, thank the Lord!

Hammelev. But how did you ever get out here, Anton? Didn't anybody come with you?

Anton (*somewhat embarrassed*). No—well—yes, you see I know the way. And—yes, I'll tell you—

Kirsten. Well, I don't want to disturb you no longer, and there's no need of no·carriage goin' to the station to-night, I guess.

Hammelev. No, I don't think so, Kirsten. But thank you just the same for your willingness. Good-by! And give my regards to your husband!

Kirsten. Good-by!

(*Shakes hands and goes out to the right.*)

Anton. Why don't you say something, mother? Was it too much of a surprise?

Mrs. Hammelev (*moves her hand to her heart; smiles*). Yes, it was a bit sudden—but now . . . Oh, Anton—when you are here, you know—don't you know . . . And how well and happy you look!

Kirsten (*puts her head inside the door*). Excuse me. I just wanted to tell you there is a strange lady standin' outside here.

Hammelev (*slightly annoyed*). A strange lady! What does she want, I wonder? Tell her to come in!

Kirsten (*calls*). Yes, you can come in, if you want to.

(*She goes out.*)

SCENE V

(LOUISE *comes from the left and remains standing right, inside the door.*)

HAMMELEV (*goes towards her*). You wish to speak with me?

LOUISE (*falteringly, embarrassed*). Yes—but I thought—perhaps I—ought not to—

ANTON. Why, of course you should. (*He feels his way to her, takes her by the hand, and leads her out into the room; the parents seem to be shocked.*) I wanted to tell you first, but as it now has happened differently than I had thought—here is the woman who has helped me to find the way out here to-day. And she has done more than that: she has led me through the darkest moments of my life.

MRS. HAMMELEV (*who, in a glance, has taken in* LOUISE; *in a voice of anxiety*). Anton—what does this mean?

ANTON. It means, father and mother, that in the last two years she and I have been one. And we will never separate from each other.

HAMMELEV (*with strained kindliness*). So—so you are engaged, poor little Anton? You haven't written and told us anything about it.

ANTON. I didn't want you to worry over me—to know that I—helpless as I was—had bound myself to another human being. I wanted you to *see* her first. (*Moved.*) For I knew that in the same moment that you saw her, you'd understand it is for our mutual happiness. Isn't that true when she has chosen to love me? As fine and beautiful as she is! You must understand how much she thinks of me. But you needn't fear for her sake, I feel sure. I can make her happy; and for her it is happiness to be able to give of her full, rich heart—to give to one who longs with all his soul for sun and light—as I do.

MRS. HAMMELEV. I think, if we should speak of the richness of heart, that few have as much to give away as you have, Anton.

ANTON. No, no! don't compare me with her. Remember—for her the whole world lies open; she need but stretch out her arms. But I—I have nothing to give up, nothing to offer. And there is nobody who asks anything from me, anyhow. Nature has now once for all—it seems to me—given me the right to be a bit selfish. . . .

HAMMELEV. We had thought that—

ANTON. Yes, father, I might have known that this would come as a great surprise to you. And I know that before long you will love Louise as much as I myself do.

HAMMELEV. Louise—so that's her name—your . . . And her last name, if I may ask?

LOUISE. Thorsen.

HAMMELEV. Louise Thorsen—oh, yes . . . (*Heartily.*) Well, well, my dear

Anton—and you also, my dear—Louise Thorsen, I suppose I ought to wish you all sorts of health and happiness.

(*Approaches* ANTON *with extended hand.*)

MRS. HAMMELEV (*goes between them*). Hammelev—I think you first ought to let us speak with the young lady. (*With an emotion that she can hardly conceal.*) May I only say this: Anton knows that I, too, wish him happiness —that nobody could wish him more happiness than I—but it is not more than right that I learn to know her a little better before I—

ANTON (*quietly*). Of course you may, mother.

MRS. HAMMELEV. You must understand me rightly, Anton. Father and I have been waiting for months for the happy day when you would come home. We spoke of it when we sat here the other evening—we thought of when you would step inside the door—we thought of how it would be with all of us together, the three of us. Now the whole thing will have to be changed. I can't quite reconcile myself to it at once. Therefore, I want to have a chance to learn to know her first—she, whom you have chosen for yourself.

ANTON. Yes, mother, since you look at it that way—I think myself it is the best way. For I know very well that when you have talked with her ten minutes you'll love her as if you had known her for many years. Father and I will take a walk in the garden in the meantime.

HAMMELEV. Anton ought to go up to his room, too. But you ought to show him that yourself, mother.

MRS. HAMMELEV (*nervously*). Do as you like. I—

ANTON (*merrily*). Let's go out in the garden. I am longing to find out how much the big pear tree has grown that I planted out there myself when I still had my sight. But I tell you this, mother: you mustn't make Louise regret that she cares for me, poor mole. For if I lose her, I'll never find my way any more in life.

(HAMMELEV *and* ANTON *go out.*)

SCENE VI

MRS. HAMMELEV. Now we'll have a talk, we two—it is necessary. You may take off your things—the large hat—the coat. (LOUISE *takes her coat and hat off and puts them away. She is dressed in a plain, simple dress.*) Yes—I like you so much better without those things on. Now sit down here at the table—right here in front of me. (*They both of them sit down.*) What I am going to tell you now may hurt you. But I trust you understand that nobody could love Anton any more than his mother. Therefore I want to speak openly to you.

LOUISE (*bows down her head*). I suppose you want me to call it off with him.

MRS. HAMMELEV. I had meant to ask you whether you yourself think that you are the kind of wife he ought to have. I don't know you, of course. But I know him, and I know that he deserves to have a good woman and a woman who is pure. Can you stand before the face of God and say that you are that? You need not answer me. It is God who awaits your answer.

LOUISE (*slowly*). I know very well I haven't always been what I should have been.

MRS. HAMMELEV (*mildly*). None of us have. But you must let your own conscience decide whether you can stand with raised head as my son's bride. If you can not, I beg of you to give him up. Yes, in such a case you *must*. Could you expect me to ask anything else of you?

LOUISE (*rocking back and forth in great agony*). I have been so fond of Anton.

MRS. HAMMELEV. Yes, poor girl! You mustn't think I am so hard-hearted that I don't feel sorry for you. But life puts its mark on each one of us. And you have received yours. I saw it on you at once.

LOUISE. I have often regretted that I gave Anton my promise. I am sorry for his sake. I have often thought that perhaps it would dawn on him some day that I wasn't fit for him. And I promised myself solemnly—if such a day should come—he should be free from me at once.

MRS. HAMMELEV. Perhaps—if you had enough strength left. But what about all the years you had taken away from him in the meantime?

LOUISE. I felt that way because he cared for me and wanted to have me near him.

MRS. HAMMELEV. But you have no right to think anything like that. We have no right to masquerade, to pretend we are what we are not. And you must remember that my son can't form an opinion for himself of human beings in the same way that we can.

LOUISE (*bravely*). You mustn't think, Mrs. Hammelev, that I have hidden anything from Anton.

MRS. HAMMELEV. Hidden! To leave things untold is the same as to hide.

LOUISE. I have told him everything that I have been—that I was once—

MRS. HAMMELEV (*sharply*). A fallen woman!

LOUISE (*bending herself down in silence, as if being struck*). That is a word which is not used by oneself about oneself. (*With strong emotion.*) Yet on the very first day we met I told him I should bring shame and sorrow to him. I told him I had done things that I couldn't even tell him about, and that I wasn't worthy of walking by his side in the street.

MRS. HAMMELEV. You did tell him that?

LOUISE. As true as there is a God! I have told him everything. Oh, but he—he only smiled. He understood so well, he said, that I had gone through so many things. But when a woman had the strength to rise again, it tended to prove that she had the real stuff in her—that's what he said. Then it seemed to him also as if it, in a way, was a sort of counter-balance to his being such a wretched human being. In a way, you understand. For we each had our own misfortune to bear.

MRS. HAMMELEV (*passionately*). Don't you dare to compare his misfortune with yours! God knows my poor boy cannot be blamed for what has befallen him. Whereas you have been a bad and weak woman. You have brought your sin and shame upon yourself, and you cannot wash yourself clean of it now. I am not judging you—don't think that! But how could you come out here with him? How could you think that we, his parents, could look on quietly and see him throw himself away on a—a woman who—who was unworthy of him?

Louise. Oh, God! I didn't think so. I didn't think so. I begged him again and again to go alone. But he wouldn't listen to me; he wasn't satisfied until I promised to go with him. And he kept on saying: "When they only see how much you are to me, they will have to like you as much as I do." And then—then—I don't know—then there were moments when I hoped myself it would be as he hoped it would.

Mrs. Hammelev. You ought to have known that, in spite of telling him about your life, you are still deceiving him; that everybody else can see with their eyes what he can't! You also have a bad conscience. It is for that reason you have tried to fix yourself up. But can't you understand that you are thus holding up my poor little boy as a target for fun-making and mockery and pity?

Louise (*struggling with her tears*). He told me to fix myself up so that you might like me. I never thought— (*Suddenly taking hold of* Mrs. Hammelev's *hand.*) You must believe me! I did it all with the best of intentions.

Mrs. Hammelev. I readily believe that. But if you really loved Anton, I do not understand why you couldn't see that you would drag him down with you. But there must be an end to this now. You must give him up.

Louise (*in a low voice*). Give up! Yes, I suppose I must—I wouldn't think of standing between him and his parents. Yes, I'll—I'll tell him we must part.

Mrs. Hammelev. No. You shan't do that. You need but leave quietly. I'll speak myself to my son.

Louise. You speak to him! Yes—if you could only get him to listen. But I know him. He'll want me back, anyway. Do you know that I left him once? No—how could you know that!—

Mrs. Hammelev. You were—you were going to—leave him!

Louise. I wanted to give him back his liberty, as you want me to give it to him now. I explained my reasons for doing it in a letter to him—I have learned the alphabet of the blind. Then I moved to some relatives of mine that I had never spoken to him of. The next day he had found out where I was and came to me.

Mrs. Hammelev. Yes, I realize that you have understood how to make him attached to you. It will be a blow to him—yes, I don't reproach you.

Louise. Reproach me!

Mrs. Hammelev. I tell you, I don't blame you. And if I could give you a helping hand, so that both you and my son could become happy and contented, I would do so. But it wouldn't be right for me to think of anything else but my son's future. Remember that I am so much older than you are and have had so many more years' experience of life. And I have learned that one cannot build a house on sand or dirt.

LOUISE (*rising*). Anton's future shan't be built on such a foundation. It is better for us—it is better for him to have the sorrow of losing me now. And this time it shall be for ever. There are places where he won't be able to find me.

MRS. HAMMELEV. Are you going upstairs to talk to him now?

LOUISE (*nods*). Yes, that is one of the conditions I want to make.

MRS. HAMMELEV. You must believe me—I am doing this with the best of intentions. It is only because I love Anton so much.

LOUISE (*with a sorrowful nod*). I know. When one loves some one—

MRS. HAMMELEV (*takes Louise's hand*). But one thing you must promise me. You must be sensible. You mustn't do anything rash or foolish. Think of Anton. His life is dark enough as it is.

LOUISE. I have already taken into consideration everything. Almost as long as I have known Anton have I had on my mind to do what I am going to do now. I shall go—far away—that's all. And then neither you nor Anton will have to see me any more.

(*She goes out to the right.* MRS. HAMMELEV *walks about the room restlessly for a moment; then she seats herself at the table in deep thought.*)

SCENE VII

(HAMMELEV *enters from the right.*)

HAMMELEV. Well, I showed Anton up to the room, mother. I thought he'd long to see—to come up there. If you had only seen how he went around and felt everything! "Oh, God!" he exclaimed, "there hangs the little rack." And he felt all the books. "There is my *Ivanhoe*—and there is Dickens' *Oliver Twist;* and there *The Last of the Mohicans!*" He felt all of them by their backs. But the shirts and the socks—you could have saved yourself the trouble of making them, mother.

MRS. HAMMELEV. Why?

HAMMELEV. A person can never get enough of such things, of course, in a way. But he is well looked after in this respect. She, his sweetheart, has sewn and fixed and looked after everything for him. She works, by the way, in a dressmaking establishment.

MRS. HAMMELEV (*with an expression of surprise*). She works—she works at a dressmaker's!

HAMMELEV. Yes—in one of those large department stores in Copenhagen. She is in charge of the dressmaking department. She makes good money, too, he says.

MRS. HAMMELEV (*as before*). Good for her!

HAMMELEV. And a good thing for him, too. How would they have got along otherwise?

Mrs. Hammelev. I should hope Anton does not have to receive anything from anybody.

Hammelev. But he had to do so once. Do you know who kept him alive? When he took lessons from that professor, you know. We thought he was living with that friend of his he wrote about.

Mrs. Hammelev. Wasn't he?

Hammelev. Well, yes—yes, he was, in a way. But his friend most of the time wears skirts, and her name is Louise Thorsen. And it was she who took care of him the best way she could.

Mrs. Hammelev (*passionately*). And stole his youth. For if they shared things with each other, it must have meant that they lived together.

Hammelev. Yes—and what is there to be said? She is a woman and he a man. And, besides, he is an artist. So we ought not to judge, I think.

Mrs. Hammelev. But we must be allowed to have our opinions. We have only this one child. And he is in need of parental love more than other children.

Hammelev. Yes, mother dear, but I think it has been a great fortune for him to have found her. What can *we* do for him, we two old cronies? We shall soon have enough to do straightening out our own affairs until we meet up there with the great Doctor who opens all eyes. And when we have gone, who would he then have to cling to? No—a young woman like her is what a man like him needs. And the old doctor said that—thank God—should he get children, there was no danger that his affliction would be hereditary.

Mrs. Hammelev. But there are greater afflictions that *can* be inherited.

Hammelev. Yes, I can see that you are not very pleased with the whole thing. Before she took off her coat it seemed to me, too, as if she looked a bit too "cityfied." But I think she really is a good girl.

Scene VIII

(Anton *and* Louise *come from the right.*)

Anton (*half outside*). No, Louise, you can't go away like this. If I can't make you stay, mother must try to. (*He pulls her, in spite of her opposition, into the room.*) Have you ever heard anything like it? Louise wants to go back to the city to-night.

Louise. Yes, I must, Anton. I didn't have the courage to tell you before. But now—I feel that I know your parents—and . . .

Anton. Know—know—one can't learn to know anybody in an hour. Anyhow, it's strange that your employer wants you to return at once. And just on this occasion! Before, you have always been able to get off whenever you wanted to be with me.

Louise. I have asked to be free too often, dear Anton. Now, you see, they must have grown tired of it in the store. I want to tell you right now that hereafter I am afraid we shall not be able to be together as often as before.

ANTON. Well, then we must get married. To think that you should be the slave of the yardstick! Now I'll dictate a letter for you. I'll say that you cannot be back until the day after to-morrow at the earliest.

LOUISE. No, it won't do, Anton—you must not ask me to do it.

ANTON. But help me, then, father and mother. Can you look on quietly and silently while your daughter-in-law, who has hardly put her foot inside your door, wants to disappear again?

HAMMELEV. No, we want, of course, to—

MRS. HAMMELEV. I think you had best let Louise go, Anton. You mustn't let her take the risk of losing her position.

ANTON. And you say that, mother! But don't you know how I had looked forward to this day—when you would see her—and learn to love her and—

MRS. HAMMELEV. You must be sensible, Anton. It might influence your future if she—

ANTON. The future! Always the future, always to-morrow and again to-morrow, and please wait like a good child! But God have mercy, I am of course, unreasonable. Go, Louise, go! Hurry, that you will not be late for the train!

LOUISE (*sadly*). Are you angry with me now, Anton?

ANTON (*softly*). With you—no! I am a bit angry, I suppose. But not with you. I want to tell you this, however, that I will let you go only on one condition: that you soon take a long vacation. And then we'll come out here again, both of us. Will you promise me that, Louise?

LOUISE (*softly patting his hand*). There shall soon be happiness for both of us, Anton.

ANTON. Y-e-s—I couldn't be angry with you now. So go upstairs to my room. At the very top of my traveling bag you'll find a little package. Bring it down to me. There is something in it for you. It was my intention not to give it to you until to-night. But as long as you can't wait—

LOUISE. You shouldn't spend your money on buying presents for me.

ANTON. What! I don't lose anything by it. I don't ruin myself by it, do I?

LOUISE. But I would rather you didn't give me anything.

ANTON. Is it your intention to make me real angry—seriously angry? I can't understand what ails you to-day. My parents have seen an engaged couple before. Or do you think, perhaps, that they, in their peasant simplicity, may take offense?

LOUISE. No, but—

ANTON. Well, if you want to leave at once, then go. And take all the time you want while you are upstairs. Five minutes, if you like. There is something I want to speak to mother about in the meantime. Can you find your way to the room?

HAMMELEV. I'll show Louise the way. At the same time I'll show her the room where she was to have slept, if she had stayed over night.

ANTON. Five minutes, Louise. But no longer. We have yet a few hours till you have to leave for the train. And we will be very greedy of these two hours—we four.

LOUISE (*bends over him and kisses him*). Anton, dear, you know I have always wished to do what was best for you. Whatever may happen or whatever I may do, you must always believe in me. Do you hear, Anton—always!

(LOUISE *and* HAMMELEV *go out, right.*)

SCENE IX

ANTON. It was only this I wished to tell you, mother: I know that you have made Louise feel sad.

MRS. HAMMELEV (*with anxiety*). Has she then told you?—

ANTON. She has told me nothing; but don't you think I know her voice? And there was a false note vibrating in it. Have you anything against her? If you have—tell me.

MRS. HAMMELEV (*avoiding the question*). Why, I scarcely know her—

ANTON. Then I can only think that you are worried on account of me. It doesn't seem to you that I ought to take the responsibility of founding a family—I who have to stumble along and feel my way like a mole here in this pitiful world.

MRS. HAMMELEV. But, my dear boy, how can you say so!

ANTON. Oh, yes, *it is that.* What else could it be? But now I want to tell you one thing. You who have your sight often think of us blind ones as of feeble-minded beings. We know nothing, we are fit for nothing. But that is where you are mistaken. We are just like other human beings: we can think and dream, can love and hate just like others. You know—sometimes when I stand before an audience, it seems to me as if I were all alone. There is nobody whose soul or thoughts reach me; nobody who can disturb me. I am like the fertile soil that is left to take care of itself; there is an abundance of sunshine saved within me. That is why I feel life so strongly—like something warm and fruitful within me. And it is this feeling that gives me faith; that tells me I have a future awaiting me in spite of all.

MRS. HAMMELEV. Thank God for that, Anton! Thank God for that!

ANTON. But perhaps you mean to say that what Louise feels for me is nothing but pity; that she will cease to care sooner or later. If that is what you think, I want to tell you something—I want to tell you how we first learned to know each other.

MRS. HAMMELEV. No, you need not tell me that, Anton.

ANTON. But I want you to listen to me. You remember, no doubt, a few years ago—I had graduated from the conservatory—had had the best of teachers—and the time came for me when I had to get something to do. But nobody wished to have anything to do with a blind musician—who could not see. So I had to take a position out of town—

MRS. HAMMELEV. In the café, yes.

ANTON. Should we, perhaps, rather say in the barroom. Or in a place still worse. All around me nothing but rough, vulgar, and drunken talk of wanton women and beasts of men. And 'midst all this noise and the smell of liquor I had to sit and play music that was disgusting to me—only for the alms that they cared to throw to me. For it was for alms that I played. Right above the place where I sat there was nailed a sign: "Don't forget the blind musician!"—

MRS. HAMMELEV. My poor boy! My poor boy!—

ANTON. It was then that I wrote to you; I had to have a human being to whom I could open my heart. It was for that reason I didn't or couldn't spare your feelings.

MRS. HAMMELEV. Nobody could be nearer to you than your mother.

ANTON. Do you remember how you answered me? That I should hope and trust that I might come to the place where all eyes are opened and all tears are dried.

MRS. HAMMELEV. I had fought with God over you. But I thought He wouldn't listen to my prayers—not as I wished Him to do. It was then I began to think there was only one consolation.

ANTON (*nodding*). Death—yes. What else could there have been? Death is charitable, if one will only wait for it. But to wait—that was what seemed so hard to me—

MRS. HAMMELEV. For God's sake, Anton.

ANTON. Don't take it so to heart, mother; it is over now—long ago. But that evening, on going home, I searched my way down to the river. Of what importance in life could a poor blind musician ever be? And the Lord would not have turned me away if I had come a little too early to Him, I don't believe.

MRS. HAMMELEV. God have mercy! And I could be at rest here at home. Why didn't I know, why couldn't I have thought, that you were so much in need!

ANTON. Probably because nothing happened; because nothing was meant to happen. It is strange to think how often a mere chance can change a whole life. Chance would have it that evening that I went astray and passed through streets where I had never been before. I had fumbled around about an hour's time when I felt somebody touch my hand, and a woman's voice asked whether I had trouble in finding my way. I have become used to judging people by their voices, and I said to myself at once: "Here is one who is also in despair and who, like you, is wishing for a river, too." And I opened my heart to her.

MRS. HAMMELEV. And that woman—that—was—

ANTON. That was Louise—yes. And I wasn't mistaken in her. She had gone through many things; as much as I had. But she didn't look for the river any more. She had got over that. Well, I went home with her to her little room. She lived in a hall-room. In the daytime she went out sewing.

MRS. HAMMELEV. You went home with her—in the middle of the night!

ANTON (*with a smile*). Yes, mother. I am not used to finding much difference between day and night. To me it is all one color. And she dared not let me go. Who knows—perhaps I might have found the river, anyhow, then. So she sat up all night and talked to me about life and its joys.

MRS. HAMMELEV. Life and its joys. And I—

ANTON. Yes, mother—that you have given to me. Well, that was not all she did. She didn't only *speak* to me. She gave me a place to sleep and she gave me food to eat, so that I shouldn't have to play any more in the bar-room. For fourteen days she shared every penny of her wages with me. And in the afternoon, when she came home from her work, we went out together to look for a position for me. She advertised and put in applications for me, and—thank God! at last I got a position as an organist. Then came the stipend and then the rest. And during all my struggles she remained by my side.

MRS. HAMMELEV (*tenderly*). She has been much to you, Anton.

ANTON. She has been everything to me, mother, everything. Should any-body take her away from me, they'll take my life at the same time.

MRS. HAMMELEV (*frightened, agonized*). Anton—Oh, no—

ANTON. Yes, for I would believe God had regretted that He did not let me go into the river that night, after all. (*He rises and gropes his way.*) It's strange—it seems to me as if the room suddenly had become so different. It is just as if I wasn't at home here any more. Isn't that Louise's steps I hear above me now?

SCENE X

(HAMMELEV *comes from the right with a little package.*)

HAMMELEV. Louise asked me to give you her regards, and say—

ANTON (*full of anxiety*). Asked you to—to say—what?

HAMMELEV (*gives him the package*). And she asked me to give you this.

ANTON (*takes it*). Thanks—it is the rings. I have bought rings for both of us. Now I must give it to her at once. I hadn't intended to do it other-wise until to-night. But why doesn't she come?

HAMMELEV. She is gone to the station.

MRS. HAMMELEV (*screams*). To the station?

HAMMELEV (*somewhat surprised*). Yes—she thought it would be better to—she wanted to spare Anton from saying farewell.

MRS. HAMMELEV. Anton, Anton! She must not go! Oh, God! It is I—it is I who have—she'll never come back—no, never. (*She wants to run out.*)

ANTON (*puts himself intuitively in her way*). Let me go, mother. I'll stop her. She wouldn't heed your voice, I fear. (*Goes to the door, but turns on the threshold.*) For I suppose you want us to come back—don't you?

MRS. HAMMELEV (*as if in a trance*). Yes—yes—and never again—never again—

(ANTON *goes out, left.* MRS. HAMMELEV *has sunk down on a chair. It is as if something had suddenly broken within her, for she bursts into tears.*)

HAMMELEV (*goes over to her; he pats her head and hair*). There—there, mother dear. You loved him too much. Mothers are the only ones who can love so much that they can kill with love. (*He goes to the window and looks out.*) He runs so safely there on the road, as if he still had his sight. Now he stops and calls her. She turns.

MRS. HAMMELEV. Are they coming back?

HAMMELEV. Of course they are coming. Now they are speaking to each other. Of course they are coming.

MRS. HAMMELEV. Not to me. I have lost Anton for ever.

HAMMELEV (*doesn't hear her*). So that was the trip to the city. (*Goes to open the door.*) Come right in, please. (ANTON *and* LOUISE *enter.*) Well, Louise—I may call you Louise, may I not? You came to stay, anyhow.

ANTON (*quietly*). Louise will stay—yes. Mother will ask her—won't you, mother?

MRS. HAMMELEV. Yes, my boy. Now I beg her to stay. And, what's more —that she will always remain with you.

ANTON (*feeling his way*). Where are you, mother? (*He turns intuitively to* LOUISE *and takes hold of her.*) There—what? No, it's you, Louise, isn't it?

(*He pulls her close to himself and is entirely taken up with her.* MRS. HAMMELEV, *who had stretched out her arms toward him, lets them sink with an expression of grief on her face.*)

HAMMELEV (*seeing it*). Yes, mother dear, now you must be content with me.

(*Puts his arms around her waist.*)

MRS. HAMMELEV. He finds me no longer. We drift from each other in the darkness. How much evil we can do where we wish to do only good!

HAMMELEV. It is we who have been blind, mother dear. It is we who cannot see. . . .

CURTAIN

PAN IN PIMLICO

A Fantasy
By Helen Simpson

CHARACTERS

Hob
Dickon
The Man
The Girl

PAN IN PIMLICO

There are certain little streets in London that go to sleep very early. They have to, because the people who live in them must be up very early, and when you are in a small way it comes expensive to burn the candle at both ends. So it happens that although it is not very late—eleven or thereabouts —this particular little street is deserted; it has ceased to be a thoroughfare and has become the perfect setting for a play without an audience. This is far too good an opportunity to lose, and naturally the drama begins at once, with a small figure seated forlornly on the curb, fingering a crude pipe with six holes, but not daring to blow. He is an odd creature to find in such a place. If you met him in Greece you would have no doubt about him; but a faun in England! Still that is what he is, and his name,. HOB, is English enough. He looks furtively up the street and down again, puts the pipe to his lips and ventures a breath. The clear sound of the note startles him. He looks about him once more; but all the windows are shut, and would remain so for any instrument under heaven, even the last trump, though exception must be made in favor of the policeman's whistle. Encouraged, he starts again, this time a tune in earnest. It is not a very sophisticated tune, because he has only six notes to make it with, but it is wistful and delicate, full of weather sounds, and the regret for wide spaces. HOB becomes engrossed in it, and plays one phrase of three notes over and over again; it sounds the same every time but he forgets it in between to remember it deliciously when it comes back a moment later.

He pipes on, one hairy leg crossed over the other, brown fingers dancing on the vents; not a window curtain stirs. He pipes on, thinking of spring and the smell of plowed earth, a host of green and brown thoughts, with now and then a silver trickle as of water; but now someone hears. Something darts round the corner of the tired little street and hides foolishly behind the lamp-post, watching, listening, then, reassured, runs forward into the outer circle of light and is revealed as another faun, similar to HOB, but rather more grown up. His name is DICKON, and he has run all the way from Chelsea, his little hoofs tapping along the hard pavements regardless of noise in his eagerness to be near the sound. He does not greet HOB, who knows very well that he is there, and plays on without turning his head. It is an invitation to dance, which DICKON accepts. But after a time the long run begins to tell on him, and he drops down on his stomach, panting. HOB takes the pipe from his lips.

HOB. Dickon!

DICKON. Sh! Wait till my bellows stop working. (HOB *realizes the point*

169

of this and waits; to pass the time he balances his pipe on his nose. A
last—) That's better. Well, what is it?

Hob. Dickon, did you hear it, or were you just passing?

Dickon. Hear it? I should think so.

Hob. Was it so loud as all that?

Dickon. I don't think the policeman heard, if that's what you'r
afraid of.

Hob. And you came? All that way?

Dickon. It doesn't seem far if you dance it. I wouldn't miss that pip
for all the policemen and elderberry wine in the southern counties. But yo
hardly ever play, nowadays.

Hob. What's the use, here?

Dickon. Why, what's the matter?

Hob. I didn't mean to play to-night. I never do mean to play, really
But sometimes I want to forget the blank walls and the chimney-pots. I wan
to think of how it used to be green, and how we used to come nearly ever
night in summer just to be alone with the trees. I can think of them whil
I play; but then it stops, and they all go, and it's chimneys again, and iro
railings again, and dirty-white lace curtains to keep out the moon.

Dickon. And the people?

Hob. I hate them. I want everything as it used to be. I want the bi
skies, and the trees.

Dickon. They don't make good company, though, trees don't. They'r
always sighing.

Hob. Poor things; they're always in love with the wind.

Dickon. What used to grow here? What were they? Oaks?

Hob. Larches.

Dickon. Larches, aye, that was it. Pretty things enough in spring, wit
their leaves like green feather; but give me an oak or a pine for comfort
something you can rub your back against. These birches and larches, they'r
too thin-skinned.

Hob. They're such dears.

Dickon. Ah, you're young yet. When you're my age—I've forgotten jus
what it is, but when you come to it, you'll look for comfort.

Hob. I'm not so young. I can remember a lot of things.

Dickon. That just shows. You haven't learned to forget.

Hob. Why should I? The old times were the best.

Dickon. The old times. The days when the streets and shops were al
green fields, with a bit of marshland there to the left where the river runs by
Yes, we were happy then, I don't deny it. But you'd do better to forget.

Hob. I can't bear to kill all the happy thoughts.

Dickon. Better that than have them nagging at you. Once you let you
memory get the upper hand you can't enjoy life. It's a youngster's disease
this everlasting harking back.

Hob. But oughtn't I to think about the old times?

DICKON. Not if it makes you look down on the new times. And if for all your trees and hedges, there's something about a chimney-pot—

HOB. No, no—!

DICKON. I say there is. You may not see it, perhaps, but it's there for all that. Why, I know one old fellow, down Eaton Square way, that turns with the wind. He's got a little vane on his head, shaped like a dolphin, and it keeps him dancing, I can tell you. Now a chimney-pot like that, he sees life.

HOB. Who wants to see that sort of life? I want to see live things everywhere.

DICKON. You've only to keep your eyes open.

HOB. Live people shut up in dead squares of brick; live people eating dead things; live people pretending to be dead themselves.

DICKON. Ah, but they haven't altered much underneath; and come to that, earth's always changing, on top.

HOB. You don't see. You don't care. Don't you want it to be like it used to be?

DICKON. I want it to be itself.

HOB. But why should the old things go?

DICKON. To make room.

HOB. But why, why? Don't you remember how one evening, long ago, a boy came past in a red cap just here where we're sitting? He was lost, and so hungry. We gave him what we had to eat, and he dipped up water from the river in his cap to drink. It was clean, then. He wasn't surprised to see us. Why should he be? And we all went to sleep under the trees, only the branches were very young and thin and the moon looked in, and woke us all, so we got up and danced.

DICKON. I've forgotten. But what is there in that?

HOB. And that other night in winter when it was very still and cold, a man came riding by with a girl behind him on the saddle. She was shivering, although his cloak was round her.

DICKON. And then what happened?

HOB. The horse saw us crouching in that warm sheltered hollow by the copse, and stopped. Then the man looked, and held out his hand to us, and said, "Help us, little brothers."

DICKON. We helped him lift her down. Her poor hands were all numb with cold. And we made a little nest of bracken for her.

HOB. She curled round like a squirrel does, and fell asleep at once with her head on the man's knee.

DICKON. But he stayed awake, and so did we, all huddled together because of the frost.

HOB. Then just at daybreak I heard the sound of hoofs two miles away and told him. He woke her, and they saddled the horse and went away together through the wood. But just before the trees hid them she turned and waved her hand to us.

DICKON. I wanted them to stay. We could have hidden them so well, so easily. They were so young, and she had hair the color of plane-tree leaves in October. Well, they're gone. Why do you fret for them? A white hand, a slender branch, a dozen daffodils in a patch of sunlight, that's all you care about. Let them go. They made us happy while we had them. Now we've other things.

HOB. But we weren't meant for the other things. We're different. We weren't meant for towns.

DICKON. Towns don't last.

HOB. But none of our things are left.

DICKON. They'll come again. These people don't know. They think a lot of themselves, but they won't be here always. Then it's our turn.

HOB. But they've spoilt the world, covered it up, hidden it all away.

DICKON. The earth comes back in the end. She's strong. She's patient. She always wins.

(HOB *shakes his head dubiously. It is evident that he remains unconvinced. He fingers his pipe listlessly, and is about to play again when* DICKON *stops him with a lifted hand.*)

DICKON. Hush! Listen.

HOB. What?

DICKON. Footsteps. (*He pricks his ears for a moment and then gives a satisfied nod.*) Only lovers.

HOB. How do you know?

DICKON. Because I do know. Haven't you learnt anything in the last couple of thousand years? Or can't you tell a lover if he hasn't got a white horse?

HOB. It doesn't seem so real without one.

DICKON. They're coming this way. They're coming here.

HOB. Well?

DICKON. I'm going to stay and watch.

HOB. What for? Such dull people; and dirty too.

DICKON. Ah, but they're such dears.

(HOB *sniffs disdainfully, and moves into the shadow of an area. Enter the couple. He is a pallid young man in seedy blue clothes with a greasy muffler; she is young, with chestnut hair and bright swift eyes. At first,* DICKON's *diagnosis would appear to be wrong, for there is nothing of affection in their attitude. They walk furtively, and occasionally the man holds a hand to his swollen eye.* DICKON, *concealed in the neatest way by lying flat in the gutter, is not disconcerted, and grins at them both with a proprietary air.* THE GIRL *pauses to listen, as though she feared to hear someone following; then relaxes, and sits wearily down on one of the mean and dirty steps.*)

THE GIRL. Can't 'ear nothing now. 'E must 'a gone on past.

THE MAN. Blast these coppers, always shoving their noses in where they're not wanted. Let 'im come, that's what I say. Let 'im come. 'E don't know me. I ain't done nothing to 'im.

THE GIRL. 'E knows me, worse luck. But this is off 'is beat; 'e wouldn't never come so far.

THE MAN. If it 'adn't been for that copper I'd 'a 'arf killed 'im.

THE GIRL. You give 'im something to remember as it was. Come and sit down 'ere by me.

THE MAN. If I go back now, 'e'll 'a gorn.

THE GIRL. You done quite enough.

THE MAN. I'd 'a liked to 'a finished 'im orf.

THE GIRL. You sit down. What's the good of talking like that? 'E's gorn 'ome long ago.

THE MAN. Yes, and if it 'adn't been for you 'anging on to me like that 'e wouldn't 'a touched me. I'd 'a marked 'im proper, only for you.

THE GIRL. You marked 'im, all right.

THE MAN. Ah.

THE GIRL. 'E won't go calling a decent girl names like that again in a 'urry.

THE MAN. 'E won't go calling nobody names for the next week or two, not with that mouth.

THE GIRL. It was grand, the way you went for 'im.

THE MAN. Grand eye, that's all I get out of it.

THE GIRL. 'Ow's it looking? Show. (*He submits to inspection. She touches it with experienced fingers and shakes her head.*) You'll want a bit of steak on that.

THE MAN. It feels all soft. It's starting to swell.

THE GIRL. Oh, it does look bad. It must 'urt something cruel.

THE MAN. 'Urt? I don't think. 'E couldn't 'urt a baby with that punch of 'is. 'E never touched me at all. I knocked my 'ead against the 'andle of the swing door, that's what done it. And if you 'adn't gone 'anging on to my arm—

THE GIRL. I know, I know. But you was grand, all the same.

THE MAN. 'E was drunk. 'E couldn't 'ardly put 'is 'ands up. 'E didn't know what 'ad come to 'im when I give 'im that left.

THE GIRL. Drunk 'e was, I know that. But all the same, 'e'd got no call to throw muck at a girl what earns 'er living decent just because she comes in at closing time for a 'arf pint. If you was out all day on a flower patch, rain or shine, with a pair of last year's boots what wanted mending, you'd need a drop of something to warm you.

THE MAN. 'E got something to warm 'im all right.

THE GIRL. Serve 'im right, too, the dirty 'ound! 'T'aint the first time I been 'ome with 'er, 'e says. Let me go, you bloody liar, I says, you been drinking. You get on 'ome, I says. All right, dearie, 'e says, I won't keep you waiting. And then you 'erd what 'e called me.

THE MAN. I 'erd 'im.

THE GIRL. The dirty beast. Charlie, the barman, 'e saw 'ow it was. You go out of 'ere, 'e says, you've 'ad enough. It's 'ard enough to keep a license what with these restrictions and women coppers and all, without we get customers fighting all over the bar. If you want to fight, 'e says, you can go outside.

THE MAN. Call that a fight? Why I could 'a pushed 'is face in, if I'd 'ad time. I could 'a chewed 'im up with one 'and tied be'ind me. Fight!

THE GIRL. I dunno what I should 'a done if it 'adn't been for you.

THE MAN. You wouldn't 'a gone with 'im?

THE GIRL. 'E's such a big feller. All the others is scared of 'im, even when 'e's 'ad too much. I couldn't 'a got away from 'im, not easy. You aren't near as big as 'im. Whatever made you do it?

THE MAN. Oh, well. I dunno.

THE GIRL. That's what I call brave.

THE MAN. Oh, shut your mouth.

THE GIRL. I didn't 'ardly know where to look when 'e come out with that before a lot of strangers.

THE MAN. 'Oo'd listen to a dirty 'og like that?

THE GIRL. You didn't believe it?

THE MAN. Believe what?

THE GIRL. What 'e said.

THE MAN. 'Oo cares what 'e said?

THE GIRL. I'm a good girl, I am.

THE MAN. Well, what of it?

THE GIRL. I mean what 'e said was a lie. 'E'd no call to say it.

THE MAN. I know that.

THE GIRL. Was that why you 'it 'im?

THE MAN. Oh—I dunno.

THE GIRL. Did you think I looked all right?

THE MAN. I didn't notice much.

THE GIRL. You are Mr. Wide Awake, aren't you? What's your name, anyway.

THE MAN. Bert McEvoy.

THE GIRL. Scotch?

THE MAN. No.

THE GIRL. Do you live round 'ere?

THE MAN. I don't live round nowhere.

THE GIRL. Ain't you got no work?

THE MAN. Work? I got work, all right. I got enough of that.

THE GIRL. Oh, all right. I'm not one to ask questions where I'm not wanted.

THE MAN. I'm a sailor, if you want to know.

THE GIRL. Fancy! 'Ave you got your arms tattooed?

THE MAN. No. What 'ud I want to do that for?

THE GIRL. I knew a sailor once, 'e 'ad a mermaid and an anchor and a true lovers' knot all on 'is right arm. 'E'd been out to India and France and all over the place. Do you have to go as far as that?

THE MAN. East coast mostly. London to Newcastle.

THE GIRL. It must be cruel cold in winter.

THE MAN. Not for me. I'm what they call a stoker.

THE GIRL. That's the man what 'as to work the engines, ain't it?

THE MAN. Keep the engines going, you mean.

THE GIRL. Same thing. Ain't you got no friends?

THE MAN. Not 'ere.

THE GIRL. Where, then?

THE MAN. Gravesend.

THE GIRL. Where are you going to sleep?

THE MAN. I dunno.

THE GIRL. You ought to 'ave something put on that eye soon.

THE MAN. I will, when I get back to the ship.

THE GIRL. The ship you're on? Where is it?

THE MAN. Wapping.

THE GIRL. That's a long way from 'ere. 'Ow you going to get back? All the trains is stopped.

THE MAN. Walk.

THE GIRL. You can't go walking about the streets all night after a fight like that.

THE MAN. I tell you I—

THE GIRL. It *was* a fight. I seen 'im 'it you twice in the chest, besides your eye. You can't go all that way, and rain coming on, too.

THE MAN. I'm all right.

THE GIRL. Tell you what—you better come along to my place.

THE MAN. Look 'ere, are you 'aving a game with me?

THE GIRL. What yer mean?

THE MAN. You said just now—

THE GIRL. I said just now I was a good girl. So I am. I don't want none of your lip.

THE MAN. No offense.

THE GIRL. And I'm not going to let a man who done what you done for me go walking about all night long in the wet.

THE MAN. I'll be all right. Don't you trouble about me.

THE GIRL. What you afraid of?

THE MAN. I'm not afraid.

THE GIRL. I tell you my old woman'll make you up a bed.

THE MAN. 'Oo's to pay for it?

THE GIRL. Nobody. You're welcome.

THE MAN. Thank you kindly. I don't want no woman paying for my doss. I'm not that sort. If I ain't got the money I can walk. 'Twouldn't be the first time.

THE GIRL. You're very grand, aren't you? If it was some lady out of a motor car it 'ud 'a been another story. Thank you, my good feller, and 'ere's five bob for your trouble. Yes, and you'd 'a taken it, too.

THE MAN. That's a lie—

THE GIRL. Just because I'm a poor girl you think you're too 'igh and mighty to take anything from me. I'd give you five bob, if I 'ad it.

THE MAN. I don't want no five bob from you nor anybody else. You get 'ome to bed. I don't want no more talking.

THE GIRL. 'Ow can I go to bed and leave you to go walking about in the wet? Why won't you let me—

THE MAN. That's enough of it. I won't take charity from no one.

THE GIRL. 'Tain't charity.

THE MAN. Well, I don't want it, whatever it is, see? 'Ere it is near on twelve o'clock and you been out on your feet all day. You go on 'ome. Don't you trouble about me. Don't you think no more about it. I done no more for you than I'd 'a done for anyone. Say good night, and I'll be getting along. (*He holds out his hand. She sits motionless, almost crying. He touches her on the shoulder.*) Won't you just say good night?

(*She leaps to her feet and strikes furiously at the outstretched hand, her eyes glazing.*)

THE GIRL. No. I wouldn't give that much for a fool like you. That's what you are, a bloody fool. You won't take 'elp from a woman. You'll walk about all night. You won't let no one do you a kindness. Oh, no! Of all the— Oh, I do wish to God there was someone 'ere that'd knock a bit of sense into your silly 'ead!

(*It is an invitation, though crudely worded.* DICKON *rises from the gutter and stands, unmistakable, in the circle of lamplight. The couple stares at him, amazed.*)

THE MAN. 'Ey, look, what is it? Lord, I never knew before what a couple of double whiskies 'ud do on an empty stomach.

THE GIRL. It must be something got loose from the Zoo.

(*They continue to stare at him.* DICKON *advances, unperturbed.*)

THE MAN. What yer want? Go on, you be orf.

DICKON. I'll be off if you will.

THE MAN. Streuth, it can talk.

DICKON. Oh, yes, but I'm not going to. There's been too much talk already.

THE MAN. What yer want?

DICKON. I want to give you a bit of advice.

THE MAN. Eh?

DICKON. Advice. You'd much better go along with her, you know.

THE MAN. What's it got to do with you? What do you know about it anyway?

DICKON. I know a lot. More than you think. I know more about you than you do about yourself.

THE MAN. Ho, do you?

DICKON. You take my advice and go with her.

THE MAN. I don't know 'er. She ain't nothing to me. I don't even know 'er name.

DICKON. That's easy enough. What is your name, nowadays?

THE GIRL. Vi'let. Vi'let Peace.

DICKON. Well, Bert, you go along with Vi'let Peace, and don't let's have any more nonsense.

THE MAN. Don't you go on at me. I'm not going to be told what to do by some one out of a circus.

DICKON. You blind boy.

THE MAN. Eh?

DICKON. Haven't you seen me before?

THE MAN. No, I take my oath I haven't. At least, I don't think so.

DICKON. Vi'let?

(*She continues to stare at him. He looks gravely back. She shakes her head slowly.*)

DICKON. Sure?

THE GIRL. No. Wait 'arf a minute. I seem to feel something—

DICKON. What?

THE GIRL. I seem to feel all cold-like.

DICKON. It was a frosty night. You had nothing to cover your hair. I couldn't see the warm color of it even in the moonlight, against the blue of the cloak—his cloak.

THE MAN. Mine? What yer talking about?

THE GIRL. My hair—the cold night— Oh, wait, wait a minute!

DICKON. Hob and I were lying hidden in the brushwood under the lee of that little hill where the 'buses have to change gear. It was the horse saw us first.

THE MAN. 'Orse? There was something red—

DICKON. His saddle was red, and there was a big wound in his shoulder.

THE MAN. That was coming through the gate. A cove went for me. A cove chucked a spear at me. What the 'ell did 'e want to do that for? I 'adn't done nothing to 'im.

THE GIRL. And I was that cold, wasn't I? I went to sleep straight off, in among the ferns.

DICKON. And then Hob heard them coming.

(*At the sound of his name* HOB *emerges from the area and runs to the corner of the street to keep watch.*)

THE MAN. Cripes! There goes another! What is it?

DICKON. That's Hob.

THE GIRL. But where was we going? What was it? Tell us, quick.

DICKON. There'd been a fight.

THE MAN. A fight?

THE GIRL. Yes, and you'd killed a man. I remember now. We was run-

ning away. You'd killed a man and we was running away, and I got that
tired I couldn't ride no more.

THE MAN. *'Er* name wasn't Vi'let.

THE GIRL. But it was me, all the same. No, I'm 'ere, it can't 'a been me.
Oh Gord, I'm going loopy!

DICKON. It was you.

THE GIRL. It was me, 'e says so. Don't you remember?

THE MAN. I sort of think I do, only I can't call these little coves to mind.

DICKON. You spoke to us. You asked us to help you.

THE MAN. Did I? So I did. Long ago. Donkey's years ago. Lord, what
a rum start!

THE GIRL. We went away together. What happened to us then? I can't
remember nothing, but the feel of the wind through my hair. They didn't
catch us, did they?

DICKON. No.

THE GIRL. And did we live 'appy ever after?

DICKON. I think you must have.

THE GIRL. 'Ear that, Bert? We lived 'appy ever after.

THE MAN. What gets me is 'ow do we come to be 'ere at all? We're both
dead, by rights.

THE GIRL. It's all the same now as it was then. That's 'ow.

THE MAN. I wonder. Maybe. Let's 'ave a look at you.

(*He puts his hands on her shoulders, and turns her towards the light, looking intently into her eyes. She twists away from him after a moment.*)

THE GIRL. You'll know me again, I expect.

THE MAN. Why, you're cold. You're shivering.

THE GIRL. I'm all right.

THE MAN. Put my coat round you.

THE GIRL. No, Bert. I'm all right, really.

THE MAN. Go on, don't keep me standing about.

THE GIRL. You'll get your death. Don't be so silly.

THE MAN. I got to look after you.

THE GIRL. Whatever for?

THE MAN. I got to.

THE GIRL. You're very uppish all of a sudden. What's come over you?

THE MAN. I dunno.

THE GIRL. You wasn't like this a minute ago.

THE MAN. It's different, now.

THE GIRL. What is?

THE MAN. Me. You.

THE GIRL. I dunno what you mean.

THE MAN. 'Ere's what I mean.

(*He kisses her suddenly. At first she stands stiffly, then her hands creep up
to his shoulders and hold him. HOB, at the street corner, turns his head.*)

HOB. Some one coming, two streets away.

The Girl. No, no. It can't be true. It can't be real, not all of a sudden like this.

The Man. It is real.

The Girl. Why, five minutes ago you was going to leave me. You was going back to your ship with your poor eye and all, and never going to see me again. Bert, you're not 'aving me on? You didn't do it just because—I swear I never thought— Oh Bert, it's true, isn't it?

The Man. True's death.

The Girl. What made you think of me like that?

The Man. It must 'a been your 'air.

The Girl. What, my old carrots?

The Man. It looked a treat with the light shining down on it, all sort of gold and brown, like good beer.

The Girl. Bert, you wouldn't 'a done it for anybody else, would you?

The Man. Not me.

The Girl. You did it because it was me. Did you think I looked all right?

The Man. I thought—

The Girl. What?

The Man. I thought you looked—

The Girl. Well?

The Man. All right.

The Girl. Did you?

The Man. By God I did.

(*He is kissing her again when* Hob *suddenly darts back.*)

Hob. The Policeman!

The Man. What?

Dickon. Quick! Run back down Barton Street. He won't get you if you're quick.

The Man. I don't care for 'im.

The Girl. I do, and any'ow we can't stay 'ere all night. Come on, 'urry, can't you?

The Man. But where are we going?

The Girl. We're going 'ome.

(*She huddles his coat round her shoulders, and they run out, hand-in-hand. Just at the corner she stops for a moment to wave; then they disappear, laughing.* Hob *gazes happily after them, and sitting down on the curb begins to coax a glad little tune from his pipe.* Dickon *dances, slapping his sides vigorously, for it has turned cold and the rain is beginning to come down in earnest. Round the corner comes the policeman, his wet cape shining in the light. For a moment he pauses, almost as though he heard the melody flowing from* Hob's *fingers; then, without so much as a glance at the two absurd figures, one leaping wildly, the other crouching by the curb, passes majestically on.*)

CURTAIN

THE FARCE OF THE WORTHY MASTER, PIERRE PATELIN, THE LAWYER

Transcribed from the Mediæval French by Moritz Jagendorf

TO
ST. CLAIRE
AND
STANLEY LADOW

CHARACTERS

THE JUDGE, *whom no man dare judge.*

PATELIN, *the lawyer, a counselor indeed, possessing all those virtues which a good counselor should possess.*

GUILLEMETTE, *his wife, a fit wife for a lawyer.*

GUILLAUME JOCEAULME, *the draper, a successful merchant who has been cheating his customers from the day he began selling.*

TIBALD LAMBKIN, *a shepherd, a fellow, who, if his lot in life had been better, might have become a lawyer like* PATELIN, *or a merchant like* JOCEAULME.

This happened in a little town in France in the Year of Our Lord, 1400.

THE FARCE OF THE WORTHY MASTER, PIERRE PATELIN, THE LAWYER*

SCENE I

(On either side of the stage is a street scene. In back, a curtain is partly drawn to each side showing the interior of PATELIN's *house.* PATELIN *sits in bed reading a large folio; on a chair next to the bed* GUILLEMETTE *sits mending an old dress. On a bench a little to the side are kitchen utensils: a frying pan, a broom, etc. On the bed lies a nightgown and a cap.)*

GUILLEMETTE. You have nothing to say now, I suppose, have you? . . . While I needs must mend rags a beggar would be ashamed to wear—and you, a member of the learned profession! . . a lawyer . . .

PATELIN (*in bed*). There was a time when my door was crowded with clients . . . when I had plenty of work . . . and fine clothes to wear too.

GUILLEMETTE. Of what good is that to-day?—eh?

PATELIN. Wife, I was too shrewd for them. Men don't like people wiser than themselves.

GUILLEMETTE. Aye, you could always beat them at law. . . . But that was long ago.

PATELIN. It hurts me truly to see you mending rags . . . and wives of men who are thick skulled asses wearing golden threaded cloth and fine wool. There is that draper's wife across the way . . .

GUILLEMETTE. Cease the cackling. (*Silently working for a while.*) I'd give something rare and costly for a new gown on St. Mary's day. Heaven knows I need it.

PATELIN. So you do and so do I as well. It is not fit to see one of the learned profession walking about like a beggar on the highway. Ah! If I could only get some clients! I know my law well enough yet. There is not many a one can beat me at the finer points.

GUILLEMETTE. A fig for it all! Of what good is it? We are all but starved . . . and as for clothes—look. (*Holds up the dress she is mending.*)

PATELIN. Silence, good wife! Could I but have some business and put my head with seriousness to it . . . Who knows but the days of plenty would soon enough return!

---

* This version was used by the Washington Square Players.

GUILLEMETTE.   There is not a soul in town but a fool would trust himself to you.   They know too well your way of handling cases.   They say you are a master . . . at cheating.   (PATELIN *rises indignant.*)

PATELIN.   They mean at law . . . at law, good wife.   Ha, I should like to see a lawyer beat me at it . . . and . . . (*Suddenly stops, thinks for a moment, then his whole face lights up.*)   I am going to market.   I have just thought of a little business I have there.   (*Gets out of bed.*)

GUILLEMETTE.   Going to market?   What for?   You have no money.

PATELIN.   I am going to market . . . on business . . . to the long-nosed donkey, our neighbor . . . the Draper.

GUILLEMETTE.   What for?

PATELIN.   To buy some cloth. . . .

GUILLEMETTE.   Holy Saints!   You know well he is more close-fisted than any other merchant in town.   He'll never trust you.

PATELIN.   Ah, that's just why I am going.   The more miserly, the easier to gull; and . . . I have thought of something fine, . . . that will get us enough cloth . . . both for you and me.

GUILLEMETTE.   You must be mad.

PATELIN (*not heeding her*).   Let me see . . . (*Measuring her with his arm's length.*)   Two and one-half for you . . . (*Measuring himself in the same way.*)   three for me . . . and . . . What color would you want it?   Green or red?

GUILLEMETTE.   I'll be pleased with any kind.   Beggars can't be choosers. But don't think I believe what you say.   I am not a fool.   You'll never get any from Master Joceaulme.   He'll never trust you, I am certain.

PATELIN.   Who knows?   Who knows?   He might . . . and then really get paid . . . on Doom's-day. . . . Ho, ho, . . .

GUILLEMETTE.   Don't you think you had better make haste, lest all the cloth be sold?

PATELIN (*offended, walking off*).   Wife, I forgive you.   You are only a woman.   I'll teach you a fine lesson now.   If I don't bring home a fine piece of cloth—dark green or blue, such as wives of great lords wear, then never believe another word I say.

GUILLEMETTE.   But how will you do it?   You haven't a copper in your pocket.

PATELIN.   Ah!   That's a secret.   Just wait and see.   So . . . (*To himself as he walks slowly away.*)   two and one-half for her and three for me. . . . Look well to the house while I am away, wife.   (*Exit.*)

GUILLEMETTE.   What fool of a merchant'll trust him! . . . unless he is blind and deaf!   (*The back curtains are closed and now only the Street Scene is visible.*)

SCENE II

(PATELIN *comes from his door and walks slowly across to* THE DRAPER'S *table.* THE DRAPER *is just coming out with a pack of cloth and wools which he throws on the table. He busies himself arranging his goods.* PATELIN *looks on for a while, then goes right up to him.*)

PATELIN. Ho, there, worthy Master William Joceaulme, permit me the pleasure of shaking your hand. How do you feel?

THE DRAPER. Very fine, the Saints be thanked.

PATELIN. I am truly happy to hear that. And business?

THE DRAPER. You know how . . . one day one way, the other, altogether different. You can never tell when ill luck may blow your way.

PATELIN. May the Saints keep it from your doors! It's the very phrase I often heard your father use. God rest his soul among the Martyrs! What a man he was! Wise! There was not an event in Church, State, or market he did not foretell. No other was more esteemed. And you—they say that you are more and more like him each day.

THE DRAPER. Do seat yourself, good Master Patelin!

PATELIN. Oh, I can well stand.

THE DRAPER. Oh, but you must. (*Forcing him to sit on the bench.*)

PATELIN. Ah! I knew him well, your father. You resemble him as one drop of milk another. Lord, what a man he was! Wise! We, among the learned, called him the weather-cock. Well-nigh every piece of clothing I wore came from his shop.

THE DRAPER. He was an honest man, and people liked to buy from him.

PATELIN. A more honest soul there never was. And I have often heard said the apple has fallen nigh the tree.

THE DRAPER. Of a truth, good Master . . .

PATELIN. It's not flattery either. (*Looking intently at him.*) Lord, but you do resemble him! No child was ever so like his father. Each marked like the other. This is just his nose, his ears, nay, the very dimple on his chin.

THE DRAPER. Yes, they do say I look much like him.

PATELIN. Like one drop of water another. . . . And kind-hearted! He was ever ready to trust and help, no matter who came along. The Lord knows he was ever the gainer by it. Even the worst scoundrels thought twice before cheating him.

THE DRAPER. A merchant must always take heed, good Master Patelin. You can never know whether a man is honest or not.

PATELIN. Aye, that's true. But he had a way of guessing whether it was an honest man he was dealing with that was a marvel to behold. Many a funny tale he told of it—when we sat over a bottle of wine. (*Feeling the cloth on the table.*) What a fine piece of cloth! Did you make it from your own wool? Your father always used to weave his cloths from the wool of his own sheep.

THE DRAPER. So do I, Sir. From the wool of my own sheep.

PATELIN. You don't say so! This is business in a manner I like to see it done. The father all over again.

THE DRAPER (*seeing the possibility of a sale*). Ah, worthy Master Patelin, it is a great hardship indeed, to which I put myself because of this. And the loss and cost! Here a shepherd kills your sheep, I have a case against one of those scoundrels right now. The weavers ask pay like goldsmiths. But to me this is all of little account. . . . I'd attend to the making of each piece myself were it to cost ten times as much as I get in return. . . . So long as I please those who buy.

PATELIN. I can see this. It would make a fine gown.

THE DRAPER. You could not get a finer piece even in the city of Paris.

PATELIN. I am sorry I am not out to do any buying just now, though I am tempted to.

THE DRAPER. Business bad? Money scarce?

PATELIN. No, indeed not. I have a nice little sum of gold crowns even now, but I am about to invest them in something profitable. . . . It's as strong as iron this cloth here. (*Examining it.*)

THE DRAPER. You may take my word for it, Master, there is not a finer or stronger in town. What's more, it can be bought cheap just now. It's a fine investment. Wool is certain to go up.

PATELIN. Aye, it's a fine piece of cloth, Master Joceaulme. . . . But then I shouldn't . . . yet . . .

THE DRAPER. Come, Master Patelin, come. You need the cloth and have the money to buy. Then you'll invest a few crowns less. A man should always have a gown tucked away in the coffer. What would you say if some fine day, comes along the town crier shouting: There has been a new judge appointed and it is Master Pa . . .

PATELIN. You must have your little joke, worthy Sir. Just like your father. I would pass his shop, a friendly chat . . . and then my purse was much the lighter for it. But I never regretted it, never.

THE DRAPER. You wouldn't now, either. It's well worth buying.

PATELIN. It tempts me. . . . It would look well on my good wife, and I could use it well for myself.

THE DRAPER. It needs but your saying. Come, what's the word, Master?

PATELIN. Well. . . .

THE DRAPER. It's yours even though you hadn't a copper.

PATELIN (*somewhat absent minded*). Oh, I know that.

THE DRAPER. What?

PATELIN. I'll take it.

THE DRAPER. That's talking. How much do you want?

PATELIN. How much is it per yard?

THE DRAPER. Which do you like best? The blue?

PATELIN. Yes, that is the one.

THE DRAPER. You want a rock bottom price, no haggling. This is the finest piece in my shop. . . . For you I'll make it twenty-one sous per yard.

PATELIN. Holy Saints! Master! What do you take me for? A fool? It isn't the first time I am buying cloth.

THE DRAPER. It's the price it cost me myself; by all the Saints in Heaven.

PATELIN. That's too much,—entirely too much.

THE DRAPER. Wool costs like holy oil now, and these shepherds are forever robbing me.

PATELIN. Well, there is truth in what you say. I'll take it at the price. I like to see every man make his honest penny. Measure it.

THE DRAPER. How much do you want?

PATELIN. Let me see. Two and a half for her, three for me, that makes five and a half.

THE DRAPER. Take hold there, Master, here they are: (*Measuring out*) one . . . two . . . three . . . four . . . five. I'll make it six. You'll not mind the few coppers more.

PATELIN. Not when I get something fine in return. Then I need a cap too.

THE DRAPER. Would you like me to measure it backwards?

PATELIN. Oh, no, I trust your honesty. How much is it?

THE DRAPER. Six yards at twenty-one sous the yard—that's exactly nine francs.

PATELIN. Nine francs . . . (*Under his breath.*) Here it goes. Nine francs.

THE DRAPER. Yes and a good bargain you got.

PATELIN (*searching his pockets*). No . . . I have but little with me, and I must buy some small things. You'll get your money to-morrow.

THE DRAPER. What!!! . . . No . . . No . . .

PATELIN. Well, good Master Joceaulme, you don't think I carry gold coin with me, do you? You'd have me give thieves a good chance to steal it? Your father trusted me many a time. And you, Master William, should take after your father.

THE DRAPER. I like my money cash.

PATELIN. It's there waiting for you, good Master Draper. You can come for it, I hope.

THE DRAPER. It's bad custom to sell on credit.

PATELIN. Did I ask you for credit: for a month, a week, a day? Come to my house at noon, and you will find your money ready. Does that satisfy you?

THE DRAPER. I prefer my money cash, right on the purchase. . . .

PATELIN. And then, Master William, you have not been to my house for I don't know how long. Your father was there many a time—but you don't seem to care for poor folk like myself.

THE DRAPER. It's we merchants who are poor. We have no bags of gold lying idle for investments.

PATELIN. They are there, Master, waiting for you. And my good wife put a fine goose on the spit just when I left. You can have a tender wing. Your father always liked it.

THE DRAPER. Perhaps. . . . It's true. I haven't been to your house for a long time. I'll come at noon, Master Patelin, and bring the cloth with me.

PATELIN (*snatching the cloth from him*). Oh, I would never trouble you. I can carry it.

THE DRAPER. But . . .

PATELIN. No, good Sir, not for the wealth of the East. I would not think of asking *you* to carry it for *me*.

THE DRAPER. I'd rather . . . well . . . I'll soon be there, Master. I'll come before the noon meal. Don't forget the nine francs.

PATELIN. Aye I'll not. And there'll be a bottle of red wine . . . and a fine fat goose. Be certain to come. (*Exit* PATELIN.)

THE DRAPER. That I will right soon. Ho, ho, ho—ha, ha, ha—the fool! A good bargain he got! Twenty-one sous the yard. It isn't worth one-half that. And on top of it a fine dinner . . . Burgundy wine and a roasted goose! For a customer like that every day! Now I'll take in my cloth. I'll soon to his house. (*Takes up the cloth and leaves.*)

SCENE III

(*The back curtains are drawn aside showing* PATELIN's *chamber.*)

PATELIN (*running in*). Wife, wife . . . (GUILLEMETTE *enters, the old gown in her hand.*) Well, Madam . . . now . . . I've got it, . . . right here I have it. What did I tell you?

GUILLEMETTE. What have you?

PATELIN. Something you desire greatly. But what are you doing with this old rag? I think it will do well for a bed for your cat. I did promise you a new gown and get you one I did.

GUILLEMETTE. What's gotten into your head? Did you drink anything on the way?

PATELIN. And it's paid for, Madam. It's paid for, I tell you.

GUILLEMETTE. Are you making sport of me? What are you plappering!

PATELIN. I have it right here.

GUILLEMETTE. What have you?

PATELIN. Cloth fit for the Queen of Sheba. (*Displaying the cloth.*) Here it is!

GUILLEMETTE. Holy Virgin! Where did you steal it? Who'll pay for it? What kind of a scrape have you gotten into now?

PATELIN. You need not worry, good Dame. It's paid for . . . and a good price at that.

GUILLEMETTE. Why, how much did it cost? You did not have a copper when you left.

PATELIN. It cost nine francs, fair Lady . . . a bottle of red wine . . . and the wing of a roasted goose.

GUILLEMETTE. Are you crazy? You had no money, no goose!!!

PATELIN. Aye, aye, that I did. I paid for it as it behooves one of the learned profession of law: in promissory statements. And the merchant who took them is no fool either, oh, no; not a fool at all; but a very wise man and a shrewd. . . .

GUILLEMETTE. Who was he? How . . .

PATELIN. He is the king of asses, the pope of idiots, the chancellor of baboons . . . our worthy neighbor, the long-nosed Draper, Master Joceaulme.

GUILLEMETTE. Will you cease this jabbering and tell me how it happened? How did he come to trust you? There is no worse skinflint in town than he.

PATELIN. Ah, wife! My head! My knowledge of the law! I turned him into a noble and fine lord. I told him what a jewel his father was; I laid on him all the nine virtues thick as wax, and, . . . in the end he trusted me most willingly with six yards of his fine cloth.

GUILLEMETTE. Ho, ho, ho, you are a marvel! And when does he expect to get paid?

PATELIN. By noon.

GUILLEMETTE. Holy Lord, what will we do when he comes for the money?

PATELIN. He'll be here for it and soon to boot. He must be dreaming even now of his nine francs, and his wine, and the goose. Oh, we'll give him a goose! Now you get the bed ready and I'll get in.

GUILLEMETTE. What for?

PATELIN. As soon as he comes and asks for me, swear by all the Saints that I've been in bed here for the last two months. Tell it in a sad voice and with tears in your eyes. And if he says anything, shout at him to speak lower. If he cries: "My cloth, my money," tell him he is crazy, that I haven't been from bed for weeks. And if he doesn't go with that, I'll dance him a little tune that'll make him wonder whether he is on earth or in hell. (PATELIN *puts on his night-gown and cap.* GUILLEMETTE *goes to the door and returns quickly.*)

GUILLEMETTE. He is coming, he is coming; what if he arrests you?

PATELIN. Don't worry; just do what I tell you. Quick, hide the cloth under the bed clothes. Don't forget. I've been sick for two months.

GUILLEMETTE. Quick, quick, here he is. (PATELIN *gets into bed and draws the curtains.* GUILLEMETTE *sits down and begins to mend the old dress.* THE DRAPER *enters.*)

THE DRAPER. Good day, fair Dame.

GUILLEMETTE. Sh . . . for the Saint's sake. Speak lower.

THE DRAPER. Why? What's the matter?

GUILLEMETTE. You don't know!

THE DRAPER. Where is he?

GUILLEMETTE. Alas! Nearer to paradise than to earth. (*Begins to cry.*)

THE DRAPER. Who?

GUILLEMETTE. How can you be so heartless and ask me that, when you know he has been in bed for the last eleven weeks.

THE DRAPER. Who?

GUILLEMETTE. My husband.

THE DRAPER. Who?

GUILLEMETTE. My husband—Master Pierre, once a lawyer, . . . and now a sick man . . . on his death-bed.

THE DRAPER. What!!!!!

GUILLEMETTE (*crying*). You have not heard of it? Alas! And . . .

THE DRAPER. And who was it just took six yards of cloth from my shop?

GUILLEMETTE. Alas! How am I to know? It was surely not he.

THE DRAPER. You must be dreaming, good woman. Are you his wife?
The wife of Pierre Patelin, the lawyer?

GUILLEMETTE. That I am, good Sir.

THE DRAPER. Then it was your husband, who was such a good friend of
my father, who came to my shop a quarter of an hour ago and bought six
yards of cloth for nine francs. And now I am here for my money. Where
is he?

GUILLEMETTE. This is no time for jesting, good Sir.

THE DRAPER. Are you crazy? I want my money, that's all.

GUILLEMETTE. Don't scream. It's little sleep he gets as it is, and here you
come squealing like a dying pig. He has been in bed for nigh twelve weeks
and hardly slept three nights.

THE DRAPER. Who? What are you talking about?

GUILLEMETTE. Who! My poor sick husband. (*Weeps.*)

THE DRAPER. Come! What's this? Stop that fooling. I want my money,
my nine francs.

GUILLEMETTE (*screaming*). Don't scream so loud. He is dying.

THE DRAPER. But that's a black lie. He was at my shop, but a quarter of
an hour ago.

PATELIN (*groaning from behind the curtain.*) Au, au, au . . .

GUILLEMETTE. Ah, there he is on his death-bed. He has been there for
thirteen weeks yesterday without eating as much as a fly.

THE DRAPER. What are you talking about? He was at my shop just now
and bought six yards of cloth . . . blue cloth.

GUILLEMETTE. How can you make sport of me. Good Master William,
don't you see how he is! Do speak lower. Noise puts him in agony.

THE DRAPER. The devil speak lower! It's you who are howling. Give me
my money, and I'll not speak at all.

GUILLEMETTE (*screaming*). He is deadly sick. This is no time for fooling.
Stop screaming. What is it you want?

THE DRAPER. I want my money, or the cloth . . . the cloth he bought from
me only a little while ago.

GUILLEMETTE. What are you talking about, my good man? There is something strange in your voice.

THE DRAPER. You see, good lady, your husband, Pierre Patelin, the learned
counselor, who was such a good friend of my father, came to my shop but a
quarter of an hour ago and chose six yards of blue cloth . . . and then told
me to come to his house to get the money and . . .

GUILLEMETTE. Ha, ha, ha, what a fine joke. You seem to be in good humor
to-day, Master Draper! To-day? . . . When he has been in bed for fourteen
weeks . . . on the point of death! (*She screams louder and louder all the*

time.) To-day, hey! Why do you come to make sport of me? Get out, get out!

THE DRAPER. I will. Give me my money first . . . or give me my cloth. Where is he with it?

GUILLEMETTE. Ah me! He is very sick and refuses to eat a bite.

THE DRAPER. I am speaking about my cloth. If he does not want it, or hasn't the money, I'll gladly take it back. He took it this morning. I'll swear to it. Ask him yourself. I saw him and spoke to him. A piece of blue cloth.

GUILLEMETTE. Are you cracked or have you been drinking?

THE DRAPER (*becoming frantic*). He took six yards of cloth, blue cloth!

GUILLEMETTE. What do I care whether it is green or blue? My husband has not left the house for the last fifteen weeks.

THE DRAPER. May the Lord bless me! But I am sure I saw him. It was he, I am sure.

GUILLEMETTE. Have you no heart? You have had enough of your fooling.

THE DRAPER. Damn it all! If you think I am a fool . . .

PATELIN (*behind the curtain*). Au, au, au, come and raise my pillow. Stop the braying of that ass! Everything is black and yellow! Drive these black beasts away! Marmara, carimari, carimara!

THE DRAPER. It's he!

GUILLEMETTE. Yes, it is; alas!

THE DRAPER. Good Master Patelin, I've come for my nine francs, . . . which you promised me . . .

PATELIN (*sitting up and sticks his head out between the curtains*). Ha, you dog . . . come here. Shut the door. Rub the soles of my feet . . . tickle my toes. . . . Drive these devils away. It's a monk; there, up he goes . . .

THE DRAPER. What's this? Are you crazy?

PATELIN (*getting out of bed*). Ha . . . do you see him? A black monk flying in the air with the Draper hanging on his nose. Catch him . . . quick. (*Speaking right in* THE DRAPER's *face, who retreats.*) The cat! The monk! Up he flies, and there are ten little devils tweaking your long nose! Heigh, ho! (*Goes back to bed, falling on it seemingly exhausted.*)

GUILLEMETTE (*in loud lamentations*). Now see what you have done.

THE DRAPER. But what does this mean? . . . I don't understand it.

GUILLEMETTE. Don't you see, don't you see!

THE DRAPER. It serves me right; why did I ever sell on credit. But I sold it, I am certain of that, and I would swear 'twas to him this morning. Did he become sick since he returned?

GUILLEMETTE. Are you beginning that joke all over again?

THE DRAPER. I am sure I sold it to him. Ah, but this may be just a cooked up story. By God! . . . tell me, have you a goose on the spit?

GUILLEMETTE. A goose on the spit! No-o-o-o, not on the spit! You are the nearest . . . But I've had enough of this. Get out and leave me in peace.

THE DRAPER. Maybe you are right. I am commencing to doubt it all. Don't cry. I must think this over for a while. But . . . the devil. I am sure

I had six yards of cloth . . . and he chose the blue. I gave it to him with my own hands. Yet . . . here he is in bed sick . . . fifteen weeks. But he was at my shop a little while ago. "Come to my house and eat some goose," he said. Never, never, holy Lord, will I trust anyone again.

GUILLEMETTE. Perhaps your memory is getting wobbly with age. I think you had better go and look before you talk. Maybe the cloth is still there. (*Exit* THE DRAPER, *across the front stage and into his shop.*)

PATELIN (*getting up cautiously and speaking low*). Is he gone?

GUILLEMETTE. Take care, he may come back.

PATELIN. I can't stand this any longer. (*Jumps out.*) We put it to him heavy, didn't we, my pretty one, eh? Ho, ho, ho. (*Laughs uproariously.*)

THE DRAPER (*coming from his shop, looking under the table*). The thief, the liar, the damned liar, he did buy . . . steal it? It isn't there. This was all sham. Ha, I'll get it, though. (*Runs toward* PATELIN'S *house.*) What's this I hear . . . laughing! . . . The robbers (*Rushes in.*) You thieves . . . I want my cloth. . . .

(PATELIN *finding no time to get back into bed, gets hold of the broom, puts the frying pan on his head and begins to jump around straddling the broom stick.* GUILLEMETTE *can't stop laughing*).

THE DRAPER. Laughing in my very nose, eh! Ah, my money, pay . . .

GUILLEMETTE. I am laughing for unhappiness. Look, how the poor man is, it is you who have done this, with your bellowing.

PATELIN. Ha. . . . Where is the Guitar. . . . The lady Guitar I married. . . . She gave birth to twenty little Guitars yesterday. Ho, ho. Come my children. . . . Light the lanterns. Ho, ho, ha . . . (*Stops, looking intently into the air.*)

THE DRAPER. Damn your jabbering. My money! Please, my money . . . for the cloth. . . .

GUILLEMETTE. Again. . . . Didn't you have enough before? But . . . Oh . . . (*Looking intently at him.*) Now I understand!!! Why, I am sure of it. You are mad . . . else you wouldn't talk this way.

THE DRAPER. Oh, holy Lord . . . perhaps I am.

PATELIN (*begins to jump around as if possessed, playing a thousand and one crazy antics.*) Mère de dieu, la coronade . . . que de l'argent il ne me sonne. Hast understood me, gentle Sir?

THE DRAPER. What's this? I want my money . . .

GUILLEMETTE. He is speaking in delirium; he once had an uncle in Limoges and it's the language of that country. (PATELIN *gives* THE DRAPER *a kick and falls down as if exhausted.*)

THE DRAPER. Oh! Oh! Where am I? This is the strangest sickness I ever saw.

GUILLEMETTE (*who has run to her husband*). Do you see what you have done?

PATELIN (*jumps up and acts still wilder*). Ha! The devil . . . the green cat . . . with the Draper. I am happy . . . (*Chases* THE DRAPER *and his wife around the room.* GUILLEMETTE *seeks protection, clinging to* THE DRAPER.)

GUILLEMETTE. Oh, I am afraid, I am afraid. Help me, kind Sir, he may do me some harm.

THE DRAPER (*running around the room with* GUILLEMETTE *clinging to him*). Holy Ghost, what's this? He is bewitching me.

PATELIN (*trying to explain the signs to* THE DRAPER, *who retreats.* PATELIN *follows him whacking the floor and furniture and occasionally getting in one on* THE DRAPER. *Finally* THE DRAPER *gets on one side of the bed, and* PATELIN *on the other. In that position he addresses him in a preachy, serious voice.*) Et bona dies sit vobis, magister amantissime, pater reverendissime, quomodo brulis? (*Falls on the floor near the bed as if dead.*)

GUILLEMETTE. Oh, kind Sir. Help me. He is dead. Help me put him to bed . . . (*They both drag him into bed.*)

THE DRAPER. It were well for me to go, I think. He might die and I might be blamed for it. It must have been some imp or some devil who took my cloth . . . and I came here for the money, led by an evil spirit. It's passing strange . . . but I think I had better go. (*Exit.*)

(THE DRAPER *goes to his shop.* GUILLEMETTE *watches, turning every moment to* PATELIN *who has sat up in bed, warning him not to get out. When* THE DRAPER *disappears, she turns around and bursts out laughing.*)

PATELIN (*jumping out*). Now, wife, what do you think of me, eh? (*Takes the cloth.*) Oh! Didn't we play a clever game? By Saint Peter, I did not think I could do it so well. He got a hot goose, didn't he? (*Spreading the cloth.*) This'll do for both and there'll be a goodly piece left.

GUILLEMETTE. You are an angel. Oh, ho! And now let us go and begin to cut it up. (*Both exeunt.*)

SCENE IV

The Street Scene.

(JOCEAULME *comes from the shop with a piece of cloth under his arm. He is much upset. Looks once more under the table for the cloth which* PATELIN *took.*)

THE DRAPER. The devil! These hounds. . . . I'll get them yet. Here a fine piece of cloth! Only the fiend himself knows who took it—and then that shepherd. To think of it . . . robbing me for years. But him I'll get surely. I'll see him hanged, yet. By the holy Lord I will. (TIBALD LAMBKIN *appears from the other side.*) Ah, here he comes. . . .

THE SHEPHERD (*stutters, thick voice; a typical yokel*). God give you a good day, sweet Sir. I greet you, good Sir. . . . I was not sure it was you, good Sir. . . .

THE DRAPER. You were not, eh? You knave; but you will soon know for certain . . . when your head is on the gallows . . . high up . . .

THE SHEPHERD. Yes, good Sir . . . no . . . I saw the constable . . . and he spoke to me that you want to see me . . .

THE DRAPER. Oh, no! Not I, my fine thief . . . but the judge.

THE SHEPHERD. Oh, Lord! Why did you summon me. I don't know why. I never killed your sheep.

THE DRAPER. Oh, no, you are a saint. It's you, you mangy dog . . . all the while you were robbing me of my sheep. But now you'll pay for it with your head. I'll see you hanged.

THE SHEPHERD. Hanged by the neck! Oh, Lord! Good Master, have pity.

THE DRAPER. Pity, eh? And you had pity when you were robbing me of my cloth . . . I mean my sheep. Thief, scoundrel, you robber . . . where is my cloth . . . my sheep?

THE SHEPHERD. They died of sickness, Sir . . .

THE DRAPER. You lie, you caitiff, you stole them and now . . .

THE SHEPHERD. It is not so, good Master. I swear. On my soul . . .

THE DRAPER. You have no soul, you thief. By all the Saints, I'll see you dangling this Saturday . . .

THE SHEPHERD. Good and sweet Master, won't you please make a settlement . . . and not bring me to court.

THE DRAPER. Away, you thief. I'll make you pay for those six yards . . . I mean those sheep. You just wait. (*Walks off in a fury.*)

THE SHEPHERD. Oh, Lord! I must quickly find a lawyer . . . I've heard of Master Patelin . . . they say no man is better at gulling. It's here he lives. (PATELIN *comes just then from his house. When he sees* LAMBKIN *he tries to get back, fearing it may be* THE DRAPER, *but on hearing his voice he stops.*) Ho, there, Master! Is it you who are Master Patelin the lawyer?

PATELIN. What is you want of him?

THE SHEPHERD. I have a little business for him.

PATELIN. Oh! is it that! Well, I am Master Patelin. Good man, tell me the nature of your business. Is it anything pertaining to the law?

THE SHEPHERD. I'll pay well. . . . I am a shepherd, good Master. A poor man, but I can pay well. I need a lawyer for a little case I have.

PATELIN. Come this way, where we can talk lower. Someone might overhear us . . . I mean disturb us. Now good man, what may your business be?

THE SHEPHERD. Good Master Lawyer, teach me what to say to the judge.

PATELIN. What is it you have done, or has someone done you an injustice?

THE SHEPHERD. Must I tell you everything . . . exactly as it happened?

PATELIN. You can tell me the truth, I am your lawyer. . . . But good friend, counsel is costly.

THE SHEPHERD. I'll pay all right. It's my Master whose sheep I stole who summoned me to the Judge. He is going to have me hanged because I stole his sheep. You see . . . He paid like a miser . . . Must I tell you the truth?

PATELIN. I have told you once. You must tell me how everything really happened.

THE SHEPHERD. Well . . . he paid like a miser . . . so I told him some sheep had the hoof sickness and died from it . . . and I buried them far . . . far . . . away, so that the others shouldn't get it. But I really killed them and ate the meat and used the wool for myself—and he caught me right so that I cannot deny it. Now I beseech you . . . I can pay well—though he has the law on his side . . . whether you cannot beat him. If you can, I'll pay you in fine, gold crowns, sweet Master.

PATELIN. Gold crowns!!! H'm, what's your name?

THE SHEPHERD. Tibald Lambkin, a poor shepherd, but I have a few crowns put aside. You just . . .

PATELIN. What do you intend to pay for this case?

THE SHEPHERD. Will five . . . four crowns be enough, sweet Sir?

PATELIN (*hardly able to contain himself for excitement*). Ah! . . . H'm . . . well . . . that will be plenty seeing that you are a poor man. But I get much greater sums, friend, I do. . . . Did you say . . . five?

THE SHEPHERD. Yes, sweet Sir.

PATELIN. You'll have to make it six. I may tell you though, that your case is a good one, and I am sure to win it. But now tell me, are there any witnesses the plaintiff can produce? Those who saw you killing the sheep?

THE SHEPHERD. Not one. . . .

PATELIN. That's fine.

THE SHEPHERD. . . . But more'n a dozen.

PATELIN. That's bad. H'm, let me see now . . . no . . . (*He seems to hold a deep and learned debate with himself.*) No . . . but . . . The book says otherwise. (*Suddenly his face lights up.*) By all the Saints, and the nine hundred and ninety-nine Virgins! I've got it . . . aye, what a wonderful idea! Two ideas in one day! You can understand a sly trick, can't you, fellow?

THE SHEPHERD. Can I? Ho, ho, ho, ho . . .

PATELIN. But you'll pay as you promised.

THE SHEPHERD. Hang me if I don't. But I can't pay if I hang, ho, ho, ho . . .

PATELIN (*gleefully*). Now, first, you have never seen me; nor heard of me . . .

THE SHEPHERD. Oh, no, not that . . .

PATELIN. Silent until I have finished. Second, you mustn't talk a single word but "Ba" . . . (*Imitating the bleating of a sheep.*) Only bleat like your sheep. No matter what they talk to you. Just say Ba. . . . Even if they call you an ass, or an idiot, or villain, or fool, don't answer anything but Ba. . . . Just as if you were a sheep.

THE SHEPHERD. Oh, I can do that.

PATELIN. Even if I talk to you, say nothing but Ba. . . . And if they split roaring at you, just say Ba . . . The rest you leave to me. I'll get you out for certain.

THE SHEPHERD. I'll surely not say another word. And I will do it right proper.

PATELIN. Your case is as good as won. But don't forget the seven gold crowns.

THE SHEPHERD. I'll sure not, wise and sweet Master Patelin.

CRIER (*is heard from afar*). "The court, make room" . . .

PATELIN. Ah, here they come. Don't forget Ba. . . . I'll be there to help you. And . . . the money . . don't forget that.

(*Attendants, constables, town clerks and villagers enter. Two clerks carry a seat for* THE JUDGE *which is placed in the center of the stage.* THE JUDGE, *fat and grouchy, comes to the front, looks about for a moment, then goes to his seat and sits down.*)

THE JUDGE. If there is any business to be done, come to it; the court wants to adjourn.

PATELIN. May heaven bless you and grant you all you desire.

THE JUDGE. Welcome, Sir. May the Saints give you plenty of clients.

(THE DRAPER *now comes running in.* PATELIN *suddenly realizes that it is against him that* THE SHEPHERD *must be defended and expresses uneasiness. He hides himself behind the crowd.*)

THE DRAPER. My lawyer is soon coming, your Worship. He has a little business elsewhere which is detaining him.

THE JUDGE. You must think I have nothing to do but to wait for your lawyer. You are the plaintiff, aren't you? Bring your complaint. Where is the defendant?

THE DRAPER. Right there, your worship; that lummox shepherd, who has been hiding behind that good citizen there as if he couldn't say ba. . . . But your Honor, it's in fear of justice.

THE JUDGE. Both being present, I will examine you. (*To* THE DRAPER.) Tell me all the facts of your case. Was he in your hire?

THE DRAPER. Yes, your Lordship. He killed my sheep and after I treated him like a father . . .

THE JUDGE. Did you pay him a good wage?

PATELIN (*edging up sideways, and covering his face with his hand*). Your Lordship, I have heard it said that he never paid him a copper for his work.

THE DRAPER (*recognizing* PATELIN). By all that's holy . . . You . . . !!!!??? 'Tis he and no other.

THE JUDGE. Why do you cover your face, Master Patelin?

PATELIN. Oh, your Lordship, I have a terrible toothache.

THE JUDGE. I am sorry for you, for I had one myself the other day. I'll tell you a fine cure, Master. Hold your feet in cold water wherein are three hoofs of a red cow from Gascogne. This'll draw the ache into the nails of your toes and you can then rid yourself of it with great ease by cutting them.

'Tis a sovereign remedy. Try it and see, Master. But let us go on. Come Master Draper, I am in a hurry.

THE DRAPER (*not heeding* THE JUDGE *but still staring at* PATELIN). It's you, isn't it? It's to you I sold six yards of cloth. Where is my money?

THE JUDGE. What is that you are talking about?

PATELIN. His mind is clouded, your Lordship. He is not accustomed to speaking clearly. Perhaps the defendant will enlighten us. You . . .

THE DRAPER. I am not speaking clearly!! You thief . . . liar . . .

PATELIN. Your Worship, I think I understand him now. It's strange how incoherently those who have no legal training speak. I think he means he could have made six yards of cloth from the sheep the shepherd is supposed to have stolen or killed.

THE JUDGE. Aye, so it would seem. Come, Master William, finish your tale.

PATELIN. Get to the facts as the judge directs you.

THE DRAPER. And you dare talk to me like that!

THE JUDGE. Master William, come to your sheep.

(*During the rest of the court scene* PATELIN *works always so as to attract the attention of* THE DRAPER *every time he tries to talk of his sheep, and so diverts his attention from that and leads him to talk of the cloth. Whenever* THE DRAPER *talks of his case,* PATELIN *either sticks his face up to him or places himself in such a position that* THE DRAPER *must see him.*)

THE DRAPER. You see, your Lordship . . . he took my six yards of cloth this morning . . . the thief . . .

THE JUDGE. Do you think I am a fool or an ass? Either you come to the point or I'll dismiss the case.

PATELIN. Your Worship, let us call the defendant. He, I am sure, will speak clearer than this Draper.

THE JUDGE. Yes, that will be wise. Step forward, Shepherd.

THE SHEPHERD. Ba . . . a . . .

THE JUDGE. What's this, am I a goat?

THE SHEPHERD. Ba . . . a . . .

PATELIN. Your Lordship, it seems this man is half-witted and thinks himself among his sheep.

THE DRAPER. Damn you! He can talk, and he is not half-witted either . . . but a thief like you. It was you who took my cloth!

THE JUDGE. Cloth! What are you talking about, anyhow? Now, you either get back to your sheep or I'll dismiss the case.

THE DRAPER. I will, your Lordship, though the other lies as near to my heart, but I'll leave it for another time. That shepherd there . . . he took six yards of cloth . . . I mean, sheep. Your Honor must forgive me. This thief . . . my shepherd, he told me I would get my money . . . for the cloth as soon . . . I mean this shepherd was to watch over my flocks and he played sick when I came to his house. Ah, Master Pierre. . . . He killed my sheep and told me they died from hoof-sickness . . . and I saw him take the cloth . . .

I mean he swore he never killed them. And his wife swore he was sick and said he never took the cloth . . . No, that shepherd there. . . . He took the sheep and made out he was crazy. . . . Oh, my Lord! I don't know what . . .

THE JUDGE (*leaping up*). Keep quiet, you don't know what you are talking about. You are crazy. I have listened to your idiotic talk about sheep, and cloth, and wool, and money. What is it you want here? Either you answer sensibly, or . . . this is your last chance!

PATELIN. There is surely something strange about this poor man's talk, and I would advise that a physician be consulted. At times though, it seems as if he were talking about some money he owes this poor shepherd.

THE DRAPER. You thief! You robber! You might at least keep quiet. Where is my cloth? You have it. . . . You are not sick.

THE JUDGE. What has he? Who isn't sick? Are you going to talk of your business or not?

THE DRAPER. He has it as certain as there is a God in heaven. But I'll speak of this later. Now, I'll attend to this thief, this shepherd.

PATELIN. This shepherd cannot answer the charges himself, your Lordship. I will gladly give my services to defend him.

THE JUDGE. You won't get much for your pains.

PATELIN. Ah, but the knowledge that I am doing a kind and honest deed, and then I may be able to stop this haggling which annoys your Lordship so much.

THE JUDGE. I'd be greatly thankful.

THE DRAPER. You'll defend him . . . you thief . . . you . . .

THE JUDGE. Now, Master William, you keep quiet or I'll have you put in the stocks. I have listened long enough to your idiotic gab. Proceed, Master Patelin.

PATELIN. I thank your Lordship. Now, come on, my good fellow. It's for your own good I am working as you heard me say. Just because I would do you a kind deed. Answer everything well and direct.

THE SHEPHERD. Ba . . . a . . .

PATELIN. Come, I am your lawyer, not a lamb.

THE SHEPHERD. Ba . . .

PATELIN. What's Ba . . . ? Are you crazy? Tell me, did this man pay you money for your work?

THE SHEPHERD. Ba . . .

PATELIN (*seemingly losing his temper*). You idiot, answer, it's I, your lawyer who is talking to you. Answer.

THE SHEPHERD. Ba . . .

THE DRAPER (*who has listened open-mouthed and bewildered*). But, your Lordship, he can talk when he wants to. He spoke to me this morning.

PATELIN (*severely*). Everything happened to you this morning, Master Joceaulme. Now it seems to me, it would be far wiser for you to send this shepherd back to his sheep, he is used to their company far more than to that of men. It does not look as if this fool had sense enough to kill a fly, let alone a sheep.

THE DRAPER. You . . . you . . . robber . . . liar!!!

THE JUDGE. I honestly think they are both crazy.

PATELIN. It seems as if your Lordship is right.

THE DRAPER. I am crazy! You scoundrel! You robber! Where is my cloth? They are both thieves . . .

THE JUDGE. Keep quiet, I say.

THE DRAPER. But, your Lordship!

THE JUDGE. All you get is vexation, in dealing with dolts and idiots, be they male or female, so says the law. To finish this wrangling the court is adjourned.

THE DRAPER. And my cloth . . . my money . . . I mean my sheep! Is there no justice? Will you not listen to me?

THE JUDGE. Eh, listen to you, you miser? You dare scoff at justice? You hire half crazy people; and then you don't pay them, then you bellow something about cloth which has nothing to do with the case and expect me to listen to you?

THE DRAPER. But he took my cloth . . . and he killed my sheep. I swear to you. There he stands, the thief. (*Pointing to* PATELIN.)

THE JUDGE. Stop your bellowing. I discharge this half-witted shepherd. Get home and don't ever come in my sight again no matter how many bailiffs summon you.

PATELIN (*To* THE SHEPHERD). Say thanks to his Lordship.

THE SHEPHERD. Ba . . .

THE JUDGE. By all the Saints, never have I come upon such a nest of idiots!

THE DRAPER. My cloth gone . . . my sheep . . .

THE JUDGE. Huh! You . . . Well, I have business elsewhere. May I never see your like again. The court is adjourned. Good day, Master Patelin.

PATELIN. A joyous day to you.

(*All leave except* PATELIN, THE DRAPER, *and* THE SHEPHERD.)

THE DRAPER. You thieves . . . you scoundrels! You . . . You . . .

PATELIN. Don't shout yourself hoarse, good Master Joceaulme.

THE DRAPER. You stole my cloth and played crazy . . . and now it was because of you, that I lost my sheep . . .

PATELIN. A fine tale! Do you think anyone will believe you?

THE DRAPER. I am not blind. Didn't I see you dancing this morning. I saw you . . .

PATELIN. Are you so certain. Good Sir, it may have been Jean de Noyon. He resembles me very much.

THE DRAPER. But I know you when I see you. You screamed and acted mad, shouting a tale of dogs and . . .

PATELIN. Perhaps you imagined it all. Go back to my house and see if I am not *still* there.

THE DRAPER (*looks much puzzled*). May the Lord . . . Perhaps . . . But I'll go to your house and if I don't find you there, I'll go to the Judge and see to it that he listens to my story. I'll get a lawyer from Paris. (*To* THE SHEPHERD *who has been standing at a safe distance.*) You thief! I'll get you yet. I'll go to your house now. (*To* PATELIN.)

PATELIN. That's a wise action. (*Exit* THE DRAPER.)

PATELIN. Now Tibald, my fellow. What do you think of me? Didn't we do a fine piece of work?

THE SHEPHERD. Ba . . .

PATELIN. Yes. Ho, ho—wasn't it great?

THE SHEPHERD. Ba . . .

PATELIN. No one is near now; your Master is gone. It was a great idea, wasn't it? This legal stroke. You may speak now without fear.

THE SHEPHERD. Ba . . .

PATELIN. I said you could speak without fear, no one is near. Where is the money?

THE SHEPHERD. Ba . . .

PATELIN. I can't stay with you all day. What is this game?

THE SHEPHERD. Ba . . .

PATELIN. How now? Come I have business elsewhere.

THE SHEPHERD. Ba . . .

PATELIN. What do you mean. You are not going to pay?

THE SHEPHERD (*with a grin*). Ba . . .

PATELIN. Yes, you played your rôle well, good Lambkin. But now it's over. Next time you may count on me again. Now my money; the six crowns.

THE SHEPHERD. Ba . . .

PATELIN (*sees the game now, stops. In a somewhat pathetic voice*). Is that all I am going to get for my work?

THE SHEPHERD. Ba . . .

PATELIN (*getting furious*). By the holy Lord, I'll have a bailiff after you, you thief . . . you scoundrel . . . you robber . . .

THE SHEPHERD. Ho, ho, ho . . . Ba . . . ! The Judge said I need never come back. And—ho, ho, ho, I never knew you . . . Ba . . . a . . . a! (*Runs out.*)

PATELIN (*silent for a time, then grinning pathetically*). Alas! 'Tis only paying me in my own coin. . . . Nevertheless 'twas a fine idea. . . . (*Exit.*)

CURTAIN

JUBILEE
(FEEST)

A PLAY

By HERMAN HEIJERMANS

Translated from the Dutch by Lilian Saunders and
Caroline Heijermans-Houwink

CHARACTERS

The Director of the Prison
The Warden
Number Seven
Number Eighty-Three
His Mother
Number Two Hundred and Fifteen
Number One Hundred and Thirteen
His Daughter
Number Sixty-Seven

JUBILEE

The DIRECTOR'S *office has through barred windows at the back a view of the courtyard of the prison. There are doors on each side. Flower pots are on the window sills. Above a filing cabinet hangs the portrait of a king. There is a small writing desk. Floods of sunlight come through the windows.*

FIRST JOY

DIRECTOR (*a gray-haired functionary, military bearing, serious manner, decorated*). Hasn't the bell rung yet?

WARDEN (*a brisk young fellow*). It must be on the stroke. (*He opens the door and listens. The prison bell begins to ring. He looks at his watch.*) Two minutes behind time, Meneer.

DIRECTOR. Let Number Seven come in.

WARDEN. It is his recreation period, Meneer.

DIRECTOR. So much the better. It will be his last time.

WARDEN (*astonished*). His last time?

DIRECTOR. Off with you. (*While the* WARDEN *is gone, he takes some documents out of the filing case and lays them on the desk, steps to the door and speaks through the opening.*) You must have patience, people. Every one his turn. And be quiet, you understand. The water works you will keep for the outside, hé? And no scenes, otherwise you delay each other. (*To* NUMBER SEVEN, *who stands hesitating in the other doorway.*) There, there, come in. (*He sits at the desk.*) Sit down there. (*He searches for a document, rummaging through the papers, then looks up smiling.*) Don't you understand? You are to sit down.

NUMBER SEVEN (*he is a sallow, bent little man, with white hair and stubbly gray beard, watery eyes, and wrinkled, skinny neck. His jaws move constantly as if chewing, and he fumbles his cap uneasily.*) Sit down? Here? In my recreation period? And I couldn't help it yesterday—I didn't—I only laughed. If they have put that in the report—

DIRECTOR (*kindly*). There is nothing in the report—or perhaps, yes—I have not looked.

NUMBER SEVEN (*interrupting him, excitedly*). Somebody sat there sneezing, sneezing so that the domenee had to stop because of him—then I got a giggling fit—then the warden said that if I laughed again—

DIRECTOR (*threatening him with his finger smilingly*). So! That was you then in the church? (*Looking at a paper*). Yes, it is in the report. (*The ringing of the bell ceases.*) Laughing during the service—I ought to give you—

203

NUMBER SEVEN. Almighty God! I didn't laugh at the domenee—for the domenee I would go through fire and water, if he would ask me—but that one sneezed so—he couldn't leave off—every time he tried, he began again in the stillness—he squeaked so, he squeaked like a mouse in the wall, héhéhé! Don't take it ill, Meneer.

DIRECTOR. Good, good—

NUMBER SEVEN. If for that you want—

DIRECTOR. I want nothing. I only want you to sit down a minute.

NUMBER SEVEN. And my recreation period? (*Whimpering.*) Anybody could get a laughing fit from nervousness—

DIRECTOR (*smiling*). We'll give you a long recreation period—uh—what is your name, now? (*He opens the cover of the dossier.*)

NUMBER SEVEN. Seven.

DIRECTOR. No, no.

NUMBER SEVEN (*firmly*). Yes, yes, Seven—the seventh cell in the first corridor.

DIRECTOR. I mean your other name—your own name.

NUMBER SEVEN (*laughing foolishly, not understanding*). Héhéhé! Héhéhé! Seven, seven.

DIRECTOR (*reading*). Gerrit Jan Muller, born—

NUMBER SEVEN (*trembling*). Is she dead?

DIRECTOR. Who?

NUMBER SEVEN. Say it out plain—without fiddle-faddles—just like before—before—five, six years ago.

DIRECTOR. Who then—what?

NUMBER SEVEN. My daughter, in the asylum.

DIRECTOR. No, Gerrit Muller—at least not that we know. You can go yourself and find out about her if you wish.

NUMBER SEVEN (*not understanding*). I can do what?

DIRECTOR. Find out for yourself. You have been by the royal decree, freed from—let me see—from the last four years of your sentence. The king has been dead for three weeks. Day before yesterday, Saturday, his successor signed a decree of pardon for you and four others. Well? ·Well? Have you nothing to say to that?

NUMBER SEVEN (*laughing foolishly*). Héhéhé! Héhé! Yes, yes.

DIRECTOR. You may go, Gerrit—uh—uh—

NUMBER SEVEN. Seven, Meneer.

DIRECTOR. From this moment you are no longer Number Seven.

NUMBER SEVEN. No, no—that—that—that—that—

DIRECTOR. You are as free as a bird.

NUMBER SEVEN. Héhéhé! As a bird! Now may I go to recreation—and laugh? I did laugh, that's true—I don't lie about that—but the warden, he jerked me—

DIRECTOR. Haven't you understood anything of what I have just told you. Gerrit Muller?

NUMBER SEVEN. Yes, yes. She isn't dead yet—it lasts a long time with her
—a long time. I know about my wife—I know about my son—but she is
tough—maybe tougher than I am. How is it that crazy people—

DIRECTOR (*with emphasis*). Gerrit Jan Muller. (*He does not listen*).
Number Seven!

NUMBER SEVEN. Yes, Meneer.

DIRECTOR. Number Seven, the new king has given orders that you are to
be set free to-day. Do you understand? You are free.

NUMBER SEVEN. That's good, Meneer.

THE DIRECTOR. You have had plenty of opportunity to think over the crime
for which you were condemned more than twenty years ago. Isn't that so,
Number Seven? You left the community as a criminal. We send you back
to it, let us hope, as a sincerely repentant man. Is that clear? You are free.
You will be paid what you have earned by your work. Your record here has
been excellent, never anything serious in your report.

NUMBER SEVEN. The report—I sat there praying with my hands folded—
you can ask anybody—the warden could have seen that himself—if he didn't
have a spite against me—

DIRECTOR (*ringing*). Yes, yes. (*To* WARDEN). Number Seven is free.
He is on the pardon list. Will you go with him to the administrator?

WARDEN. You might give us your fist on that, Seven.

NUMBER SEVEN. What do you mean?

DIRECTOR (*to the* WARDEN). It is impossible to make him understand—he
can't take it in.

WARDEN. You don't have to go back to your cell any more, Seven. (*Laughing.*) You're put out in the street, man!

NUMBER SEVEN (*feebly*). In the street? Not back—not back any more?
Who said that?

DIRECTOR (*laughing*). The new king.

NUMBER SEVEN (*slowly, his understanding wavering*). I can't stay here
any longer? Why? What—what have I done?

DIRECTOR. Your conduct has been excellent all these years, both under me
and under my predecessor, Gerrit Jan Muller.

NUMBER SEVEN (*as if at last waking up*). Why don't you say "Seven"
any more? Why do you call me by my name? Yes, that used to be my
name.

DIRECTOR. I call you by your name as every one will do from now on since
you are not to stay here any longer.

NUMBER SEVEN. I can't stay any longer?

DIRECTOR. No, and now go with the warden—others are waiting.

NUMBER SEVEN (*excitedly*). I won't go with him—I don't know anything
outside any more—nothing at all—I thought I could stay here until I died—
domenee always said so—what can I do outside—outside—?

DIRECTOR (*pointing to the window*). That you will soon see when you get
out into the sunshine.

Number Seven (*dully*). What month is it?

Director (*making a sign to the* Warden *to leave the room*). June.

Number Seven (*counting on his fingers*). June, June—What day?

Director. Monday, the fourteenth. Is that enough?

Number Seven. Monday—Monday. June—June. What year have we? (*Laughing feebly.*) I don't know anything any more.

Director. 1906. In 1885 you were condemned for—for the poisoning—

Number Seven (*holding up his hands as if warding off some horror*). Of two—of two! (*He sinks into a chair and begins to cry shudderingly.*) Don't make me go away—what can I do outside—what can I do outside!

Director. Come, come. You have perhaps friends—acquaintances?

Number Seven. No.

Director. Will you go back to your old home? One of the guards will take you to the station.

Number Seven. No.

Director. Have you had no visitors in these last few years?

Number Seven. No.

Director. If you would like to go to the domenee's house—

Number Seven. No. Yesterday I laughed. So he would—

Director. Gerrit Muller, we can't keep you here.

Number Seven (*stammering with agitation*). If I promise never to laugh in the church again? What can it matter to the new king if I stay here? The domenee promised me—you can ask him. What could I do outside—outside—to have mud flung on me in the street again—like when I came from the judges, after they had condemned me for—for—

Director. For the murder of two—

Number Seven. Yes, "Thou shalt not kill"—but I was as crazy as my daughter then—and the money of—of—

Director. Of the legacy.

Number Seven. Of the legacy—yes, yes—I couldn't get it out of my head and my wife—my wife would say—if only they—if only they were out of the way then we wouldn't be beggars any more. (*Suddenly bursting out in despair.*) Why did you have to drag all that out again? When I was so quiet, when I had forgotten—after all those years—all those years—when it ate into my brain as I lay awake in my cell. Will they stand outside again yelling and screaming, "Poisoner! Poisoner! Poisoner!"

Director. Muller, control yourself. No one will recognize in you the man of twenty years ago.

Number Seven. Yes, yes they will know me—all of them!

Director. Oh, come! There hangs a looking glass. If you don't believe me, look in it. Be reasonable. You are leaving the prison with a nice little sum of money. The domenee will keep an eye on you.

Number Seven (*gets up slowly, looks timidly in the glass, starts back*). Is that—is that—*me?*

Director (*kindly*). Do you think they will recognize you?

NUMBER SEVEN (*still looking in the glass*). How many years is it since I have looked in a glass?

DIRECTOR. Over twenty. (*Clapping him on the shoulder.*) Ask the administrator for anything you need, and come tell me good-bye when you are through.

NUMBER SEVEN. No, no, that's not me—that's somebody else, hé?

DIRECTOR (*a little impatient*). Yes, yes. (*He goes to the door and beckons to the* WARDEN.)

NUMBER SEVEN (*thoughtfully*). Was I brown or black? Brown, brown. And now like this! Now like this! Héhéhé! That's queer, that you can forget your own face—

WARDEN (*at a sign from the* DIRECTOR). Ready, Seven? We'll get a top notch outfit for you.

NUMBER SEVEN. Tha's good.

DIRECTOR. Well, Muller, don't you say thank you?

NUMBER SEVEN (*again vacantly*). Yes, yes—but now can I (*speaking slowly and with difficulty*)—now can I go to recreation? And for the laughing —that won't happen any more—no, no—no matter what goes on in the church.

DIRECTOR (*to the* WARDEN). The next. (*He looks in the papers.*) Number Eighty-three.

WARDEN. Jawel, Meneer.

(NUMBER SEVEN *has been standing before the mirror, his lips mumbling stupidly, he cries out as the* WARDEN *takes him by the arm, then goes off with him as if in a dream.*)

* * *

SECOND JOY

DIRECTOR (*rising up with the paper in his hand, he opens the door, and speaks into the next room*). Is there any one here for Eighty-three?

WOMAN'S VOICE. I, Meneer.

DIRECTOR. The mother?

MOTHER. Yes, Meneer.

DIRECTOR (*with a sign that she is to wait a minute*). No, no, Juffrouw! Presently, presently. Not until I ring. He is not here yet. (*He closes the door. There is a knock at the other door.*) Yes?

WARDEN. Eighty-three, Meneer.

DIRECTOR. Eighty-three?

EIGHTY-THREE (*a young fellow with a crop of unruly brown hair, brown mustache, strong, large-boned face, defiant expression, distrustful manner, a scar on the left temple*). Yes, Meneer.

DIRECTOR. Melchert de Waal?

EIGHTY-THREE. Yes, Meneer.

DIRECTOR. Melchert de Waal, in 1904 you were sentenced to three years imprisonment for assault with intent to kill, upon a certain Jan Smees—

EIGHTY-THREE (*quickly*). Not with intent to kill.

DIRECTOR. It doesn't matter, I am not the judge. These distinctions do not concern me. De Waal, I have good news for you. Your mother, who is waiting for you in the next room, whose sole support you were, I believe—(*the prisoner nods stolidly*)—your mother has made such an earnest appeal, supported by the burgemeester of your town, who seems to interest himself in you —your exceptional record as soldier in the colonies—did you bring back that scar from there? (*The prisoner nods.*)—Your exemplary conduct in the prison, with the exception of your obstinacy toward the domenee, during the first month, when you stubbornly refused food—

EIGHTY-THREE. Yes, I wanted to croak.

DIRECTOR (*kindly*). Exactly—in which we did not assist you—and not so unkind on our part, Eighty—(*He corrects himself.*)—de Waal—because if we had let you have your way then, my friend, I should not now be announcing to you the pleasant surprise that the last nine months of your sentence have been remitted, by grace of the new king, crowned to-day. You are free!

EIGHTY-THREE (*brightening up*). At once.

DIRECTOR. Within the hour, after a few formalities.

EIGHTY-THREE (*joyfully*). Thank you.

DIRECTOR. You must understand that the royal pardon must be accompanied on my part by an admonition to you, probably superfluous in this case, to repent—

EIGHTY-THREE. Jawel, jawel!

DIRECTOR. No, de Waal, it is not well. In your report I find the statement that you adopted a very insolent attitude—let me finish my sentence, will you —especially toward the domenee, when he visited you in your cell.

EIGHTY-THREE. I never had any use for domenees.

DIRECTOR. That is no excuse. Instead of insulting him, which of course we could not have allowed, you took the method of refusing to answer him. If I had added that to your report, I doubt if—

EIGHTY-THREE. To talk of repentance, when I felt no repentance—that I could not do. I have never lied—not before the judges—not before anyone.

DIRECTOR. Not repent! You feel no repentance? You who in your rage almost cut a man to pieces!

EIGHTY-THREE. I would to-day—

DIRECTOR (*sharply*). You would what?

EIGHTY-THREE (*sullenly*). Nothing.

DIRECTOR. Are you going back into the community after more than two years of imprisonment, with such resentment in your heart?

EIGHTY-THREE. I did not say that. I have no resentment. But, I have no remorse. You wouldn't have either, Meneer, if you saw a girl that you were crazy about running with another man, once, and then again and then a third time—making a fool of you—always lying. Didn't she say herself before the judges that she had treated me like a dog? Dogs bite. So do I. Eight hundred and twenty-seven slowly counted days—yes, slowly counted—

I saw her face as she sat on the witness bench crying—and that helped my defense. And her letters, in the beginning, now and then—for she knew how to write—kept my heart warm. When I am free, and go with my mother to see her—if she is not waiting for me at the gate—I shall not have to lower my eyes before her. It was my duty, because I was her protector and because she went with the other because she was afraid of him. I could not let her be afraid. Eight hundred and twenty-seven days—and nights—and nights— I thought always "Dirty rascal, you with your Judas tricks to take away my girl." My girl, all mine, for I brought her from the East—hired her to help my mother in the shop. "Dirty rascal, to make her afraid, to set her against me." If I had killed him, I might have felt remorse, but since they patched him up in the hospital, he got only what he deserved, only what he deserved. I couldn't go to the judges—how they would have laughed—to lay a complaint that a rascal wouldn't let my girl alone. A man has to attend to such things for himself. I'll marry her within the month—even if we haven't a penny to live on, I'll marry her. You can't think, Meneer, how that thought kept me up—held me steady when the whole damned prison began to turn—to turn— to turn. When I marry her, my eight hundred and twenty-seven days and nights will be the proof that I fought like a man to get her.

DIRECTOR. Let me hope for you then, de Waal, that you, as the husband of that girl, will be contented and never again give up to your anger like a wild beast.

EIGHTY-THREE. Now, that you can count upon, surely, surely.

DIRECTOR. The administrator will pay you what you have earned for your work. Your mother has clothes for you. (*He rings.*)

WARDEN (*entering*). Yes, Meneer?

(*The* MOTHER *coming through the other door, at almost the same moment, begins to cry.*)

DIRECTOR (*to the* WARDEN). Just a minute. (*The* WARDEN *goes out.*) Have you clothes for your son in that valise, Mother?

MOTHER (*a little old middle-class woman with a care-worn face, eyes red from weeping, and a bent back*). Yes, Meneer, a new suit and a shirt front, and a—(*bursting into tears.*)

EIGHTY-THREE (*making a desperate effort to control himself by an assumption of jollity*). Now! Hé! Hé! Now! Come, come! It is finished, Mother? Is it for that you came here? Why should you stand there blubbering when I am going away with you? (*She flings herself upon his neck.*) Now! Hé! Hé!

MOTHER. The first time that I don't see you behind bars!

EIGHTY-THREE (*with a pretense of gayety*). You mustn't take it ill of her, Meneer. She keeps a fire and water shop—always showers!—Hé! Hé! Now!

DIRECTOR. You can take him right through the door, vrouwtje. The Warden will show you the way.

MOTHER (*with repressed agitation*). May I say something first—just a little minute?

DIRECTOR. If you don't make your minute too long.

MOTHER (*greatly agitated*). I wish that you—that you—I don't dare—

DIRECTOR. What is it then?

EIGHTY-THREE (*tense with anxiety*). Is it anything—wrong with Marie

MOTHER (*agitatedly*). No, no. Why should you think of that?

DIRECTOR. Then why don't you tell him? My time is limited, Mother.

MOTHER. It's nothing. It's my nerves.

THE DIRECTOR (*ringing*). Then I wish you the best of luck—and to you de Waal, I wish the fighting strength of a fine fellow who has a mother and a good wife to look out for. (*To the* WARDEN.) The next. Three hundred and fifteen.

MOTHER (*sinking into a chair in a nervous palsy and turning to the* DIRECTOR *in fear of her son*). Ach, God, Meneer, tell him—you tell him—while he is here yet—while we are not alone—before he is free—tell him that this wretch of a girl that helped to put him in prison and brought ruin on his whole life—the trollop—the trollop—to help send my boy to prison—

EIGHTY-THREE (*controlling himself in torture*). Tell me yourself—I am no child—I can stand it.

DIRECTOR. She refuses to see him?

MOTHER. Ach, God, no! If it was only that—if it was only that! She took up with that scoundrel—they are off to America—and I couldn't help it —it wasn't my fault—as true as the good God hears me—I did everything—everything I could for her—

EIGHTY-THREE. To America? When?

MOTHER. A year ago, jongen. I couldn't help it—I went after them—I—

EIGHTY-THREE (*dully*). Why are you only telling me now? Didn't you have the chance before when you came to see me?

MOTHER. I didn't dare—I was so afraid, Meneer, that he would make way with himself in prison—he loved her so, the trollop, the slut, the huzzy—more than he ever loved me—

DIRECTOR (*after a pause*). After all you have just said, de Waal, I understand fully that your mother's news is a crippling blow to you. Bear it like a man. Nobody can help you or advise you. Try to be a good son—that is all that is left to you.

EIGHTY-THREE (*staring in front of him with the eyes of a hunted animal*). With—with—with him!

DIRECTOR. And perhaps in the end it may turn out to be not the worst thing for you—isn't that true, juffrouw?

MOTHER. I say that too—if he will only—

EIGHTY-THREE (*breathing heavily, hearing nothing*). With him! With him!

WARDEN (*at a sign from the* DIRECTOR). Come, Eighty-three, others are waiting.

EIGHTY-THREE (*unheeding*). With him—him—oh, Jesus, Jesus!

MOTHER (*anxiously*). Tell him that I did everything I could.

DIRECTOR. He will not doubt that, moedertje. (*Going up to the prisoner and giving him his hand.*) Good-by, de Waal, and be brave.

EIGHTY-THREE (*staring straight before him*). Thank you.

DIRECTOR. Your mother has clothes for you.

MOTHER. Yes, Meneer, underclothes and a new collar and a fine suit. (*Beginning to cry again.*) ,Come now, jongen, don't stand there so unhappy— there are plenty of others—besides that huzzy that helped put you in prison—

EIGHTY-THREE (*absently*). Don't cry. Be quiet. It is all right. It's all right. Good-by, Meneer, good-by. (*He follows the* WARDEN, *the* MOTHER *takes up the valise and carries it after them.*)

* * *

THIRD JOY

DIRECTOR (*stands in thought for a few moments, looking into the court, then takes a chair behind the desk and lights a cigar. There is a knock*). Yes?

WARDEN. Two hundred and fifteen, Meneer.

TWO HUNDRED AND FIFTEEN (*a young man, bald on the crown, with a face worn by dissipation, a mustache with turned up points, a nonchalant manner*). *Merci,* Meneer! If it were permitted I would like to fall on your neck!

DIRECTOR. How do you know?

TWO HUNDRED AND FIFTEEN (*pointing to the* WARDEN). From him! I could dance for joy! This I must say, that the new king seems like an angel to me.

DIRECTOR. Calm yourself. (*To the* WARDEN.) And will you in the future be so kind as to hold your tongue as I instructed you?

WARDEN. Jawel, Meneer—but he—

THE DIRECTOR. That will do. Keep to your instructions. (*He motions to the* WARDEN *to go out.*) Two hundred and fifteen—Bastiaan van—

TWO HUNDRED AND FIFTEEN. Bastiaan van Velsen, *à votre service*—

DIRECTOR. It is certainly not necessary, van Velsen, for me to bring to your memory that in 1905—

TWO HUNDRED AND FIFTEEN (*airily*). No, bring nothing to my memory.

DIRECTOR. Will you take it so flippantly when you realize that in the waiting room outside there is absolutely no one of your family—neither your father nor your mother—

TWO HUNDRED AND FIFTEEN. Mother would find it rather impossible, Meneer—she died when I was still in swaddling clothes.

DIRECTOR. She was then more fortunate than your father who has had to live through the whole scandal.

TWO HUNDRED AND FIFTEEN. You may say so! You may say so! *A qui la faute?* If papa had just paid up for me, I should never have had to take advantage of your hospitality!

DIRECTOR. Bastiaan van Velsen, I appeal earnestly to your conscience—

TWO HUNDRED AND FIFTEEN. Excuse me, Meneer, for interrupting you—please put down that exquisite cigar—or at least let me have a pull at it—now that I don't bear my number any more. For eight months every kind of smell except that of an after-dinner cigar! (*The* DIRECTOR *gives him one smiling.*) *Merci!* (*He lights it and takes a whiff.*) Divine! You are a gentleman from top to toe.

DIRECTOR. Meneer van Velsen, you should remember—

TWO HUNDRED AND FIFTEEN. Everything! Everything! Now, don't let me get sentimental—I suffocate with remorse—*parole d'honneur!* But the little ladies, Meneer! That rabble of little ladies!—and thousands of dollars lying every day under your nose—and your sworn oath that you will put it back again! Ach, ach! Yes, look serious, now. In a prison for men—for men only, you could not lose as much hair as I have lost.

DIRECTOR. Through the pressing request of your brothers, who were present at the audience of the king, and through my somewhat—colored report, as you know—

TWO HUNDRED AND FIFTEEN. *Merci,* you are a gentleman.

DIRECTOR. You were given your pardon. Your father has sent me this envelope for you with the understanding that you are to be out of the country in twenty-four hours. If you behave yourself in foreign lands they will not leave you in want.

TWO HUNDRED AND FIFTEEN (*taking the envelope without opening it*). Now look at the logic of an old man! If he had handed over that gold a year or so ago—(*Opening the envelope.*)—four figures! More than I expected! Must I sign a receipt for it? No?

DIRECTOR (*laughing*). We hope you will not come back for it a second time.

TWO HUNDRED AND FIFTEEN. Very well, Meneer, very well!

DIRECTOR (*holding out his hand*). *Adieu,* Meneer van Velsen.

TWO HUNDRED AND FIFTEEN. We won't say "See you later." How shall I cash this little scrap of paper?

DIRECTOR. The administrator will cash it, and at the same time pay you what (*smiling*) you have honorably earned.

TWO HUNDRED AND FIFTEEN. Still more money! It is a joy to live! *Adieu,* Meneer, and many thanks for the pleasant visit. (*Twisting his mustache in front of the glass.*) I have actually put on weight. (*To the* WARDEN *at the door.*) No, don't take me out yet, I feel so at home here. *Après vous.* (*Turning back at the door.*) Do you buy those cigars somewhere in the neighborhood?

DIRECTOR (*laughing*). From Bon in the Langstraat—La Estrella.

TWO HUNDRED AND FIFTEEN. *Merci, merci.* I shall take a box with me to Paris—smuggle them in! Ha ha ha! A new crime—incorrigible! Ha ha ha! Paris! The city of light! The city of little ladies—Galette! Pognon! Ha ha ha! (*He goes out.*)

* * *

FOURTH JOY

DIRECTOR (*with papers in his hand at the left door*). Who is here for One hundred and thirteen? (*Voices are heard in the waiting room*—"One hundred and thirteen! For you, One hundred and thirteen! One hundred and thirteen.") Quietly, quietly! Not all at once. (*A voice*—"She is deaf and dumb, Meneer.") Come in. (*Speaking louder.*) Hundred and thirteen.

(*The* DAUGHTER, *looking closely at his lips, nods.*)

DIRECTOR (*using gestures when possible*). Are you the daughter? (*She nods.*) Couldn't your mother come? (*She controls a sob.*) Now, now, now! Is mother sick? (*She takes a pencil out of her pocket, writes a few words in a note book and gives it to him.*) So? In the hospital? Very sick? (*She writes the answer.*) You have just had word that she cannot live? Very sad! Very sad! Now go back into the waiting room until I call you. (*He rings. To the* WARDEN.) Hundred and thirteen. No, don't stay here, juffrouw. (*Louder.*) Wait in there—There. (*She writes.*) Will I tell him about your mother? Yes, yes.

ONE HUNDRED AND THIRTEEN (*a short, heavy set man with a lean, sharp face, black hair, gray on the temples, stooped shoulders*). Don't take it ill, Meneer, that I left my pen behind my ear. (*He fingers it awkwardly.*) I'm through.

DIRECTOR. Through what?

ONE HUNDRED AND THIRTEEN (*timidly, not looking at the* DIRECTOR). Through with the copying.

DIRECTOR. Oh, yes, yes—you have copying. (*He reads.*) Hendrik Leendert van Buren, born December 14, 1859, printer and book binder—a year and a half for manslaughter, with extenuating circumstances—

ONE HUNDRED AND THIRTEEN (*flinching*). Why must that—

DIRECTOR. Van Buren—(*Interrupting himself.*) lay your pen down—you do not need to use it here any more.

ONE HUNDRED AND THIRTEEN. Why not, Meneer? Isn't my work satisfactory?

DIRECTOR. On the contrary. Sit down. (ONE HUNDRED AND THIRTEEN *does so uneasily.*) It has pleased His Majesty, the new king, to grant you a pardon, taking effect to-day.

ONE HUNDRED AND THIRTEEN (*looking quickly at the* DIRECTOR). No.

DIRECTOR. Yes, yes.

ONE HUNDRED AND THIRTEEN. No, that cannot be.

DIRECTOR. Cannot be?

ONE HUNDRED AND THIRTEEN. No, I cannot accept that.

DIRECTOR. The responsibility does not rest with you. The Warden will take you to the administrator for your earnings in prison—and in the waiting room—

ONE HUNDRED AND THIRTEEN. No, it must be fully expiated—fully, fully—

DIRECTOR. That is an extraordinary way to show your gratitude for the royal decree—

ONE HUNDRED AND THIRTEEN. You will find here a hundred more worthy of it than I.

DIRECTOR. Should you not let us decide that?

ONE HUNDRED AND THIRTEEN. No, I will not accept it. The words of the domenee are here. (*He touches his forehead.*)

DIRECTOR. So much the better. Keep them in mind when you go back into the world.

ONE HUNDRED AND THIRTEEN. I did it.—There—this is the first time that I have admitted, except to the domenee, that I killed it—that it had lived.

DIRECTOR. Van Buren, you are intelligent enough to understand that your admission has nothing to do with what I have the pleasure to announce to you now. Your sentence is remitted.

ONE HUNDRED AND THIRTEEN. I want to confess to the worldly judge what, too late, I confessed to the Heavenly Judge.

DIRECTOR. If you have settled your case with the Heavenly Judge, the worldly judge has no jurisdiction over the pardon of His Majesty. But for your own satisfaction let me tell you that not one of the judges believed in your denial of your guilt. Still, in consideration of your previous unblemished reputation—

ONE HUNDRED AND THIRTEEN. I am not entitled to that consideration—

DIRECTOR. Reason the more to be thankful. Now I will have your daughter come in.

ONE HUNDRED AND THIRTEEN (*angry and agitated*). My daughter—No. no!

DIRECTOR. No nonsense, van Buren. Your wife cannot come, she is—unable.

ONE HUNDRED AND THIRTEEN. Then nobody had to come for me—nobody—I will not go home with my daughter.

DIRECTOR. My friend, you cannot complain that I have not treated you with consideration—but I have no more time—others are waiting. If you will not meet your daughter, then I will let her know. (*Sharply.*) But this I must say, that I find a pardon in your case almost misplaced. Such an attitude toward an afflicted child—it is unheard of! No, don't detain me any longer. (*He is about to ring the bell.*)

ONE HUNDRED AND THIRTEEN. Just a minute. I don't want to leave in this way.

DIRECTOR. Ach, come, this is too much. You force me to tell you what the poor thing wrote just now, that your wife lies sick in the hospital.

ONE HUNDRED AND THIRTEEN (*scarcely hearing*). I will not go with my daughter.

DIRECTOR. Even if you know that your wife lies at the point of death?

ONE HUNDRED AND THIRTEEN. Even then not.

DIRECTOR (*sitting down in amazement*). That is strong. I did not expect that—certainly not from you. (*The prison clock strikes.*)

ONE HUNDRED AND THIRTEEN (*after sitting listening a moment*). The child that I—that I—murdered—for that there is only one word—murder—if a creature is two hours old or eighty years old. Life is life and death is death. That child was hers—that child was my grandchild—that child was her shame. But for her shame I would not be sitting here, with the sound of that clock in my ears, and would have no fear of the day of judgment. (*He tries to control himself with hands trembling and lips quivering.*)

DIRECTOR (*seriously*). I know from the documents, van Buren, that it was the child of your deaf-mute daughter that you—

ONE HUNDRED AND THIRTEEN. The illegitimate child.

DIRECTOR. That you—

ONE HUNDRED AND THIRTEEN. Yes, yes—that I murdered—between two pillows—smothered—but you don't know all. Nobody knows all. I said nothing even to my own lawyer, afraid that he might let it slip—and I made up my mind firmly to lie, to lie, to lie—to keep us out of the hands of the law—all three of us.

DIRECTOR. All three?

ONE HUNDRED AND THIRTEEN. My wife, myself, and that shameless creature that they call my daughter.

DIRECTOR. Not with such hatred, van Buren—she waits for you outside that door. You will have to pass the rest of your life together.

ONE HUNDRED AND THIRTEEN (*inflexibly*). No, you can send her away quietly. I will never see her again.

DIRECTOR. Come, come!

ONE HUNDRED AND THIRTEEN. If you, Meneer—if you are not offended by the comparison—if you had an only child, an only daughter, and she dragged you down from an honorable position in the world and set you in one of these cells—would you then meet her with open arms if you were sitting here in my chair?

DIRECTOR. An afflicted child you forgive more easily than another.

ONE HUNDRED AND THIRTEEN. Orphans in their orphan clothes and afflicted children are protected by everyone—that I thought and said, year in and year out, as I stood by her bed with wild eyes—you don't have to fear for the deaf-mute, I said to my wife, she will find people everywhere who will stand by her if she has need of help—just like the blind. And then—then with a soldier from the camp—a stranger—one whose name even is not known—one who left with his company—gone—can't be found—and if you should find him—he can't be punished—can't be punished—

DIRECTOR. Don't you think, van Buren, that that wretch is more to blame than she?

ONE HUNDRED AND THIRTEEN. No.

DIRECTOR. If I insist it is because I feel it a duty to give to all those leaving the prison an admonition and a word of encouragement. You have no other family—it is your duty as a father.

ONE HUNDRED AND THIRTEEN. No, no, Meneer. We did more for her than other parents do because she came into the world afflicted—she could not talk as we did, she could not hear as we did—she missed much—but she had her eyes, her eyes with which she saw as well as we, her eyes with which she could read the commandments in the Bible, her eyes that saw more clearly than those of other children—saw when we were distressed. And she held her tongue—nine months without a single word, nine months of deception. If she had told her mother—a girl doesn't take her father into her confidence—if she had told her mother, there would not have been such a calamity that night, through fear of the neighbors, the neighbors, the neighbors! Above lived a deacon from my congregation; below, my landlord. You could hear every word spoken if you wanted to. The three families, each on his own floor sat evenings reading a chapter from the Bible—paid no attention to each other—even in a little quarrel we used to whisper. We were the quietest of the three because we spoke with our fingers to our daughter, always with our fingers, the way she had learned in the city. Until that night, that night that made of me a criminal, a murderer—that night, in the middle of August, suffocatingly hot—so hot that you smothered and you couldn't throw open a window. Oh, that heat, that heat! The sweat that rolled trickling, trickling, down your face, as if you were standing in the broiling sun! And your brains that throbbed! My daughter (*bitterly*), my daughter did not cry out, did not complain, did not groan. Tears, the neighbors could not hear, thank God— she lay like a corpse. But then, in the stillness, in the stillness—through the whole horror we were walking in our stockings for fear of the landlord, downstairs, and the neighbors upstairs who were lying awake on account of the heat —we heard them speaking in whispers—then in the stillness the child began— the child not yet a half hour old! My wife took it in her arms—it cried harder—and then, because the neighbors called out to know what was going on—I—I—without my wife making any effort to prevent me—without a movement from my daughter—all three—all three, in that moment, thought it was the best solution. At daybreak I took the bundle—the rest you know. Three accomplices, but only one before the judges, one who denied, denied, denied that it had lived—in order to save what might yet be saved. There was nothing to be saved. Not even the honor of my daughter. Nothing. Nothing. And it did live. I shall never again lay my head on a pillow, never again. I can feel yet how the pillow moved that night—how it—how it —moved no more. Neighbors make you forget conscience and God.

DIRECTOR. Since you have been pardoned so short a time after your sentence, it is almost certain that all that has been taken into consideration. Go now with your daughter to the hospital.

ONE HUNDRED AND THIRTEEN. No, Meneer—leave me my freedom there. From a decent man, who believed in God's word and led his family in daily prayer, I became in that one night a convict. I almost hope that when I reach the hospital, she will have closed her eyes, never again to look into mine. In the days before it all leaked out we did not look into each other's eyes, and the Lord be praised, she never came to visit me although we were to have celebrated our silver wedding. No, she never came to see me, because, as she wrote, she did not want to see me in convict clothes—clothes that I would never have dreamed—that I would have to wear—

(*He drops his head on the arm of the chair to hide his tears. The* DIRECTOR *opens the waiting room door slowly and beckons. The* DAUGHTER *comes in— starts back. He signs to her to stay and be quiet, goes out himself through the other door. The father gets up slowly, sees the* DAUGHTER, *draws back, looks around as if seeking the* DIRECTOR, *turns away. She gives a cry, throws herself on his neck. He pushes her away, tries to loosen her arms, ends by kissing her and weeping with her.*)

ONE HUNDRED AND THIRTEEN. Don't cry any more! Don't! Come now! (*He makes her sit down.*) How is it with Mother? (*She answers in the sign language.*) So. Then we'll go at once. In what hospital? (*She answers.*) Good.

DIRECTOR (*coming back*). I thought so. Wasn't I right to insist?

ONE HUNDRED AND THIRTEEN. Thank you. May I go immediately?

DIRECTOR. Immediately.

ONE HUNDRED AND THIRTEEN. Thank you. Good-by, Meneer.

DIRECTOR. Good-by.

ONE HUNDRED AND THIRTEEN. One thing I would like to know.

DIRECTOR. Yes?

ONE HUNDRED AND THIRTEEN. May I write the king a letter of thanks?

DIRECTOR. You may do that if you want to.

ONE HUNDRED AND THIRTEEN. Then I will do it certainly, certainly. And must I have a seal for that?

DIRECTOR. No, no, only a stamp.

ONE HUNDRED AND THIRTEEN. Yes, of course. (*To his daughter.*) Why do you stand there? Do you want to stay? And no more crying. Good-by, Meneer. (*They go out.*)

* * *

FIFTH JOY

DIRECTOR (*looking after* ONE HUNDRED AND THIRTEEN *through the waiting room door, to the* WARDEN). Pietersen!

WARDEN (*coming in*). Yes, Meneer?

DIRECTOR. Bring Sixty-seven, the last one on the list.

WARDEN. Do you know that a carriage with two horses stands waiting for him outside, and that there are fifty men watching for him?

DIRECTOR. The same demonstration as the last time.

WARDEN. Yes, Meneer. They tried to come into the courtyard and the corporal had to call his men to keep them back.

DIRECTOR (*smiling*). Very good. That is a comrade whom we shall have back here a few more times. Call him.

WARDEN (*smiling also*). I think, Meneer, that he has smelt the news—for the last half hour they have been standing by the north wing, near his cell, singing their song of freedom.

DIRECTOR (*opening the window, laughing. The song of freedom rings out in the distance*). Mountebanks! Just go on! (*He listens a minute, then shuts the window. The* WARDEN *goes out. The* DIRECTOR *sits down again at his desk. Almost immediately* SIXTY-SEVEN *comes in.*) Number Sixty-seven? Herman de Wilde? (*Sarcastically.*) A landau is waiting for you outside with an escort of your followers.

SIXTY-SEVEN (*a slender, gray haired man, with intelligent features, a high forehead and a large, imperious nose. He wears glasses with black mountings. His hair, which is thin on the crown is still thick at the temples. It, like his thick beard and his mustache, is entirely white. He speaks quietly and in a cultured manner.*) That means—?

DIRECTOR. That to-day there is some reason to sing for you the famous song of freedom. (*Pointing to the portrait of the king above the filing cabinet.*) The king, whom you insulted in open meeting, is dead. The successor to the throne, the new prince—

SIXTY-SEVEN. Has some compunctions against burying me here.

DIRECTOR (*quietly*). I do not think that His Majesty gave you his pardon because of conscientious scruples.

SIXTY-SEVEN (*disdainfully*). Jawel—I know all about it. "Let him out," they apparently advised him. "That will be a clever bit of politics. In place of posing as a martyr, he will have to thank you." Jawel! I'll look out for that. I won't be a dupe.

DIRECTOR (*jestingly*). I think you would do better to keep what you have to say for your followers. Speeches for my benefit—don't you think—are a little bit misplaced. Only as director of the prison, I advise you to avoid a third or fourth sentence.

SIXTY-SEVEN (*smiling*). Pardon—my sixth sentence.

DIRECTOR. You can get what you have earned from the administrator.

SIXTY-SEVEN. I shall not make use of that opportunity.

DIRECTOR. Then will you tell me what use I shall make of the money?

SIXTY-SEVEN. Were others pardoned to-day?

DIRECTOR. Yes.

SIXTY-SEVEN. How many?

DIRECTOR. Four besides you, from this prison.

SIXTY-SEVEN. Divide it among the four.

DIRECTOR. That wouldn't go very well. Three of them would not take it. One of them, perhaps—one who has been here since 1885.

SIXTY-SEVEN. Since 1885! Is such an unfortunate still living? May I ask who he is?

DIRECTOR. Certainly. (*Looking in the papers.*) Gerrit Jan Muller.

Sixty-Seven. Then will you be so kind as to give Gerrit Jan Muller my honorarium.

Director. That can be done if you will sign a receipt. (*Holding out his hand.*) And now, Meneer Herman de Wilde, to the pleasure of not seeing you again. Preach as much revolution as you will, but keep yourself outside the law.

Sixty-Seven (*smiling*). Perhaps in a couple of centuries we shall be so far along that there will be no more prisons for solitary confinement—because of the lack of directors.

Director. Or the lack of criminals—if your theory works out practically.

Sixty-Seven (*jestingly*). You've hit the bull's-eye!

Director (*as* Sixty-Seven *turns to the door*). And do me a favor—ask the gentlemen waiting outside not to sing quite so loud as you step into the landau.

Sixty-Seven (*jestingly*). You don't think much of singing?

Director. Songs of freedom in these surroundings? No.

Warden (*appearing at the door in much agitation*). Meneer the director—Number Seven—Number Seven—(*Controlling himself as he sees* Sixty-Seven.)

Director. What is it, Pietersen? Why do you stand there? (*The* Warden *indicates that he cannot speak before* Sixty-Seven.) Go on, speak. (*To* Sixty-Seven.) Number Seven, that is your new protegé, to whom your money is to be given. (*To the* Warden.) Go on. What is it?

Warden. We couldn't make him go—

Director. Do you hear that, Meneer de Wilde—one who has so little to complain of that he does not want to leave the prison. (*To the* Warden.) Go on, what has he done? (*The* Warden *does not answer.*) Now, then, Pietersen.

Warden (*under his breath*). He has hung himself, Meneer.

Director (*standing up horrified*). Hung himself! Hung himself, with so many guards about?

The Warden. He had just got his pay, said good-by to everybody—and then—and then—it happened. They have cut him down—no more life in him —nobody was in fault.

(*The* Director *goes out quickly with the* Warden. Sixty-Seven, *who has listened, shocked, sits down in front of the desk, stares thoughtfully before him. The* Director *comes back, takes his place at the desk. There is a long, oppressive silence. The two men look at each other.*)

Director (*troubled*). I am sorry, Meneer de Wilde, that it was just *you* who had to hear this.

Sixty-Seven (*thoughtfully*). One who did not want his freedom—(*He stands up, goes to the door, stops and says earnestly.*) Do not be uneasy—I shall not take advantage of this—and—there shall be no singing outside.

CURTAIN

THE BRIDEGROOM

A PLAY

By Lajos Biro

Translated from the Hungarian by Charles Recht

CHARACTERS

THE BRIDE
THE FATHER
THE MOTHER
ONE OF THE SISTERS
ANOTHER SISTER
THE OLDEST BROTHER
THE THIN AUNT
THE STOUT AUNT
THE POOR RELATIVE, *the Stout Aunt's husband.*
A PHYSICIAN
THE IRRATIONAL BARON

THE BRIDEGROOM

Just one bit of comment about the poor relative; and about him only this much. He is in no sense a parasite. He doesn't belong to the tribe of the submerged tenth; on the contrary, he isn't even poor—he is only, so to speak, constantly embarrassed in his intercourse with his wealthy relatives. He feels that the gods have favored him in giving him the entrée into these happier circles. He is charmed and enthusiastic, and struggles anxiously and painstakingly to confirm their favorable opinion. He drinks in their words—he even snatches them before they have been fully uttered, and he hurries his assent so quickly that his words form a continuous stuttering—a constant monotonous murmuring.

The irrational baron is, of course, called irrational merely because he is very rational. His soul is the survivor of those barbaric, chivalrous, self-sacrificing knights whom humanity pensioned off long ago.

The oldest brother is the heir, though his estate does not consist of a castle and acres, but of a business house and ledger accounts.

(The two sisters are arranging the bridal gifts on a table. THE BRIDE leans out of the window toward the street, waving greetings.)

BRIDE. Good-by, sweetheart . . . good-by, my dear, my darling. (*Frightened, she peers out anxiously.*) Carl, for God's sake! (*In despair.*) Carl! (*She screams.*) Carl!

(*With a piercing shriek, she staggers back and falls.*)

BOTH SISTERS. Renee, Renee! For God's sake, Renee, what's wrong with you? What's happened?

ONE OF THE SISTERS. Help, quick, help!

THE OTHER. Papa, papa, mama!

ONE OF THE SISTERS. Help, Alfred!

(*THE FATHER, MOTHER, OLDEST BROTHER and both aunts rush in.*)

FATHER. What's happened?

MOTHER. Great Heavens, who tripped Renee?

ONE OF THE SISTERS. She was looking out of the window and waving good-by to Carl.

THE OTHER SISTER. Then suddenly she cried out and fainted.

FATHER. Where has Carl gone?

THE OLDEST BROTHER. To meet the baron. We were waiting only for him.

THE STOUT AUNT. Hans went with him. I saw Uncle Hans go downstairs with him.

(*THE POOR RELATIVE appears on the threshold, all upset, hatless, and wiping the perspiration from his forehead.*)

THE STOUT AUNT (*with a shriek peculiar to marital affection*). Hans, Hans, has anything happened to you?

(THE POOR RELATIVE, *still trying to get his breath, shakes his head.*)

FATHER. What's wrong with Carl? Where is Carl? What's happened to him?

(THE POOR RELATIVE *gasps for breath.*)

FATHER (*with the imperiousness of a Cæsar*). What's—happened—to—Carl?

THE POOR RELATIVE. Terrible! Awful! . . . He went to meet the baron. . . . I accompanied him. . . . I went with him. . . .

FATHER. But tell us finally what's happened to him.

THE POOR RELATIVE. He started to cross the street, he turned to look at this window, was waving greetings. . . . He didn't see an automobile approaching . . . wanted to jump to the side . . . but he was run over.

MOTHER. God! God!

(*She bursts into sobs. This is a signal for the two sisters to begin to sob. The two aunts make awful faces.*)

FATHER. A doctor, quick—run for a doctor! Did you ask someone to get a doctor?

THE POOR RELATIVE. Yes, we got one from the street.

THE OLDEST BROTHER. But where is Carl? Where did they take him?

THE POOR RELATIVE. Down in the janitor's flat.

FATHER. To the janitor's? I'm going to have him brought right up here.

THE OLDEST BROTHER. Father, you stay here. I'll take care of that. Your place is with your family.

FATHER. A doctor from the street! Call a specialist! Two specialists!

THE OLDEST BROTHER. I'll look after everything. If possible I'll bring him up. Is he badly hurt?

THE POOR RELATIVE. I don't know. . . . I believe so. . . . Very likely. . . .

THE OLDEST BROTHER. I'll hurry. You'll soon know about it.

(*He goes out.*)

FATHER. Did he faint?

THE POOR RELATIVE. I believe so. I don't know.

FATHER. Didn't you look at him?

THE POOR RELATIVE. Certainly.

FATHER (*cross-examining him*). Did he faint? Answer yes or no.

THE POOR RELATIVE (*frightened*). Yes . . . he fainted . . . that is, I don't know exactly. If you think so . . .

FATHER. But he will soon recover?

THE POOR RELATIVE (*agreeing with all enthusiasm*). Certainly . . . I hope so . . . soon . . . very soon . . .

MOTHER (*she has been busying herself about the prostrate daughter and is surrounded by the other women*). The waist . . . open the waist . . . take her corset off.

THE STOUT AUNT. Rub her forehead with vinegar.

THE THIN AUNT. Vinegar is no good.

ONE OF THE SISTERS. Let's put her to bed.

MOTHER. Yes, to bed.

THE THIN AUNT. Haven't you any sense? I often fainted but they never put me to bed.

FATHER (*imperiously*). Put her to bed!

(*The women carry* THE BRIDE *out of the room.*)

FATHER. Let's hope that to-morrow the wedding need not be postponed.

THE POOR RELATIVE (*agreeing eagerly*). Quite likely. Quite likely. Why should it not be possible . . . yes, possible?

FATHER. The ceremony can take place in the house. Carl can sit in an armchair.

THE POOR RELATIVE (*agreeing and demonstrating his contempt of death*). In an armchair . . . excellent . . . in an armchair . . . he can sit in an armchair . . .

(THE OLDEST BROTHER *with a tragic expression appears on the threshold.*)

FATHER. Well, how is it? Will he recover soon?

(THE OLDEST BROTHER *shakes his head dismally.*)

FATHER. No? No, you say? What does that mean? Will there be no wedding to-morrow?

(THE OLDEST BROTHER *shakes his head and assumes a dramatic mien.*)

FATHER. Will he be sick a long time?

(THE OLDEST BROTHER *nods resignedly.*)

FATHER. But he will recover?

(THE OLDEST BROTHER *shakes his head.*)

FATHER. Will he die?

THE OLDEST BROTHER. He has two or three minutes . . .

FATHER. Impossible . . . no, no, no . . . that's impossible . . . that must not happen, you must be mistaken.

THE OLDEST BROTHER. The doctor is coming up. Here he is.

(THE DOCTOR *appears on the threshold. He is serious and respectful.*)

FATHER. Is it true? Doctor, is it true?

DOCTOR. Alas, it is all over.

FATHER. But there must still be some hope. A specialist quick! A specialist can surely help him.

DOCTOR. You can call a specialist . . .

FATHER. We can, of course we can, can't we?

DOCTOR. But no specialist in the world can cure the dead.

FATHER (*shocked*). Is he dead?

DOCTOR. He died a minute ago.

FATHER. A minute ago.

DOCTOR. He died of a fractured skull and concussion of the brain. The medical science with all her Latin words can do nothing more for him.

FATHER. But how could it have happened? How can such things be possible.

Doctor (*sympathetically*). My task, unfortunately, is finished.
(*He bows slightly and is about to depart.*)
One of the Sisters (*she rushes in*).   . . . The doctor . . . the doctor
. . . Renee is still unconscious.
Father. Quite true. God, God! Doctor . . . if you please, Doctor!
Doctor. You wish me to examine the patient?
Father. Please do. I'll settle with you later.
Doctor (*annoyed*). Very well. (*He goes out with one of the sisters.*)
Father. How terrible. What an unheard of misfortune!
The Oldest Brother. The Baron has just come. I heard his cab pull up.
Father. What a fatal day!
(The Irrational Baron *enters much excited.*)
The Irrational Baron. What have I heard . . . What a misfortune . . .
How's Carl? Where is he? Is he very ill?
Father. My dear Baron, it is all over.
The Irrational Baron. All over! Will he die?
Father. He's dead.
The Irrational Baron. Where is he?
The Oldest Brother (*introducing himself*). Alfred Tureczi, lieutenant in
reserve of his Majesty's Huzzars.
(The Irrational Baron *nods in recognition.*)
The Oldest Brother. He is lying in the janitor's flat. He was carried
there after the accident.
The Irrational Baron. Dead?
The Oldest Brother. Dead.
(*The women, with the exception of* The Mother, *come in.*)
One of the Sisters (*falling around* The Father's *neck*). Oh, papa, papa,
papa!
The Other Sister (*embracing the father*). Papa, papa, papa!
Father. Poor Renee, poor Renee!
(*The women wipe their eyes.*)
Father. How is our poor Renee? Does she know yet?
The Stout Aunt. She is still unconscious. The doctor told us to go out.
One of the Sisters. He told only mama to stay.
The Stout Aunt (*sobbing*). Poor Renee!
(*All the women are weeping.*)
The Irrational Baron (*speaking to* The Father). Terrible! A terrible
catastrophe.
Father. Terrible.
The Irrational Baron. On of the eve of his wedding.
Father. Yes, on the eve of his wedding. And everything was ready, and
such a lot of wedding presents and the entire family was invited, even you,
my dear baron, even you. And now this misfortune happens.
The Irrational Baron. When his young life was about to blossom . . . the
poor bride . . .

FATHER (*sobbing*). Poor Renee!

(*All the women are weeping again.*)

THE IRRATIONAL BARON. And you, my poor brave big boy. My poor, poor Carlo.

ONE OF THE SISTERS (*moaning*). Poor Carlo!

FATHER. My dear Baron, you loved him.

THE IRRATIONAL BARON. I loved him more than anyone in the world! With my heart and soul! He was my only friend! He was like a son or brother to me!

FATHER. We all loved him so much.

THE OLDEST BROTHER (*crying*). We all loved him so much.

THE STOUT AUNT. We all loved him, all of us.

FATHER. He was one of the best men in the world.

ONE OF THE SISTERS. And so charming.

THE OTHER SISTER. And so handsome.

THE STOUT AUNT. He was a gentleman.

THE THIN AUNT. And rich.

FATHER. And he was so well-informed.

ONE OF THE SISTERS. And he could play the violin so beautifully.

THE OTHER SISTER. And he played football on the 'Varsity.

THE STOUT AUNT. And he was so gentle to every one of us.

THE POOR RELATIVE. Gentle, yes, he was gentle. . . . He invited me to accompany him to meet the Baron.

FATHER. And he was always so attentive.

ONE OF THE SISTERS. He always brought us flowers.

THE OTHER SISTER (*sobbing*). And candy.

FATHER. And how they two were attached to each other! How they loved each other!

THE STOUT AUNT. They were together all the time . You couldn't separate the two. They sat or stood together holding hands by the hour.

ONE OF THE SISTERS (*sobbing, but still charmed with the memory of it*). They—were—kissing—each—other—all—the—time—and—everywhere.

(THE OTHER SISTER *sobs, but with ecstasy.*)

THE STOUT AUNT. He would have made a model husband. He never contradicted women.

THE THIN AUNT. Perhaps it was all too fortunate.

ONE OF THE SISTERS. How happy they were!

THE OTHER SISTER. How happy we all were!

FATHER. I could hardly wait to rock the first little grandchild in my arms.

THE IRRATIONAL BARON. Poor Carlos.

THE STOUT AUNT. He was a perfect man.

THE OTHER SISTER. A gentleman from his head to his heels.

FATHER. He would have been my son. I loved him more than my own child.

ONE OF THE SISTERS. I loved him more than my own brother.

THE STOUT AUNT. We loved him best of all the family.

FATHER (*sobbing*). My dear Baron, we all loved him so.

THE IRRATIONAL BARON (*sighing*). My poor Carlos. (*The loud wailing irritates* THE BARON.) I'm going down to him. Can I see him?

THE OLDEST BROTHER. I'll go down with you, my dear Baron.

(THE IRRATIONAL BARON, *downcast, goes out.* THE OLDEST BROTHER *follows him.*)

FATHER. What a gruesome, fatal day. What a catastrophe. What are we going to do with all these wedding presents? Even the spare room is full of them.

THE STOUT AUNT. You'll keep the presents, anyhow.

THE THIN AUNT. You must send all the presents back.

THE STOUT AUNT. You can't send them back. You aren't going to insult people.

THE THIN AUNT. The presents were meant for a wedding.

THE STOUT AUNT. Good; let them stay here until there is a wedding. Renee is going to get married some day.

FATHER. Marry! God only knows when. They loved each other so. That makes it worse than if she were only a widow. That reminds me that we have to cancel the order for the wedding dinner.

(THE OLDEST BROTHER *comes in.*)

FATHER. Where is the Baron?

THE OLDEST BROTHER. He wanted to remain alone with the dead.

FATHER. Yes, and what are we going to do with the body? Shall we have him brought up here? Will he be buried from here?

THE THIN AUNT. No, no, no. Don't you bring him up here.

THE STOUT AUNT. Wasn't he one of the family?

THE OLDEST BROTHER. We'll arrange that later. Don't profane sorrow with such discussions. How's Renee?

FATHER. Good God, yes! How's Renee? What's wrong with her?

ONE OF THE SISTERS (*opening the door into the next room and looking in*). The Doctor is speaking to Mama. He'll be here presently.

(THE DOCTOR *comes in.*)

FATHER. How is she? How is she, Doctor? Nothing serious, I hope.

DOCTOR. Fortunately, it is not. She is now completely out of danger. She is conscious, but she is still a little weak.

FATHER. Thank God!

THE GIRLS. Thank God!!

THE STOUT AUNT (*pathetically*). Thank God!

THE THIN AUNT. I told you!

DOCTOR (*speaking to* THE FATHER). I would like to have a few confidential words with you, sir.

FATHER. With me?

DOCTOR. Yes.

FATHER. At your service.

DOCTOR. But this is confidential.

FATHER (*excited*). Go out all of you! Get right out! (*The others go out.*) May my son remain, my oldest son?

DOCTOR. Yes, he may remain.

FATHER. What is it? Anything serious, Doctor?

DOCTOR. Oh no, nothing serious. Considering all the circumstances, the patient is entirely normal.

(THE OLDEST BROTHER *quivers all over.*)

DOCTOR. Nevertheless, as I said, the patient requires the kind of quiet care and nursing which every young mother needs.

FATHER (*stammering*). All mothers . . . mothers . . . you don't mean that . . .

DOCTOR. On the condition and care of the patient two lives are now depending.

FATHER. No, no; that's impossible! You must be mistaken!

DOCTOR. It's important that during the next six months she should be free from all mental exertion and should have a perfect rest.

FATHER. That's a silly joke. What you are saying is a mistake. It's impossible, I tell you.

DOCTOR. A mistake is out of the question. As soon as the patient recovered consciousness I spoke to her, and she herself confirmed my suppositions.

FATHER. Impossible, impossible. . . . (*Racing up and down.*) Impossible. (*Calling.*) Cecilia! Cecilia! (*Wildly excited.*) Cecilia, where the devil are you? Cecilia?

(*He rushes out.*)

DOCTOR (*addressing* THE OLDEST BROTHER). What I enjoined your father, I would strongly recommend to you.

THE OLDEST BROTHER. Then it is really true?

DOCTOR. Yes; now I will have to go.

THE OLDEST BROTHER. As the oldest son, I would beg you, Doctor, that you consider this affair as wholly confidential.

DOCTOR. You need not ask it, my boy. My profession demands that I keep professional secrets.

THE OLDEST BROTHER. Oh, yes, pardon me. . . .

DOCTOR. Good-by.

(*He leaves.*)

THE OLDEST BROTHER. Good . . . B—.

(*Perplexed, he stares pensively into space.*)

FATHER (*rushing in*). Where is Mama? Where did she go?

(*He goes out through the other door.*)

THE OLDEST BROTHER. Papa, papa, calm yourself.

(*He rushes out after him.*)

THE STOUT AUNT (*rushing in.*) Alfred.

(*Seeing no one in the room, she is about to leave.*)

THE THIN AUNT (*comes hurrying in*). What has happened? Why are you carrying on? The whole house seems to have gone mad.

(THE STOUT AUNT *clasps her hands and bows her head.*)

THE THIN AUNT. What's happened? You were with Renee—what's happened to her?

(THE STOUT AUNT, *horrified, remains silent.*)

THE THIN AUNT (*out of temper, very impatient*). What has happened?

(THE STOUT AUNT *draws her head toward* THE THIN AUNT'S *mouth, looks carefully about, shakes her head with evident horror and whispers into her ear.* THE THIN AUNT *listens with amazement. When the narrative evidently reaches its most delicate point, she begins to grin with satisfaction, then her malignant joy gives place to indignation. The aunts face each other, puzzled and speechless, and make a face as though they meant to say,* "You can expect almost anything to happen in this house.")

THE THIN AUNT (*pointing to the next room*). And what do they think of it?

THE STOUT AUNT. I have not heard yet.

THE THIN AUNT. Come, let us find out.

BOTH SISTERS (*rushing in*). Mama, mama!

(*They remain standing and stare at each other, embarrassed and silent.*)

FATHER (*he rushes in*). Cecilia! Cecilia!! (*To the two girls.*) Where did your mother hide?

(*The Sisters, perplexed, do not answer him.* THE MOTHER *comes in at opposite door. She has been crying out and is drying her tears with a handkerchief.*)

FATHER. Where the deuce were you? Why did you hide from me?

MOTHER. I was . . .

FATHER (*imperiously*). Cecilia, woman, how did you allow this to happen?

(THE MOTHER *weeps gently.*)

FATHER. How could you be so careless? . . . Is this the protection you give your daughters? . . .

(*The Aunts,* THE POOR RELATIVE *and* THE OLDEST BROTHER, *all greatly interested, come in through different doors.*)

FATHER. You were a nice sort of mother!

MOTHER. Forgive—

FATHER. That is the way you take responsibility for your daughters!

MOTHER. But she was a bride.

FATHER. Certainly she was . . . a bride . . . yes. But does that make allowances for everything? . . . Now see what it leads to.

MOTHER. But how could I suspect . . .

FATHER. A careful mother suspects everything. You should never have permitted them to be alone. You should have followed their footsteps all the time!

MOTHER. The wedding was to be to-morrow.

FATHER. Was to be. But it will not be. . . . And now we—you—have . . .

you have her on your hands for good . . . this daughter of yours . . . this wretched . . .

MOTHER. Don't insult Renee!

FATHER. No? Don't insult her? Perhaps I shall even thank her for this! For this disgrace which she has brought on my home! For the dishonor which she has attached to my name! From this day on she is my child no longer!

ONE OF THE SISTERS (*sobbing*). Renee is not to blame.

FATHER. Who else is to blame? Perhaps I am. . . . And besides, who gave you the right to chatter? What are you both doing here? Clear out!

THE OTHER SISTER (*sobbing*). Poor Renee!

FATHER. How dare you interfere here? Leave at once. Go to your rooms. Clear out—out, I say.

(*Both girls leave.*)

MOTHER. Renee is not to blame.

FATHER. Who then, who then, who then?

MOTHER (*weeping with a drawling wail*). Carl . . .

FATHER. Carl?

MOTHER. We trusted him blindly. He alone is to blame.

FATHER. He alone? . . .

MOTHER. Renee was so inexperienced. . . . He took advantage of her innocence.

THE OLDEST BROTHER (*firmly*). He slyly abused our confidence.

THE STOUT AUNT. The confidence of the entire family.

FATHER. He was going to marry her . . . how could he know . . .

THE STOUT AUNT (*warmly*). He should have considered this. An upright man remembers that he'll die.

THE THIN AUNT. Oh, what does a man of that sort, of that type, care what becomes of a poor girl whom he has (*moralizingly*) sacrificed to his bad, his bad passions?

THE STOUT AUNT. Such . . . such infamy!

THE POOR RELATIVE. A man who can do a thing like this is a bad man.

MOTHER. He bears all the blame. He was a bad man.

THE THIN AUNT. I always had my suspicions about him. I never had any confidence in him. His sweet, sly talk never caught me; but you, you always petted and fussed about him so.

MOTHER. He did this behind our backs . . . he made us all believe that he was a very upright man.

THE POOR RELATIVE (*now brave*). He was not an upright man; no, he was not.

THE THIN AUNT. All his softness was nothing but pure sham.

MOTHER. He put that on so that he could sneak here and ruin our poor child.

FATHER. And he ruined us all.

THE STOUT AUNT. Behind his outward appearance was hidden a scoundrel.

FATHER. He brought disgrace on us all.

(THE IRRATIONAL BARON *appears in the doorway.*)

THE STOUT AUNT. He was a scoundrel.

FATHER. A good-for-nothing, a scamp.

THE POOR RELATIVE. That's just what he was—a scamp, a good-for-nothing.

THE OLDEST BROTHER. He was no gentleman.

THE IRRATIONAL BARON (*dumbfounded*). Who are you talking about? (*Embarrassed, they all remain silent.*) Who were the gentry discussing?

FATHER. Who? Who else . . . but this—

THE IRRATIONAL BARON (*indignant*). Carlos?

FATHER. Yes, indeed.

THE IRRATIONAL BARON. What in the world has happened?

FATHER. What has happened? Plenty has happened. . . . He has ruined me. . . . He has destroyed our girl.

THE IRRATIONAL BARON. But explain what has really happened.

FATHER. The Doctor examined her . . . she has brought shame on my house . . . this girl . . . before she became his wife . . . he betrayed us . . . he took advantage of our confidence.

THE IRRATIONAL BARON (*now understanding*). Oh . . . (*There is a pause.*) Poor Carlos!

FATHER. Poor—poor . . . but we—we have her on our hands.

THE IRRATIONAL BARON (*consolingly*). But they loved each other so.

FATHER. Loved—loved? And does that excuse the man from being a scoundrel? He cannot marry her now, can he?

THE IRRATIONAL BARON. But the poor boy is dead.

FATHER. Dead? Of course he is dead. . . . Every one can say that. . . . But that's just what he should have considered.

THE IRRATIONAL BARON (*excited, but controlling himself, softly*). But you could hardly wait till you could rock your first grandchild.

FATHER. My first grandchild. . . . Do you suppose that I will recognize that child as my grandchild? . . . Do you think that I will have anything to do with that child?

THE IRRATIONAL BARON. But what is going to become of the poor child?

FATHER. That I don't know. . . . I suppose we will board it out.

THE IRRATIONAL BARON (*his anger mastering him*). A nice sort of a grandpapa—and what is going to become of the mother?

FATHER. That's just what I don't know. That's the worst of it. Who will marry that kind of girl?

MOTHER (*sobbing*). Yes, who will marry that kind of girl?

THE OLDEST BROTHER. Such a shame!

THE STOUT AUNT (*taking courage*). Such a piece of scoundrelism!

THE THIN AUNT. To bring us to this misfortune! To bring such a catastrophe on us! To abuse our confidence that way! That's nothing but scoundrelism!

THE IRRATIONAL BARON (*almost beside himself with rage*). Oh, gentle female souls, may I remind you that there is only one catastrophe here in question—only that misfortune which happened to poor Carlos. It is he who is dead.

FATHER. He is, sure . . . but we . . .

THE IRRATIONAL BARON. The gentry are enjoying the best of health, but are complaining about what has happened. My Carlos is dead, and you are complaining. I must say, I would to God the reverse were the case.

FATHER (*insulted*). How dare you insult an unfortunate father? . . . Who will marry this helpless creature? Who will marry her?

THE STOUT AUNT. The poor creature!

THE THIN AUNT. The unfortunate victim!

THE IRRATIONAL BARON (*beside himself, no longer able to master his rage, he thunders*). Silence! Silence! (*Frightened, they all are silent.*) Silence! . . . I will marry her.

FATHER. What . . . what's that?

(*All appear amazed.*)

THE IRRATIONAL BARON. I'll make her my wife! No objections, I hope!

FATHER (*more amazed*). Of course not; but . . .

THE IRRATIONAL BARON (*permitting no interruption*). I dared to hope so. You can take my word for it though, ladies and gentlemen, that I would never have mixed with the like of . . .

THE OLDEST BROTHER. Pardon me!

THE IRRATIONAL BARON (*shouting*). Silence! (*Firmly.*) I would have never mixed with the like of you, but I want to provide a father for the child of my Carlos. I will make good his shortcomings.

FATHER. But the child . . .

THE IRRATIONAL BARON (*in a rage*). I know that child was expected here (*sarcastically*) with a great love. But I hope that this feeling will change if it bears my name.

FATHER (*breathlessly*). You, you . . . your name!

THE IRRATIONAL BARON (*pitilessly*). To unite my name with the pickle company for which your family name stands, that I would never do! But Carlos' child must not suffer. I will give it my name.

FATHER. You alone . . . what do you think!

THE IRRATIONAL BARON (*sharply interrupting him*). I will now take my leave of you, ladies and gentlemen. In four weeks I will return. Then we will hold the wedding in this house. . . . The prospective bride will in the meantime recover sufficient strength to withstand the painful ceremonies. Immediately after the wedding I will go traveling. The Baroness will give birth to the child while I am away. I hope that the Baroness will get all the necessary care. In a half a year she will begin divorce proceedings against me. A divorced Baroness, I hope, will not be a discredit to the firm, nor will the grandchild if it bears my name.

FATHER (*overflowing with gratitude*). Of course not, of course not . . . now everything will run smoothly again. Your generosity, my dear Baron . . .

THE IRRATIONAL BARON. Don't deceive yourself that I am doing this for your sake. I am only doing this for Carlos.

FATHER. Of course, of course . . . but we are . . .

THE IRRATIONAL BARON. Well, then I shall return four weeks from to-day. (*He goes out. The rest stare at each other in utter amazement.*)

THE OLDEST BROTHER. Such a change!

FATHER (*with relief*). What a splendid man!

MOTHER. Now everything is in order again.

THE THIN AUNT. If Renee will only agree to this!

FATHER (*angrily*). Why not? She will be very happy.

THE STOUT AUNT. Some one ought to go and tell her.

ONE OF THE SISTERS (*she rushes in*). Papa, listen—we are with Renee. . . . She says that Carl made a will three months ago.

FATHER. When?

ONE OF THE SISTERS. Three months ago.

FATHER. Yes? And what?

ONE OF THE SISTERS. She inherits everything.

FATHER. She? Renee?

ONE OF THE SISTERS. Yes.

FATHER. Is it certain?

ONE OF THE SISTERS. Certain.

FATHER. Certain? Then I'll go to her. I will tell her the great news. Come!

(FATHER *and daughter go out. There is a pause.*)

THE STOUT AUNT. Everything is turning out well.

MOTHER. Yes, yes; let's thank the good Lord for all this.

THE THIN AUNT. If only people don't find out about it.

THE OLDEST BROTHER. Suppose they do? If any one dares to look askance at Renee, he'll have to settle with me.

THE POOR RELATIVE. Renee will be a Baroness now.

MOTHER (*with bliss*). Yes!

THE POOR RELATIVE. And she will be a very rich woman as well.

MOTHER (*beaming*). Yes!

THE THIN AUNT. How lucky your family is!

MOTHER. Lord be praised! We can now all be very happy.

FATHER (*entering*). Renee has told me all about it. The last will has been properly made out. It is in the lawyer's office.

MOTHER. Wasn't it kind of Carl?

FATHER (*in a tone of appreciation*). It was a beautiful deed. Men who are as farsighted as he are rare . . .

THE POOR RELATIVE. A rare man—a very rare man. In every respect he was a rare man.

THE STOUT AUNT. He was a good man, too; and how devotedly he loved our Renee!

THE THIN AUNT. He was almost too good, I would say.

FATHER. He was goodness itself, and every inch a man of honor.
THE POOR RELATIVE. Every inch a man of honor.
FATHER. An honorable, sincere and very straightforward man.
THE OLDEST BROTHER. A gentleman!

CURTAIN

THE MARRIAGE

A PLAY

By DOUGLASS HYDE

Translated from the original Gaelic by Lady Gregory

CHARACTERS

MARTIN, *a young man.*
MARY, *his newly married wife.*
A BLIND FIDDLER.
NEIGHBORS.

THE MARRIAGE

SCENE—*A cottage kitchen. A table poorly set out, with two cups, a jug of milk, and a cake of bread.* MARTIN *and* MARY *sitting down to it.*

MARTIN. This is a poor wedding dinner I have for you, Mary; and a poor house I brought you to. I wish it was seven thousand times better for your sake.

MARY. Only we have to part again, there wouldn't be in the world a pair happier than myself and yourself; but where's the good of fretting when there's no help for it?

MARTIN. If I had but a couple of pounds, I could buy a little ass and earn a share of money bringing turf to the big town; or I could job at the fairs. But, my grief, we haven't it, or ten shillings.

MARY. And if I could get but a few hens, and what would feed them, I could be selling eggs or rearing chickens. But unless God would work a miracle for us, there's no chance of that itself. (*She wipes her eyes with her apron.*)

MARTIN. Don't be crying, Mary. You belong to me now; am I not rich so long as you belong to me? Whatever place I will go to I will know you are thinking of me.

MARY. That is a true word you say, Martin; I will never be poor so long as I know you to be thinking of me. No riches at all would be so good as that. There's a line my poor father used to be saying:

> "Cattle and gold, store and goods,
> They pass away like the high floods."

It was Raftery, the blind man, said that. I never saw him; but my father used to be talking of him.

MARTIN. I don't care what he said. I wish we had goods and store. He said the exact contrary another time:

> "Brogues in the fashion, a good house,
> Are better than the bare sky over us."

MARY. Poor Raftery! he'd give us all that if he had the chance. He was always a good friend to the poor. I heard them saying the other day he was lying in his sickness at some place near Killeenan, and near his death. The Lord have mercy on him!

MARTIN. The Lord have mercy on him, indeed. Come now, Mary, eat the first bit in your own house. I'll take the eggs off the fire. (*He gets up and goes to the fire. There is a knock at the half-door, and an old ragged, patched fiddler puts in his head.*)

FIDDLER. God save all here!

MARY (*standing up*). Aurah, the poor man, bring him in.

MARTIN. Let there be sense on you, Mary; we have not anything at all to give him. I will tell him the way to the Brennans' house; there will be plenty to find there.

MARY. Indeed and surely I will not put him from this door. This is the first time I ever had a house of my own, and I will not send anyone at all from my own door this day.

MARTIN. Do as you think well yourself. (MARY *goes to the door and opens it.*) Come in, honest man, and sit down, and a hundred welcomes before you. (*The* OLD MAN *comes in, feeling about him as if blind.*)

MARY. O Martin, he is blind. May God preserve him.

OLD MAN. That is so, acushla; I am in my blindness; and it is a tired, vexed, blind man I am. I am going and ever going since morning, and I never found a bit to eat since I rose.

MARY. You did not find a bit to eat since morning! Are you starving?

OLD MAN. Oh, indeed, there was food to be got if I would take it; but the bit that does not come from a willing heart, there would be no taste on it; and that is what I did not get since morning; but people putting a potato or a bit of bread out of the door to me, as if I was a dog, with the hope I would not stop, but would go away.

MARY. Oh, sit down with us now, and eat with us. Bring him to the table, Martin. (MARTIN *gives his hand to the* OLD MAN, *and gives him a chair, and puts him sitting at the table with themselves. He makes two halves of the cake, and gives a half to the blind man, and one of the eggs. The* OLD MAN *eats eagerly.*)

OLD MAN. I leave my seven hundred thousand blessings on the people of this house. The blessing of God and Mary on them.

MARY. That it may be well with you. O Martin, that is the first blessing I got in my own house. That blessing is better to me than gold.

OLD MAN. Aurah, is it not beautiful for people to have a house of their own, and to have eyes to look about with?

MARTIN. May God preserve you, right man; it is likely it is a poor thing to be without sight.

OLD MAN. You do not understand, nor any person that has his sight, what it is to be blind and dark the way I am. Not to have before you and behind you but the night. Oh, darkness, darkness! No shape or form in anything; not to see the bird you hear singing in the tree over your head; nor the flower you smell on the bush, or the child, and he laughing in his mother's breast. The morning and the evening, the day and the night, only the same thing to you. Oh, it is a poor thing to be blind. (MARTIN *puts over the other half of the cake and the egg to* MARY, *and makes a sign to her to eat. She makes a sign to him to take a share of them. The* BLIND MAN *stretches his hand over the table to try for a crumb of bread, for he has eaten his own share; and he gets hold of the other half cake and takes it.*)

MARY. Eat that, poor man, it is likely there is hunger on you. Here is another egg for you. (*She puts the other egg in his hand.*)

BLIND MAN. The blessing of the Only Son and of the Holy Mother on the hand that gives it. (MARTIN *puts up his two hands as if dissatisfied; and he is going to say something when* MARY *takes the words from his mouth, laughing at his gloomy face.*)

BLIND MAN. Maisead, my blessing on the mouth that laughter came from, and my blessing on the light heart that let it out of the mouth.

MARTIN. A light heart, is it! There is not a light heart with Mary to-night, my grief!

BLIND MAN. Mary is your wife?

MARTIN. She is. I made her my wife three hours ago.

BLIND MAN. Three hours ago?

MARTIN (*bitterly*). That is so. We were married to-day; and it is at our wedding dinner you are sitting.

BLIND MAN. Your wedding dinner! Do not be mocking me! There is no company here.

MARY. Oh, he is not mocking you; he would not do a thing like that. There is no company here; for we have nothing in the house to give them.

BLIND MAN. But you gave it to me! Is it the truth you are speaking? Am I the only person that was asked to your wedding?

MARY. You are. But that is to the honor of God; and we would never have told you that, but Martin let slip the word from his mouth.

BLIND MAN. Oh, and I eat your little feast on you, and without knowing it.

MARY. It is not without a welcome you eat it.

MARTIN. I am well pleased you came in; you were more in want of it than ourselves. If we have a bare house now, we might have a full house yet; and a good dinner on the table to share with those in need of it. I'd be better off now; but all the little money I had I laid it out on the house, and the little patch of land. I thought I was wise at the time; but now we have the house, and we haven't what will keep us alive in it. I have the potatoes set in the garden; but I haven't so much as a potato to eat. We are left bare, and I am guilty of it.

MARY. If there is any fault, it is on me it is; coming maybe to be a drag on Martin, where I have no fortune at all. The little money I gained in service, I lost it all on my poor father, when he took sick. And I went back into service; and the mistress I had was a cross woman; and when Martin saw the way she was treating me, he wouldn't let me stop with her any more, but he made me his wife. And now I will have great courage, when I have to go out to service again.

BLIND MAN. Will you have to be parted again?

MARTIN. We will, indeed; I must go as a spailpin fanac, to reap and to dig the harvest in some other place. But Mary and myself have it settled, we'll meet again at this house on a certain day, with the blessing of God. I'll have the key in my pocket; and we'll come in, with a better chance of stopping in it. You'll have your own cows yet, Mary; and your calves and your firkins of butter, with the help of God.

MARY. I think I hear carts on the road. (*She gets up, and goes to the door.*)

MARTIN. It's the people coming back from the fair. Shut the door, Mary; I wouldn't like them to see how bare the house is; and I'll put a smear of ashes on the window, the way they won't see we're here at all.

BLIND MAN (*raising his head suddenly*). Do not do that; but open the door wide, and let the blessing of God come in on you. (MARY *opens the door again. He takes up his fiddle and begins to play on it. A little boy puts in his head at the door; and then another head is seen, and another with that again.*)

BLIND MAN. Who is that at the door?

MARY. Little boys that came to listen to you.

BLIND MAN. Come in, boys. (*Three or four come inside.*)

BLIND MAN. Boys, I am listening to the carts coming home from the fair. Let you go out, and stop the people; tell them they must come in: there is a wedding-dance here this evening.

BOY. The people are going home. They wouldn't stop for us.

BLIND MAN. Tell them to come in; and there will be as fine a dance as ever they saw. But they must all give a present to the man and woman that are newly married.

ANOTHER BOY. Why would they come in? They can have a dance of their own at any time. There is a piper in the big town.

BLIND MAN. Say to them that I myself tell them to come in; and to bring everyone a present to the newly-married woman.

BOY. And who are you yourself?

BLIND MAN. Tell them it is Raftery the poet is here, and that is calling to them. (*The boys run out, tumbling over one another.*)

MARTIN. Are you Raftery, the great poet I heard talk of since I was born! (*Taking his hand.*) Seven hundred thousand welcomes before you; and it is a great honor to us for you to be here.

MARY. Raftery the poet! Now there is luck on us! The first man that brought us his blessing, and that eat food in my own house, he to be Raftery the poet! And I hearing the other day you were sick and near your death. And I see no sign of sickness on you now.

BLIND MAN. I am well, I am well now, the Lord be praised for it.

MARTIN. I heard talk of you as often as there are fingers on my hands, and toes on my feet. But indeed I never thought to have the luck of seeing you.

MARY. And it is you that made *County Mayo*, and the *Repentance*, and *The Weaver*, and the *Shining Flower*. It is often I thought there should be no woman in the world so proud as Mary Hynes, with the way you praised her.

BLIND MAN. O my poor Mary Hynes, without luck! (*They hear the wheels of a cart outside the house, and an* OLD FARMER *comes in, a frieze coat on him.*)

OLD FARMER. God save you, Martin; and is this your wife? God be with you, woman of the house. And, O Raftery, seven hundred thousand welcomes before you to this country. I would sooner see you than King George. When they told me you were here, I said to myself I would not go past without seeing you, if I didn't get home till morning.

BLIND MAN. But didn't you get my message?

OLD FARMER. What message is that?

BLIND MAN. Didn't they tell you to bring a present to the new-married woman and her husband. What have you got for them?

OLD FARMER. Wait till I see; I have something in the cart. (*He goes out.*)

MARTIN. O Raftery, you see now what a great name you have here. (OLD FARMER *comes in again with a bag of meal on his shoulders. He throws it on the floor.*)

OLD FARMER. Four bags of meal I was bringing from the mill; and there is one of them for the woman of the house.

MARY. A thousand thanks to God and you. (MARTIN *carries the bag to other side of table.*)

BLIND MAN. Now don't forget the fiddler. (*He takes a plate and holds it out.*)

OLD FARMER. I'll not break my word, Raftery, the first time you came to this country. There is two shillings for you in the plate. (*He throws the money into it.*)

BLIND MAN.   This is a man has love to God,
                 Opening his hand to give out food;
                 Better a small house filled with wheat,
                 Than a big house that's bare of meat.

OLD FARMER. Maisead, long life to you, Raftery.

BLIND MAN. Are you there, boy?

BOY. I am.

BLIND MAN. I hear more wheels coming. Go out, and tell the people Raftery will let no person come in here without a present for the woman of the house.

BOY. I am going. (*He goes out.*)

OLD FARMER. They say there was not the like of you for a poet in Connacht these three hundred years back. (*A middle-aged woman comes in, a pound of tea and a parcel of sugar in her hand.*)

WOMAN. God save all here! I heard Raftery the poet was in it; and I brought this little present to the woman of the house. (*Puts them into* MARY'S *hands.*) I would sooner see Raftery than be out there in the cart.

BLIND MAN. Don't forget the fiddler, O right woman.

WOMAN. And are you Raftery?

BLIND MAN.   I am Raftery the poet,
                            Full of gentleness and love;
                            With eyes without light,
                            With quietness, without misery.

WOMAN. Good the man.

BLIND MAN.   Quick, quick, quick, for no man
                            Need speak twice to a handy woman;
                            I'll praise you when I hear the clatter
                            Of your shilling on my platter.

(*A young man comes in with a side of bacon in his arms, and stands waiting.*)

WOMAN. Indeed, I would not begrudge it to you if it was a piece of gold I had (*puts shilling in plate.*) The *Repentance* you made is at the end of my fingers. Here's another customer for you now. (*The young man comes forward, and gives the bacon to* MARTIN, *who puts it with the meal.*)

MARY. I thank you kindly. Oh, it's like the miracle worked for Saint Colman, sending him his dinner in the bare hills!

BLIND MAN.   May that young man with yellow hair
                            Find yellow money everywhere!

FAIR YOUNG MAN. I heard the world and his wife were stopping at the door to give a welcome to Raftery, and I thought I would not be behindhand. And here is something for the fiddler. (*Puts money in the plate.*) I would sooner see that fiddler than any other fiddler in the world.

BLIND MAN.   May that young man with yellow hair
                            Buy cheap, sell dear, in every fair.

FAIR YOUNG MAN (*to* MARTIN). How does he know I have yellow hair and he blind? How does he know that?

MARTIN. Hush, my head is going round with the wonder is on me.

MARY. No wonder at all in that. Maybe it is dreaming we all are. (*A gray-haired man and two girls come in.*)

GRAY-HAIRED MAN (*laying down a sack*). The blessing of God here! I heard Raftery was here in the wedding-house, and that he would let no one in without a present. There was nothing in the cart with us but a sack of potatoes, and there it is for you, ma'am.

MARY. Oh, it's too good you all are to me. Whether it's asleep or awake I am, I thank you kindly.

BLIND MAN. Don't forget the fiddler.

GRAY-HAIRED MAN. Are you Raftery?

BLIND MAN.   Who will give Raftery a shilling?
                            Here is his platter; who is willing?
                            Who will give honor to the poet?
                            Here is his platter: show it, show it.

GRAY-HAIRED FARMER. You're welcome; you're welcome! That is Raftery, anyhow! (*Puts money in the plate.*)

BLIND MAN. Come hither girls, give what you can
To the poor old traveling man.

GRAY-HAIRED MAN. Aurah Susan, aurah Oona, are you looking at who is before you, the greatest poet in Ireland? That is Raftery himself. It is often you heard talk of the girl that got a husband with the praises he gave her. If he gives you the same, maybe you'll get husbands with it.

FIRST GIRL. I often heard talk of Raftery.

OTHER GIRL. There was always a great name on Raftery. (*They put some money in the plate shyly.*)

BLIND MAN. Before you go, give what you can
To this young girl and this young man.

FIRST GIRL (*to* MARY). Here's a couple of dozen of eggs, and welcome.

OTHER GIRL. O woman of the house! I have nothing with me here; but I have a good clucking hen at home, and I'll bring her to you to-morrow; our house is close by.

MARY. Indeed, that's good news to me; such nice neighbors to be at hand. (*Several men and women come into the house together, every one of them carrying something.*)

SEVERAL (*together*). Welcome, Raftery!

BLIND MAN. If ye have hearts are worth a mouse,
Welcome the bride into her house.

(*They laugh and greet* MARY, *and put down gifts—a roll of butter, rolls of woollen thread, and many other things.*)

OLD FARMER. Ha, ha! That's right. They are coming in now. Now, Raftery, isn't it generous and open-minded and liberal this country is? Isn't it better than the County Mayo?

BLIND MAN. I'd say all Galway was rich land,
If I'd your shillings in my hand.

(*Holds out his plate to them.*)

OLD FARMER (*laughing*). Now, neighbors, down with it! My conscience! Raftery knows how to get hold of the money.

A MAN OF THEM. Maisead, he doesn't own much riches; and there is pride on us all to see him in this country. (*Puts money in the plate, and all the others do the same. A lean old man comes in.*)

MARTIN (*to* MARY). That is John the Miser, or Seagan na Stucaire, as they call him. That is the man that is hardest in this country. He never gave a penny to any person since he was born.

MISER. God save all here! Oh, is that Raftery? Ho, ho! God save you, Raftery, and a hundred thousand welcomes before you to this country. There is pride on us all to see you. There is gladness on the whole country, you to be here in our midst. If you will believe me, neighbors, I saw with my own eyes the bush Raftery put his curse on; and as sure as I'm living, it was withered away. There is nothing of it but a couple of old twigs now.

BLIND MAN. I've heard a voice like his before,
And liked some little voice the more;

I'd sooner have, if I'd my choice,
A big heart and a small voice.

MISER. Ho! ho! Raftery, making poems as usual. Well, there is great joy on us, indeed, to see you in our midst.

BLIND MAN. What is the present you have brought to the new-married woman?

MISER. What is the present I brought? O maisead! the times are too bad on a poor man. I brought a few fleeces of wool I had to the market to-day, and I couldn't sell it; I had to bring it home again. And calves I had there. I couldn't get any buyer for at all. There is misfortune on these times.

BLIND MAN. Every person that came in brought his own present with him. There is the new-married woman, and let you put down a good present.

MISER. O maisead, much good may it do her! (*He takes out of his pocket a small parcel of snuff; takes a piece of paper from the floor, and pours into it, slowly and carefully, a little of the snuff, and puts it on the table.*)

BLIND MAN.   Look at the gifts of every kind
                Were given with a willing mind;
                After all this, it's not enough
                From the man of cows—a pinch of snuff!

OLD FARMER. Maisead, long life to you, Raftery, that your tongue may never lose its edge. That is a man of cows certainly; I myself am a man of sheep.

BLIND MAN. A bag of meal from the man of sheep.

FAIR YOUNG MAN. And I am a man of pigs.

BLIND MAN. A side of meat from the man of pigs.

MARTIN. Don't forget the woman of hens.

BLIND MAN.   A pound of tea from the woman of hens.
                After all this, it's not enough
                From the man of cows—a pinch of snuff!

ALL.   After all this, it's not enough
                From the man of cows—a pinch of snuff!

OLD FARMER. The devil the like of such fun have we had this year!

MISER. Oh, indeed, I was only keeping a little grain for myself; but it's likely they may want it all. (*He takes the paper out, and lays it on the table.*)

BLIND MAN. A bag of meal from the man of sheep.

ALL.   After all this, it's not enough
                From the man of cows—a half-ounce of snuff!

(*One of the girls hands the snuff around; they laugh and sneeze, taking pinches of it.*)

OLD FARMER. My soul to the devil, Seagan, do the thing decently. Give out one of those fleeces you have in the cart with you.

MISER. I never saw the like of you for fools since I was born. Is it mad you are?

ALL.   From the man of cows, a half-ounce of snuff!

MISER. Oh, maisead, if there must be a present put down, take the fleece, and my share of misfortune on you. (*Three or four of the boys run out.*)

OLD FARMER. Aurah, Seagan, what is your opinion of Raftery now? He has you destroyed worse than the bush! (*The boys come back, a fleece with them.*)

BOY. Here is the fleece, and it's very heavy it is. (*They put it down, and there falls a little bag out of it that bursts and scatters the money here and there on the floor.*)

MISER. Ub-ub-bu! That is my share of money scattered on me that I got for my calves. (*He stoops down to gather it together. All the people burst out laughing again.*)

OLD FARMER. Maisead, Seagan, where did you get the money? You told us you didn't sell your share of calves.

BLIND MAN.
    He that got good gold
    For calves he never sold
    Must put good money down
    With a laugh, without a frown;
    Or I'll destroy that man
    With a bone-breaking rann.
    I'll rhyme him by the book
    To a blue-watery look.

MISER. Oh, Raftery, don't do that. I tasted enough of your ranns just now, and I don't want another taste of them. There's threepence for you. (*He puts three pennies in the plate.*)

BLIND MAN.
    I'll put a new name upon
    This strong farmer, of Thrippeny John.
    He'll be called, without a doubt,
    Thrippeny John from this time out.
    Put your sovereign on my plate,
    Or that and worse will be your fate.

MISER. Oh, in the name of God, Raftery, stop your mouth and let me go! Here is the sovereign for you; and indeed it's not with my blessing I give it.

(BLIND MAN *plays on the fiddle. They all stand up and dance but Seagan na Stucaire, who shakes his fist in* BLIND MAN'S *face and goes out. When they have danced for a minute or two,* BLIND MAN *stops fiddling and stands up.*)

BLIND MAN. I was near forgetting: I am the only person here gave nothing to the woman of the house. (*Hands the plate of money to* MARY.) Take that and my seven hundred blessings along with it, and that you may be as well as I wish you to the end of life and time. Count the money now, and see what the neighbors did for you.

MARY. That is too much indeed.

MARTIN. You have too much done for us already.

BLIND MAN. Count it, count it; while I go over and try can I hear what sort of blessings Seagan na Stucaire is leaving after him.

(*Neighbors all crowd round counting the money.* Blind Man *goes to the door, looks back with a sigh, and goes quietly out.*)

Old Farmer.   Well, you have enough to set you up altogether, Martin. You'll be buying us all up within the next six months.

Martin.   Indeed I don't think I'll be going digging potatoes for other men this year, but to be working for myself at home.   (*The sound of horse's steps are heard.   A young man comes into the house.*)

Young Man.   What is going on here at all?   All the cars in the country gathered at the door, and Seagan na Stucaire going swearing down the road.

Old Farmer.   Oh, this is the great wedding was made by Raftery.   Where is Raftery?   Where is he gone?

Martin (*going to the door*).   He's not here.   I don't see him on the road. (*Turns to young farmer.*)   Did you meet a blind fiddler going out the door— the poet Raftery?

Young Man.   The poet Raftery?   I did not; but I stood by his grave at Killeenan three days ago.

Mary.   His grave?   Oh, Martin, it was a dead man was in it!

Martin.   Whoever it was, it was a man sent by God was in it.

CURTAIN

A SNOWY NIGHT
A Play

By Roberto Bracco

Authorized translation from the Italian original by Arthur Livingston

CHARACTERS

SALVATORE
GRAZIELLA
FRANCESCA

PLACE: *Naples, in our own time.*

A SNOWY NIGHT

A room in a ground floor tenement, on a side street, in the poorer quarters of Naples. The room is miserably furnished, but neat: a double bed, the usual cheap affair of iron, with clean pillows and blankets, however; a wooden table, a couple of wooden chairs, a bench, a dresser, a few other indispensable articles. Standing in the center of the room is a large brazier for burning charcoal. There is no fire. At the head of the bed hangs a small crucifix, though the walls are otherwise quite bare.
The room must seem cold and empty.
In the back drop, a heavy folding door opens directly upon the street. High up, in one of the wings of the door, a tiny window has been cut—too small for a person to put his head through. Two iron bars, crossing at right angles, make it look like the window of a prison-cell. It has also a wooden shutter fastening with a hook.
The door and the window are closed. It is night. The room is almost dark.

*   *   *

Graziella *is lying stretched out on the bed, her shawl thrown over her. In the dim light she looks more like a corpse than like a person sleeping.*
After a period of silence, a song (sung to the music printed at the end of the Act) comes slowly drawling in from the street. It is the jest of a gang of night hawks—a canto a dispetto.

A Voice (*singing*).   Tu stai dormendo
                      e mon lo sai che noi stiamo svegliati—
                      e siamo dieci
                      a cantare per te che si hai lasciati . . .

All The Gang (*in refrain*).   Che ci hai lasciati.
Graziella (*wakening; sits up on the bed and shudders*).   Oh!
(*A period of silence. Then the song begins again. She sits there, listening.*)
A Different Voice.   Ti sei scordata
                      Che quando stavi al vicolo Schiavone
                      noi passavamo—
                      e ci chiamavi tu,
                      dal tuo balcone . . .

The Gang (*in refrain*).   Dal tuo balcone.
One of The Gang (*raising his voice, to be sure he is heard, but with a mocking drawl*).   Nothing doing around here any more!
Graziella (*almost to herself, quivering with anger*).   A plague on the lot of you!

ANOTHER VOICE. Only one man good enough for this queen now!

ANOTHER VOICE. And he—aha!—he's coming!

GRAZIELLA (*to herself*). He's coming! Oh—if they say anything to him—what will happen? . . . (*She slips down from the bed, gropes her way to the dresser, and lights a little oil lamp. Then she hurries to the window, opens the wooden shutter, and standing on tiptoe, looks out.*) They're going away—they're going! Oh! . . . (*Much relieved.*) I'm so glad! (*She closes the shutter again, hooks it, and stands there listening, waiting for the usual signal from* SALVATORE. *A long, shrill whistle—*GRAZIELLA *brightens.*) He's coming—he's coming! (*She listens eagerly again. Another long whistle, nearer and louder this time.* GRAZIELLA *hurriedly unlocks the door, and pulls open one of the wings.*)

(SALVATORE *appears. He is wearing a plain cloth cap, pulled down over his eyes, and a shabby coat with the collar turned up.*

GRAZIELLA *throws her arms about his neck and nestles against him like a child. They stand there for a moment in this embrace.*)

SALVATORE. My! What a night! I don't remember anything like it. More like the North Pole than like Naples. It freezes you to the bone! And I knew you wouldn't have a fire. . . . You are out of money. . . . Well—so am I!

GRAZIELLA. The man in the wine-shop on the corner gave me a few pieces of charcoal. It lasted for a while; after that—

SALVATORE. Didn't I tell you never to accept presents from anybody?

GRAZIELLA. But it was so cold! I had to—I couldn't say no. It was just a handful—see the ashes there. (*A period of silence. She goes over and locks the door, looking out into the street, however, before she closes it. With the door still open.*) Why, Salvatore—

SALVATORE. What?

GRAZIELLA. It's snowing!

SALVATORE (*throwing his hat angrily on the bed*). I wish it would snow from now till Kingdom Come! (*Sits down in a chair.*)

GRAZIELLA (*approaching him tenderly*). You told me you would cheer up!

SALVATORE. Cheer up! . . . Cheer up! A pretty time to cheer up! I've lost my job!

GRAZIELLA. Lost your job?

SALVATORE. That's what I said—I've lost my job. When we were closing up this evening, the boss came around and told me I was getting through . . . Didn't need me any longer!

GRAZIELLA. He's a crook!

SALVATORE. Crook? Why is he a crook? Not at all! He gave me two months' in advance, last pay day, didn't he? Well, he said I could keep the money. So why is he a crook? When you get money from a man, you have to give him something for it, don't you? Well, I had nothing to give him—there! Good intentions don't count—you have to be good for something. And what am I good for? . . . Bumming around all my life between one dive and another! Why, work was the last thing on earth I ever thought of. I had plenty of money, and I was pretty good with the cards. I got along. I didn't need to work. And then I met you—in one of those dives—and we thought we'd try to get on our feet—break away from all that life. We didn't realize what it was going to be like. So now, here we are—fighting a battle with empty guns. We're living in this hole just now—but to-morrow, or the day after, we'll be on the sidewalk!

GRAZIELLA. Oh no!—You'll see. . . . Little by little—

SALVATORE. No, you never can make a man out of stuff like me—Just get this into your head good and solid. I'll never be able to earn a cent, honestly!

GRAZIELLA. But think of all you might do! You've a fine education. You've been to school!—You told me once you even went to boarding school, somewhere away from Naples.

SALVATORE. I should say I did! And I was the first in the class, too. Huh! A boy of promise I was! A coming genius! To keep me from getting conceited, the teachers used to say, "You ought to thank your father for giving you such a splendid brain!" Well, mother had let me believe that I really had a father, and that he died before I was born. So I sent him my thanks, to the other world! Yes—all the prizes I got! We had pretty uniforms, too. It was a military school. (*He laughs bitterly.*) Huh! . . . Real class in that school! Nobody without a title . . . Counts, dukes—huh!—real aristocracy. You see, she (*meaning his mother*)—well, she had money enough to keep me in such company—poor fool that she was! Thought she could make a gentleman out of me. Thought she could paint me up to look the part. But it never got deeper than my skin. . . . The blood she gave me came from the sewers of Naples!

GRAZIELLA. But she must have been fond of you to do all that. . . . She must have meant well.

SALVATORE (*leaping to his feet*). Don't you defend that woman! Don't you dare say a word for her!

GRAZIELLA. But she's your mother! Salvatore. She must have meant well. . . .

SALVATORE. She had no right to bring me into the world! (*A brief pause.*) But once she had me, she had no right to keep me way off there, letting me grow up in ignorance of what she really was. If she had kept me with her, I would have taken it all quite naturally—the filth around her would have entered my flesh and bones, become part of my soul, part of me! And then, when I was a man, I would have loved my mother, and thought it quite natural to be living quietly on the proceeds of her shame!

GRAZIELLA (*humbly*). But you forget that I was like her! (*A silence*).

SALVATORE (*approaching her, and taking her head gently in his hands*). I shouldn't have said that to you, should I? Forgive me if it hurt! (*A pause.*) Besides, with you, it's different. You had the courage to break away from all that, and you didn't wait till you got too old to play the game any longer.

You were so anxious to live a different sort of life that I was sorry for you, and you have been all this time such a good, good girl, that really I never think of you in that connection. No—you are white, all the way through. I know. . . . You would have worked at anything to keep us going. You would have gone and washed dishes for somebody, if I had let you. You've stuck it out—ready for anything. There are few people in this world good enough to kiss the ground you walk on, Graziella. . . . That's the gospel truth. And if you keep it up—

GRAZIELLA (*starting*). If I keep it up?

SALVATORE. Yes . . . because anything may happen, you know.

GRAZIELLA (*vehemently*). No!—With you, Salvatore, always—always with you! . . . Cold, hunger—everything . . . but always with you, till the very end—until I die! And when I die, I shall die with you—with you! Don't you know that? (SALVATORE *looks the other way to hide his emotion,* GRAZIELLA *clinging to him passionately.*) You are weeping! There are tears in your eyes! . . . Let me see them—let me see them! Why do you deny me that joy? . . . You are weeping! And that means that you still love me—you do, don't you!

SALVATORE (*gently, his voice husky with tears*). I thought I could come to you some day, and say, "Look, Graziella! We were out there in a boat, on a stormy sea, and we thought we were going to drown. But I brought the boat ashore, with your help, and you brought the boat ashore with my help!" . . . But am I able to say that to you, really? Can I honestly say so? Is there any reason to hope I shall ever be able to say so?

GRAZIELLA. I have that hope still, even if you have not, Salvatore. I am not discouraged. I believe in you. I am so sure that everything will come out all right, that even now, as you stand here, despondent, hopeless, my heart is just overflowing with happiness, and I kiss you—there—and there—and there—and there—as if this were a night of joy, and a bed of roses were waiting for us! (*She kisses him repeatedly.*)

SALVATORE (*strangely moved by her passionate appeal, drawing her to him, and whispering in her ear*). Shall we pretend that it is a bed of roses?

GRAZIELLA. Yes. (SALVATORE *catches her up in both his arms. The song of the gangsters again drawls down the streets.*)

A VOICE. Con un geloso
       Ti sei voluta chiudere in prigione—
       A pane ed acqua
       Campate tutti e due di passione . . .

THE GANG (*in chorus*). Di passione.

SALVATORE (*hearing the first notes, throws* GRAZIELLA *off, as though in shame at having been surprised in such intimacy. Then he stands there, listening in fury, his face distorted with atrocious suffering*). Do you hear that?—Your old friends! They are making fun of you!

GRAZIELLA. The dogs!

ANOTHER VOICE. Prima con noi
               Passavi allegramente le nottate—
               E mo suspiri
               Per quante lire noi t'abbiamo date . . .

THE GANG (*in chorus*). T'abbiamo date.

(SALVATORE, *unable to control himself, dashes for the door.*)

GRAZIELLA (*throws herself desperately upon him*). No, Salvatore—don't—don't! You are only one, and there is a crowd of them. They'll kill you—they'll kill you!

SALVATORE (*throwing her off*). If I get one of them first, I don't mind if they kill me!

GRAZIELLA (*her back to the door*). No, Salvatore. Throw me out to them, rather! . . . Let them insult me! Insult me yourself! But don't go out there! Don't go out there to be killed by those people, who have already been my ruin!

SALVATORE (*hesitates for a moment, then sinks into a chair. There is a long pause*). Well—why not? I suppose I might as well be a coward into the bargain—a coward . . . why not? To-morrow night they'll be back here again, hanging around in front of the house to pass a pleasant evening at our expense. And they'll come back the night after that, and the night after that; and I'll sit here and listen to them, because there's a crowd of them, and I'm alone. I'll listen to them respectfully, also—yes, yes—respectfully!—tipping my hat because they . . . they are many and gave you at least a living, while I—I'm only one, and I give you nothing!

GRAZIELLA. Oh, Salvatore! . . .

SALVATORE. Well, you—then—you do something about it! You do something to get us out of this!

GRAZIELLA. Plenty of people have gone away from Naples before this. Let's you and I go away off somewhere—

SALVATORE (*jumping to his feet, vehemently*). And how will we go, pray? The tickets—for example! You don't know what you are talking about. Where's the money? Oh, you women!—It's just sentiment with you! You think people can live on love. We love each other, eh? And so—let's go away—away off somewhere! Where, in God's name? No! Our place is here—here—in prison—as those fellows just said in their song! In prison—on bread and water, and around us the Carnival of all those who can boast of having given you real money! (GRAZIELLA *crushed, shrinking, sinks to a chair, and says nothing. A long silence.* SALVATORE, *resuming bitterly.*) Why go on this way? We ought to have brains enough to go back to the point where we started four months ago. Everybody comes into this world with an address written here—(*He points to his forehead*). He is like a letter pushed into a mail-box. Whether he likes it or not, he must go to that address.

GRAZIELLA (*timidly*). That's the way you talk; but you know you would never leave me. I'm sure of that!

SALVATORE (*pretending not to hear, and continuing*). We got the jolly notion of walking on our heads, with our feet in the air. It's amusing, I admit, for other people to look at! But for us—for us, there can be only death. Let's have done with this crazy nonsense about love! (*He crosses the room to the bench, and lies back on it, his legs sprawling out in front of him. A long silence. Their next words are pronounced softly, slowly and sadly, every word distinct, however, with a solemn, almost funereal resonance.*)

GRAZIELLA (*drawing her shawl tightly about her*). Uh!—how cold it is!— it's getting worse! If you don't intend to go to bed to-night, at least take one of the blankets.

SALVATORE. And you?

GRAZIELLA. I have my shawl.

SALVATORE. But you are shivering!

GRAZIELLA. It doesn't matter.

SALVATORE. You go to bed.

GRAZIELLA. No, Salvatore—I won't. (*A long silence. Suddenly a knock is heard at the door. GRAZIELLA leaps to her feet.*)

SALVATORE (*also rising*). Who can that be at such an hour?

GRAZIELLA (*clinging to him in great alarm*). Oh, Salvatore! (*Another moment's silence.*)

SALVATORE. Some one going along the street thought he would contribute his bit, too! (*The knock is repeated.*)

GRAZIELLA. No. . . . It's some one who wants to come in! (*Shuddering with terror.*) Do you think it's those fellows? (*SALVATORE bites his lips, and writhes with an anger mingled with perplexity. GRAZIELLA going to the little window, opening the shutter, and looking out.*) No, Salvatore. It's a woman. (*With great relief.*)

SALVATORE (*startled*). A woman?

GRAZIELLA (*closing the shutter again*). I don't know who it is. She has a big bag on one shoulder—I couldn't see her face, but it's a woman.

SALVATORE (*with sudden understanding, running to the door and calling harshly to the person on the other side*). Who are you? What do you want? Who are you?

VOICE OF FRANCESCA (*coming indistinctly from outside*). It's I—It's I!

SALVATORE (*furiously*). You just move on! Get away from here!

GRAZIELLA (*timidly, trying to soften him*). Oh, no, Salvatore! Don't drive her away like that!

SALVATORE. But what does she want? What is she doing here? She's always following me around—dogging my tracks, wherever I go. I can't turn around but I see her somewhere, watching me, spying on me! And now she has followed me here, to this place, on this terrible night! . . . Ah!—she's the ghost of my loathesome lot in life!

VOICE OF FRANCESCA (*from outside, faintly*). I'm bringing you this bag of charcoal—it's snowing hard. . . . Please let me in! You'll need it! . . . (*A silence.*)

GRAZIELLA (*timidly imploring*). Salvatore!

SALVATORE (*steps to the door and draws the bolt, but then an uncontrollable revulsion comes over him. He turns to* GRAZIELLA, *and with lowered eyes, says softly*) You can let her in, if you want to. (GRAZIELLA *opens.* FRANCESCA *peers through the opened door, looking about the room, half fearfully. She is bent low under the weight of the bag of charcoal she is carrying. She is a woman in her sixties, but she seems much older than that: the wear and tear of a hard life. She is dressed in rags. On her unkempt hair, and scattered over her clothing, as over the bag of charcoal, flakes of snow can be seen.*)

GRAZIELLA. Let me help you.

FRANCESCA. It's too heavy for you. I'll attend to it.

GRAZIELLA. Let me just get a hold.

FRANCESCA. Thanks. (*Together they carry the bag and set it on the floor near the brazier.* SALVATORE *has stepped back, and avoids meeting* FRANCESCA'S *eyes. Confused between the instinctive passion within him, and his own sense of shame, he cannot endure the situation any longer. He picks up his hat, and while the women are busy with the charcoal, slips out through the door without their noticing.*)

GRAZIELLA (*questioning the old lady with a shy yet affectionate intimacy*). How did you know we were cold?

FRANCESCA. Oh, I watch you—I keep my eye on you. Sometimes I stand for two or three hours here on the street, in front of your door. Then again, I sit down on your doorstep, and pretend to be sleeping. But I'm listening, you see, with my ear against the door. And sometimes, in the silence, I can hear you talking. . . . And some of the words I understand. I was there before he came. I saw those boys, as they came along to sing their song out in front here. Then I saw him coming up the street, and I slipped away, so that he wouldn't notice me. But I didn't go very far. . . . I noticed how you opened the window, and I was sure you were as frightened as I was! "God bless you," I said to myself. "In any case there will be four arms to help him, if there's a fight." Fortunately the gang moved away in the other direction. By the time he got here, everything was quiet. Your door opened— he stepped in. The door closed again . . . and I kissed the ground in thankfulness!

GRAZIELLA (*looking at her with a surprise mingled with deep sadness*). So you are always watching over us?

FRANCESCA. Always!

GRAZIELLA. There, Salvatore, do you hear that? (*She turns, and not finding him, she is alarmed.*) Where is he? Where is he? (*She runs to the door, and sees him standing outside in the street. She calls to him pleadingly.*) Oh, Salvatore—please come in—you'll catch your death of cold out there!

VOICE OF SALVATORE (*bitterly*). I don't want to hear what you are saying!

GRAZIELLA. But what are we saying that you can object to? Come in . . . please come in!

FRANCESCA (*anxiously, but resignedly*). No, Graziella—don't call him . . . don't call him again. It's just as well he's not here. (*Hurriedly, in a low tone.*) Listen! He mustn't know—but here's a little money for you!

GRAZIELLA (*joyously, radiant*). Money? . . . Money? (*Then changing tone.*) But you—poor as you are . . .

FRANCESCA. No. . . . It's money I have been keeping for him for years— oh, for so many years. . . . But to-night, I thought it would be a mortal sin to keep it any longer!

GRAZIELLA (*suddenly paling with fright, and stammering*). But that money! —He won't accept it!

FRANCESCA. If you tell him you are a mother, how would he dare refuse?

GRAZIELLA (*starting with surprise*). But how did you know that I am a mother?

FRANCESCA. Oh, I knew you were—I guessed it—and I'm sure you never told him so, either!

GRAZIELLA. I kept it from him, for fear he might be angry. But how did you ever understand?

FRANCESCA. I understand everything, as though I were living here with you!

GRAZIELLA. Because you saw me visiting Donna Concetta these last few days?

FRANCESCA. Yes. I saw you going there. I often follow you like that along the streets.

GRAZIELLA. Yes. She is a good midwife. And I was not feeling well. I wanted baby to have the best!

FRANCESCA. And you were so beautiful. And I knew you were a good girl, and I just didn't want you to worry any longer. I wanted you to know that this child which is to come into the world would have comfort enough and grow up strong and healthy and happy. Because I have the money here—yes, here it is . . . here it is—take it—take it! . . . I would have said that to you long ago, but I was afraid of Salvatore, as you were, and I delayed until now. However, I never hoped I would be able to have a talk with you alone to-night, so I put the money there, in the bag, along with the charcoal.

GRAZIELLA. In the bag? . . . Quick—quick—we must hide it! He mustn't know! I'll give it to him when you have gone, if I have the courage to. (*Looking anxiously at the door, she bends over the bag, opens it and rummages around.*) It would be unwise to show it to him while you are here. It would be terrible!

FRANCESCA (*bending over the bag, and finding the money 'at once.*) Here it is! But put it out of sight!

GRAZIELLA (*takes the purse, and hides it under her shawl*). Yes—yes!

FRANCESCA (*whispering in a very low voice, for fear* SALVATORE *will hear*). If you continue living this way, it will not be good for the baby.

GRAZIELLA. Better death for me and Salvatore, than that any harm should come to our child!

FRANCESCA. Hunger is a terrible thing, and this is a cold winter. (SALVA-
TORE'S *steps are heard approaching.* GRAZIELLA *motions to* FRANCESCA *to be
silent.*)

SALVATORE (*enters, and stops when barely through the door. A brief silence.
Then, to* FRANCESCA). Do you stop talking when I come in!

GRAZIELLA. You said you didn't want to hear what we were saying!

SALVATORE (*looking first at one, and then at the other*). That's not why she
broke off! There's something else in the air!

GRAZIELLA. Nothing to your disadvantage—that you well know.

SALVATORE. Ah—I wonder!

GRAZIELLA. Your mother has always loved you, and she loves you now—as
I do!

SALVATORE (*advancing menacingly upon* GRAZIELLA). I ask you a question.
And you answer me—yes, or no! . . . Could you think of earning money for
me, by returning to the life you once led?

GRAZIELLA. No!—No!—I wouldn't do that even to save your life!

SALVATORE. Well, then—you have no right to say that she has loved me as
much as you do!

FRANCESCA (*humbly*).When you were a child, I didn't realize. How could I
realize? I was so different from the women you came to know. I saw only
with the eyes I had then. I lived the life I had always lived. There was no
one to make me think of anything different. It was the contempt you had for
me that opened my eyes! . . . It was the curses you heaped upon me! And
from that day to this, I have been a different woman. I have chosen to live in
poverty—to deserve something else from you! I was twenty-eight at that
time, to be sure. But people told me I was prettier than I had ever been.
. . . I had always taken care of myself. But, from what you taught me, I
came to hate myself! And I mortified my flesh, standing by day under the
burning sun, and at night out under the rain. . . . I went into the churches,
and pressed my face to the floor which other people walked with their feet!
I lived on the crust of bread that the charity of Christians gave me. And at
times, as this girl here goes without food to deserve your love, so I went without food to deserve your forgiveness!

SALVATORE (*moved, in spite of himself*). The sufferings you have chosen to
inflict upon yourself may save your soul when you have ended your sufferings
on earth, and that, perhaps, will be justice. But, unfortunately, anything you
endured could not save me from the poison you had given me to drink, and
which was to spoil my blood for all my life! (*Approaching her, and opening
his coat as though to uncover his heart.*) Look at me! Just try to realize
what a torment of hatred and bitterness and sorrow has piled up inside me
here! (FRANCESCA *draws back, and hides her face.* SALVATORE *insisting.*)
Look at this offspring of yours! Look at this man I am! Half gentleman,
half vagabond; half ignorant, half educated; half hero, half coward; half man,
half beast! . . . Ah! You can't imagine what a horror it is to live this way!
I have a loathing for the disgrace that lies upon me! And yet my mind lingers

upon it continually. I cannot reconcile myself to this life of squalor, and yet I am the lowest of the low. From a life of vice I take a woman who loved me—and yet I curse that impulse of kindness, and I have to stand around while you, of all people, come and offer her something which I have not the money to buy her! Oh—if only I had the power to forgive you!—I could escape, perhaps, part of the weight of this crushing humiliation.

FRANCESCA (*trembling*). I didn't come for your forgiveness, Salvatore. I have long since abandoned hope of ever getting that. Because I understand that you cannot—that you simply cannot!

SALVATORE (*still more deeply moved*). I see you, sometimes, standing there, trembling and afraid—your face wan, emaciated—your deep-sunk eyes as bright as two candles lighted in a tomb. And a great cry rises within me. . . . I feel like screaming to you: "Oh—Mother, Mother!—come to me! Come to me, as a mother to her child!" . . . But then, the poison in my blood rises to my head, and fills my brain. It makes me drunk. It sets me all on fire! I wrestle with myself—I seem to have two hearts in my breast, knocking against each other, breaking each other to pieces. . . . And I could tear out these eyes of mine, in order to escape the sight of your eyes which fill me with such bitter torment!

FRANCESCA. Well—I promise you. . . . I promise you, that from now on, you will never see me again! I will keep out of your sight. Oh, I will watch you—I will keep watching you—but without your seeing me—without your seeing my eyes that hurt you so. In that way you won't have to be in torment all the time—you will not be tortured with the thought that I stand there, hoping for your forgiveness. You have let me enter your house—you have let me talk with her—(*She points to* GRAZIELLA)—and for that I thank you. Because of that, I can go away content. I had waited for this moment for so long. (*She wipes the tears from her eyes.*) And if—if you can grant a prayer of mine—a prayer which I offer with this little bag of fuel that I have brought —I beg of you, Salvatore—I beg of you, never to abandon this dear, good child! She is such a good girl. . . . And nothing can so comfort an unhappy man as to know that he has saved a poor woman who had fallen in sin! (GRAZIELLA *bursts into sobs, and throws her arms round the old woman's neck.* FRANCESCA, *weeping, presses* GRAZIELLA *to her breast, and kisses her on the forehead.*) This for you—and this (*kissing her again, longer this time, and more passionately*) for him! . . . (*Gently she frees herself from* GRAZIELLA'S *embrace, and with a glance at her son, walks slowly from the room.* SALVATORE *sinks into a chair at the table, and rests his head heavily on his arms.* GRAZIELLA *wipes her eyes, and swings the door to, being careful to leave it open a few inches; then she goes to the brazier. She brushes up the ashes, goes to a corner, returns with an old newspaper, and prepares to make a fire.*)

SALVATORE (*raises his head, as though to make sure that* FRANCESCA *has gone. He sees the door half open, and, somewhat puzzled, asks*). Why didn't you shut the door tight?

GRAZIELLA. You are still suspicious? I left it open because I am going to ight the fire. (*She touches a match to the waste paper in the brazier, throw-ng a handful of charcoal on the blaze, and later adding some larger pieces, neanwhile fanning the fire with a palm leaf fan.* SALVATORE *rises with some rritation, goes to the door, shuts it tight, locks it, and puts the key in his pocket. Then he opens the window. He goes back to his chair.*)

SALVATORE. Well now, if you don't mind, you'll just tell me what my mother had to say.

GRAZIELLA (*laying down the fan and hesitating*). She said . . . if you would only be more reasonable. . . . If you didn't hate her quite so much. . . .

SALVATORE (*bitterly*). You will never understand what I have suffered—what I am still suffering on her account. And yet, she is not the one I really hate—I hate myself! (*Earnestly.*) Look—if I were not as poor as I am, my first thought would be—well—to help her—help her without her noticing, to be sure, and to get her out of the streets, where she is living like a beggar. No—it isn't hatred. I am more reasonable than you think. And for that reason there is no use in your trying to keep what she really said from me.

GRAZIELLA (*hesitating*). Your poor mother!—Well, we talked of how hard it was to get along. . . . The help you would like to give to her, she wants to give to us.

SALVATORE. Divide up the pennies she gets from begging, I suppose!

GRAZIELLA. No—it wasn't that—

SALVATORE. Well, what did she say then? (*A pause.*)

GRAZIELLA. The fire is burning. Come, Salvatore—it's warmer here.

SALVATORE. No. (*A pause.*)

GRAZIELLA (*rising; stepping around behind* SALVATORE'S *chair, and gently, tenderly, putting an arm around his shoulders*). Salvatore! (*She hesitates.*)

SALVATORE. Well?

GRAZIELLA. Supposing your mother . . .

SALVATORE (*in feigned encouragement*). Well?

GRAZIELLA. Suppose your mother, in addition to the charcoal, had also brought—

SALVATORE (*leaping to his feet*). Money?

GRAZIELLA. Oh, please—don't be that way!

SALVATORE (*glaring at her*). Where is that money? Where is it? Show me that money! Where is it?

GRAZIELLA (*trembling*). I'll give it to you by and by.

SALVATORE (*almost screaming*). Where did you put that money? Where did you put that money?

GRAZIELLA. Don't be that way, Salvatore!—You frighten me!

SALVATORE. Give me that money—and right away! or there will be trouble. . . .

GRAZIELLA. I have it here—I have it here. But let me give it to you later— (SALVATORE *seizes her, and begins feeling about over her shawl to find the purse.*) Wait!—Wait!—Wait a moment!

SALVATORE (*finding the purse, drags it out from under her arm, and sneers*).

Ah!—I see! So now, again—after twenty years—again this little treasure of shame is offered me. The same money with which she tried to keep me twenty years ago, when I came back from school to the luxurious home she was then maintaining—and then deserted her in loathing! On that day I turned my back upon her forever! And ever since that miserable woman has been living in the gutter, begging her way about the streets, but forcing herself to keep the savings of those years for her child—for me! . . . Now, to you—I understand—all that must seem sublime! In your heart I can read admiration, joy, gratitude—ah! (*With a gesture and an expression of disgust, he starts to throw the money into the fire.*)

GRAZIELLA (*interfering, with a cry*). ·No! . . . (*A brief pause.*)

SALVATORE (*tossing the purse upon the bag of coal instead*). Well, after all, it's natural! You two women—why not? You understand each other perfectly!

GRAZIELLA (*resolutely, firmly, with a vehemence unusual in her, she draws back her shoulders, and her voice is strong and resonant*). Shall I tell you, then? Very well. I will tell you. It is not for me, nor even for you, that I ask you not to destroy that money. No, Salvatore—the truth is that I am to have a child myself! . . . Yes, I am going to have a child—and that child I look forward to the way the poor people who are out there, sleeping on the streets to-night, must be waiting for the warm sun to rise to-morrow morning!

SALVATORE (*with desperate exasperation*). What! You are sure? You are sure you are going to have a child? . . . And you haven't let me know?

GRAZIELLA (*sorrowfully*). I didn't let you know, because you keep telling me every day that it is a crime for women like me to become mothers. But that crime I committed—for you . . . and it seemed beautiful to me!—a joy I could not surrender! And so I shrank from telling you. . . . (*Changing her tone, almost imperiously.*) But now I have told you! The confession has come from the depth of my soul—to ask you to take pity on our child that is to come. And now it is for you to decide. If you don't care whether our child is to be born in a house of desolation and poverty, throw this money into the fire! But prepare to render an accounting to God for the crime you will be committing in doing so. As for me, you know that I am resigned to everything. . . .

SALVATORE (*feverishly, caught between a deep anguish and a ferocious rage*). Yes! . . . You say that—you say that. . . . The rest was not enough! Out of the compassion I must have for this child who is to come, you would tear my conscience to bits—you would tear the last remnant of my sense of honor to shreds, and use those shreds to make a cradle for your child! . . . No!— No! . . . I will not accept that accursed money! I will go back to the life I left! I will become a vagabond once more! I will go about from dive to dive —a gambler—yes—a pickpocket, if necessary! I will become a thief, if I have to. . . . I'll go to jail . . . but in any case, I will free myself at last from all these torturing passions that bind me to women from your world!

GRAZIELLA (*as though a chasm had suddenly opened beneath her feet*).

Salvatore!—Salvatore. . . . Remember. . . . If you leave me now, there will be no further reason for me to live!

SALVATORE. You can live for that child of yours! He is worth much more to you than I will ever be!

GRAZIELLA (*screaming*). No!—No! Don't say that! It isn't true!

SALVATORE (*his breast heaving, his voice choking with the sobs gathering in his throat*). It is true!—It is true! . . . And you yourself have just given me the proof of it! Well, of one thing you may be sure. . . . I will render an accounting to God for what I do! Certain, as I shall be, to have done the best for you I could do!

GRAZIELLA. Salvatore!—please. . . . Listen to me, Salvatore. . . .

SALVATORE (*without heeding her*). That money, which I refuse for the second time, is yours. It's yours. You can find nothing wrong with it. In view of so much money, there will be no danger of your child coming into the world in a house of desolation and of poverty.

GRAZIELLA. Salvatore—listen to me!

SALVATORE (*insisting*). My mother has given you this money. Well, you won't need me any longer to keep you out of trouble!

GRAZIELLA. Salvatore—listen to me! (*She throws her arms passionately about him.*)

SALVATORE (*trying to shake her off*). And I—I will get back all my freedom!—I shall be free!—free!—free! . . . And if ever again, along my path I meet a woman like you, and like her . . . well, I will run away from her, as I would run away from the plague! . . . Good-by—good-by! . . .

GRAZIELLA (*clinging to him to keep him from going out of the door*). Stay with me, Salvatore! . . . Don't go away! Don't go away!

SALVATORE. Let me alone!

GRAZIELLA. Please stay!—Please stay! . . . (*Two heavy knocks on the door interrupt their scuffle.* SALVATORE *and* GRAZIELLA *both stop and stand there, listening.*)

SALVATORE. Some one is knocking. (*Furiously.*) It is she—back again!

THE VOICE OF A MAN. Anybody h-home in there? (*The man is evidently drunk.*)

SALVATORE. What do you want?

THE VOICE. N-nothing. . . . B-but I thought I would l-let you know. Here in your d-doorway is an old l-lady l-lying on the ground. . . .

SALVATORE. Are you a policeman? Tell her to move on!

THE VOICE. N-no. . . . I'm not a p-policeman. . . . I'm j-just d-drunk! B-but anyh-how, s-she won't move on, b-because she's d-dead! . . .

SALVATORE (*staggers, his hands to his head*). Dead!

GRAZIELLA (*looking at him in terror*). Dead!

THE VOICE. And s-she has a n-knife w-with her! . . . (SALVATORE *sinks to a chair, a flood of remorse sweeping over him.*)

GRAZIELLA (*staggers to the door, and tries to open it; then turning to* SALVATORE). You have the key. . . .

SALVATORE.   Yes.

GRAZIELLA.   Give it to me.

SALVATORE (*taking the key out of his pocket. He has not the strength to rise from his chair. He holds it out at arm's length, waiting for her to take it. His hand can be seen shaking like a branch of a tree blowing in the wind*). Here it is.

GRAZIELLA (*goes to the door again. She has hardly the strength to turn the key*).   Just a moment. . . .

THE VOICE.   G-good n-night!

CURTAIN

THE CHERRY BLOSSOM RIVER

ADAPTED FROM THE JAPANESE

By COLIN CAMPBELL CLEMENTS

CHARACTERS

A Slave Merchant
A Mother
Sakura, *her son*
A Priest
Villagers
The Chorus

THE CHERRY BLOSSOM RIVER

Scene I

A street in Tsukushi at dusk. The only light comes from two large oiled-paper windows of a Japanese house at the back. Between the windows is a small sliding door. The Chorus, a man in a long blue kimono, sits on a low bench near the edge of the stage at the extreme right. As the curtain rises a villager wanders in from the left and from the right enters the slave merchant.

MERCHANT. Ho, fellow, do you live hereabouts? (THE VILLAGER *nods.*) I am a child-merchant from the East and just came down to Tsukushi yesterday. Toward evening I bought a young boy and he begged me to take the money I paid for him with this letter to the mother of young Sakura and to deliver both safely to her. Can you tell me where she lives?

VILLAGER (*he points toward the house and mutters as he goes on his way*). That is the place.

MERCHANT (*he knocks at the door. An old woman opens it*). Pray is the mother of Sakura here?

WOMAN. Who art thou?

MERCHANT. Here is a letter from young Sakura. He also bade me safely to deliver this money, so I have brought it hither, and hereby do deliver it.

WOMAN. This is strange. First let me see the letter. (*She reads.*) 'For many months it has grieved me to look upon your wretched state, and as I have sold myself to a child-merchant and am going eastward—' (THE MERCHANT *slips out.*) Stay, what does it mean? My child was not for such as they. Ah, he is gone—lost from sight! (*She resumes reading.*) 'I pray thee to come closer to the Father of all. A thousand times I regret that I must part from thee.'

CHORUS (*chanting*).

> Why, if the parting is so bitter, does
> He leave his mother all alone to grieve?
> The mother in her humble cot alone
> Day in, day out, with naught to comfort her.

WOMAN (*chanting*).

> O Holy One in whom I put my faith,
> Great Lady of the Cherry Trees-that-Blossom,
> The lovely Konohasakuyahimo,
> At birth to thee my son was dedicated,
> Canst thou not stay him now—my Sakura?

CHORUS (*chants as the curtain falls*).

> For otherwise
> How can she live the weary days alone,
> In this old home where grief has come to her?
> She will seek out whither her child has gone,
> Weeping, with empty heart she wanders forth.

SCENE II

Near the banks of the Cherry-Blossom River, three years later. It is Spring and the cherry trees are in full bloom. A priest is talking to a villager. A young boy stands near.

THE PRIEST.

> Long have we waited, and the Cherry Time
> Has come at last. So hasten we along
> The hill-path gay with Spring's returning flowers.

I am the new priest in the temple of Isobe in Hitachi. This youth begged me to take him under my care, so we have made a vow of teacher and disciple. We have come down here near the river's edge to study the new blossoms.

> On Tsukuba the bloom is at the full
> And in the sky a myriad colors glow.
> The fir trees wear new signs of Spring.
> The hills are billows of a flowery sea in motion;
> Below us glides the mighty Sakura,
> It is the river of the cherry blossoms.

VILLAGER. Thou comest late. I've waited long for thee.

PRIEST. We stopped to gather flowers along the way. That is why we are late. The whole world is a flowery kingdom to-day.

The boy wanders out, picking flowers and singing as he goes:

> The Autumn days are pale, all silvery white:
> Then tell me, if thou canst, oh, tell me why
> These silvery dews so marvellously dye
> The falling leaves a myriad colors bright?

VILLAGER. Indeed it is, and good to look upon. But there is another sight to see. Among the flowers is a strange bird, a mad-woman, with a beautiful hand-net, with which she catches the blossoms floating on the stream. Her songs are most strange and diverting. Wait here a little time and we will bring her to you. Listen!

A woman's voice is heard chanting:

> Tell me,
> Doth any know the dark recess
> Where dwell the winds
> Which scatter the white flowers?

O sin of sins!
By all the heavenly powers
I'll search them out to upbraid their wickedness.

(THE VILLAGER *beckons to some one below who enters, leading a woman.*)

WOMAN (*falling on her knees*).   Tell me, O Wayfarer, are the blossoms falling on the Sakura River?

PRIEST.   The flowers are falling on the water.

WOMAN (*chanting*).

> The blossoms are about to fall, you say?
> O woe is me! that would entice the flowers
> As floating slowly down the stream they come,
> The silver stream whose waters hurry past
> As quickly as the fleeting days of Spring.
>> 'Whirled willy-nilly on the stream
>> The fallen petals hurry down—
>> A sign that from the mountain-side
>> Up yonder also Spring has flown.
>> And so are men and women hurried
>> Like petals down the stream of life.'
> So runs the song, but I must not delay.
> It were unkind of me to come too late
> Upon the blossoms that have turned to snow.
> In anger at the wind that sheds the blooms
> The waves have risen like an angry sea!
> Deep as my love the flowers lie like snow
> That fall and melting make a stream of tears.
> I lost my loved son, my heart was torn
> With grief, and I have crossed o'er many mountains
> And seas to Hakozaki, where the waves
> Arise, and thence by Suma's shore, and on
> Past Suruga to Hitachi at last
> I come.   I must always go on and on;
> By this way surely does not lie the path
> Of mother searching for her son, alas,
> I must be on my distant journey hence.

This is the famous river, Sakura.   In truth, a lovely place that well deserves its name.   The child from whom I parted was named Sakura, and this remembrance and the season both make dear to me this river with the name I love and where—

> 'I plunge my net in, gathering
> The snow-white blossoms floating by,
> A keepsake of the lovely Spring.'

CHORUS (*chanting*).

> Now parted are the parent and the child,
> The little bird has flown out of the nest,

> The mother left alone has traveled far,
> She is worn out with her long journey through
> The wilds, distant as earth is from the sky.
> But what if they should meet, mother and son,
> And neither recognize the other's face?
> Nay, nay, it cannot be! 'Twas winter dark
> That he was lost from view, but now the Spring
> Has come, shall he not blossom out again?

PRIEST. Pray tell me, what is it that hath made thee mad?

WOMAN. Because I have been parted from my only child.

PRIEST. That is sad to hear. I see thou dost carry a lovely net to catch the blossoms floating by. Moreover thou dost wear an earnest look of faith. What is the meaning of all this?

WOMAN. It is because the goddess who guards my native place is called the Lady-of-the-Trees-that-Blossom. On earth her presence is a cherry tree. My lost child was dedicated to her and was brought up with the name Cherry-Blossom. So as the goddess is called the Lady-of-the-Blossom, and this child I seek is named Cherry-Blossom, and the river is the Cherry-Blossom River, I fain would save these fallen flowers which bear the name I love.

PRIEST. Unhappy mother! True, indeed, there is a cause to each result and this has brought thee so far eastward to the Cherry River here.

WOMAN. This river is very distant famed. What says the verse that Tsurayuki made?

PRIEST (*chanting*).

> Ah, true, 'twas Tsurayuki sang of old.
> Hearing that in a land he had not seen—

WOMAN. In Hitachi there ran a stream men called—

PRIEST. The River-of-Blossoms, the Sakura-Gawa.

CHORUS (*chanting*).

> Methinks when Spring has come the waters rise
> And ever beat the waves more than their wont
> Upon the margin of the River-of-Blossoms.
> To-day the flowers and the poet, too,
> Have vanished like the snow, and left behind
> Only a name; the river still flows on
> And shallow after shallow lightly bears
> The foaming blossom where the waves have beat.

VILLAGER. Look! A sudden blast from the mountain-tops is scattering the blossoms on the water!

WOMAN. What sayest thou? The evening breeze down from the mountains brings the blooms. 'Tis well. I'll catch them in my net before they float away.

PRIEST (*chanting*).

> See, see, the wind from the hills beating on every treetop!

WOMAN. A flood of flowers rising white.

PRIEST. The waves that break from above—
WOMAN. Are they blossoms?
PRIEST. Are they snow?
WOMAN. Are they waves?
PRIEST. Are they flowers?
WOMAN. The hovering clouds—
PRIEST. By the river breeze—
CHORUS (*chanting*).

> Are scattered now and the swift waves flow on,
> O waves of the flowing River of Cherry Blossoms,
> Give them to me; let me catch them as they pass!
> Look how the water flows and the flowers are falling,
> But Spring, the sunny Spring, will last forever.
> The flowers that grow between the mossy rocks
> Are scarlet and shed light along the stream,
> The trees that grow beside the shadowy caverns
> Hum softly, gently, in the rising wind;
> The blossoms are unfolding like brocade,
> And all the brimming pools are deep and blue.

WOMAN (*chanting*).

> My straying footsteps brought me here at last
> To the river that rouses a longing deep within me
> For him, my Sakura, who now is lost.

CHORUS (*chanting*).

> Alike the name, alike the place. They must
> Be bound together by a former life.
> The water is the mirror of the flowers,
> But as the year grows old the blossoms slowly,
> So slowly fade and fall, then can ye say
> The crystal mirror tarnishes? What shall
> We do, well knowing that the blossoms fade
> And later turn to dust? 'Tis vain to hold
> Them, blossoms which in truth are only dreams;
> For from the treetops scattered and to naught
> They fall upon the waters and too soon
> They vanish as mere bubbles and are gone.
> What looked like clouds were the swift eddies on
> The silent pools of blossoms on Miyoshino.

WOMAN (*chanting*).

> Although I catch them in my golden net
> The cherries, flowers, and the clouds and waves
> Are but the blossoms from the boughs. Not these—
> Indeed I seek but my beloved son,
> My Sakura, my son, my cherry-flower.

PRIEST. Strange, O strange, are these poor woman's words to hear!

WOMAN (*chanting*).

> Mountains and distant sky
>   Around me lie;
> Forever the mountain chains
>   Tower to the sky;
> Fixed is the earth
>   Immutably;
> Man is a thing of naught
>   Born but to die.

PRIEST. Pray tell me, from what province and from what town dost thou come?

WOMAN. Why dost thou ask this of me for whom none until to-day has cared? Tsukushi was once my home.

PRIEST. Tsukushi! Why should we hide it from thee? Lo! The bloom of love that doth not fade.

(*He beckons to the boy, who enters singing:*

> Compassionate one, do you not heave a sigh
> When o'er your head the withered cherry-flowers,
> Like loosened butterflies new learned to fly,
> Come fluttering down? Perhaps the Autumn showers
> Are fervent tears shed by the sorrowing sky!

PRIEST. Behold thy Sakura!

WOMAN. A voice I hear—is it a dream? I cannot tell—my child?

CHORUS (*chanting*).

> The days of three long years have passed and many,
> Full many a league has lain between this mother
> And her son. His form has also greatly changed,
> But gazing on his countenance she sees
> The bright and blooming face of—

WOMAN. Sakura, my blossom!

THE BOY. Mother!

(*They embrace as the curtain falls.*)

THE SENTENCE OF DEATH

A PLAY

By Teresa Farias de Issasi

Translated from the Spanish by Lilian Saunders

CHARACTERS

Carlos Fernandez de Lara
Antonio Esparza
A Priest
A Warden

THE SENTENCE OF DEATH

SCENE. *A cell with stone walls. A cot bed covered with a gray blanket. A wooden chair, a table, a lighted candle on the table. A grated window high up in the wall looking out on a starless night.* ANTONIO *is sitting on the cot, his elbows on his knees, his head in his hands. He does not look up as the door opens and the* WARDEN *admits* CARLOS.

The action takes place in a prison cell in Mexico City.

CARLOS (*after waiting a moment for* ANTONIO *to speak*). Antonio, will you speak to me? I am your brother.

ANTONIO (*raising his head*). They said you would come.

(*He looks* CARLOS *over from head to foot, taking in every detail of his appearance . . . his aristocratic air, his expensive clothes, his diamond scarf pin, his elegant overcoat . . . all the outward signs which show him to be one of the favorite sons of fortune. His forehead darkens.*)

ANTONIO. So we are brothers! Who would believe it. Yes, I remember well, my mother told me long ago, that I had a brother—a twin brother—who was rich and high up in the world. I think she even told me his name . . . Carlos . . . isn't that it?

CARLOS. Yes. Carlos Fernandez de Lara.

ANTONIO. Why "de Lara"?

CARLOS. That is the name of our father. Didn't she tell you that?

ANTONIO. No, she never told me that. If I had known your name, perhaps I would have written to you. . . . I thought of it sometimes.

CARLOS. Why didn't you ask her my name?

ANTONIO. I don't know . . . perhaps I was too lazy, perhaps I thought you wouldn't pay any attention to me.

CARLOS. I wish you had written.

(*They are silent. Neither one knows what to say.* CARLOS, *in his turn, observes his brother intently.* ANTONIO *has none of the characteristic marks of the criminal. The two are much alike.* ANTONIO'S *skin, sallow from malnutrition, and the bluish shadow of the half grown beard which covers the lower part of the face, lessen the resemblance but do not succeed in effacing it. His manner is taciturn. A somber reproach, an obscure resentment seem to lurk in his melancholy eyes, in the bitter, disillusioned expression of his mouth.*)

ANTONIO (*breaking the silence*). My mother only told me that she found

275

herself unable to support twin babies, so she sent one of us to our father, who was rich, and raised the other herself. You see, I have had bad luck from the beginning. (*Resentfully.*) Why should you have been the lucky one instead of me?

CARLOS. But I ask that too, brother! Why has our fate been so different? We were equally innocent and unformed. Who directed our mother's choice? Was it accident? Was it God?

ANTONIO. How could it be God? They say that God is just. What sort of justice have I had? Neither of us had done anything to deserve a good or evil fate. One of us was doomed to misery and misfortune . . . why I instead of you?

CARLOS. There are things we cannot understand. We must not doubt God. Perhaps we were only apparently equal. Perhaps our souls had a different past . . . lived other lives, had different experiences, and our present destiny is only the just consequence of acts which we do not remember.

ANTONIO (*violently*). I do not believe that. If our mother had sent me to our father and kept you, who will say that you might not have been the criminal and I the honest man! What merit have you in being good . . . you were educated, cared for, set in the way of good, I was thrown on the refuse heap . . . who is responsible for the evil I have done?

CARLOS Don't be angry, brother. It is true that you have been a victim. And perhaps your fate will seem only the more cruel when I tell you that our father tried to find you after our mother sent me to him. He would have raised us both. He felt responsible for both of us. But she had concealed herself too well.

ANTONIO (*gloomily*). My mother loved us. It would have been too much if she had had to give up both of us. And since our father, rich, of exalted family, could not marry a humble working girl, she did the only thing she could do. So much the worse if I was the sufferer. And perhaps I am not altogether to be pitied. I love my mother.

(*A sentinel passes down the corridor, his gun rattling.* ANTONIO *shudders at the sound, a tremor of anguish shakes his body.*)

ANTONIO. The time is passing and the pardon does not come.

CARLOS. It will come, brother, there is no doubt that it will come. I shall wait with you until it comes. They have given me permission to spend the night with you.

ANTONIO. What time is it?

CARLOS (*looking at his watch*). Half past nine.

ANTONIO. It is late.

(*He rises, unbuttons the collar of his blouse as if it hindered his breathing, looks from side to side as if in fear, walks back and forth a moment, then sits down again on the cot.*)

ANTONIO. When did you find out that we were brothers?

CARLOS. Yesterday.

ANTONIO. Did my mother write telling what had happened to me?

CARLOS. Yes, she asked me to use my influence to have you pardoned, and I have not rested a moment since then. I have left nothing undone.

ANTONIO (*looks at* CARLOS *sharply . . . there is a pause*). Poor woman! she was nearly crazy when she heard my sentence. It was to see her that I came to the city. I knew that if I came they might catch me, but she was very sick—they thought she was dying. So I came, and they got me. It couldn't be helped.

(*He takes a package of cigarettes from his pocket and offers it to* CARLOS.)

CARLOS. Thank you, brother, I do not smoke. (*Hastily.*) Don't be offended. Take a cigarette yourself. In a little while they will bring the supper I have ordered and then we will eat together.

ANTONIO. A little wine, then? (*Taking up the bottle.*) Is is good wine. The warden gave it to me. He's a good fellow.

CARLOS. I don't drink either, brother. I have never tasted wine.

ANTONIO (*bitterly*). You, they educated! Me, no! When I was nine years old I began to smoke and when I was fourteen I used to get drunk.

CARLOS. You didn't go to school?

ANTONIO. No, I never went. I don't even know how to read. And the truth is that I am ashamed.

CARLOS. Did you learn a trade?

ANTONIO. No, I never learned anything. I was a gutter brat. I liked to be idle. I liked to run the streets. All the same, about fifteen years ago, we were so poor that I had to go to work. I worked in a factory. The patron said I was clever and he pushed me along. I began to like work and I stopped drinking. After a few years I married.

CARLOS. You are married?

ANTONIO (*with a profound sigh*). Yes, brother, I have had a home, even I. Very humble, but it was my own home. What good times those were! I worked with enthusiasm, with joy. We had two children. I bought a little piece of ground . . . one of those that is sold on long payments. What hopes my poor Rosario and I built on that scrap of ground! Every Sunday we went to walk around it. The thought of paying for that ground and building our home there was heaven to us. We were not too ambitious, *verdad?* We did not ask for great fields and grand palaces. Just a few yards of earth, a *casita* of adobe was the object of our hopes. Ay! Poor people should not have hopes, it seems, for ours, humble as they were, could not be realized!

(*He is silent for a moment, filled with emotion at the memories he has evoked.*)

ANTONIO. Have you land?

CARLOS. So much that I am ashamed of it. So much that I have never even seen it all!

ANTONIO (*hardly hearing the answers, full of his memories*). One evening, as I left the factory, a sergeant stopped me and ordered me to follow him. He took me to the barracks where they put a uniform on me and assigned me to a battalion that was to leave the next day for Morelos.

CARLOS. They took you like that, without notice?

ANTONIO. Yes, and I cannot tell you the indignation I felt at being disposed of so, without my consent. I had never felt hatred before—but at that moment I began to hate power . . . injustice. But I was not wicked then, no. When they first put a gun into my hands—my hands which only understood handling tools—my heart turned over and I felt myself lost. I will confess— I was afraid! I felt a horror of killing! (*He laughs bitterly.*) What an idea! They taught me to kill and now they want to kill me because I have used the knowledge they forced on me! Listen, brother, I, who am condemned to death for homicide, I, who do not know exactly how many men I have killed—I felt my eyes blur, and my heart leap out of my breast when for the first time I formed part of a firing squad and executed an unfortunate Indian, who on his knees begged for mercy!

CARLOS. How horrible!

ANTONIO. Yes. What anguish when, obeying the commands of the General, I helped to hang the rebels we had taken prisoner! I swear to you, brother, many times when I was alone, I cried! Yes, I, the bandit chief, Antonio Esparza, I cried!

CARLOS. I pity you.

ANTONIO. One day a company of rebels put the Federal forces to flight and I was taken prisoner. At first I tried to escape, but little by little they attracted me. The leader of the band talked to us of liberty, of equality. He said that their cause was just and noble. That when the government was overthrown there would be an end of oppression, that everyone would be happy, that there would be no more poor, that there would be land for everybody. And much more besides. I ended by believing that their rebellion was a work of redemption. I believed it so fully that I, in my turn, became a leader. I felt myself ennobled because I no longer thought of myself, of my own good, but of the good of the whole race. I wanted the earth to belong to all. I wanted all to be brothers. I wanted bread for everyone. I said to myself, hiding in the woods of Morelos, "The sun is for everyone, the air is for everyone, the earth should be for everyone too." (*His eyes glow with fervor, his surroundings are forgotten.*) They told you I was a bandit—they were wrong! I am not a bandit, I am a revolutionary—a liberator!

(CARLOS *is silent.*)

ANTONIO (*angered by his silence*). Why are you silent? Do you think my cause was wicked? Do you think I am a criminal? Yes, that's it! You are rich. Naturally you think of things in a different way. You, who by no virtue of your own find yourself the owner of a great fortune and much land, you could not possibly have the same point of view as I, who, after long years of effort could not even succeed in owning a few feet of ground. The one who enjoys the plunder does not judge things in just the same way as the one who has been robbed. You don't have the same thoughts when your stomach is empty as you do when it is full. But understand this (*somberly*), understand this—I am not the only one who is responsible for the blood I have shed. (*His lips quiver.*)

CARLOS. My poor brother, I believe that you were honest and good at heart. I believe that but for the injustice of humanity you would have remained so. Your hatred was born from the selfishness and indifference of the rich—it is true that they are your accomplices in the flow of blood that you have caused. . . .

ANTONIO (*his eyes lighting up*). Ah! You approve of our revolution! You approve of my conduct and that of my followers!

CARLOS. No, because you have only changed one kind of harmful force for another, and by hatred you will never bring about fraternity. You have been misled by those who were themselves misled by false teachings.

ANTONIO (*obstinately*). The land should be for the people.

CARLOS. But that is what we think too . . . we who want to save the country, just as you do. We have come to the same conclusion by different roads. . . you having nothing and we having more than we are entitled to. It is true, we have no right to more than we can use when you and others like you have nothing.

ANTONIO (*dejectedly*). Even my little scrap of earth was taken away from me.

CARLOS. Brother, I swear to you that, in memory of this solemn hour I will persuade my father to divide one-third of his land among his peons.

ANTONIO. For that I thank you.

(*The warden brings in a tray with the lavish supper which* CARLOS *has ordered. They sit down and try to eat but the food chokes* ANTONIO. *He gets up and begins to walk about nervously.*)

CARLOS. You must try to eat. You will sleep better if you eat.

ANTONIO. Sleep! I can't sleep. I feel a weight here. (*Touching his breast.*) How can I sleep! If the pardon does not come, to-morrow morning . . . early . . .

CARLOS. It will come.

ANTONIO. You believe it?

CARLOS. Assuredly.

ANTONIO. Don't think I am afraid. I am not a coward, no. For myself I am not afraid to die. But to leave my wife and my children. . . . She can't earn enough for all of them, and they are too little to work. They would have to beg.

CARLOS. No, of that you need have no fear. Your wife and children shall be under my protection. You will tell me where I shall find them.

ANTONIO. You will not have to hunt for my wife. If she is not sleeping at the gate of the prison, she will be here at dawn. We have already said farewell . . . she brought the children . . . pobrecitos! (*He chokes with emotion, gets up and takes a swallow of wine.*) I have an intolerable thirst. I am burning up. I think I must have a fever. My bones ache and my mouth is dry. I can't breathe. This is atrocious! Let them kill me. . . . I can stand that . . . but this waiting . . . this waiting is frightful!

CARLOS. The pardon will come I am certain. If you would only try to sleep. It would make the waiting easier. Lie down. Take off your coat and your shoes. There. That is better.

(*He takes a book from his pocket and sits down near the candle.*)

ANTONIO. What are you going to do?

CARLOS. I am going to read to you. Perhaps it will quiet you. It is a very beautiful book.

ANTONIO (*starting up violently*). Yes, yes, for you! You who can leave this cursed place at any time you wish . . . for you, who will see the sun to-morrow! But for me . . . (*He sits despondently on the cot.*) The sun! What happiness it would be to walk in the sun again! Tell me . . . if they pardon me . . . if I get out of here, you will give me a little piece of ground, *verdad?*

CARLOS. Yes, yes, of course, as much as you want.

ANTONIO. I will work. I know how to work. You will see. And Rosario and the children will be there. And we shall sit in the sun. How happy we shall all be! (*He lies back on the cot.*) The casita! We shall build the casita . . . at last. We shall have a garden . . . there will be flowers . . . and vines . . . Rosario will . . .

(*His voice drifts into silence and he sleeps. The silence is profound, oppressive, almost terrifying.* CARLOS' *gaze is fixed upon the peacefully sleeping man. There are traces of nobility in his face—perhaps also in his soul! The ferocity, the unspeakable cruelty of the death penalty rises before* CARLOS' *mind in all its sinister nudity. This man, whose instincts were for good, is condemned to die, like a dangerous wild beast for crimes which unjust laws have forced him, in his ignorance, to commit! A phrase which he once read came into his mind, "Human justice has found no better way to punish murder than to imitate it," and he murmurs . . .*)

CARLOS. Absurd! To blot out one stain with another! To wash out blood with more blood! And who in truth is the culprit? This man who has made so much blood flow . . . is he anything more than the instrument of those above him . . . an instrument which they have fashioned for their own uses and which has slipped and turned in their hands? Murder is a crime. Yes. Then why commit this crime in the name of the law? Who can dare say that one murder is more justifiable than another in the eye of God? For in each case a sacrilegious hand throws open the gates of eternity, violates the mysterious dignity of death, disarranges a system, launches a challenge in the very face of the Almighty! . . .

But evolution? Evolution which has given us the ineffable certainty of the solidarity of mankind! Evolution, which tore down the Bastille, shattered its chains, abolished the frightful dungeons of the past! Evolution which has snatched the instruments of torture from the hands of executioners and quenched the fires of the Inquisition! Must evolution stop helpless before the atrocious anachronism of the death penalty? Impossible! Evolution cannot be arrested. The dawn of justice is at hand . . . of fraternity . . . ignorance is the cause of crime . . . ignorance must be destroyed. . . .

(*Gradually his thoughts become confused and slumber vanquishes him also. Folding his arms upon the table he rests his head upon them and sleeps deeply. Hours pass. He wakes with a start at the grating of the heavy door. A figure like a black shadow stands beside him. It is the priest. The hour has come.* CARLOS *looks towards his brother with eyes filled with horror.*)

CARLOS. Is it . . . is it morning?

THE PRIEST. It is the hour.

CARLOS (*crossing himself*). Santa Maria!

ANTONIO (*waking and leaping to his feet*). What is it? (*He looks from one to the other . . . to* CARLOS.) I understand. You deceived me. You did well.

THE PRIEST (*laying his hand on* ANTONIO'S *arm*). My son, within an hour you are to die. Your soul will appear before your God. You must make your peace with him, so that he may be with you and uphold you in your last moments.

CARLOS. My brother, I did what I could . . . forgive me that I failed. Why did we not meet sooner . . . so that I could have helped you . . .

(*He throws his arms around* ANTONIO *and the two brothers hold each other in a long embrace.*)

THE PRIEST (*to* CARLOS). My son, if you have failed in your duty to this man, it may be that in your contrition you will be led to use your great possessions in the service of his unfortunate brothers, those whom he so unwisely tried to help. May God aid you.

(*He signs to* CARLOS *to leave them alone . . . wringing his brother's hand passionately, the young man goes out, pale and trembling, walking as if in a horrible nightmare, his whole body shaken by the pounding of his heart.*)

THE PRIEST. Kneel down my son and confess your sins.

(ANTONIO *kneels, crossing his hands on his breast.*)

CURTAIN

IN CONFIDENCE

A PLAY

BY ALVILDE PRYDZ

Translated from the Norwegian by Arvid Paulson

CHARACTERS

Miss Karlsen
Miss Barth

Reprinted from the Appleton Modern Plays

IN CONFIDENCE

A room in a boarding house. On the left there is an open door leading to an alcove. A red lantern throws a faint light from above. There is a table with a lamp and several pieces of embroidery. A young girl, MISS KARLSEN, sits en déshabillé on a chaise longue with her legs crossed and both elbows on the table before her, reading a book. She is exerting herself to read, but sinks down over the book, rises again suddenly, and goes over to a door on the right and stands there listening.

MISS KARLSEN (*to herself*). I wonder whether she has gone to bed; if she hasn't, I should think there would be no harm in having a little chat with her, since we live right next to each other. (*Aloud.*) Miss Barth! Oh, Miss Barth, may I not open the door just a little? I am so terribly lonesome to-night, and when I am in a bad humor it is so terribly unpleasant to have to be alone. You can't imagine how glad I was when I came home the other day and heard that somebody had moved into the room next to mine. Won't you be sweet enough to let me? Just a wee bit—it will help me at once!

MISS BARTH (*inside, a trifle sullen and cross*). You think so! I was just about to go to bed!

MISS KARLSEN. Well, but that's just the time it is the nicest—when one has gone to bed. For then one thinks of so many things that one would like to ask and know about! Tell me, what did you think of the soup and the fish we had for dinner to-night? That's what auntie gives us every Tuesday evening for dinner!

MISS BARTH (*as before*). It was very plain, indeed; but is that anything to keep the door open for? I tell you I must go to bed now; I am so tired, and not feeling awfully well, either!

MISS KARLSEN (*returns to her sofa*). But, my dear! Couldn't we have a little intimate chat—a chat in confidence—anyhow?

MISS BARTH. I don't remember having seen you until to-day!

MISS KARLSEN. What's the difference? We have now lived beside each other for two days—that helps a little, doesn't it? And then I liked you so much the moment I saw you! That's the most important thing of all, it seems to me. Besides, I noticed that you sat and played with the soup to-day just as I did, and that gave me at once such a tremendous feeling of sympathy for you. Tell me, what do you really think of being engaged? I mean—*really!*

MISS BARTH (*in a white kimono, comes to the door, with a yawn*). Oh! V-e-r-y w-e-ll!

285

MISS KARLSEN (*with a deep sigh*). Yes, I say the same! It's great, isn't it! (*There is a pause.*)

MISS BARTH. No, now I *must* go to bed. Good night, Miss Karlsen! (*She wants to shut the door.*)

MISS KARLSEN. Yes, I, too. Good night! But, dear, won't you leave the door open—just a little, won't you, please?

MISS BARTH (*with a glance expressing displeasure*). Oh, yes; why, certainly —of course!

MISS KARLSEN (*searching for something on the table*). Tell me, what do you think of sewing monograms, anyhow? . . . I mean on everything—on everything you own? I don't think I like it! (*Takes a deep breath. After a pause, in a careless tone of voice.*) And what do you think of men and such things—I mean in general? I believe you prefer the young men . . . auntie has no use for them; they do nothing but sit and pick at the food, she says. But on the other hand—the old, they never come here for their meals; Nikolai —he never takes his meals here with auntie . . . never! Just think of Nikolai, he is soon forty! Your fiancé is young, I'm sure! Isn't he?

MISS BARTH (*who has remained standing in the doorway; with apparent dislike for the subject, mockingly*). "Your fiancé!" . . . His name is Falck— that's the rascal's name, and he's old enough, believe me . . . for what he has done in the world! It's true, as your auntie says, that the old are the best— I'm sure it's so; . . . so *you* haven't anything to regret. (*She sighs.*) Good-night, Miss Karlsen! Don't you think we had best leave each other alone now? (*Goes inside, but comes back after a moment and makes the opening a trifle bigger.*) What are you thinking of, Miss Karlsen?

MISS KARLSEN. Oh! . . . of life in general! And you?

MISS BARTH. Of Nature!

MISS KARLSEN. . . . and Nature comes before discipline, doesn't it?

MISS BARTH. Just so! Good-night! (*She goes inside.*)

MISS KARLSEN (*after a silence, in a low voice.*) Miss Barth! Have you put out the light in there? Have you gone to sleep?

MISS BARTH. Why, yes; it's late. Haven't you?

MISS KARLSEN. Oh, yes, I'm in bed, too. Good-night, Miss Barth! (*Turns down the light. After a pause.*) Booh, it's so dark and strange here. No, I can't go to sleep! Can you? Why, you are crying! You are not crying, are you?

MISS BARTH (*in an injured tone*). I? How can you think so? *I* thought it was you!

MISS KARLSEN. No; but I can plainly hear you, too!

MISS BARTH (*again in the doorway*). Ah, me! It's terribly lonesome here, isn't it?

MISS KARLSEN. Have *you* found it out, too? Are you at home in the forenoon, may I ask?

MISS BARTH. That depends upon how I feel.

MISS KARLSEN. Did you feel like it to-day?

Miss Barth. Yes, it so happened, I must confess!

Miss Karlsen. Oh, dear me! Then you must have heard how Nikolai came into my room and how we had a tiff—Nikolai and I!—Every word, I suppose?

Miss Barth. Well, just about!

Miss Karlsen. Well, of all things! But you may be sure *I* have heard a few things, too, if you want to know!

Miss Barth (*angrily*). You are perfectly welcome! If it pleases you, keep right on listening! It doesn't bother me, you may be certain of that!

Miss Karlsen (*rising*). Listen, Miss Barth! Do you mind if I open the door wide? (*Teasingly.*) Do you mind? But come inside, my dear; come into the room, and let me see whether what you say is really true.

Miss Barth (*crying*). No, I am not coming in; I feel more comfortable sitting in my own chair.

Miss Karlsen (*opens the door wide*). Then bring your chair along.

Miss Barth. No, I can't do it. (*But, nevertheless, she comes dragging the chair a moment later. It is an American rocking chair.*)

Miss Karlsen (*smiles contentedly and claps her hands*). Well, and now— I'll tell you, Miss Barth! As long as you have heard everything that happened this forenoon, you may as well hear the rest, if you want to. Isn't it dreadful—simply appalling—that one is obliged to marry some time or other, simply because one is engaged! Just think of it! What do you think of it, Miss Barth?

Miss Barth (*with regained presence of mind*). I didn't know one was obliged to.

Miss Karlsen. No-o? Oh, yes, certainly; that's always the way. (*Jumps up and paces up and down.*) I assure you Nikolai would never listen to me if I suggested anything like that. Young girls never know what they want, he says. They *want to*—in spite of all that they say to the contrary—they want to, nevertheless, he maintains—think of it! And Nikolai has a tremendously keen mind. (*She stops.*) But tell me, what did you really mean, Miss Barth —for in the end, of course, we must get married to the man we are engaged to, mustn't we? . . .

Miss Barth (*with sudden determination*). Not I! It has never even entered my mind!

Miss Karlsen (*shocked*). Then, my dear, what *do* you think?

Miss Barth. I don't think at all!

Miss Karlsen (*moving restlessly in her chair*). Yes, but . . . yes, but . . . oh, you can't mean what you say! . . . And your fiancé who is so—so dear, I don't believe you know yourself how crazy he is about you!

Miss Barth (*depressed*). I don't know anything at all—except that it was pleasant—but it is no longer!

Miss Karlsen (*surprised*). Yes; but, my dear, you are fond of him, aren't you?

Miss Barth (*excitedly*). Of *him?* Of one like that—who has even been in

America!—just because he was so stubborn and impossible—and who has been engaged many times before! He told me that himself yesterday!

Miss Karlsen (*rises feverishly*). Yes; but Heavens! Can it really pass over like that, Miss Barth? For, of course, you *must* have been fond of him—that's plain!

Miss Barth (*indignantly*). That doesn't follow! A man like *him!*

Miss Karlsen. *He!* Why, both auntie and the others say that he is such a nice man. But tell me, how about *yourself,* Miss Barth?

Miss Barth. I? I was not at all bad when I was at home! *That's* what hurts me! (*She begins to weep.*)

Miss Karlsen. No, you must not sit here and talk badly about yourself! I won't have it! You don't know how sweet you are! Everybody says so!

Miss Barth. No, I'm not sweet. I am only ashamed for mother's sake, and for father's sake, and for the sake of all of them at home. For I must tell you there isn't a soul at home—not even a cat—that knows I am engaged. They think I am visiting in the home of a girl friend of mine, and here I am at a boarding house, and have to pay for every little thing I get! And all the money that I had I have taken out of the bank! Falck has borrowed some of it, too. I only hope father doesn't find that out; that would be a nice thing, an amusingly pleasant little thing—that would be.

Miss Karlsen. Yes; but tell me—how is it that you are not living with your friend's parents?

Miss Barth. Yes, why! . . . If my friend only *had* any parents . . . and if I had only had . . . a . . . girl friend . . . but . . . well, I must tell you that I have always had a weakness for telling lies; but never so badly as now, because . . . it is Falck who is the girl friend! And you can't imagine how my folks . . . they are such nice people, all of them, and then they think I, too, am like them. . . . (*She is crying.*)

Miss Karlsen (*flies up from the chair*). I must tell you, Miss Barth, that this is worse than it ever was for me. (*Enticingly.*) But listen, dear, it would be *so* exciting to hear you tell . . . a *little* more . . . for it is exactly as if I were reading the sort of novels Nikolai has forbidden me to read.

Miss Barth. Yes, but then you must change your seat. I can't stand to have anybody sit like that and look at me. (*Places herself in a comfortable position.*) I met him at a picnic dance this summer and I . . . well, he fell in love with me the moment he saw me; that's what he said at least. I wore a light-blue dress and lilies-of-the-valley, and it *was* fun! The woods were so green, and it was such a beautiful day! And we danced, and we walked, and we talked . . . and all the time he suggested that there was no reason why I should be held to such strict conventions as they imposed upon me at home . . . entirely away from life and development . . . he could tell that by my conversation, he told me; and then he asked me whether I knew how delightful it was to love a human being, and if I wouldn't try to feel a little love for him. And we were walking along, and finally he wanted me to become engaged to him. "It's only a test," he said. "You needn't tell anybody about it, not

even your mother," he said; "for if you find you don't like me, it is much
easier to undo it, and the family doesn't have to come with a lot of nonsense" . . .

MISS KARLSEN. He certainly was right in that!

MISS BARTH. Yes; but anyhow, it isn't the thing to do. I told him so at
the time; and that I was sure I didn't love him enough, for I knew, of course,
that love is a wonderful feeling, something that grips you and takes a hold of
you, and I have read that in many places, too. . . . But Falck assured me that
it was not at all necessary, nor was it customary, either. And if I wanted to,
we could begin merely as friends, platonic friends, as if we had both of us
been of the same sex, like the friendship between two boys or two girls; I had
no idea how elevating and developing it was, he said. Parents did not understand such things, he contended, and as far as the love was concerned—the
real love—I didn't need to worry about that; it would come later—it always
does. That's what *he* said! (*She becomes pensive.*)

MISS KARLSEN. Oh, but Miss Barth! More, more!

MISS BARTH. Well, then we took another little walk again, and it had
become so beautiful out there in the woods . . . it *was* so beautiful there; and
even *he* was almost beautiful, I assure you . . . that evening, I mean. And
then—then the moon came out, and . . .

MISS KARLSEN. Oh, Heavens, yes! If I could only have been there, too!
But I don't believe I could ever get Nikolai to do anything like that! He is
so terribly particular and precise about such things!

MISS BARTH (*continues*). Well, after all, we became engaged out there in
the woods, for I thought that since he was so eager about it that I . . .

MISS KARLSEN. Oh, I think it's perfectly wonderful that you dared to . . .
right at once, on the spur of the moment. . . . I think it's perfectly delightful;
and how brave! And out there! In the moonlight . . . and the dark woods!
. . . Nikolai—he wrote at once to mother, *he* did—you see I was going to
school here then—and then came uncles and aunts, and there was a long story
of all sorts of things! (*Sighs, and becomes eager for more again.*) But please
tell me some more; it's disgusting how inquisitive I am, isn't it? Besides, I
know it will turn out that I am right, Miss Barth; you liked him after all,
didn't you?

MISS BARTH (*interrupts her*). My dear, I did tell you; it *was* nice that
time in the woods—it *was* . . . and a few times *after* that, too; I have never
said anything but that.

MISS KARLSEN. But, nevertheless, I can't quite understand how you
dared . . . .

MISS BARTH. My dear, he was going there, teasing and enticing me . . .
that I didn't belong anywhere but in the nursery, and things like that he said
. . . so it *wasn't* so strange, after all, was it? (*Rises abruptly.*) But, after
all, there wasn't anything to it; it hasn't come—this great love; it hasn't come
at all . . . it has only taken away the little there was of it; and when I now
have found, too, that Falck himself is not the man I thought he was, I can't

possibly. . . . But now I won't say another word, for I know you must have very little respect for me . . . you, who want to marry the man you are engaged to.

MISS KARLSEN. Not at all! I don't think it's nice of you to have such a bad opinion of me! Now, please, tell me the whole story, or I'm sure I'll be very sick, for it's just exactly as if I were in the midst of an exciting novel and Nikolai would come and take it away from me. Tell me how you happened to invent the friendship story—you haven't told me that!

MISS BARTH (*seats herself again*). That was Falck's idea, of course! Uf— that's his Christian name—he lives here in town, you see—and I decided to correspond. But, you see, mother always reads all my letters—which is something entirely out of date, Falck says—and so we thought it best to call each other "friend," and I was to tell mother that his letters were from a daughter of Doctor Berg's in town. But in every letter I got, Falck asked me to come to town for a visit and stay with his parents. . . . At last mother thought I answered my friend in a very impolite way, and it seemed to her I ought to go to town and see Miss Berg, since she was so insistent. Mother said I needed a little amusement, too, which was true. *I* would never have dared to think of anything like that; but since mother herself began to persuade me and was bent on my going, I couldn't resist any longer. So I went, and when I came here, Falck met me at the station. And then he took me up here to your aunt, after having first had dinner at his home; and it was awfully nice there. He lives very beautifully!

MISS KARLSEN. Heavens! It must have been wonderful!

MISS BARTH. I'll tell you: we had champagne . . . and cigarettes—that I had never smoked before . . . and we two who were supposed to be girl-friends! But it's just *that* I won't be any longer, and I certainly can't be engaged to him any longer, either. Now—do you think it's my fault, do you? I can't go out and stamp love out of the ground, can I? . . . And now . . . what do you think he is going to do? . . . He is going to announce our engagement, and I am going with him to his sister—he has never said a word about any sister before—he has invented this story in order to compel me to go. Just think, I am invited to a dance there to-morrow, and I am to be presented to the whole family—now that I don't want to, and only wish there was an end to it all. What have I to do at his sister's? And he won't get me to go there, either. (*Absorbed in thoughts.*) Do you know what I dreamed one night here, when I couldn't go to sleep? I dreamed that some one came and took me by the hand and asked me: do you know what is the greatest thing in the world? It is when a human being loves another one so much that one feels as if one had come away from everything that is small and petty, and low, and evil, and had entered a huge, beautiful temple. And I suggested that we go into such a beautiful place as that—but then there was again someone who said: dare you go in?—Oh, how miserable that made me feel!—Then I awakened. And I felt so ashamed that I couldn't do anything but cry; but, nevertheless, I was glad that I had seen it in such a light! . . . I think I must go back home again, first of all.

MISS KARLSEN. Mr. Falck has told aunt you were going to be here for the winter!

MISS BARTH. Oh, my parents would never give their consent to that! And now I am terribly afraid that mother may come down here to Doctor Berg's to take me home—but the dance is almost the worst of all! That was something I had never even thought of—that I would have to go to a dance at his sister's!

MISS KARLSEN. Oh—if it isn't anything worse than that . . . but why was he in such a bad humor when he came here to-day? Forgive me, if I seem horribly inquisitive!

MISS BARTH. I don't mind! He acts like that because he always wants to sit on the sofa when I sit there. He says I am so all-devastatingly stupid, and that I have fooled him—I thought it was *he* who had fooled *me!* (*She sighs.*) And how awful it is not to know how one is going to come out of it; for he has no desire to understand me in anything.

MISS KARLSEN. Quite seriously, Miss Barth, do you think one *can* get out of it? A promise is a holy thing; that's what Nikolai says. (*She wipes her eyes.*)

MISS BARTH. Then there must be many kinds of promises, for mine is only such a very little one, you understand—and Falck's! If you think there is anything at all to his, you are mistaken!—But why are you crying? What is the matter, Miss Karlsen—what is the matter?

MISS KARLSEN. Nikolai wants to get married! That's what I think is so disgusting!

MISS BARTH. Let him do it! If only Falck thought the same way; that would be joy!

MISS KARLSEN. Yes, but it's with me, can't you understand! And in March! To be engaged is all right; it's quite a lot of fun, even, for if we have a quarrel we can stay away from each other for a few days. But when you are married, it's another thing! It must be terrible. Although Nikolai is very nice and charming, as you yourself can hear . . . but he insists that when one has become engaged, one must get married as soon as possible: after *a* comes *b,* he says.

MISS BARTH. When *a* stands alone, nothing comes after it, *you* ought to say.

MISS KARLSEN. Yes, if I could only get Nikolai to realize that! Now! Now you can see what a good thing it really was that we got together and had this little confidential chat to guide and to strengthen each other! . . . What would you say if I should write to him that now, since I have had experience. . . . No, experience won't do; Nikolai wouldn't tolerate that . . . but I feel that there is something wrong with things as they stand between Nikolai and myself! Heavens, I thought it would be something so wonderful to be engaged! People seem to think it is an everlasting happiness—I gather that from Nikolai! Oh, he says so many things, Nikolai does! He says that the men should first use their own youth, and then ours—they must ferment away—there can be no wine before that's done, says Nikolai!

MISS BARTH (*smiles*). According to Mr. Nikolai's prescription, we must become grape juice—to be taken at once for fear it will turn sour . . .

MISS KARLSEN. Yes, but let us speak seriously, Miss Barth! I have been thinking it over from all angles—now don't you think it would be best for me to wait a while? For I am really not ready for this step yet.

MISS BARTH (*as before*). Yes, but perhaps it is with us as it is with asparagus; which must be picked before it is ripe. (*Suddenly serious.*) But, anyhow, now I know what I will do. I will never get engaged again . . . never, I believe! At any rate, I will wait until something comes along that takes a real good hold of me.

MISS KARLSEN. But if you wait too long, nothing will come, speaking seriously.

MISS BARTH (*smiles*). Oh, if nothing else còmes, I can always get one of those well-seasoned ones; according to your friend Nikolai's recipe, they are best. You know, it did me, too, some good—what he told you here to-day of all the virtues that develop when one has passed the hairy stage.

MISS KARLSEN. I don't remember that! But now, just think of me! Wedding in March! Married woman! Married people are awful! Sit around with the old women, drink tea, and knit! How would you like that, if I may ask? Nikolai will be my murderer!

MISS BARTH. Tell him that!

MISS KARLSEN. I don't dare! And I can't help liking him, either, for he is really not like the rest, you know; he *is* lovely. And when he is in good humor, he calls me his summer-bird!—Oh, but then he ought to give me a chance to use my wings first! There is no room for that over in the bank building!

MISS BARTH. Oh, yes, yes; he is in the bank, isn't he, and that's where you are going to live also? That looks dark!—If you could do as I!—I am going away! . . . You are sitting there playing with a book—what is it, if I may ask?

MISS KARLSEN (*timidly*). It is poems. . . . Nikolai wants me to sit and read poetry, too, because *he* is poetic! Isn't that a fine reason? When I am married I shall simply cease to exist.

MISS BARTH. Certainly! But men have written so much, it seems to me. Isn't there anything that they have written on this subject that you could tell to your Nikolai? Find a little poem that will suit him . . . and send it to him.

MISS KARLSEN (*eagerly turning the leaves*). I don't believe so! Who should it be, do you mean? (*Looks at the index.*) It is all so . . . terribly arranged, and awfully confusing; it is only Nikolai who understands it! No, no, there isn't anything here!

MISS BARTH. Supposing you wrote something yourself, then!—Come, let us both of us write! (*Goes inside and fetches writing material.*) Now—at once! And then we can read it to each other!—For I won't go to that dance at his sister's—I won't! That's certain. I am leaving to-morrow—so he will get my letter when he comes here to fetch me. I am not going to be engaged, and you are not going to be married! That will be splendid! Now write! (*Writes.*)

MISS KARLSEN (*excitedly*). Yes. (*Writes.*) I am going, too—out to the country to uncle; I am going to-morrow, early in the morning; so he will get it when he comes here to take me for a walk! I'll have auntie give it to him herself! And then, well, then I am really going to Aunt Kirsten, at Mentone; now when I can have company on the way . . . Aunt Kirsten has written to me so often . . . and what a burning desire I have had to go . . . but Nikolai has never wanted to give me his consent. (*Writes eagerly.*) Nikolai will go crazy; I am sure he will . . . but I don't care. . . . (*Writes, stops suddenly, reflects, writes, throws the pen away, takes a deep breath, smiles.*) Good heavens, what have you made me do! But I don't regret it! I am so happy that I could . . . I could. . . . Are you ready? Read, read, please! Won't you hurry? Please do!

MISS BARTH (*writes*). Be patient, my dear; I am ready now! Listen to me! (*Reads.*) "My unfortunate friend; I regret everything I have done and said while I have known you—especially since yesterday, when you told me all about your affairs with Augusta and Laura and the others. I hope you yourself understand, too, how badly it is with the advancement and the development of the things you promised so surely would follow, and it ought not to surprise you that I now say thanks and good-by. Ask never again for your friend; she exists no longer."

MISS KARLSEN. Oh, that's perfectly fine! I do think he will realize it himself, as you have told it to him; but now you must hear my letter! (*Reads.*) "Dearest Nikolai; Let us cease being engaged for a while, for I can't get married in March anyhow, dear! And if you really love me—(*wipes her tears*) —you know you have told me I have wings! Well, then let me try them first for a while—otherwise what would be the fun of having them! And now I am going to tell you I am flying away—out in the sun and the blue sky and the great flower-gardens, far out and away, where my aunt lives! But if you think that I stay away too long, then . . . well, then you don't love me the way I had thought you did!"

MISS BARTH. Now I wonder whether he'll understand that?

MISS KARLSEN (*wiping her tears*). I believe it is very badly put together! If I could only have got it to sound like the poems! But Nikolai will understand it, I think; Nikolai always understands everything!

MISS BARTH. But these are different figures from the ones he usually counts with! Well, now it seems to me we ought to go to bed in all seriousness, since we are going traveling to-morrow! Heavens, how sleepy and tired one feels after a session like this! But I must have a cigarette first, or I can't sleep; I have learned that from Falck—so you see he really has taught me *some-*

thing; I think, nevertheless, I'll ask him not to be too angry with me. (*Writes swiftly still a few words.*) Now, let him console himself with this. . . . How about you? (*Offers* MISS KARLSEN *a cigarette.*)

MISS KARLSEN (*looks at the cigarettes; then she suddenly turns around.*) No, I won't. Nikolai can't bear it; really he can't! In *that* much, at least, he shall have been obeyed, poor Nikolai! But now, Miss Barth, now we simply *must* go to bed. You know we are going to travel to-morrow! For the last time, good-night! (*They embrace each other.*)

MISS KARLSEN (*turns to the window*). And look at the moon! (*Blows out the light.*) Do you see the light there, how it comes stealing in, right through the acacia leaves? Can you see it—it is in its last quarter; oh, that's when I love it, for then it is so still and fine! Oh, you father man in the moon, who has heard every single word! Good-night! (*Kisses her fingers and throws a kiss to the moon.*)

(*There is a knock at the wall from within.*)

MISS KARLSEN. Now we have awakened auntie. (*Cries.*) Yes, yes, I am just going to bed, auntie! I am just going now!

CURTAIN

ON THE HIGHWAY

A Dramatic Sketch

By Anton Chekov

Translated from the Russian Original by David A. Modell, A.M.

CHARACTERS

TIKHON YEVSTIGNEEV, *keeper of the tavern on the highway.*
SEMION SERGEEVITCH BORTSOV, *a ruined landowner.*
MARIA YEGOROVNA, *his wife.*
SAVVA, *a wandering old penitent.*
NAZAROVNA *and* YEFIMOVNA, *pilgrim women.*
FEDIA, *a transient workman.*
YEGOR MERIK, *a tramp.*
KUZMA, *a passer-by.*
A POSTMAN.
MARIA YEGOROVNA'S DRIVER.
Pilgrims, merchants, travelers, and others.

ON THE HIGHWAY

The action takes place in a province of South Russia. The stage represents
TIKHON'S *tavern. To the right is the bar, with shelves holding bottles.*
Beyond is a door leading outside. Over the doorway, on the outside, hangs
a red, greasy little lantern. The floor and the benches lining the walls are
entirely taken up by pilgrims and other travelers. Many, for lack of room,
sleep in a sitting posture. It is late at night. As the curtain goes up,
thunder is heard and lightning is seen through the doorway.

TIKHON *is behind the bar. On one of the benches lounges* FEDIA *playing a*
harmonica. Near him sits BORTSOV *dressed in threadbare summer clothes.*
On the floor, by the benches, lie SAVVA, NAZAROVNA, *and* YEFIMOVNA.

YEFIMOVNA (*to* NAZAROVNA). Shake the old man there, *Mátushka.*[1] He
seems to want to give up his soul to God.

NAZAROVNA (*lifting from the wanderer's face one end of his great-coat*).
Hey, you man of God, are you still alive or are you dead already?

SAVVA. Why dead? Alive, *Mátushka.* (*He raises himself on his elbows.*)
Please cover my feet, my poor woman. So! The right one a little better.
That's it, *Mátushka.* God bless you!

NAZAROVNA (*covering* SAVVA'S *feet*). Sleep, *Cátyushka.*

SAVVA. How can one sleep? Would I had the patience to bear this suffering; as for sleep—that doesn't bother me. Sinners don't deserve rest, anyway.
What's that noise, pilgrim-mother?

NAZAROVNA. The Lord sends thunder. The wind blows and the rain keeps
on beating on the roof and the windows like fine peas. Do you hear? The
floodgates of heaven are ajar. (*Thunder is heard.*) Mercy, mercy, mercy!

FEDIA. It thunders, rattles and howls, and there's no end to it! Oo-oo-oo
. . . as if the forest murmured. Oo-oo-oo . . . the wind howls like a dog.
(*He huddles himself together.*) It's cold! My clothes are wringing wet, and
the door is wide open. (*He plays quietly.*) My harmonica has swelled up
from the rain, boys, or I would give you such a concert as would lift you off
your feet. Something grand! A quadrille, say, or a polka maybe, or some
Russian couplet. We can do all that. In the city, where I served as hallman
in the Grand Hotel, I saved no money, but in the harmonica's estimation I
outdid myself at every note. And I play the guitar, too.

---

[1] A Russian diminutive derived from the word for mother, but used indiscriminately
as a term of address among friends or acquaintances or even strangers. For this and the
corresponding masculine term—*Cátyushka* (from the Russian for father)—which I am
here introducing, English has no equivalents. The general sense is vaguely expressed by
"My dear lady" and "My dear sir," respectively.—Translator.

A VOICE FROM THE CORNER. A fool and foolish talk!

FEDIA. From a fool I hear that. (*A pause ensues.*)

NAZAROVNA (*to* SAVVA). You, old man, had better lie in the heat awhile and warm your foot a bit. (*A pause ensues.*) Sir! Man of God! (*She shakes* SAVVA.) Not going to die, are you?

FEDIA. You, grandfather, had better take a sip of vodka. It'll scorch your insides a bit as you drink, but it'll brace you up afterwards. Take a drink.

NAZAROVNA. Stop your jabbering, lad. The old man is perhaps giving up his soul to God and repenting of his sins, and you keep on like that—and with a harmonica. Stop that music, you impudent fellow!

FEDIA. And why don't you leave him in peace? He's not feeling well, and here are you keeping up an old woman's prattle. He's too good to say a rough word to you, and you, fool that you are, are only too glad that he listens to you. . . . Sleep, grandpa; pay no heed to her. Let her chatter—don't you care. An old woman's tongue is like the devil's broom; it'll sweep the wisest man out of the house. Don't you care! (*He clasps his hands.*) But you are skinny, brother! Awful! Just like a dead skeleton—no vitality at all. Not dying, are you?

SAVVA. Why die? God forbid—just simply to die! I'll bear it a bit and then, with God's help, I'll be up again. The Holy Virgin won't let me expire in a strange land. I'll die at home.

FEDIA. Are you from far?

SAVVA. From the district of Vológda. From Vológda itself—I'm a citizen there.

FEDIA. And where is Vológda?

TIKHON. Beyond Moscow. It's a government.

FEDIA. Whew! How far you have wandered, graybeard! And all on foot?

SAVVA. On foot, my boy. I was at Tikhon beyond the Don and am now bound for the Holy Mountains. From there, by God's leave, I'll make for Odessa. Thence, they say, one can get to Jerusalem very cheaply—for some twenty-one rubles even.

FEDIA. And were you ever in Moscow?

SAVVA. I should say so! About five times.

FEDIA. A fine city? (*He lights his pipe.*) Worth seeing?

SAVVA. Many holy places, lad. It's always nice where holy things abound.

BORTSOV. (*He approaches the bar and* TIKHON.) Once more, I beg of you, serve a drink, for Christ's sake.

FEDIA. The main thing about a city is that it should be clean; to be sprinkled when dusty and cleaned when dirty; to have high buildings, a theater, police, cabs that— I've lived in cities myself; I understand.

BORTSOV. Just a wine-glass—here this small one. It's only on trust. I'll pay you.

TIKHON. Yes, yes!

BORTSOV. I beg of you! Do a favor!

TIKHON. Go on.

BORTSOV. You don't comprehend me. Understand, you scamp, if your peasant blockhead contains any brains, that it isn't I that ask, but, putting it in your peasant language, my inside asks. My sickness craves! Understand!

TIKHON. There's nothing for us to understand. Get out!

BORTSOV. But if I don't have a drink right now—if I don't satisfy my craving, mind you—I'm likely to commit a crime. God knows what I may do! You have seen, fool, many drinking folk in your saloon life—don't you know yet what such people are? They are sick folk. Chain them, beat them, cut them up, if you will, but don't deny them vodka. Well, I humbly beg of you! Do a favor! I humiliate myself. My God, how I humiliate myself!

TIKHON. Up with the money; then there'll be vodka.

BORTSOV. But where am I to get money? Everything is gone for drink! Everything, to a thread! Then what can I give you? Only this overcoat is left; but I cannot give you that. . . . It's over a bare body. . . . Want the cap? (*He takes off his cap and hands it to* TIKHON.)

TIKHON (*examining the cap*). Hm! . . . There are caps and caps. It's as full of holes as a sieve.

FEDIA (*laughing*). A noble's! To wear in the street and to tip to ladies. "Hello! Good-by! How do you do?"

TIKHON (*returning* BORTSOV'S *cap*). I wouldn't take it as a gift. It's a dunghill!

BORTSOV. You don't like it? Then trust me. I'll be passing here on my way back from town and bring you your five kopéks. May you choke with it. Yes, choke! Let it stick right in your throat. (*He coughs.*) I hate you!

TIKHON (*pounding his fist on the counter*). What do you want of me? Who are you, anyway? What kind of a crook? What brought you here?

BORTSOV. I want a drink. Not I—exactly I, either; my sickness wants it. Understand!

TIKHON. Don't try my patience, or you'll be out on the steppe in a jiffy.

BORTSOV. What shall I do? (*Walking away from the bar.*) What shall I do? (*He meditates.*)

YEFIMOVNA. It's the evil one that's torturing you. Just snap your fingers at it, sir. The cursed thing whispers to you: "Drink! Drink!" But you answer: "I won't! I won't!" and it'll leave you alone.

FEDIA. Must have wheels in his head—hi-hi-hi! It's enough to turn one's stomach. (*Giggling.*) You're queer, sir. Go to sleep! It's no use hanging around like a scarecrow in the middle of the saloon. This is not an orchard.

BORTSOV (*viciously*). Shut up! Nobody is asking you, you jackass!

FEDIA. You may talk and talk, but don't go too far. I have met your kind before. There are many such as you sauntering up and down the highway. And as for "jackass," I'll give you such a box on the ear that you will howl louder than the wind. You're a jackass yourself, you good-for-nothing! (*A pause ensues.*) Rascal!

NAZAROVNA. The old man is praying perhaps and giving up his soul to his

Maker, and they, the blasphemers, keep on picking quarrels with each other—and what language! Shame on them!

FEDIA. And you, cabbage-stalk, should not grumble once you are in a saloon. In saloons there's saloon manners.

BORTSOV. But how can I? What shall I do? How make him understand? Is eloquence necessary? (*To* TIKHON.) The blood clots my heart. Uncle Tikhon! (*Weeping.*) *Uncle* Tikhon!

SAVVA (*groaning*). I have a shooting in the leg as from a bullet of fire. . . . Pilgrim mother, *Mátushka!*

YEFIMOVNA. Well, *Cátyushka?*

SAVVA. Who is weeping?

YEFIMOVNA. The nobleman.

SAVVA. Ask the nobleman to shed a tear for me, that I may live to die at Vológda. A tearful prayer is more acceptable.

BORTSOV. I am not praying, sir. Nor are these tears; it's sap. The heart contracts and makes the sap run. (*He sits down at* SAVVA'S *feet.*) Sap, this is! But how could you understand? It isn't for your dark mind, sir, to understand. You people are sitting in the darkness.

SAVVA. But are there any who have the light?

BORTSOV. There are such, grandpa. *They* would understand.

SAVVA. Indeed, there are, my friend. The saints had that light. They understood all suffering—understood it without your ever telling them anything, either. They just looked into one's eyes, and they had it. And what comfort their understanding brought one! It was as if you never had any woe—'twas gone as by a touch of the hand.

FEDIA. And have you ever seen saints?

SAVVA. Occasionally, my boy. There are many people of all kinds on earth. There are the sinners, and there are the servants of God.

BORTSOV. I don't understand this at all. Talk is addressed to the understanding, but have I any reason now? I have only feeling—thirst! (*He suddenly walks up to the bar.*) Tikhon, take the overcoat. Understand? (*About to take it off.*) The overcoat.

TIKHON. And underneath is what? (*He peeps under* BORTSOV'S *overcoat.*) The bare body? No, don't remove it; I won't take it. I won't take sin upon my soul. (MERIN *enters.*)

BORTSOV. Well, I take the sin on myself. All right?

MERIK. (*He quietly takes off his great-coat, remaining in a sheepskin jacket. In his belt is an axe.*) Some feel cold, while bears and those who forget their kin always feel hot. I'm perspiring! (*He puts the axe on the floor and removes his jacket.*) Before one drags a foot out of the mud he's in a pool of perspiration. You drag one foot out, and in goes the other.

YEFIMOVNA. That's so. . . . The rain hasn't slackened, has it, friend?

MERIK (*glancing at* YEFIMOVNA). I don't talk with old women. (*A pause ensues.*)

BORTSOV (*to* TIKHON). I take the sin on myself. Do you hear or not?

TIKHON. I don't want to hear, either. Leave me alone!

MERIK. It's pitch-dark, as if someone had smeared the sky with tar. Not a soul is to be seen. And the rain keeps beating in one's face like a snowstorm. (*He takes his clothes and axe under his arm.*)

FEDIA. For such as you—thieves—that's just the thing. Beasts of prey lie in hiding, and for you, merry Andrews, it's a holiday.

MERIK. And from whom do I hear this?

FEDIA. Look and see. Not blind, are you?

MERIK. I'll make note of this. (*He walks up to* TIKHON.) Hello, big mug! Or don't you recognize me?

TIKHON. If one should remember all you drunkards who pass on the highway, it would add ten furrows to his forehead.

MERIK. Then, take a look. (*A pause ensues.*)

TIKHON. I have you already, what do you think of that! I recognized you by your optics. (*He holds out a hand.*) Andrei Polikarpov?

MERIK. I was Andrei Polikarpov, but now call me Yegor Merik.

TIKHON. Why so?

MERIK. Whatever passport it pleases the Lord to give me, by that name am I known. I've been Merik for about two months. (*Thunder roars.*) Te, te, te! Fire away! Who's afraid? (*He surveys the room.*) Any police spies here?

TIKHON. What spies? Mostly gnats and mosquitoes. A tame lot this is. The police must now be sound asleep in their featherbeds. (*Aloud.*) Say, *právoslávnyé,*[2] watch your pockets and clothes if you wouldn't be sorry. A crook! Might steal!

MERIK. Let 'em watch their cash, if they have any; but as for their clothes, I won't touch 'em. Nowhere to take 'em.

TIKHON. Where the deuce are you going?

MERIK. To Kuban.

TIKHON. Oho!

FEDIA. To Kuban? Upon your word? (*He rises.*) Fine places! It's such a region, friends, that you can't even dream of it though you should sleep three years. Such profusion! They say the birds there, the game, the animals of all kinds, and—my God! Why, the grass grows there all year round, the people live like brothers, and they have more land than they know what to do with. The government, they say—a soldier told me the other day—grants one hundred *dessiatins*[3] per head. That's happiness, by golly!

MERIK. Happiness. . . . Happiness follows behind one's back. It can't be seen. You'll not be happy sooner than you can bite your own elbow. It's all nonsense. (*He surveys the benches and the people.*) Looks like a prisoners' halting-place. What poverty!

---

[2] Another untranslatable term. It means, literally, "true believers," but is used by Russian peasants to express more the idea of comradeship—something like "countrymen"—than any religious connotation. The word, which is a pronominal adjective, is here used in the plural.—Translator.

[3] A dessiatina is equal to a little more than 2½ acres.

YEFIMOVNA (*to* MERIK). Such fierce eyes! There's enmity in you, lad. Don't stare at us!

MERIK. Such poverty!

YEFIMOVNA. Turn away! (*She pushes* SAVVA.) Savva, dear, a wicked man is staring at us. It bodes no good, my dear. (*To* MERIK.) Turn away, I say, you serpent!

SAVVA. He won't touch you, *Mátushka,* he won't. God won't permit it.

MERIK. What true believers! (*He shrugs his shoulders.*) So quiet! Why, you are not asleep, you bow-legged ones. Why do you keep quiet?

YEFIMOVNA. Turn away your eyes—turn away your devil's look!

MERIK. Shut up, you crooked old thing! It was not with the devil's look, but with kindness and good cheer, that I noticed your sad lot. You huddle up from the cold like flies; so I took pity on you and wanted to say a kind word—wanted to comfort you—and there you turn away your faces. Well? All right! (*He walks up to* FEDIA.) Where do you hail from?

FEDIA. From hereabouts; Khamonovsky Zavód—from the brick yards.

MERIK. Get up, sir.

FEDIA (*rising*). Well?

MERIK. Up, up, altogether. I'll lie down here.

FEDIA. Not your place, is it?

MERIK. It is. Go spread on the floor.

FEDIA. Pass on, wayfarer. I am not afraid of you.

MERIK. Saucy? Well, go and don't argue, or you'll cry, fool.

TIKHON (*to* FEDIA). Don't cross him, lad. Do as he says.

FEDIA. What right have you? You bulge out your pike eyes and think I'm afraid of you. (*He gathers up his belongings under his arm and proceeds to make his bed on the floor.*) Devil! (*He lies down and covers his head and all.*)

MERIK (*making his bed on the bench*). Then you haven't seen the devil, if you call me one. Devils aren't like that. (*He lies down and places his axe beside him.*) Lie down, dear axe, comrade mine. Let me cover you, axie.

TIKHON. Where did you get that axe?

MERIK. Why, I stole it; stole it, and now must carry it about as a fool would some gaudy-colored bag: I hate to leave it behind and yet have nowhere to keep it—it's like a loathesome wife. . . . No, friend (*he covers himself*), devils aren't like that.

FEDIA (*poking his head out from under his great-coat*). How, then?

MERIK. They are like vapor, spirit, like a puff of air (*blowing*)—that's how they are. One can't see them.

A VOICE FROM THE CORNER. If he should sit under hedges, he might.

MERIK. I tried and didn't see. They lie, the old women and silly peasants. Neither the devil, nor the wood-nymph, nor the dead can be seen. The eye isn't made to see everything. When I was a lad I used to go to the woods at night in order to see the wood-nymph. I would yell and shout with all my might, calling the goddess of the forest and never winking an eye. Well,

I imagined all sorts of queer things, but I saw no nymph. I would go to cemeteries at night to see ghosts, but the old women lie. I saw all kinds of beings, but as for that Awful One—I couldn't see him to save my life. We haven't the eye for it.

A VOICE FROM THE CORNER. Don't be so sure about that; sometimes one can see. A peasant in our village once killed a pig. He ripped his belly open when out leaped the—

SAVVA (*rising.*) Boys, don't be mentioning the Evil One. It's a sin, my friends.

MERIK. Ah, you graybeard! You skeleton! (*He laughs.*) We needn't visit cemeteries; our own dead creep out here from underground to read us sermons. A sin! It's not for those with your foolish ideas to read people lectures. You are a gloomy lot, steeped in ignorance. (*He lights his pipe.*) My father was a peasant and also liked to read us sermons. One night he stole a bag of apples from the parson. He brought it to us and said: "Boys, don't munch any apples before the great fast—it's a sin." You act the same way. The devil must not be mentioned, but it's all right to cuss. Take this hag here, for instance. (*He points to* YEFIMOVNA.) In me she saw a wicked man, and yet she herself, from woman's folly, has yielded her soul to the devil some five times, no doubt.

YEFIMOVNA. Fie, fie, fie! Christ protect us! (*She covers her face with her hands.*) Savva, dear!

TIKHON. Why do you scare them? And glad! (*The wind slams the door.*) Jesus Christ, what a wind!

MERIK (*stretching*). O, if one could but show his strength! (*The door slams again in the wind.*) Pit it against this wind here! It can't tear the door off its hinges, while I could, if it came to that, pull this tavern up by the roots. (*He rises and lies down.*) What a bore!

NAZAROVNA. Say your prayers, you heathen! Why are you restless?

YEFIMOVNA. Leave him alone, the plague take him! He is again staring at us. (*To* MERIK.) Don't stare, wicked man. What eyes! What eyes! Like the demon's before early mass.

SAVVA. Let him stare, pilgrim-mothers. Offer up a prayer and his eye will bring you no harm.

BORTSOV. No, I cannot—it's beyond my endurance! (*He walks over to the bar.*) Listen, Tikhon, I ask you the last time: half a glass!

TIKHON. (*He shakes his head.*) Money!

BORTSOV. My God, but haven't I told you already? Everything is gone for drink. Where shall I get you money? And will it ruin you to give me a drop of vodka on trust? A glass of vodka stands you but two kopéks, but for me it means deliverance from suffering. How I suffer! It's not caprice, but suffering! Understand?

TIKHON. Try it on somebody else. Go ask those *právoslávnyé* there—let them treat you for the sake of Christ, if they will—but I give only bread for Christ's sake.

BORTSOV. You can skin those paupers yourself, but I would rather be excused. It's not in me to rob them. Not in me! Understand? (*He pounds his fist on the bar.*) Not in me! (*A pause ensues.*) Hm . . . but wait. (*He turns to the pilgrims.*) And that's not a bad idea, either—*právoslávnyé,* won't you sacrifice five kopéks? It's the inside that begs. I'm sick!

FEDIA. Oh, you! "Sacrifice." Cheat! Isn't water good enough for you?

BORTSOV. But how I lower myself! My, how I humiliate myself! Never mind! I don't want anything—I was only joking.

MERIK. You won't move him, Boss. He's a noted miser. Wait, I must have a five-kopék piece somewhere. We'll have a glass together, half and half. (*He fumbles in his pockets.*) Got stuck somewhere, damn it! I thought I heard something jingling in the pocket recently. No, it's gone. Gone, friend. Such is your luck! (*A pause ensues.*)

BORTSOV. I can't go without a drink. I'll commit some crime—or else decide on suicide. What shall I do? My God! (*He looks to the door.*) Go away, perhaps? Go forth into this darkness, lead wherever chance may?

MERIK. Why don't you, dear pilgrims, read him sermons? And you, Tikhon, why don't you put him out? He hasn't paid for his night's lodging, you know. Kick him out; take him by the collar! Oh, how brutal people are nowadays! They have no sentiment or kindness. Fierce folk! A man is drowning, and they shout to him: "Drown faster. We haven't time to watch; this is our busy day." As for throwing him a rope, that's out of the question. Rope costs money!

SAVVA. Don't censure, kind man.

MERIK. Shut up, you old wolf! You are a cruel lot. Monsters! Soulmongers! (*To* TIKHON.) Come over here and pull off my boots. Quick!

TIKHON. Ho, ho, what airs! (*He laughs.*) It's awful!

MERIK. Come on, I say. Quick! (*A pause ensues.*) Do you hear or not? What am I talking to? (*He rises.*)

TIKHON. Say, say, that'll do.

MERIK. I want you, bloodsucker, to pull the boots off me—me, a poor tramp.

TIKHON. Well, well, don't rage. Have a drink. Come have a glass.

MERIK. Folks, what am I asking? That he treat me to drinks or remove my boots? Have I expressed myself inaccurately? (*To* TIKHON.) You didn't hear me right, it seems. I'll wait a minute—perhaps you'll get me. (*There is considerable commotion among the pilgrims and others. They get up and stare at* TIKHON *and* MERIK *in silent suspense.*)

TIKHON. The evil one brought you! (*He comes out from behind the bar.*) What a lord we have here! Well, come on, then. (*He pulls off* MERIK's *boots.*) What a rogue!

MERIK. That's right. Place them alongside each other. That's it. Now go!

TIKHON. (*He returns behind the bar after removing the boots.*) But my, how you like to joke! Another one of your jokes here and out you go in a jiffy. Sure enough! (*To* BORTSOV, *who is approaching.*) You again?

BORTSOV. You see, I could give you some gold trinket. It's yours, if you want it.

TIKHON. Why do you stutter? Talk like a man.

BORTSOV. Though it is very mean on my part, what else can I do? Being dead broke, I bring myself over to this meanness. Even a court would acquit me. Take it but on condition that you return it to me later when I come back from town. I hand it to you before witnesses. Ladies and gentlemen, you be the witnesses! (*He takes from his bosom a golden locket.*) Here it is. I ought to remove the picture, but I've no place to keep it; I'm all wet. Well, grab it—picture and all. Only remember: your fingers must not touch this face! I beg of you. I was rude to you, dear sir, and foolish, but you will pardon me and not touch it with your fingers. Don't let your eyes rest on this face. (*He hands* TIKHON *the locket.*)

TIKHON (*examining the locket*). A stolen little watch. . . . Well, all right, drink. (*He pours out a glass.*) Drink till you burst!

BORTSOV. But don't let your fingers touch it. (*He drinks slowly and spasmodically.*)

TIKHON (*opening the locket*). Hm, a lady! Where did you get such a one?

MERIK. Let's see it. (*He gets up and walks over to the bar.*) Let's have a look.

TIKHON (*pushing* MERIK'S *hand away*). Stand back! See it in my hand.

FEDIA (*gets up and goes to* TIKHON). Let me see it, too.

(*From all sides pilgrims and others approach the bar, forming a crowd.*)

MERIK (*with both his hands he tightly holds* TIKHON'S *hand with the locket and silently eyes the picture. A pause ensues*). A handsome little devil. From the nobility.

FEDIA. Yes, from the nobility. What cheeks! What eyes! Get your hand out of my way; I can't see. Hair down to the waist. Just as if alive! Was about to speak. (*There is silence.*)

MERIK. For a weak man this is the greatest curse. Once such a woman gets astride a fellow, he (*waving his hand in despair*)—he's done for. (*The voice of* KUZMA *is heard.* "Ho! Ho, you fowl!")

KUZMA (*entering*). The tavern standing on the way tempts the traveler by night and day. One may pass his own father in broad daylight without noticing him, but a tavern can be seen in the dark a hundred versts away. To one side, all ye who believe in God! Well. (*He knocks a five-kopék piece on the bar.*) A glass of real Madeira! Quick!

FEDIA. O, you reckless devil!

TIKHON. Don't swing your arms; you'll knock this out of my hand.

KUZMA. That's what God intended them for, to be swung. She's all melted, the sweetmeat—your aunt, the chicken. Scared by the rain, the tenderfoot! (*He drinks.*)

YEFIMOVNA. Who wouldn't be afraid, my good man, to be out on the road in such a night as this? Now, thank God, there are plenty of villages and farms along the way where one may find shelter from the elements, but formerly it was something terrible. You could go a hundred versts and not only come upon no farms or villages, but not see a chip of wood. You had to sleep on the ground.

Kuzma. And how long, old woman, have you been knocking about in the world?

Yefimovna. Going on eighty, *Cátyushká.*

Kuzma. Going on eighty! Why, you'll soon be as old as a crow. (*He looks at* Bortsov.) And what sort of bird is this? (*He eyes* Bortsov *closely.*) A nobleman!

(Bortsov *recognizes* Kuzma *and, blushing, goes off to the corner and sits down on the bench.*)

Kuzma. Semion Sergeévitch! Is that you or not? Hey? How come you to be in this tavern? Is this the place for you?

Bortsov. Hush!

Merik (*to* Kuzma). Who is that?

Kuzma. An unfortunate sufferer. (*He nervously walks about by the bar.*) Ah! In a saloon! What do you think of that? In rags! Drunk! I am shocked, friends, shocked! (*He talks in a half-whisper to* Merik.) This is our master—our landlord, Semion Sergeévitch Bortsov. Did you notice his condition? Doesn't look much like a man, does he? Thus does drinking— Another glass! (*He drinks.*) I come from his village, from Borstóvka— maybe you've heard of it—two hundred versts from here, in the district of Yegórov. We were his father's serfs— 'Tis a pity!

Merik. Was he rich?

Kuzma. Very.

Merik. Squandered his father's wealth?

Kuzma. No; ill luck, my friend. He was a fine gentleman—rich and temperate. (*To* Tikhon.) You may have seen him pass this tavern on his way to town. Fine, spirited horses and a carriage on springs—first class! He kept fifteen horses, my friend. About five years ago he was crossing the Mikishkin Ferry here, I remember, and instead of five kopéks he tossed a ruble. "No time," says he, "to wait for change." What do you think of that?

Merik. He must have been out of his mind.

Kuzma. He acted like one in his senses. It all came from being chicken-hearted—from too much riches. To begin with, boys, there was a woman in the case. He fell in love, that good man, with a city-bred girl and imagined her the most beautiful woman in the whole world. The crow fell in love worse than a falcon. Comes from a respectable family, she does; not a loose woman or anything like that, but simply a flirt. Just went about twisting and twirling and making eyes all the time. Always laughing and smiling— no brains at all. The nobility like that; they think her clever. Our peasant way would be simply to chase her out of the house. Well, she returned his love, and the nobleman's fate was sealed. He commenced to take her out and all that—treat her to teas and sweetmeats, all-night rowing and piano-playing.

BORTSOV. Don't tell, Kuzma. Why should you? What have they to do with my life?

KUZMA. Beg pardon, your honor. I just told the least bit—a mere trifle—and that'll do for them. Just a bit, because I was shocked—very much shocked, I was. Another glass, there! (*He drinks.*)

MERIK (*in a half-whisper*). And did she love him?

KUZMA (*in a half-whisper which gradually rises to regular speech*). How could she fail to love him? He's no insignificant nobleman. Who wouldn't fall in love when there are a thousand *dessiatins* and money to burn? He himself was a man of parts, dignified and temperate, hobnobbing with every government official, like you and me here, shaking their hands (*He takes* MERIK *by the hand*)—"hello" and "good-by" and "by your leave." Well, one night I was passing through the noble's park, a park, friend, five versts long. I was walking quietly. I looked around and there were they sitting on a bench (*He imitates a kiss*) kissing each other—he her once and she, the serpent, him twice. He takes her snow-white hand in his, and she's all aglow, hugging him and hugging him, the devil take her. "I love you, Senia," says she. And Senia, like one dazed, from sheer good nature, goes about from place to place bragging about his happiness. He gives one a ruble, another two; gives me money to buy a horse. Exempts all his debtors for joy!

BORTSOV. But, why be telling about it? These people have no sympathy! It's torture!

KUZMA Only a trifle, sir. They're inquiring, and why not tell a bit? But if it makes you angry, then I won't, that's all. I don't give a hang for them. (*The postman's bells are heard.*)

FEDIA. Don't holler; talk low.

KUZMA. I'm talking low as it is. He won't have it, and that's all there is to it. And there's nothing more to tell, anyhow. They got married—that's all. Nothing more to it. Fill another glass, there, for Kuzma, the temperate. (*He drinks.*) I don't like drunkenness! After the wedding, just as people were about to have supper, what should she do but run away in a cab. (*In a whisper.*) To the city to a lawyer, her lover! How's that? What do you think of her? At that very moment, mind you. Killing her wouldn't be enough!

MERIK (*thinking*). Yes; and then what?

KUZMA. Lost his reason. As you see, he started out to kill a fly and now, I hear, he's up against the bumble-bee.[*] Those were flies, but now it's bumble-bees! And he still loves her; you can see that he does. He must now be going to the city on foot to glance at her. He'll have a look and return.

(*The mail coach arrives at the tavern. The postman enters and drinks. The postman silently pays and goes out. The mail coach, with bells tinkling, leaves.*)

A VOICE FROM THE CORNER. In such weather to rob the mail would be a cinch!

---

[*] A Russian proverb whose meaning must be gathered from the context.

MERIK. I have lived thirty-five years in the world and never once robbed the mail. (*A pause ensues.*) Now it's gone—too late! Too late!

KUZMA. Want a taste of Siberia?

MERIK. Some rob and don't taste it. And even if Siberia! (*Bluntly.*) What next?

KUZMA. You refer to the unfortunate one?

MERIK. Whom else could I mean?

KUZMA. The next question, friends, how came his ruin? A brother-in-law, his sister's husband. He took a notion to guarantee a loan of some thirty thousand rubles made by this man from a banking house. That brother-in-law is a grafter; he knows his business, the rascal—no flies on him, I tell you. He took the money, and as for paying it back—why, what's the use? And so our man just had to come across with that thirty thousand! (*He sighs.*) Foolish fellow, and it's his own foolishness that he is paying for. His wife had children by that lawyer, and his brother-in-law bought an estate near Poltava, while this here fellow goes about the saloons and, like a fool, complains to us, peasants: "I've lost all faith, my friends. I have no one, that is, to pin my faith to." Chicken-heartedness! Everyone has his troubles. The serpent gnaws at the heart, hence men take to drink. Take, for instance, the head of our *vólost.*[5] His wife brings a man teacher to the house in broad daylight, spending on drink the money of her husband, while he just walks about and smiles. Grub a bit thinner, that's all.

TIKHON (*sighing*). It's all according to the strength God's given one.

KUZMA. That does vary, it is true. . . . Well, what's coming to you? (*He pays.*) Take the bloody money! Good-by, boys. Good night, sleep tight! I must run; I'm late. I'm bringing a midwife from the hospital to a lady. She must have grown tired waiting, the good-natured thing, and wet to the skin. (*He hurries out.*)

TIKHON (*after a pause*). Hey, there! What's your name? Unhappy man, come have a drink. (*He fills a glass.*)

BORTSOV. (*He approaches the bar hesitatingly and drinks.*) It means I now owe you for two drinks?

TIKHON. O, never mind. Drink, that's all. Drown your woes in sorrow.

FEDIA. Have one on me, boss. Alas! (*He throws a five-kopék piece on the bar.*) One dies if he drinks, and dies if he doesn't. It's all right without drink, but with it, by Jove, is pleasanter. Even sorrows grow lighter with drink. Drink away!

BORTSOV. Whew! It's hot!

MERIK. Let's have it. (*He takes the locket from* TIKHON *and studies the picture.*) Hm! Ran off after the wedding, eh? Is that the kind you are?

A VOICE FROM THE CORNER. Fill another glass, Tisha. Let him have one on me, too.

MERIK (*dashing the locket to the floor.*) Damn you! (*He walks quickly to his place and lies down with his face to the wall. A commotion follows.*)

---

[5] A rural district.

BORTSOV. What's this? What do you call that? (*He picks up the locket.*) How dare you, brute! What right have you! (*Wailing.*) D'you want me to kill you, do you? Peasant! Ruffian!

TIKHON. It's enough to rage, boss. It's not made of glass; it didn't break. Have another drink and go to bed. (*He fills a glass.*) I lingered too long to listen to you fellows; it was time to close up long ago. (*He goes and locks the outside door.*)

BORTSOV (*drinks*). How dared he? And such a fool, too! (*To* MERIK.) Understand? You are a fool—an ass!

SAVVA. Friends! Honorable gentlemen! Give your tongues a rest. What's the good of noise? Let people sleep.

TIKHON. Lie down, lie down. Enough of that! (*He goes behind the bar and locks the drawer containing the day's receipts.*) It's time to sleep.

FEDIA. I should say it is! (*He lies down.*) Good night, folks.

MERIK (*he gets up and spreads his sheepskin coat on the bench*). Here, boss, lie down.

TIKHON. And where will you sleep?

MERIN. Anywhere; even on the floor. (*He spreads his great coat on the floor.*) It's all the same to me. (*He places his axe beside him.*) For him it's a hardship to sleep on the floor. He's used to fine linen and cotton mattresses.

TIKHON (*to* BORTSOV). Lie down, sir. It's enough to stare at the picture. (*He blows out the candle.*) Be done with her!

BORTSOV (*tottering*). Where am I to lie down?

TIKHON. On the tramp's place. Didn't you hear him give it to you?

BORTSOV (*he approaches the above-mentioned place.*) I'm—rather drunk. Is this it? Here am I to sleep, eh?

TIKHON. Here, here; lie down, don't fear. (*He stretches himself on the bar.*)

BORTSOV (*lying down*). I—am—drunk. All about is. (*He opens the locket.*) Got a light? (*A pause ensues.*) You, Masha, are a queer little woman. You look at me from the frame there and smile. (*He laughs.*) Drunk! But is it fair to laugh at a fellow who's drunk? You overlook this, as *Stchastlivtoev* [6] would say, and fall in love with a drunkard.

FEDIA. How the wind howls! It's terrible!

BORTSOV (*he laughs*). You're funny! How can you spin like that? No one can catch up with you.

MERIK. He's raving—bewitched by the picture. (*He laughs.*) Here's a curious situation! Learned men have invented all kinds of machines and medicines, but no wise man has yet found an antidote for the female sex. They study how to cure every disease, but it never even occurs to them that more people perish through women than from disease. Sly, mercenary, ungracious creatures, with no brains at all! Mothers-in-law intriguing against

[6] An obscure reference inexplicable by anything in the play. The word itself is a proper masculine noun derived from the Russian for "happiness."—Translator.

their daughters-in-law, the latter trying to blacken their husbands, and so on without end.

TIKHON. The women have pulled his ears and now his hair's on end.

MERIK. I am not the only one. From the beginning of time, ever since the world was created, people have been complaining. It's not for nothing that in stories and songs woman and the devil are linked together. Not for nothing! It's true, even if only half true. (*A pause follows.*) That noble there is making a fool of himself. It wasn't from too big a head, either, that I left my parents and went tramping.

FEDIA. Women?

MERIK. Like that nobleman, I, too, walked about like one under a spell, boasting of my happiness, day and night like a man in a fever. But the time came and I opened my eyes. It wasn't love—just deceit!

FEDIA. What did you do to her?

MERIK. None of your business. (*A pause ensues.*) Killed her, you think? I didn't have the courage. I not only spared her, but pitied her besides. Live and be happy! Only keep out of my sight, and may I forget you, you venomous snake? (*A knock is heard at the door.*)

TIKHON. Who the devil's this? Who's there? (*The knocking continues.*) Who's knocking? (*He gets up and goes to the door.*) Who's knocking? Pass on your way; we're locked up!

A VOICE FROM BEHIND THE DOOR. Let me in, Tikhon; do a favor! A spring's broken in the carriage. Help a fellow out; be a friend in need. If we could only fasten it with some rope, we might get there somehow.

TIKHON. Who are you driving?

A VOICE FROM BEHIND THE DOOR. A lady going from the city to Varsónsfievo. Only five versts farther. Help me out!

TIKHON. Go tell the lady that if she'll pay ten rubles we'll get a rope and fix up that spring.

A VOICE FROM BEHIND THE DOOR. What! Are you crazy? Ten rubles! You mad dog! Exulting in people's misfortunes?

TIKHON. Just as you like. If you don't want to, very well.

A VOICE FROM BEHIND THE DOOR. Well, all right; wait a while. (*A pause follows.*) The lady says it's all right.

TIKHON. Come in! (*He opens the door and admits the driver.*)

THE DRIVER. Hello, *právoslávnyé!* Well, fetch the rope! Quick! Boys, who'll lend a hand? There'll be tips.

TIKHON. Oh, what's the use tipping? Let them sleep. We two can manage it ourselves.

THE DRIVER. Whew, how tired I am! The cold and the mud—not a dry spot anywhere! Another thing, friend: Haven't you a room here for the lady to get warm? The carriage has tilted so that there is no sitting up in it.

TIKHON. A room! What ever put that into her head? Let her thaw out here if she is frozen; we'll find a place. (*He goes to* BORTSOV *and dusts off a place near him.*) Get up, get up! Lie on the floor an hour or so while a lady gets warm. (*To* BORTSOV.) Rise, sir! Sit up awhile. (BORTSOV *rises.*) Here's a place for you. (*The driver goes out.*)

FEDIA. Here's a fine guest for you; the devil sent her! Now there'll be no sleeping again before daybreak.

TIKHON. Sorry I didn't ask fifteen! She'd pay. (*He stops before the door in an expectant attitude.*) You people don't be so rough. Don't use such language. (MARIA YEGOROVNA *enters, followed by the driver.*)

TIKHON (*bowing*). Welcome, your highness! Ours is but a peasant's hut— a rat-hole. Don't scorn it.

MARIA YEGOROVNA. I can't see a thing here. Where am I to go?

TIKHON. This way, your highness. (*He leads her to the place by* BORTSOV.) Here, please. (*He blows away the dust.*) I have no private room; I'm sorry. But, madam, have no fear; these are good, quiet people.

MARIA YEGOROVNA (*sitting down beside* BORTSOV). My, how terribly close it is here! Open the door at least!

TIKHON. All right, madam. (*He runs over and opens the door.*)

MERIK. People are freezing here and they throw the door wide open! (*He gets up and slams the door shut.*) What a boss you are! (*He lies down.*)

TIKHON. I beg your pardon, your highness. That's our jester; he's a little off. But don't fear, he won't touch you. Only—excuse me, madam—I can't take ten rubles. Fifteen, if you please.

MARIA YEGOROVNA. All right, only be quick about it.

TIKHON. This minute. We'll have it fixed in a twinkling. (*He pulls a rope from under the bar.*) This very minute. (*A pause follows.*)

BORTSOV (*gazing at* MARIA YEGOROVNA). Mary! Masha!

MARIA YEGOROVNA (*looking at* BORTSOV). What now, I wonder?

BORTSOV. Mary, is this you? Where do you come from?

(MARIA YEGOROVNA, *having recognized* BORTSOV, *shrieks and bounds off to the center of the tavern.*)

BORTSOV (*following her*). Maria, it's I! (*He giggles.*) My wife! Maria! And where am I? A light, folks!

MARIA YEGOROVNA. Go away! You lie—it isn't you. It's impossible! (*She covers her face with her hands.*) It's a lie—a joke!

BORTSOV. The voice, the gait! Maria, it's I! I'll soon—get sober. My head swims. My God! Wait, wait—I don't understand anything. (*He shouts.*) My wife! (*He drops by her feet weeping.*)

(*A group gathers around the couple.*)

MARIA YEGOROVNA. Stand back. (*To the driver.*) Dennis, let's start. I can't stay here any longer.

MERIK. (*He jumps up and stares at her face.*) The picture! (*He grabs her by the hand.*) That's her! Hey, folks, it's the noble's wife!

MARIA YEGOROVNA. Get away, fool! (*She tries to free her arm.*) Dennis, why do you look on? (DENNIS *and* TIKHON *run up to her and take* MERIK *by the arms.*) This is a murderer's den! Let go my hand! I'm not afraid. Be off with you!

MERIK. Wait, I'll let go soon. Let me say just a word to you, one word, that you may understand—wait. (*He turns to* TIKHON *and* DENNIS.) Away with you, blockheads; don't hold me! I won't let go before I have said that word. Wait—just a second. (*He strikes his forehead with his fist.*) No! God has denied me the wisdom; I can't hit upon a word for you!

MARIA YEGOROVNA (*freeing her hand*). Get away with you! Drunkards! Dennis, we are off! (*She starts for the door.*)

MERIK (*blocking her way*). Well, just glance at him with but one eye! Caress him with but a single word of love; I beg of you, in the name of God.

MARIA YEGOROVNA. Take this madman away from me!

MERIK. Then perish, you damned thing! (*He swings his axe. A terrible commotion ensues. Every one jumps up with noise and shrieks of horror.* SAVVA *gets between* MERIK *and* MARIA YEGOROVNA. DENNIS *forcibly pushes* MERIK *aside and carries the lady out of the tavern. Then every one stands as though stunned. A long pause follows.*)

BORTSOV (*beating the air with his hands.*) Maria! Where are you, Maria?

NAZAROVNA. My God, my God! You have broken my heart, you murderers! Oh, what a cursed night!

MERIK (*dropping his arm that holds the axe*). Have I finished her or not?

TIKHON. Thank God, your head is safe.

MERIK. Then I didn't kill her! (*He walks unsteadily to his bed.*) It's not my fate to meet death through a stolen axe. (*He drops on his bed and weeps.*) How sad! How terribly sad! Pity me, *právoslávnyé!*

CURTAIN

THE STREET SINGER

A PLAY

By José Echegaray

Translated from the Spanish by John Garrett Underhill

CHARACTERS

ANGUSTIAS
PEPE, *her lover*
SUSPIROS, *a young girl*
CÓLETA, *a beggar*
PASSERSBY AND TOWNSPEOPLE

THE STREET SINGER

*The stage represents a square or street. There may or may not be trees;
there may or may not be seats; there may or may not be lighted lamps.
Several wine shops, lighted and standing open, may or may not be seen.
The only thing which is essential is the wall of a house facing the front,
or but slightly inclined to it, near the principal entrance used, so that the
beggars and the singer may take their places against it.*
The time is night.
Coleta, *fifty years of age, degraded, addicted to drink, a beggar by profession,
and* Suspiros, *a girl of sixteen, attractive, soft-mannered, but sickly, who
begs incidentally, are standing before the wall waiting to solicit alms.*

Coleta. Hello, Suspiros! Begging again to-night?

Suspiros. Yes, Señor Coleta. My stepmother made me. She says if I
don't bring back two pesetas she'll give me a bigger cuff than she did yesterday.

Coleta. Did you get a good one yesterday?

Suspiros. Ay! Señor Coleta!

Coleta. You're not beginning to cry already?

Suspiros. If I didn't cry, I'd die of my troubles. My poor mother used
to say that sighs are wings that you give to troubles and they fly away.

Coleta. Don't you want to lend me something?

Suspiros. What do you want me to lend you?

Coleta. Some of those lovely sighs of yours, which you say are wings.
I might be able to use them.

Suspiros. Everybody has sighs of his own.

Coleta. I haven't; not if that's what they're like. When my troubles
come, they come on all fours, like stray dogs. When I slip out of the tavern
—just over there—and meet the police, my trouble is running; it's not flying.
Never! That is—not flying with wings. Let me tell you, child, they say it
is drink. Bah! They will say anything to ruin a man's reputation.

Suspiros. They'll ruin you any way they can.

Coleta. That's right. But to-night, when it's dark—you're not going to
beg here?

Suspiros. I'm used to it; I'm not so much ashamed.

Coleta. But nobody goes by.

Suspiros. Ay! That's the reason I like it!

Coleta. You don't know how to beg.

Suspiros. Yes, sir, I know how to beg; the trouble is, people don't know

315

how to give. I say: "A penny for my poor mother who is sick!" And you ought to see how sick she is! She died two years ago. Well, I get nothing. Or else I say: "A little penny for God's sake, for my mother, who is in the hospital, in the name of the Blessed Virgin! I have two baby brothers." No one gives, either.

COLETA. They don't, eh? And how many brothers are you going to have to-night?

SUSPIROS. Ay, Señor Coleta! I had two and nobody gave me anything; I had three and they didn't give me anything. Last night I tried four and I got six pence, so to-night I mean to have five and see what they give me, or whether I just get the cuff from my mother.

COLETA. Just in the family, how many brothers have you, really?

SUSPIROS. Really, I had two. But they died—like my mother. Ay! They died because of the way my stepmother treated them—as she does me; and I am dying! Listen! If I can make two or three dollars I am going to run away to Játiva, and live with my aunt.

COLETA. Listen! If I didn't have so much to do in the tavern over there—you know—I'd take you for my daughter, and then we could beg together. Because I know how to beg, with my education; but a man can't beg here; this place is a desert.

SUSPIROS. There was a new girl here last night. She looked like a lady, the way she was. She didn't sigh, though; she was crying.

COLETA. Well, if she can cry, I'll take you both for my daughters; I need a family. You with your sighs and she with her cries, and me with my poor old eyes, we'd do twenty *reals* a day and live like kings. It's a great life. I was a gentleman once; I was a school-teacher. Then I was an undertaker; Then I drove an ox-cart; and then—I didn't drive it; and here you have me.

SUSPIROS. I'd be better off with anybody else than my stepmother.

COLETA. That girl certainly did look like a lady.

SUSPIROS. That's why she was afraid to beg—she was ashamed.

COLETA. Was she? She stood here by the wall half an hour, glued to it; and then she went away without saying a word.

SUSPIROS. A good beggar ought to be able to do something; that's what I say. The old man who stands there with the violin, he makes a lot of money because he plays the violin. Take the little girl in the square—it's easy for her; she can sing. But you and I, we can't do anything. I wonder if she can —I mean that girl that was here last night?

COLETA. I think so. She began—like this—Ahem!—as if she was trying to sing.

SUSPIROS. No; she was crying. Between saying to herself, "I'm crying," and "I mustn't cry!" she gave such a gulp—

COLETA. She did? But then you saw what happened?

SUSPIROS. I? No.

COLETA. A young fellow came around the corner. He was pretty slick—yes, he was—and well dressed.

SUSPIROS. And he was generous and good! That's the man who gave me a handful of coppers and said, "I am sorry I can't give you any more!"

COLETA. Well, he said to me, "Get out of my way, damn you! You smell of wine." Lord, what does he expect a man to smell of when he's coming out of a tavern? People don't stop to think. And that wasn't the worst of it; what I smelled of was beer.

SUSPIROS. What did that gentleman want with the señorita?

COLETA. She saw him and ran away, like that!

SUSPIROS (*innocently*). I wonder why?

COLETA. Oh! I don't know. Though I was a teacher, I don't have to teach you. You will find out for yourself soon enough—when you get over these sighs.

SUSPIROS. Look! Look! There she comes now.

COLETA. That's her. Move up in the corner and give her room.

(ANGUSTIAS *enters at the rear.*)

ANGUSTIAS. Here it is. Here is where I stood last night. I am afraid— I am such a coward! But this time—I'll shut my eyes—I'll pretend that I am alone. I'll be blind—I must!—My poor mother suffering and dying so! And nothing in the house for to-morrow! How can I buy bread? How can I buy medicines? The doctor wants so many medicines. Prescriptions and pawn-tickets—I've nothing else in my pocket. Ah, at it, Angustias, at it! This is not begging. I can sing: I am not begging. People pay or don't pay, as they like. It's the same as if I were singing in a theater. An opera out-of-doors. Of course! I'll be a street singer. That's no disgrace; I am not afraid! I am not ashamed! What a coward I am! My mother would beg on her knees for me—and I can do as much for her!

(*She goes toward the spot where* COLETA *and* SUSPIROS *are waiting, but hesitates.*)

COLETA (*to* SUSPIROS). Here she comes.

SUSPIROS (*to* COLETA). Give her room.

COLETA (*to himself*). She'll sing to-night. I can see she's made up her mind to it.

SUSPIROS (*to herself*). She's made it up to cry till her heart breaks.

(ANGUSTIAS *takes her place in line with* COLETA *and* SUSPIROS, *standing with her back against the wall. A pause ensues.*)

ANGUSTIAS (*making an effort*). I can't—I can't sing—

COLETA (*to* SUSPIROS). She's beginning.

SUSPIROS. Beginning what?

COLETA. To sing.

SUSPIROS. To cry, I say.

COLETA. Humph! It's a sentimental song, take it from me, child.

ANGUSTIAS (*to herself*). If he comes again as he did last night, I can't do it.

SUSPIROS. Is the señorita going to sing?

ANGUSTIAS. Yes—I think so.

SUSPIROS. Something sad?

ANGUSTIAS. Very sad.

SUSPIROS. I love songs that make me cry.

ANGUSTIAS. So do I! Let us cry!

SUSPIROS. Are you ready to begin?

ANGUSTIAS. Yes. Let's begin.

COLETA. Hadn't you better clear your throat first?

ANGUSTIAS. No.

SUSPIROS. Don't keep us waiting then.

ANGUSTIAS. There's nobody here. Don't you see? There's nobody here.

SUSPIROS. There will be as soon as you begin.

COLETA. Take it from me, don't sing too good music; it's above the people's heads.

ANGUSTIAS (*passing her hand across her forehead*). It must be late—it must be very late—

COLETA (*assuming a grand air, about to pay a compliment*). The nightingales sang all night in my country when I was a boy.

SUSPIROS. When I was a little girl in Játiva the larks sang at daybreak.

COLETA. And daybreak is the end of the night.

SUSPIROS. And the beginning of the morning.

COLETA (*to* ANGUSTIAS; *he says this advancing a step*). So begin.

SUSPIROS. Begin.

ANGUSTIAS. Yes—thanks. Now we'll show them.

SUSPIROS. Stand close by me.

ANGUSTIAS (*indicating* COLETA). Is he your father?

SUSPIROS. Oh! He's Coleta. He has a good heart. And he's not drunk to-night.

ANGUSTIAS. Then I'll begin. (*She attempts to sing.*) My voice shakes.

COLETA. All the better. For the *tremolo,* it's better to have the voice shake.

SUSPIROS. Don't do that. (*Then to* ANGUSTIAS.) When you get through each verse, I'll go around and take up the money, if you want me to. I've a plate here my stepmother gave me.

COLETA. Yes! It's politer to beg with a plate.

ANGUSTIAS. It is? Thank you.

COLETA. And I'll go down the other side so that nobody escapes.

SUSPIROS. You'll see the pennies drop.

COLETA. And if that young fellow comes who was here last night, there'll be *pesetas* and *duros.*

ANGUSTIAS. What? Who did you say?

SUSPIROS. You know. The fellow who came when—when the señorita went away.

ANGUSTIAS. No! Have him hear me? Have him see me? I'd rather die first. No, no! Not to-night! I'll wait till to-morrow—to-morrow will do—
(*Leaving the wall and coming forward.*)

COLETA. Here he is now.

ANGUSTIAS. Yes! It is he! Great Heaven!

COLETA (*to* SUSPIROS). She'll sing now.

(ANGUSTIAS *begins her song. Meanwhile* PEPE *enters. It is easy to see by his dress that he is a gentleman.*)

SUSPIROS (*to* COLETA). He's looking for her.

COLETA. They can sing a duet.

PEPE (*watching from the rear*). Yes, it is she. And it was last night. (*Coming forward.*) Angustias! Angustias!

ANGUSTIAS. What do you want?—Go away!—Let me be—

PEPE. Ah! it was you!—I knew it. I could not be deceived!

ANGUSTIAS. Leave me!—Leave me!—Great God! I am free.—Let me go!

PEPE. No! Wait! You cannot go without hearing me. Are you in such a hurry to go?

ANGUSTIAS. I cannot hurry enough.

PEPE. Have I hurt you so?

ANGUSTIAS. Was it a little?

PEPE. To love you with all my soul—was that to hurt you?

ANGUSTIAS. Love *me?*

PEPE. Whom, then?

ANGUSTIAS. I found that out.

PEPE. You never found it out. Did I leave you, or was it you who sent me off? Tell me that—tell me the truth! Don't I always come back to you? All day long at your door, and all day long it is closed! All night long at your window, and all night long it is dark! I follow your steps when you go out, to see if I can put my feet where you have set yours; that is the only consolation you have left to me. And when I lose sight of you it seems as if my soul would rush out of my body after you; for the soul is lighter than the body, and can travel faster. My Angustias—for you were my Angustias—you were happiness to me!

ANGUSTIAS. You know how to talk. The more fool I, to have believed you at first! But since I believed you then, I cannot believe you now. No! though you were to do what you never do—speak the truth!

PEPE. Have I deceived you?

ANGUSTIAS. Do you ask me that?

PEPE. How?

ANGUSTIAS. In everything! Did you tell me who you were when you came to see me? No, you did not! You came to me as if you had been a man of my own class, a poor man who had to work for his living as I had for mine. And then what a game you played with my heart! Your cap and flannel shirt— Oh! they were honorable; yes, they were!—but they covered up a heart that was evil. You didn't wear a mask, for your face is a mask. It always is. Can you deny it? You can't deny it. Deny that you hid your position, your money, your name! Yes, your name! for it burns in my throat, it has been such a shame to me!

PEPE. I don't deny it. But if I had come to you in any other way—you are so proud, so jealous—you would never have loved me.

ANGUSTIAS. How could you tell that I was so proud, before you know me?

PEPE. Couldn't I see it in your face?

ANGUSTIAS. Proud, no; but honest—yes!

PEPE. I told you the truth at last.

ANGUSTIAS. At last? The truth? When I know it, and you know that I know it, why do you have to lie? You never told me the truth. I found it out! I found it out because God willed it so—He would not stand by and see a poor girl deceived. And He put you in my way and revealed you to me as you were—rich, deceitful, vain! Yes, a gentleman—without a particle of conscience!

PEPE. Angustias! Don't say such things!

ANGUSTIAS. Your memory is weak. One winter night, when it was dark— dark nights were not made for nothing—what have the nights done that they should be so dark?—well, one night I was in the heart of Madrid, delivering some work. When there is work to do, I work. You—when do you work? When you want to make people believe you! Well, I was passing the door of a theater—

PEPE. Angustias!

ANGUSTIAS. Do you remember? No, let me finish. Can't you see it? I can— I can see it as if it were happening now. I had to stop because a carriage drew up by the sidewalk—a carriage with two horses, a coachman and a footman. The footman opened the door, and with the door he took up the whole sidewalk so I couldn't pass; and I stood still. I waited to see the gentleman get out; and he got out. What clothes! How he did shine! A great fur coat, and the white bosom of his shirt was glistening in the fur. I had to laugh, he looked so like my Pepe. "I am a fool," I thought—and then I thought—I tell you I am a fool! "No; Pepe would be handsomer in clothes like those." I thought so, because I loved you—because I adored you—yes, I adored you! My God! Love like that should never die! The sun and the sky may, and life itself go out, but not love—no! For without love there is nothing!

(*She begins to cry.*)

PEPE. Angustias—let me explain. You don't understand. There are things in life—facts sometimes—parents—and sometimes they don't understand, either!

ANGUSTIAS (*interrupting*). There is nothing to explain. Listen! Suddenly you turned; that is, the gentleman with the coat turned, and the white bosom gleaming in the fur. Who knows?—I may have ironed that shirt myself. Well, he turned, and he said to the footman, "Remember, at twelve; be there!" Great God, what a jump my heart gave! It was your voice. Your voice! And what you said to the lackey you had said to me, oh, so many times! "Remember—at twelve; be there!" I leaped forward; I couldn't hold back. I gave a cry. I caught you by the arm—no, not by the arm! What I caught was the coat, not you. When you wore a blouse I could touch you—I have, so many times! But in that greatcoat, my hand was lost in the fur and my fingers couldn't reach you.

PEPE. No more, Angustias! No more!

ANGUSTIAS. Why not? Wasn't it so? I cried out: "Pepe, Pepe! Is it you?" And you, with another cry, answered "Angustias!" And the people stood still in the streets and laughed. And the lights of the theater beat on us with a fierce burning glare. And I blushed red, with shame—and I ran! I got home, I don't know how—I stumbled up the stairs, I threw myself into my mother's arms, and, choking with tears, I cried out: "Pepe is not Pepe! It is all over! He is rich! He has a carriage!" "But you—you have your honor," my mother said; and, as I have no furs, her poor old fingers sank deep into my arm. We are poor—when we embrace our embraces are real, body to body and soul to soul. There come between us no sables and no ermines.

PEPE. But the next day I came—

ANGUSTIAS. The next day my mother saw you. "We live up too many flights for you to climb to see my daughter," she said, "and my daughter would have to go down too many if she were to go to see you. Please don't take the trouble."

PEPE. But I—

ANGUSTIAS. You said nothing. As you were silent then, be silent now. And remember to respect a woman.

PEPE. Angustias—

ANGUSTIAS. Not another word.

PEPE. Give me hope!

ANGUSTIAS. Hope? Have I hope?

PEPE. If, without thinking of hindrances, of anybody, of anything, I said to you: "Be my wife!"

(*Seizing her hand.*)

ANGUSTIAS (*moved in spite of herself*). Is the pretense still on? Well!—when you slip that ring on my finger, we shall see whether the pretense is on.

PEPE (*endeavoring to remove the ring*). At once!

ANGUSTIAS. No, not that bright one. No; that costs too much! It sparkles too brightly for a girl like me. I can't afford to wear it. It would be a disgrace. It is for gentlemen like you. I mean the other, the guard, the little gold band that looks like a wedding-ring. Don't say that I am proud. But I can tell you this: My mother has a ring like that, and though we are dying of hunger, she will carry it with her to her grave. Well, I shall be carried to mine with one like that—or without one! I have done with you.

PEPE. Angustias!

ANGUSTIAS. You may go! If you don't, I'll go myself—I'll run away—jump from the viaduct—kill myself!—

PEPE. I'll go, Angustias. I'll go— But, ah—who knows?— Good-by— Good-by.

(*He goes out.*)

ANGUSTIAS. I know! I know! He won't come back. Good-by! (*Various persons enter. As* ANGUSTIAS *begins to sing, they form a group about her.*) And now to sing—to earn money for my mother—to buy her medicines. To sing—though it tears out my throat! (*She goes up to the wall by* SUSPIROS *and* COLETA.) Here I am. I am ready now. I am going to sing.

(*She begins to try her voice.*)

COLETA (*to* SUSPIROS). Now she'll begin. Ddin't I tell you that man would make her sing?

SUSPIROS. Keep quiet—I want to listen.

(ANGUSTIAS *begins to sing.*)

COLETA. Here come more people.

SUSPIROS. Go on! Go on! The flies flock to the honey.

(*The crowd grows greater as* ANGUSTIAS *sings. The scene should be one of animation. Some applaud at appropriate moments; others shout out disconnected phrases such as* "Good!" "Brava!" "Olé for the street-singer!" "Encore!" "Encore!" "Another!" "Sing something lively!" "Something sad!" "Ole!" PEPE *returns. Little by little he draws nearer and mingles with the crowd, however without attracting attention.*)

PEPE (*to himself*). What is this?— Great God!—My Angustias!— Ah!— No, no! Never!— Let them say what they will, I cannot—

SUSPIROS (*producing a tray*). Now leave it to me. I'll take up the money.

ANGUSTIAS (*supporting herself against the wall*). I can't sing any more. Do what you like.

SUSPIROS. Come on!— Oh, come on! Throw in the pennies—don't be stingy. It's worth it. I have seven little brothers—

(*She goes through the crowd passing the tray.*)

PEPE (*in a low voice*). Here—take this—

(*He throws in several duros, and the gold ring of which* ANGUSTIAS *spoke, along with them.*)

SUSPIROS. Ave María! What a lot of money! Goodness!—*Duros!* Look! Look! (*Running up to* ANGUSTIAS.) And a gold ring. He threw it in—the man who was here last night!

ANGUSTIAS. What? What's that you say? Ah! (*Seizing the ring.*) Yes, it is his! But where is he? (*Breaking through the crowd to find him.*)

PEPE (*rushing to meet her*). Here I am! Now come with me to your mother.

ANGUSTIAS. Swear to me by yours first, that you don't deceive me.

PEPE. I do; I swear it. Will you come? Do you want to?

ANGUSTIAS. What shall I do?

PEPE. Come.

SUSPIROS. Señorita, you forget the money—

PEPE. It's for you.

SUSPIROS. Hurrah! Now I can run away to Játiva.

COLETA. Promise me to let me buy your ticket.

ÁNGUSTIAS. My Pepe!

PEPE. This is the end of the song, for I am carrying off the Street Singer.

CURTAIN

POVERTY

A Play

By Hans Alin

Translated from the Swedish by Arvid Paulson

CHARACTERS

THE FATHER
THE MOTHER
THE DAUGHTER
THE SON

POVERTY

THE SCENE: *A small-sized room—gloomy and dark and poorly lighted. Its walls are bare and show signs of dampness. The furniture indicates dire poverty. At the back there is a door, leading to the hall; on the right a door opening into another room. On the left a single window. In the center of the room a round table, surrounded by four chairs. A lamp is burning with a dim light. The room gives the impression of gloom and dreariness.*

THE FATHER, *bent, wrinkled, dressed in a shabby, brown bathrobe, sits on the right of the table, his face half turned away; his head is resting in his hand.*

THE MOTHER, *worn and furrowed; poorly dressed, with a thin, motheaten, threadbare shawl over her shoulders; she sits facing the audience, mending old clothes.*

THE DAUGHTER, *emaciated, lean, sits to the left of the table; her chair is pushed away from it. She is staring into vacancy.*
There is a long, oppressive silence.

THE MOTHER (*sighs*).
THE FATHER (*moves uncomfortably*).
THE MOTHER (*looks up and sighs*). Are you cold?
THE FATHER (*turns away*).
(*Silence.*)
THE MOTHER. What are you thinking about, pa?
THE FATHER (*gives her a short answer*). Nothing.
(*Silence.*)
THE MOTHER (*resumes her mending. Another pause. Again she looks up. Turns to the daughter*). Why are you sitting like that—idle, doing nothing? Can't you find something to do?
THE DAUGHTER (*doesn't reply*).
THE MOTHER. Didn't you hear what I said?
THE DAUGHTER (*with a sneer*). No-o!
THE MOTHER. Why can't you find something to do? Do you hear?
THE DAUGHTER. I ain't got nothing to do.
THE MOTHER. You can always find something. A big girl like you sitting there, doing nothing!
THE DAUGHTER. I tell you I ain't got nothing to do.

THE MOTHER. Mend your rags.

THE DAUGHTER. I ain't got none. Not even rags.

THE MOTHER. Take a book and learn something then.

THE DAUGHTER. Book! Where would I get that from? You know just as well as I that we ain't got any. We can't even afford to buy a newspaper—the only one we see is the one the grocer wraps around the herring—when he wants to be generous.

THE MOTHER. You can borrow one of Sven's.

THE DAUGHTER. The books he's got are too highbrow for me—you never gave me enough of an education for them.

THE MOTHER (*in a temper*). What! Didn't we send you to school till you was fourteen? And ain't we been paying for your piano lessons for nearly five years?

THE DAUGHTER. Well—what good is that, now that you have taken away the piano from me?

THE MOTHER. Taken away! You know very well why we had to sell it—so that Sven would have money to continue his studies.

THE DAUGHTER. And I quit mine, ha!

THE MOTHER. You know well enough he's our only hope—that we want him to finish his studies so that he can help us.

THE DAUGHTER. A lot of help he'll be. All you do is think of yourself, anyhow. Do you think it's right to take the bread from the children and throw it to the dogs?

THE MOTHER. Do you mean to call us dogs?

THE DAUGHTER. No—I didn't mean that exactly—the words just happened to come that way. . . .

THE MOTHER. Now you are stupid, Gerda.

THE DAUGHTER. That shows I am really related to you.

THE MOTHER. You never forget to talk back.

(*There is a silence.*)

THE MOTHER (*heaving a sigh*). Don't be sitting there thinking forever, pa. Smoke your pipe instead.

THE FATHER. No tobacco.

THE MOTHER. Borrow ten cents from Sven and let Gerda go down and buy you some.

THE DAUGHTER. I ain't going into any cigar store buying tobacco for anyone!

THE FATHER. Nobody is going to ask you to. I don't intend to borrow money to buy tobacco with from any son of mine. I can go without it.

THE DAUGHTER. That's just what I say. Poor people can't afford to have vices.

THE MOTHER. Ain't you got enough to buy your father some tobacco, Gerda?

THE DAUGHTER. No, I ain't. And if I did, I wouldn't spend it on tobacco. I'd buy a bit of bread first so we wouldn't have to be starving.

THE MOTHER. Buy your own bread then, why don't you?

THE DAUGHTER. Because I ain't got the money. I can't give piano lessons on the sink or the dust bin.

(*There is a pause.*)

THE MOTHER (*wrapping the shawl tighter around her*). It's cold in here—I feel a draught. (*To* THE DAUGHTER.) Did you fix the fire in Sven's room—so that he at least will be warm? Did you?

THE DAUGHTER. Yes—you needn't worry about him; it's roasting hot in there. But we—we have to sit and freeze to death, of course. Can't he leave the door open?

THE MOTHER. He needs to have it warm—he is working. And his hands are always so cold.

THE DAUGHTER. The poor fellow! Ain't he got cold feet, too?

(*Silence.*)

THE MOTHER. What time is it, anyhow? (*Looking up.*) It looks sort of bare on the wall since the clock went. It was like company, anyhow. (*Rising.*) I suppose it's about time to get something ready for supper. Are you hungry, pa?

THE FATHER (*does not answer*).

THE MOTHER (*with a sigh*). Poor pa!— Would you like to help me, Gerda?

THE DAUGHTER. No—I wouldn't.

THE MOTHER. That's nice of you. I should think you'd be a little more considerate of your mother. It's always I who have to do it all—always have had—all my life. I am beginning to feel like an old dishrag—too worn-out to be used any longer—ready to be thrown on the ash heap any moment.

THE DAUGHTER. Besides, I suppose all you've got to eat is the putrid, stinking fish that we had for dinner. If you intend to heat that up for supper—then I don't want any, thank you. I have had enough of the heartburn it gave me all day long.

THE MOTHER. I suppose you want eggs for supper—they ought to be expensive enough for you!

THE DAUGHTER (*maliciously*). Eggs! Ha—just listen to her! Oh, no—eggs are for Sven! If ever you gave me one—then I am sure it would be a poisonous snake egg. I have put some oatmeal on the stove, too.

THE MOTHER. And blue, skimmed milk—no, thanks.

THE MOTHER (*flaring up*). You'll go without food, then. "He who does not work shall not eat!"

THE DAUGHTER (*with icy scorn*). How wise you are!

THE MOTHER. Be careful, Gerda—you'll never get along in the world if you keep on like this.

THE DAUGHTER. Are you telling my fortune for me?

THE MOTHER. No—not that—but he who don't respect his parents. . . .

THE DAUGHTER (*impudently*). Respect?! Respect such as you? . . .

THE FATHER (*bangs the table with his fist*). That's enough! Now shut up! Not another word, or out you go!

THE DAUGHTER (*rising from her seat, the chair topples over. She makes no effort to lift it up. In a cold, hard voice*). You needn't show me the door—I'll go myself.

THE FATHER (*brutally*). Well—get out, then!

THE DAUGHTER. Don't worry. I'll go. I ain't going to trouble you no longer. But before I go, I got something to tell you that you ain't going to forget in a hurry. . . . Don't think I made up my mind just this minute—oh, no, I've been meaning to do it for a long time—but it's taken me a long time to get the guts to do it . . . to quit this miserable life. Have I ever done anything but starve and freeze, maybe? How could I ever learn anything but meanness and hate, the way I've been shut in here with you! With every breath I've drawn, I've sucked in nothing but ill-will and hatred and poison—from these mouldy, dirty walls. They've poisoned me! They've killed my youth—they've made me waste away like a consumptive without air . . .

THE MOTHER. You talk as if you were crazy.

THE DAUGHTER. No, I ain't yet, but I would go crazy if I stayed here much longer. But I know what I'm doing—don't you fool yourself. I ain't worrying a minute—not even for what's the worst hell to me—you. The street will grab me with open arms, and the gutter will bawl out a noisy welcome.

THE MOTHER. So—you want to turn into a streetwalker—that's what you want. Well, I always thought you leaned that way. I just wonder what'd have become of you, if I hadn't kept an eye on you all this time.

THE DAUGHTER (*cynically*). Oh, yes—thank you for all the good advice you've given me—and thanks for the fear you've put into me for the men, the wild beasts—you've frightened me of them so that I ain't dared to look at them for fear of getting a baby! Ha—Ha—Ha!

(*She laughs hysterically.*)

THE MOTHER. You ought to be ashamed of yourself! Out with you! I don't want to hear another word from you!

THE FATHER (*rises menacingly*). Ain't you gone yet?

THE DAUGHTER (*going toward the door*). I'll be gone—don't you worry. I won't bother you any more, I swear. (*In the doorway, she turns to face them.*) Trash!

(*She leaves, closing the door with a bang. There is a moment of silence.*)

THE MOTHER (*nervously pulling at her shawl*). Do you think she means to go?

THE FATHER. Let her go—we can't keep her here any longer.

THE MOTHER (*with a sigh*). May God help her.

(*She goes out.*)

THE FATHER (*rising, begins to pace up and down*).

(*A pause.*)

(THE MOTHER *enters. She puts the supper on the table; then picks up the chair and places it by the table. The sound of a door being shut is heard from the hall.*)

THE MOTHER (*listens*). Some one slammed the door to the hall—could it be Gerda, do you think? (*Goes to the window.*) Yes, God have mercy—it was Gerda! (*She turns around.*) Run after her, Emil. Hurry up, Emil! We can't let her go out in the streets at this time of the night. . . .

THE FATHER. No, I ain't going to run after her. I wouldn't move as much as a finger—if that would make her come back. . . . The way she sat there to-night, answering you back. It made me boil inside. I felt every time like going over and giving her a slap in the face. (*Pacing the floor.*) Don't you worry—she'll be back—when it gets to be late enough.

THE MOTHER. No, not Gerda. She will never come back. I know her. She would rather go to the bottom. (*She sighs.*) Now we have only Sven left. (*She goes out.*)

THE FATHER (*still paces the floor*).

THE MOTHER (*enters with the oatmeal*). Sit down, pa—I'll go and call Sven. But don't tell him—it'll only upset him. And maybe she'll come back when she's cooled off. (*She goes to knock at his door. Opens it timidly.*) Do I disturb you? Have you time to come and eat? The supper is on the table.

(*Goes to the table—fixes* SVEN'S *chair for him. Sits down.*)

THE SON (*enters. Thin, pale, ·wears glasses; looks tired out from over-study*). How dark you have it in here—is there no oil in the lamp again?

THE MOTHER. Yes, but we screwed down the wick in order to save a little.

THE SON (*sits down. Takes some of the oatmeal. Then he looks around.*) Where is Gerda?

THE MOTHER AND THE FATHER (*remain silent*).

THE SON. What is the matter? Where is Gerda?

THE MOTHER (*avoiding the question*). She's gone out.

THE SON. Out? At this time of the day! Alone? What is the idea?

(*No one answers him.*)

THE SON. Where is she?

THE MOTHER (*with a trembling voice*). Gerda has—has gone away. She has left us.

THE SON. Left?

THE MOTHER. Yes—she was nasty and mean and treated pa and me like two thieves because we had sold the pian . . .

(*She leaves the sentence unfinished.*)

THE SON (*rising, in a rage*). What do you mean? Have you sold Gerda's piano? You didn't tell me anything about it. And you didn't have to? You had already finished paying my school debt. (*Sits again.*) Where did she go?

THE MOTHER. I don't know. She was nasty to me, and then pa told her if she didn't behave and keep quiet, he would show her the door—and—then she —went. . . .

THE SON. Then she'll never return of her own free will. . . . And all this because of me. . . .

(*He rises.*)

THE MOTHER. Aren't you going to eat your supper?

THE SON. No—I can't eat now. (*He goes to his room.*)

(*There is a tense silence.* THE FATHER *and* THE MOTHER *resume eating. Some one is heard out in the hall—and the sound of a closed door.*)

THE MOTHER (*listening*). Some one in the hall! She has come back—thank God! Sven took it so hard. (*While still listening, she rises.*) Or maybe it was . . . (*She goes to* SVEN'S *door, listens, knocks. Knocks again, cautiously opens the door, little by little, until it is wide open.*) It was Sven—he is gone to look for her—he has left the lamp burning. (*She goes into* SVEN'S *room. Suddenly there is a scream from within—she comes out, her face white and anguished. In her hand she clutches a piece of paper.*) The Lord save us! Emil—read—read!

THE FATHER (*takes the note with trembling hand and reads*). "I have gone to look for Gerda. If I find her, I shall return—otherwise I am gone for good. Good-by! Sven!"

THE MOTHER (*sinking together in a chair, covering her face with her hands, sobs violently*). Sven. . . . Sven. . . .

(THE FATHER *sits staring into space,* THE SON'S *note clutched in his hand.*)

CURTAIN

THE DISENCHANTED

A Turkish Play

By Izzet-Melyh

Translated from the French by Helen Tilden

CHARACTERS

JULIETTE SÉNIRE, *30 years old, beautiful and a coquette.*
LÉÏLA HANOUM, *23 years old, pretty and refined, from a great Turkish family.*
    Wife to
NAZMI BEY, *28 years old, son of a pasha, educated in France. Head of the*
    Bureau of Foreign Affairs.
CONSTANTIN SÉNIRE, *Husband of Juliette, 45 years old, a banker.*
A SERVANT.
    The action takes place at the present time, in Constantinople.

THE DISENCHANTED

A drawing room, richly furnished, in the home of NAZMI BEY. *It is a mixture of Oriental and European styles. At the back a door opening into the apartments of* LËÏLA HANOUM *of which the portière, embroidered in silk and gold, is completely lowered. A door at left communicates with a second salon. The door at right gives onto a stairway. One sees at the left a table covered with cups and plates full of cakes. Coffee has been served. At the rise of the curtain* NAZMI BEY *is standing talking with animation.* MONSIEUR *and* MADAME SÉNIRE *follow him attentively.*

NAZMI BEY. But my dear lady, you are too well acquainted with my ideas to accuse me of fanaticism. If I speak as I am about to do, it is only to establish the reality of things and to show you several little distinctions. In the first place you must not suppose that all Turkish women are unhappy. The majority of our wives live tranquilly in the spirit of their beliefs and traditions, and do not think of any existence beyond that which destiny has meted out to them. They are moreover convinced, rightly or wrongly, that their religion prescribes this manner of living.

JULIETTE. And those who are beginning to know the world? Those who read and think, those in a word, whom a well known author has called "the disenchanted," do they not suffer?

NAZMI. I have never denied that. I only affirm that the number of these disenchanted ones is restricted, and I assure you that there are among our most cultivated and well informed women those who are not at all rebellious. Take my wife Léïla, for example: have you ever heard her complain?

CONSTANTIN. If Léïla Hanoum cherishes an exceptional love for her husband which makes her forget all . . . that proves nothing my dear Bey.

JULIETTE. I am not so polite and I reply to Nazmi Bey, "What do you know about it?" And then, too, why do you wish to make us believe in any case that you are a partisan of imprisonment and of slavery? Is it a new fad that you are adopting for a caprice?

CONSTANTIN. Nazmi Bey considers perhaps that the number of those who rebel against the old régime having grown so large, it is no longer fashionable to speak against the harem.

NAZMI (*smiling*). How do you draw that conclusion?

JULIETTE. From your own words, from your manner of proving that the harem is a cause of suffering only to the minority.

CONSTANTIN. Yes, to what must we attribute this fixed idea of yours?

335

Nazmi (*in the same tone*). Simply to the desire to console myself in the thought that those who are cognizant of the evil are less numerous.

Juliette. Ah!—and then!

Nazmi. After all, what good is it to plague oneself? This matter of the harem depends upon other questions, political and social, that must be left to a slow evolution to decide. Nevertheless there are people who reverse the proposition and who declare that our social and political future is, on the contrary, dependent to a great extent upon the future condition of our women. This idea has the flavor of a paradox, but it is a very fertile one, and to be just, one of my friends in Paris has developed it in a very clever manner in one of his letters. First, he said in substance, a woman who lives far from society, who does not see at close range the intrigues and the contentions of modern life is incapable of giving to her child a solid and uniform education, compatible with the demands of its life. Since there is the harem, there is no social life. How can politics and above all diplomacy survive? What is a minister or an ambassador without the support of his wife?

Juliette. Your friend is indeed paradoxical.

Nazmi (*continuing*). There is more. How do you pretend, he adds, to fraternize with the several elements in your country since there exists practically no relationship between their families and yours? All conquerors have assimilated the conquered peoples by imposing on them their languages and their customs, and above all by giving to them their sons and daughters in marriage. . . . Doesn't the harem deprive you also of the most charming thing in the world, the society and the friendship of women? Without them your turquoise sky, your blood-red sunsets, your fairylike moonlight and your divine Bosphorus—do they not appear insignificant and somber? Without them can you have delicacy, refinement and poetry? Can sculpture and music, the theater and literature, live without them? To conclude, do you not run the risk of remaining always an incomplete people?

Constantin. Those are words that you young Turks who have been affected by progress and rebirth should meditate seriously. There is, besides, a danger which to my mind is very great. The number of Mohammedans who receive a modern education and who travel in Europe increases constantly. When they marry these gentlemen naturally wish to go about with their wives, to receive in their homes, to lead a life compatible with their ideas as much as with their actual needs. But the harem intervenes. What happens then? Either your men marry Christians more and more (which would bring about a dearth of husbands for your young girls), or else they leave their wives behind the grilles of their harems and continue to go about in society from habit, for pleasure, or from a sense of duty.

Nazmi. I admit that you are right, as I have observed these things myself from experience. But what is one to do about it?

Juliette. Simply what you should have answered your clever Parisian friend.

Nazmi. I have written him a dozen pages.

JULIETTE. And what conclusion did you draw?

NAZMI. I no longer remember. Moreover all my dissertations could have had no practical result.

JULIETTE. But it is unkind of you not to tell us.

NAZMI. Use your imagination. I have held forth too long already, and to what purpose? Let us allow Time to work out her own fate. Then you see this question makes me too sad.

CONSTANTIN. Let us be discreet (*rising*), and let us know enough to leave on time. I have several calls to make. (*Offering his hand to* NAZMI.) Au revoir, dear friend, and thanks for the delightful afternoon that we have spent with you. You will not forget, I hope, to speak to his Excellency on the subject of my concession.

NAZMI. Rest assured that I will speak to my father this evening.

CONSTANTIN. That is very decent of you. (*To his wife.*) Are you coming, Juliette?

JULIETTE. No, I do not wish to leave without seeing Madame Nazmi Bey.

CONSTANTIN. Hanoum Effendi has not gone out? It seems to me that you were saying just now . . .

NAZMI. She isn't here now, but she will not be long in coming home. Léila went to the home of the Rechad Beys, quite near here. She left several minutes before you arrived.

JULIETTE (*looking about her*). I am sure that Léila Hanoum has arranged in person the thousand and one little things that make the presence of a woman felt in this room. The flowers in these vases, the arrangement of these trinkets, little nothings—but which have their own particular charm.

CONSTANTIN. To my mind the thing that above all has a special charm and a touching delicacy is the purity, the sweetness of this woman who, after having prepared everything for her husband's guests, effaces herself with a good grace and in an unselfish spirit.

NAZMI. I thank you for Léila. She will be very pleased when I repeat your compliments to her.

CONSTANTIN (*as though speaking to himself*). The heart of a woman is ever a mystery. But the heart of a Turkish woman must contain both mystery and devotion.

JULIETTE. You hear, Nazmi Bey? My husband is revealing himself as a poet and psychologist.

CONSTANTIN. Naturally you don't think so. (*Sententiously and teasingly.*) One never appreciates the being one possesses! Well, well—thanks once more my dear Nazmi Bey. May I see you soon again! (*He takes* NAZMI's *hand again and before going out says to* JULIETTE.) I will send the carriage for you.

(NAZMI BEY *accompanies Sénire.* JULIETTE, *left alone, walks about the salon. As she stops to look at a picture,* NAZMI *reënters, goes stealthily up to her, kisses her neck. She gives a little cry.*)

JULIETTE. Please don't. Do you know that I am very, very angry? Why didn't you come yesterday?

NAZMI. I had some urgent business. . . .

JULIETTE. You could have put it off till later. To begin with I don't believe in your urgent business.

NAZMI (*after a moment's hesitation*). Very well, I don't want to lie. Here is the truth. After dinner I was about to dress when Léïla said to me: "Are you going out again this evening?" And there was in her voice such a touching supplication, in her eyes such sadness, that I had to stay, all the more so because of late her manner has been very strange.

JULIETTE. What an idea! Wouldn't she have said something to you?

NAZMI. Oh, no, no! You don't know Léïla! She is very good, very gentle, at times even a little naïve. But she has pride, a great deal of pride. She is capable of suffering for months without letting anything be seen. It would be imprudent, all the same, to try her too far.

JULIETTE. Ah! You are afraid of disturbing the peace of your married life. You *are* admirable, I assure you! But how about me?

NAZMI. Pardon me, there is a difference. Let us speak frankly of these things. Your husband dosen't count with you, while I have an affection for Léïla. I swear that I would never consent to make her unhappy.

JULIETTE. You love your wife. Perfect. Very well! That is your right after all. So much the better for her, and, who knows, for yourself also perhaps . . . only it was not necessary to lie to me until to-day. It wasn't necessary to tell me that you loved me (*a little ironical smile*) more than all the world.

NAZMI. It is strange how nervous you are!

JULIETTE. I don't think that I am wrong.

NAZMI. Yes, you are wrong, and you are committing a grave injustice. Juliette, be reasonable (*approaching her*), you know very well that I love you.

JULIETTE. That doesn't prevent you from adoring Léïla and doing everything that she asks of you.

NAZMI. I swear to you that you need not envy her. Ah no! Poor little thing! I said just now that Léïla wasn't one of the disenchanted. I spoke the truth from the point of view of our customs to which she submits without too many regrets. But is she satisfied with her husband? I doubt it very much. That is why I cannot prevent myself from pitying her. If you call that love! While you, Juliette, you are the woman who rules my dreams, my desires and my passions. Léïla brought sweetness, devotion and affection. That was beautiful but not sufficient. I needed love with its emotion, its ecstasy, love diabolical and divine, torturing, deceiving and exquisite, love which makes you clever and foolish, cruel and generous, a madman, but which also makes you understand the real meaning of life.

JULIETTE. What eloquence! Where have you read all these beautiful things?

NAZMI. Everywhere and nowhere. I have learned them from you. One cannot express these things well until the day when one has analyzed and penetrated them by experience. Then each one is convinced that he is the discoverer of these eternal truths. And each one is right since all appears new when one loves. So you see, since we love each other (*he speaks close to her face and caresses her hands*), since I love you, I think myself living in an eternal springtime, a springtime filled with perfumes, with drunkenness and with pleasure. I am always thirsty for your kisses and your caresses. And, if I was not at your house yesterday, if I let pass any opportunity of meeting you outside, it is a little on account of my very love, on account of the cruel jealousy which tortures me. I experience an almost physical pain when I see these eyes and these lips smile with complacence at the lusts which surround you.

JULIETTE. Then egoism and jealousy are your outstanding qualities. After all, I comprehend, since, like all Turks, you are in the habit of locking up your women and of wishing to possess even their most intimate thoughts. . . . (NAZMI *tries to embrace her but she turns her head away from him.*) Let me be! Let me be!

NAZMI (*moving away sullenly*). You have had enough of my love! Say so frankly, that would be better!

JULIETTE (*coquettishly*). Sulky boy! How bad you are! Stop this scowling air which does not become you at all. (*Seriously.*) Nazmi, do not be ungrateful. (*Caressingly.*) Have you forgotten already the delicious hours we have passed together?

NAZMI (*taking her hands*). It is just because I remember these hours so well that I want to find again the maddening charm of your lips. Oh, if you knew, Juliette, how I never cease to want you!

JULIETTE. And I? What of me? You cannot yet convince yourself that if I gave myself away just now, if I appeared nervous it is because . . .

NAZMI. Tell me, tell me Juliette, I have always the need, I am always happy to hear this divine and banal word.

JULIETTE (*passionately*). I love you! But you, you think only of your desire.

NAZMI. Yes, it is true. I am a primitive man, governed by instinct, and it is your fault, for your eyes and your lips have bewitched me.

(JULIETTE *and* NAZMI *embrace passionately. Just at this moment the portière at the back is raised.* LÉÏLA *is seen veiled in the Turkish manner. She opens her mouth to cry out, but controls herself and disappears.* JULIETTE *and* NAZMI *have seen nothing. They separate.* JULIETTE *arranges her hat and her hair. A moment of silence.* LÉÏLA *enters by the door at left. She is still veiled. She starts to lift her veil and her cape as she talks, during the following scene.*)

LÉÏLA (*pretending to have seen nothing. Nevertheless her voice trembles and her smile is sad*). Good day, Madame. You are kind to have waited.

JULIETTE. I wanted so much to see you again, and you come so rarely to my house.

LÉÏLA. Oh, you must excuse me. I go out so little. My husband goes often to see you, does he not? That makes up for it I suppose.

A SERVANT (*enters bringing a card on a tray*). This gentleman says that you expect him, monsieur.

NAZMI (*looking at the card*). That is so. Show him into my study.

SERVANT. Yes, sir.

(*He exits.*)

NAZMI. It is a business man with whom I have an appointment.

JULIETTE. You needn't stand on ceremony with me, you know.

NAZMI. Oh, he can wait. (*To his wife.*) How is Madame Réchad Bey and her son's marriage?

LÉÏLA. It appears that young Férid does not wish to marry. He declares that he is not sure of remaining faithful to her for whom he is destined and whom he does not know at all. His mother is in despair, but I approve and admire him. Here at least is a man who is not like all the others, those who say to themselves, "I must have a wife who will look after me when I am old, children that I will have the satisfaction of seeing grow up. As to love, one can very well find that outside one's own home."

JULIETTE. I approve of him also. It is really mad to join one's life to that of another being who is absolutely unknown to you.

NAZMI (*to* JULIETTE). Oh, with you as with us, marriage is a lottery. For my part I have nothing to complain of since I have won first prize!

LÉÏLA. You see, dear Madame, my husband is always very chivalrous and very polite.

JULIETTE (*to* NAZMI, *slightly ironical*). My compliments!

NAZMI. Compliments! I make my escape! I must get rid of the gentleman who is waiting. (*To* JULIETTE.) Your pardon, madame.

JULIETTE. Of course, you leave me in such good company that . . .

NAZMI. That you do not think you have anything to complain of, on the contrary.

JULIETTE (*laughing*). I didn't say that!

NAZMI (*kissing her hand*). But you thought it. (*He exits at left.*)

(LÉÏLA *remains silent. Her looks have altered. One can see that she is the prey of a painful inner struggle. An embarrassing silence.* JULIETTE *tries to find a subject of conversation.*)

JULIETTE. The soirées in Péra have become so monotonous, so boring! Gambling has killed gayety. Then the intrigues and the gossip . . . it's frightful . . . there are so many evil tongues. The best method is to let people talk. But one cannot always remain indifferent to gossip! . . . Oh, how happy you ought to be to live far removed from that sort of life.

(LÉÏLA *has not even listened to her words. She remains pensive, her eyes fixed on space. Finally deciding to unburden herself of her bitterness and her grief.*)

LÉÏLA (*fiercely*). We are alone now. Let us speak seriously.

JULIETTE. What is the matter? How pale you are! One would think that . . .

LÉÏLA (*interrupting her*). Oh, I beg of you. Let us not waste words. *I know!!* (*A pause.*) For months everything aroused my suspicions. Nazmi was absent-minded, preoccupied. He hadn't the same pleasure, the same eagerness in being with me and my life has been shattered by it. It was torture every moment. I kept quiet, I hoped I was mistaken. But I can do so no longer. I am suffocating and I rebel. I rebel against this fate that I do not deserve in any way. I revolt against the woman who has brought misery to a household which was united, peaceful, happy . . . and I say to her, to this woman, *I love Nazmi*. He is mine. I demand that you renounce him.

JULIETTE (*moved and perplexed—trying, however, to smile ironically*). My friend, you are in a state of strange excitement. . . . I prefer to leave you for the present. . . . I am sure that you will repent later when you understand your mistake!

(*She starts to exit.*)

LÉÏLA (*overcoming herself—subdued*). I was wrong to speak to you in that way. I was wrong. But I am so broken, so unhappy. You cannot imagine what the husband represents to Mohammedan women. We live closed in, hidden behind the iron grills of our windows, not being able to see any man unless he is our nearest relative. We know only what we see in books—we have no balls, no flirtations, nothing. . . . Our lives as young girls slip by thus, filled with dreams and waiting. One fine day we are told in a mysterious tone—"Here is your husband," and we are taken into the presence of a Bey or a Pasha of whose ideas and character we are ignorant, just as on his side he is ignorant even of what we look like. This man—either we love him little by little, and then he is in our eyes desire, passion—a god! Or else he is odious, cruel, insupportable and then—through honesty or through weakness, through pride or for our children we live on in this hell which is called the home, with death in our souls, but stoical and pure. And I, I have loved Nazmi with the tenderness and the exaltation of a simple and unblemished soul. The pain which is tearing my heart out is unendurable. I make superhuman efforts not to burst into sobs, not to cry out. (*In a voice full of revolt and pleading.*) Do you, at least, understand me?

JULIETTE. But I swear that there exists between Nazmi Bey and myself only the most casual relationship, friendly, if you will, nothing more.

LÉÏLA. No, madame, be frank. Forget that we are rivals. Look at me! I have no longer hatred or anger in my eyes. I appeal to your heart, and I do not wish to be anything now but your friend.

JULIETTE (*taking her hand*). I also, I am your friend.

LÉÏLA. Then, madame, confess. That is the best and the only way to straighten things out a little.

JULIETTE. I repeat—I have nothing to confess!

LÉÏLA (*overcome by anger, withdraws her hand and removes herself*). Very well, then—I saw you in his arms! (*A pause.*) In my own house! Now, no

more equivocation! (*A pause.*) And last of all, you do not love Nazmi!
(JULIETTE *slowly shrugs her shoulders, turns her head away and does not
answer.* LÉÏLA *goes up to her and continues with a singular insistence.*)
What does this silence mean? My God, if it should be more serious than I
thought! No, it is not, it cannot be more than a caprice!

JULIETTE. That is the opinion that you have of us, that we are only capable
of giving ourselves for a whim, from coquetry, from vice . . . even for self-
interest, whereas you are the only faithful wives, the only true lovers.

LÉÏLA. I do not say that. But one hasn't the right, I believe, to steal
another's husband, above all when that other is, like me, without defense and
without protection against society.

JULIETTE. If you think that we are better equipped than you, you are very
much mistaken. In this respect we are all alike. We differ only in appearance, and that on account of our ancestors, of our environment, our customs
and reciprocal traditions. Otherwise we are all women, that is to say, the
weaker sex. We suffer the same ills and in the same manner. We also are
deceived and abandoned, we also have to fight against rivals and intruders,
and, if one day, bruised and desperate, we wish to wrest from life our portion
of happiness, if we take a lover, that often costs us too dear. For we also
know the meaning of sincerity, duty, and remorse.

LÉÏLA. Oh, but all that is so weak, so lacking in character!

JULIETTE. One can see that you look at life through your veil. How far
you are from reality! Poor women, or rather poor children, I pity you!

LÉÏLA (*indignantly*). We do not need your pity. We are very happy as
we are!

JULIETTE. Then do not be so proud of your good morals, your virtue. It
is compulsory! There is no merit in it. If you are beyond reproach it is
because you are not able to be otherwise. You are faithful and devoted wives
because you remain secluded, subject to the will of your masters. You would
be like us if you were left free. . . .

LÉÏLA. Never, oh never!

JULIETTE. Do not say that. It is your pride speaking.

LÉÏLA (*in the same tone*). No, no, we will never fall so low. And if liberty
for women has as its price such vileness, such baseness, we do not want it,
we do not want it! Your liberty, your civilization, your luxury are at bottom
only intrigues, hypocrisy and decadence.

JULIETTE. As your harem and your purity are but slavery and blindness.

LÉÏLA. *That* is cleaner!

JULIETTE. It is more foolish. While you remain in your harems, that is to
say, in your sublime ignorance, your men come to us looking for the social
relaxation that your customs do not offer them. They pay court to us,
and wish to find at our sides the joys which you are incapable of giving
them.

LÉÏLA. If our men are vile enough to despise our qualities and to deceive
us, is it our fault?

JULIETTE. Certainly not . . . but you haven't the . . . you haven't the . . . I do not know what, that holds them, that . . .

LÉÏLA. Hold your own husbands then, since you pretend to have the power to do so! In spite of what you say our strength is much greater than yours. The charm of our purity is our strength, and this charm is sufficient for us. We have a horror of lying, and we have no desire to be coquettes.

JULIETTE (*losing her composure more and more*). You are only little dolls, little commonplace creatures. That is why your men prefer us. That is why you cannot contend against us.

LÉÏLA (*very pale, laughing nervously and painfully*). Ah, you think so!

JULIETTE. That is why they must be pardoned if they love us.

LÉÏLA (*making a great effort to control her tears; with terrible wildness*). You lie! You lie! He doesn't love you! It is I whom he loves! I have only to make a sign for him to come back to me.

JULIETTE. You? You haven't and you could not have any influence over him. You do not matter any more than an odalisk. And, if he respects you a little, it is out of regard for the children which you give him.

LÉÏLA (*falls in an armchair, weeping*). Go away! (*She rises.*) No, stay! (*Movement by* JULIETTE.) You will stay! (LÉÏLA *runs to the door at left and calls.*) Nazmi, come here, come quickly, I beg of you!

JULIETTE. What are you doing? You are mad! (*A moment of silence full of agony.*)

(*Enter* NAZMI. *He remains a moment, painfully bewildered; looks in turn from* LÉÏLA *to* JULIETTE, *then trying to rise above his emotion.*)

NAZMI. What is going on here—why these cries? . . .

LÉÏLA (*interrupting him*). Your mistress is insulting your wife. Choose! You must choose between us!

JULIETTE. Nazmi Bey, your wife is a child who doesn't know what she is saying.

NAZMI (*does not answer at once, hesitates, then to* JULIETTE). I do not understand exactly what has happened, but believe me, Madame, I am pained about it.

JULIETTE. Let me explain to you and you will see that . . .

NAZMI (*interrupting*). Madame, I beg of you! It is better not to continue! it is better if we leave Léïla alone.

JULIETTE. Oh, very well!

(JULIETTE *proceeds haughtily towards the door at right.* NAZMI *accompanies her and speaks to her in a low tone.*)

LÉÏLA (*reflecting, profoundly sad, is left alone. Finally she makes a decision and goes and sits in front of a little desk at right. She writes slowly, searching for words.*) "My dear father, come to see me as soon as you receive this note. Your daughter has much sorrow. I know that I am going to give you trouble, my dear, adored papa. But I have no longer the will to keep silent. I have too much need of consolation and comfort, and there is only you in the world who can give it to me, through your affection and tenderness . . ."

NAZMI (*who has approached her quietly during these last words*). Léila, Léila. (*She starts, crumples up her letter and hides it.*) I am miserable, brokenhearted. Madame Sénire has told me what has passed between you. It is serious, very serious. I am responsible, alas, but I do not wish to despair, for I know that you are good and indulgent. (*He tries to take her hand. LÉILA refuses it with a movement of impatience.*) Listen my dearest, it is always evil not to wish to hear. To become unnerved and angry only serves to make things worse. Do me the favor of allowing me to speak.

LÉILA. What is the good! I have nothing new to learn.

NAZMI. You think then that you know all!

LÉILA. Yes, since your . . . friend, has confessed all frankly, without any shame!

NAZMI. You know the facts and you judge me accordingly. You are right, that is the justice that obtains to-day, that is human justice. But think a moment! What importance have brutal facts in the face of powerful and profound psychological truths?

LÉILA. Then what is the way to judge you? Your acts are not then sufficient to enlighten me as to your sentiments? No, no, do not try to defend yourself. Your words only make my wound reopen. You have deceived me and you love me no longer. That is the only powerful and profound truth as you say. That is the cruel and irrevocable truth.

NAZMI. You certainly have the upper hand. You can condemn me irretrievably. You have moreover the right to do so, and every woman would act the same in your place. But you alone Léila—you ought not to act like everyone else. You are superior, understanding; you ought to admit that I am able to love you in spite of my faults, in spite of all.

LÉILA. To believe in such an anomaly would be childish. You know very well that I am not one of those fearful and submissive wives who easily put up with the caprices and the whims of the Master, and who even submit to sharing him. And you know also that our union has not been analogous like most Turkish marriages. We were both of us given over to new ideas. We had the conviction that a wife is not, as our men think, an inferior being, a slave of pleasure. We wished that our union should be based on equality and love. I gave you immediately all my heart, and I believed that I had conquered yours. I was confident and happy. I believed in the eternity of the beautiful dream. And suddenly I receive this terrible blow full in the face. And I tell myself, stunned and quivering, it is finished, it is finished!

NAZMI. No, it is not finished, dear Léila. Our love is strong enough to pass through this ordeal and to triumph over it. Yes, I say our love, for I swear to you that I love you as sincerely as on the first day.

LÉILA. Do not go on. I suffer to see you lie with this terrifying composure, which is a new proof of your indifference.

NAZMI. But I do not lie, I do not lie. I would have wished to open my heart to you, to show you that it is intact. This was only an infatuation, a passing fancy. What would you! Our customs are the real miscreants. Yes, it is above all our customs, which are contradictory to the ideas to which you made allusion just now.

LÉÏLA. Do not search for subtleties which have nothing to do with the question.

NAZMI. What, do you not think it very dangerous, for example, that a husband, obliged for all sorts of reasons to go about socially, is forced to leave his wife in the harem and to go everywhere alone? Are we not men, that is to say very weak, fatuous and insatiable beings? Are we not liable, drunk with the atmosphere of pleasure and of sensuality that surrounds us, to forget for a moment the far away wife and, . . .

LÉÏLA (interrupting him). There is no reason why you will not begin all over again from to-morrow on with Madame X or Madame Y. There is no reason either, why it should be a passing fancy and not a great love. Oh, all that means nothing!

NAZMI. I see that no word of mine will excuse me in your eyes. But still I ask you to have a little confidence in me. You will see how time will efface this bad memory. You will see above all how I shall by means of faithfulness, gentleness and tenderness, recapture your faith and your love, that I will make you forget all and win your pardon. (LÉÏLA makes a move as though to speak, but NAZMI does not give her the time to continue. His face is near that of his wife.) Do not answer, Léïla. All discussion to-day would be futile and dangerous. Have confidence and wait. Only tell me that you will pardon me later, much, much later. Tell me Léïla, will you pardon me?

LÉÏLA (in a very sad voice). I do not know—I do not know! I am so unhappy!

CURTAIN

JOE

A Hudson Valley Play

By Jane Dransfield

CHARACTERS

Mrs. Mason
Mrs. Tern
Lou Cosgrove
Joe, *Lou's son*
Ed Tern
Dr. Wekeland
Attendant to the Doctor

JOE

A Hudson Valley Play

SCENE: LOU COSGROVE'S *cottage in a lonely spot in Hudson Valley.*

A bare and comfortless room, with low ceiling, floor of uneven boards, none too clean, faded wall paper hanging loose here and there, disclosing dingy plaster beneath, woodwork of a sickly blue, evidently painted as a "home job." In the rear there is a door opening upon a narrow porch from which steps lead down to the road. To the right of the door is a small square window at which hang a shade, and cheap cretonne curtains of bright color, an evident effort of the occupant toward cheerfulness. Against the left wall stands a tall cupboard painted blue like the woodwork, of which it appears almost to be part. Behind this cupboard, but hidden when the cupboard is in place, is a low door leading to a vegetable cellar beneath the house. To the right is a cook stove, upon which steams a pot of soup. A table covered with a faded red "spread" stands in the center. In the rear to the left is a dresser, over which hangs a mirror, and upon which are a kerosene lamp, a few books, a comb and brush, and other toilet articles. A rocking chair stands near the stove, a deal chair near the door, and two chairs at the table. A door right leads to a bedroom.

It is just after sunset of an Indian summer day in November. The door rear stands open, and through it and the window the red flare of sunset flings itself into the room. There is a vista of the river with a ridge of hills on the opposite shore. MRS. MASON, a shrunken and timid little woman of middle age, sits in the rocker beside the stove, holding out her hands to the heat. Occasionally, as she feels the outside chill, she draws her shawl closer about her shoulders. MRS. TERN, a younger woman than MRS. MASON, plump, and by her dress evidently in more prosperous circumstances, stands in the doorway, looking out. Her hat and coat lie on the chair by the door.

MRS. MASON. Wull, do yo' see her?

MRS. TERN. Not yit.

MRS. MASON. Funny she's so late. Must be near six.

MRS. TERN. It 'ull be dark in a half hour, pitch dark.

MRS. MASON. Yes, sun goes quick in November. Better shet the door, hain't yo'? It's gettin' chilly. Days is warm in Indian summer in the Valley, but nights is cold.

MRS. TERN (*closes the door*). It sure is queer what's kept Lou. She allas quits washin' at five, an' she's only over at Mis Beebe's, jist a half-mile off.

349

Mrs. Mason. Mebbe she's got Joe hid somewheres off in the woods, an' is gone ter see him. Pity the poor boy ef he war out in the thunder storm we hed this afternoon.

(Mrs. Tern *opens the oven door, and bastes a duck roasting within.*)

Mrs. Tern. No, Lou ain't hid Joe off in the woods. She's never stand to hev him so fur off as thet, 'specially now.

Mrs. Mason. You think Lou 'ull let Joe go when the authorities cums?

Mrs. Tern (*closes the oven door, and opens the stove drafts*). Oven ain't hot enough fer duck. Yes, I kinder think Lou 'ull hev to let Joe go.

(*Draws the pot of soup forward, stirring it.*)

Mrs. Mason. What 'ud thet letter say agin, Ann?

(Mrs. Tern *crosses to the dresser, takes a letter from one of the books, unfolds it, holding it out before* Mrs. Mason.)

Mrs. Tern. Read fer yerself.

Mrs. Mason. Yo know right wull, Ann Tern, I kin't read writin'.

Mrs. Tern. This ain't writin'. It's type-writin', with a printed letter-head.

Mrs. Mason. It don't make no difference. What does it say?

Mrs. Tern. It says exactly what I told yo' afore Ed said it said, thet as Lou refuses to give Joe up of her own accord, "voluntarily" is the word they use, the town authorities wull cum an' take him.

Mrs. Mason (*startled*). To-night?

Mrs. Tern (*warily*). Oh, I dunno. Mebbe not.

(*Lays the letter on the table, takes her knitting from her coat pocket, sits by the table, opposite* Mrs. Mason, *knits.*)

Mrs. Mason. Where 'ull they put him?

Mrs. Tern. Where they put all crazy people.

Mrs. Mason. Ain't thet interferin' with folks' rights? Joe ain't exactly crazy. He never did no harm to anybody.

Mrs. Tern. Joe ain't good fer the neighborhood. He frightens the chuldren, danglin' thet foolish string of his, an' bleatin' like a lost sheep. Mis Clark says he marked her baby with thet smile of his. She cud never git it out of her head all the time she war on the way.

Mrs. Mason. I know she said thet.

Mrs. Tern. An' once Joe ran out of the house naked. Yo' remember thet time, surely.

Mrs. Mason. Yes, I remember.

Mrs. Tern. Got nearly to Mis Beebe's. Oh, it 'ud be better fer Lou, an' fer all of us, to hev Joe put away.

(*As* Mrs. Tern *speaks,* Mrs. Mason *hears something that startles her. She turns quickly to* Mrs. Tern.)

Mrs. Mason. What war thet? Didn't yo' hear somethin'?

Mrs. Tern. Can't say as I did.

Mrs. Mason. Wull, I did.

Mrs. Tern. Most like the wind, risin' after sundown.

Mrs. Mason. Didn't sound like the wind. It sounded like Joe, thet funny laugh of his, like a bleatin' lamb, jist as yo' said. Ann, where's Lou hidin' him?

Mrs. Tern. I don't know, an' I don't want ter know.

Mrs. Mason. Wull, I dunno as I want ter know, either. Only, I war wonderin'. (Mrs. Tern *rises, and goes to the window, looks out.*) Do yo' see Lou yit?

Mrs. Tern. No.

Mrs. Mason (*rises, to depart*). Wull, I dunno, as after all, I want ter help yo' make Lou give up Joe. She's allas believin' somehow he'll get his mind back some day, and mebbe, who knows, he wull. Strange things happen in this world. (*Draws her shawl about her, crosses to the door, her hand upon the knob to open it.*) Besides he's the only child she's got left, an' a son's a son, after all, even ef he ain't jist right. I'm kinder sorry fer Lou.

Mrs. Tern (*rises, turns sharply on* Mrs. Mason). Sorry! after what she's done, shamin' us all these years by livin' with her own half brother, an' hevin' chuldren. Now she's got a chance ter live decent, she's got ter live decent. Thet's what I say, an' Ed, too. Dulk's dead, an' the other two' children besides Joe. An' now the authorities is willin' ter take Joe. She owes it ter Ed an' me ter let Joe go, ef ter no one else.

Mrs. Mason (*opens the door, the sunset is fading*). Wull, I know yo' ain't got much softenin' in yo', Ann Tern, 'specially sence yo' an' Ed's bought the brick house, an' got set up. But don't be too hard on Lou.

Mrs. Tern. God's curse is on her, fer what she's done. Joe shows thet, an' her two dead chuldren. Mercy, though, they died.

Mrs. Mason. Wull, some folks as has been married by the minister has got dead chuldren, too. An' some of 'em has got foolish chuldren, an' bad chuldren, chuldren what's a disgrace an' a sorrow to 'em. You see, yo' ain't never hed no chuldren, Ann Tern.

Mrs. Tern (*tersely*). Shet the door, ef yo' be agoin'. The mists is creepin' up from the river.

Mrs. Mason (*tersely also*). I'm goin'. Good-night.

Mrs. Tern. Good-night.

(Mrs. Mason *steps out upon the porch, looks down the road, returns to the doorway.*)

Mrs. Mason. Lou's cumin'. She's carryin' a big bundle. She walks tired, an' her face has got thet white look as ef her heart war bad agin'. Ann, let her keep her Joe boy. It 'ull kill her ef he's tuk away. She loves him like as ef he war still her baby.

Mrs. Tern. I know my business.

Mrs. Mason (*bitterly*). Yes, I guess most successful folks does.

(*Goes out.* Mrs. Tern *crosses quickly to the table, takes the letter, replaces it in the book on the dresser, and going to the store, stands stirring the soup.* Lou *enters. She carries a large box, new, with the imprint of a clothing store on the cover. About thirty-five,* Lou *is slight, sensitive, quick in motion, totally different from her half-sister. She is thin and worn, but her fine features show good blood somewhere back in her ancestry. Her dark eyes flash, and her abundant dark hair is still untouched by gray. At present, though, on first appearance, she is only a hard working woman of the Valley. Her hat and coat are out of date, bought from a rummage sale, or given her by her employers. Her manner is nervous and weary. She sees* MRS. TERN, *but gives no greeting. She places the box down, and removes her hat and coat, hanging them on a peg by the dresser. Her dark dress is also out of date.* MRS. TERN *tastes the soup, adding a pinch of salt from a salt box on the wall. She assumes a casual manner.*)

MRS. TERN.   Hello, Lou, is thet you?

LOU (*laconically, as she closes the door*).   Yes, it's me. Who did yo' think it war?

MRS. TERN.   Yer late.

LOU.   Yes, I guess I be.

MRS. TERN.   Thought I'd hev the soup all het up fer yo', when yo' cum in.

LOU.   Yo' ain't stayin' ter supper, be yo'?

MRS. TERN.   Thought I might, ef it's convenient.

LOU.   Wull, it ain't.

MRS. TERN.   Anyhow, I'll jist set awhile, then, an' chat with yo', while yo' git ready. (*Sits by the table.* LOU *goes to the dresser, lets down her hair, and brushes it.* MRS. TERN *knits.*)   Still proud of yer hair, ain't yo', Lou?

LOU.   Kinder rests me ter let it down, after workin' the hull day.

(*Silence.* LOU *continues to brush her hair,* MRS. TERN *to knit, though her mind is on the conversation she wishes to open, but does not know exactly how. She looks at* LOU, *about to speak, changes her mind, returns to her knitting. Suddenly a queer sound like the distant bleating of a lamb is heard.* LOU *starts, instantly controls herself, and turns to* MRS. TERN, *to see if she has heard also.* MRS. TERN *has heard, but before* LOU *turns, resumes her stolid position, so that* LOU *will suspect nothing. She hastens to resume the conversation.*)

MRS. TERN.   Yo' war a mighty pretty girl onc't, Lou Cosgrove.

LOU (*with relief, again brushing her hair*).   Oh, thet's as it may be.

MRS. TERN.   The prettiest about these parts, darin' proud creature of the Valley, yo' war, runnin' wild through the woods an' over the hills. An' yo' might be good lookin' agin, ef yo'd a mind. Yo' ain't old yit.

LOU.   Mebbe I ain't, an' mebbe I be.

MRS. TERN.   Put a duck in the oven to roast fer your supper. It's jist about done to a turn, now. Ed brought down a lot of 'em this mornin'.

LOU.   There's plenty of duck about this fall. Seen full thirty jist now, as I war cumin' up the hill. Flew so close over my head, I cud hear their wings whirrin', an' the kind of low singin' they make to each other, friendly like.

MRS. TERN (*determines to delay no longer, rolls up her knitting, turns toward* LOU.)   What be yo' goin' ter do about thet letter?

LOU.   Nothin'.

(*Twists up her hair.*)

Mrs. Tern. Nothin', eh? Wull, mebbe the authorities are on their way here now ter git Joe.

Lou (*unmoved*). They won't git him.

Mrs. Tern. They won't, eh? What's goin' ter prevent 'em?

Lou. There's ways.

(*Opens the cupboard, and takes out a flintlock gun, which she lays on the table.*)

Mrs. Tern (*rises, aghast*). Yo' don't mean, yo're goin' ter shoot?

Lou. Yes. I'm goin' ter shoot, the first man thet enters my door ter git Joe.

(*Takes up the box she brought in, and goes out with it through the door at the right, leaving the door open.* Mrs. Tern *raises her voice so that* Lou *will surely hear.*)

Mrs. Tern. Lou Cosgrove, yo've been enough trouble as it is. (Lou *returns from the bedroom, closing the door.*) Don't yo' go makin' any more. Yo' let Joe go, peaceful like, when they cum ter git him.

Lou (*closely watching* Mrs. Tern). I suppose yo' think yo' know where Joe is.

Mrs. Tern. It ain't hard guessin'.

Lou. Then see to it yo' hold yer tongue, Ann Tern.

(*Sinks wearily into the rocker by the stove.*)

Mrs. Tern. Gosh! Lou, yo' look bad.

Lou. I ain't been feelin' good, lately. (Mrs. Tern *puts her knitting back in her coat pocket, takes from another pocket a small flask of brandy, and goes to the cupboard for a cup. The bleating sound, faint, is heard again.* Mrs. Tern *pauses to listen, and observing this,* Lou *talks on quickly to cover the sound*). Ain't been sleepin' much nights, an' can't eat. (Mrs. Tern *pours the brandy into the cup.*) It's hell, doin' washin' fer folks, six days in the week, an' cleanin' up yer own place Sundays. How's a woman to hold on, week in, an' week out, in all kinds of weather?

(Mrs. Tern *offers the brandy to* Lou.)

Mrs. Tern. Ed got it fer me from the doctor, fer the chills.

Lou (*pushes the cup away*). Ed! No thanks. I dont accept no favors from Ed.

(Mrs. Tern *places the cup on the table, sits opposite* Lou, *determined now to speak out her mind.*)

Mrs. Tern. Ed's a good man.

Lou. Thet's as it may be.

Mrs. Tern. Lou, how yo' cum ter do what yo' did, about Dulk, I mean, war allas a mystery ter me, yo' a girl as cud hev hed any man hereabouts.

Lou. Dulk war fifteen years older an' me. He war your brother, not mine.

Mrs. Tern. His mother, an' yer mother, an' mine, war the same woman. Different fathers, thet war all.

Lou. Listen ter me, Ann Tern. In them days, I war too skeered to think whether Dulk war my brother, or whether he warn't. Yo' remember my father, though mebbe yo' don't much, cus yo' went away from hum to work, as far back as I can think. Yo' never cum hum ter visit much. Wull, when my father war drunk, he war hell. An' most of the time he war drunk. My mother war as skeered as I. She cudn't do nothin' fer me. Dulk war all there war. He stood atween me an' Pa, tuk the beatin's fer me. An' we kind of drifted togither, thet war all.

MRS. TERN. Yo' speak as ef yo' ain't got no repentance in yer soul.

LOU. I ain't.

MRS. TERN. An' neither had Dulk. Afore he died, the rector tried ter git him ter say he war sorry, an' all Dulk would say war thet yo' war a good woman. Yo' got some kind of hold over him, I don't know what. Why! yo' an' Dulk war like animals.

LOU. Thet ain't true!

MRS. TERN. Why ain't it true? Yo've brought disgrace on all of us as has tried to live decent.

LOU. Yo' mean, yo' an' Ed.

MRS. TERN. Yes. Not a week passes, but I git it thrown at me, somehow, that I'm the half-sister of that woman who married, so they calls it, her own half-brother. An' God cursed her by makin' her son foolish.

LOU (*springs up, cut to the quick*). Quit yer talkin'.

MRS. TERN. Not afore I'm through, this time. It ain't fair ter me an' Ed, ter hold us up in front of folks like thet. Thet's why I say yo've got ter let Joe go. Him out of the way, yo' cud make a fresh start. Folks wud soon fergit.

LOU. What's the use of a fresh start? Jist ter work harder?

(*The sunset light has now about faded. LOU rises, lights the kerosene lamp on top of the dresser.*)

MRS. TERN. Ain't it worth while, livin' decent?

LOU. Why ain't I lived decent? I ain't stole, or lied, or got drunk. I'm as good as most folks.

MRS. TERN Yo're a smart woman, Lou Cosgrove. Yo' cud make somethin' out of yerself, ef yo'd let Joe go.

LOU. I ain't goin' ter let Joe go.

MRS. TERN (*magnanimously*). Ed an' me ud let yo' cum live with us till yo' got started agin.

LOU. I ain't got no hankerin' ter live with yo' an' Ed.

MRS. TERN (*rises*). Yo' won't do it, then? Yo' won't let Joe go?

LOU. Ed 'ull be missin' yo'. (*Opens the door.*) Yo'd better be going' up ter hum, now. It's getting darker, every minute.

MRS. TERN (*puts on her hat and coat*). Very wull. Go yer own way. Yo're an ungrateful sinner, thet's all I can say. (*Points to the gun.*) But ef yo' should git into trouble with thet, don't cum ter Ed an' me ter help yo' out. I'm through with yo' fer good. Fer good, do yo' hear? (*Crosses to the door, turns, as she stands in the doorway.*) God's curse is on yo'!

(*At the word "curse"* Lou *shrinks.* Mrs. Tern *goes out, closing the door sharply.* Lou *rushes to the door, opens it, calls out.*)

Lou. Ann Tern, take thet back! (Mrs. Tern *either does not hear* Lou, *or does not care to heed.*) Ann! (*Seeing her entreaty is useless,* Lou *returns into the room, closes the door, leaning against it, a look of terror on her face.*) God's curse! No! no! not thet! . . . (*The bleating sound is heard, more plainly than before. It recalls* Lou *to herself. She quickly locks and bolts the door.*) Yes, yes, Joe boy. (*She crosses to the cupboard, pushes it aside with all her strength, revealing a low door in the wall, which she opens. It gives upon a narrow staircase leading down. She peers down. The laugh comes again. She calls, in a half whisper.*) Joe! Joe! Joe boy! (*On hands and knees* Joe *comes up the stairs, crawls into the room;* Lou *assists him to rise. He is almost as tall as* Lou, *about sixteen, and painfully thin. Like* Lou's, *his features are fine, his eyes dark, his skin white, with a mass of dark unkempt hair. Lit by intelligence his face would have been beautiful, but it is vacant, and he smiles foolishly, as he dangles a soiled string. His shirt and khaki trousers are old, and ragged, and he is dirty as if he had been groveling in earth. He moves forward slowly toward the table with a curious sinuous motion, giving the bleating laugh. He sits down at the table.* Lou *at once removes the gun, laying it on top of the dresser, which she shoves into place.*

Joe *dangles the string into the cup on the table into which* Mrs. Tern *had poured the brandy.* Lou *draws the shade at the window, weighting it down with a flatiron, so that it lies closely, leaving no openings at the sides for some one to look in.*) Don't want no one lookin' in here to-night, Joe boy.

(*Draws the cretonne curtains together across the shade, then comes forward to* Joe, *turning his face toward her, then looking at his hands.*) My! but yo're dirty. No place fer yo' at all, down there in the vegetable cellar. Never mind, we'll soon hev yo' clean, shinin' as the first clothes out on the line in the sunshine on a Monday mornin'. (*All of* Lou's *talk to* Joe *is as one speaks to an infant, or a dog, for the comfort of it, not in the least in expectation of an answer. Throughout occasionally* Joe *gives the bleating laugh.* Lou *prepares a basin, water, towel, and soap at the dresser, and bringing them forward to the table deftly washes* Joe's *face and hands.*) Gosh! Joe boy, I does hate ter leave yo' down there in the dark the hull day. But it's better, ain't it? than bein' tuk off. Yo' wouldn't be wantin' 'em ter take yo' off, yo're Ma knows thet, wull enough. (*Turns his face up for inspection.*) That's better. (*Washes his hands.*) War yo' much skeered this afternoon when it thundered an' lightened? Hell! I war. Stopped ironin' over at Mis Beebe's, an' went down cellar jist like yo'. Mis Beebe said I might sort out the rotten pertatoes, ter use my time. Folks as pays yer money sees to it, yo' bet, thet yo' don't waste no time. (*Replaces the basin, and other things she has been using.* Joe *starts to rise. She pushes him back into his chair.*) Set still! See what I brung yo'. (*Goes into the bedroom at the right, brings out the box, lays it on the table, untying the string.*) Funny Ann Tern warn't curious what I hed in this box. Most like she thought it was some more old clothes Mis Beebe give me fer myself, like these I got on. Or else her mind war all tuk up with how she war ter git yo' out of here, so she an' Ed can rise up a little higher in the world. She's ashamed of us, but we'll show her. (*Proudly lifts out of the box a suit of cheap ready made man's clothing.*) This is fer yo', Joe boy. Yo' ain't hed no regular suit of clothes, all yer life long. No, yo' ain't, yo' son of a bitch! So, says I, Joe boy is goin' ter hev a suit, a bran new one, nobody's cast offs. Nobody ain't ever wore this afore. Thet's what made me late. Walked into town, after I'd finished at Miss Beebe's, an' cum hum by trolley. Stand up! Try the coat on. (*She pulls* Joe *up, and slips the coat on. It hangs limply, much too large for him.*) My! but it's goin' ter fit yo' grand. An' when yo' has a bath all over, and gits the hull suit on, we'll take a walk out togither. We'll show folks we're somebody, too. (*Removes the coat, replacing it in the box.* Joe *sits down again.*) Been savin' up all summer fer this. Didn't say nothin'. Wished ter surprise yo'. (*Returns the box to the bedroom, and coming back, goes to the cupboard for the supper things.*) Now we'll hev supper. Guess yo're hungry. (*Places soup and bread before* Joe.) An' there's a fine duck in the oven, too. (*Laughs harshly, opens the oven door, takes a "holder" from its peg on the wall, draws out the pan in which the duck is cooking, puts it on top of the stove, closes the oven door.*) Ann Tern's mistuk ef she thinks anybody in this house is goin' ter eat any duck what Ed brings down. (*Opens the door, returns for the pan, tosses pan and duck into the night, as it is now dark.*) Mebbe the crows 'ull eat it, or the skunks. Hope they'ull enjoy it. They're welcome ter hev it. (*Closes the door.*) Pitch dark, now, outside. No moon to-night. Nobody cud git here, now. (Joe *is eating the soup and bread.* Lou *comes forward to him.*) Glad ter see yo' eat so hearty, Joe boy. (Joe *pauses, as if dimly conscious of her presence.*) No, I ain't sittin' down with yo' to-night. Somehow, I ain't hungry. But yo' take yer fill, now, comfortable. (*Examines the gun on the dresser, to see if it is in working order, satisfies herself that it is, returns it to the dresser.* Joe *takes up the cup in which is the brandy.* Lou *snatches it from him, pours out the brandy into a waste bucket by the stove, gets a pitcher of water from the cupboard, and fills the cup with water. She hands the cup to* Joe, *who drinks the water, holding the cup out for more.* Lou *is refilling the cup when a motor horn is heard. She instantly places the cup and pitcher down on the table, frightened.*) What's thet? (*Stands listening, tense. The motor horn sounds again. Oblivious of* Lou's *fear,* Joe *snatches a piece of bread, and gnaws it.* Lou *runs to the window, as if to look out, checks herself.*) No! they wud see the light. (*Stands at the window listening. As there is no further sound, she shakes off her fear, and returning to the table fills the cup with water.*) What am I afraid of? No one can git in here to-night, anyway. The planks over the bridge is loose. Noticed 'em jist now as I cum in. Nobody cud drive a car over thet bridge. (*Laughs again, harshly.*) As fer them rich authorities walkin' up the hill, watch 'em doin' it. They don't know where ter find this house, anyhow. Only someone as knows us, cud find us. (JOE *gives his laugh.* LOU *turns on him.*) Shet up, Joe! Stop yer noise. (JOE *sinks down in his chair, his head falling forward.* LOU *throws her arm about him.*) There now, I ain't meanin' ter skeer yo', Joe boy. I'm jist nervous, thet's all. But nobody's cumin'. Here, take yer string, while I clear off the things. (*Gives* JOE *his string. He plays with it again, while* LOU *clears the table, leaving, however, the cup of water. Then she goes to the door.*) Guess I'll jist take a look around the house. (*Slips out of the door, closing it after her. For a moment after* LOU *has gone,* JOE *sits quietly dangling the string. Then he touches the cup of water. Feels the water, laughs. Takes the cup, and pours out a little onto the string, as if giving it a drink. Laughs again. Rises, and with the cup in hand wanders about aimlessly. Pours a little water onto the stove. Goes to a chair, pours some water on the back, as if giving the chair a drink. Laughs. Wanders about again, comes to the dresser, discovers the gun. Places the cup down on the dresser, takes the gun, and looks down the barrel. Laughs. Places the gun on the floor, barrel up, takes the cup, and with the idea of giving the gun a drink, pours the water down the barrel. This wets the powder, rendering the gun harmless. He uses all the water in the cup, which then he replaces upon the table. He looks down the gun again, then puts it on the dresser, as he had found it, recrosses to the table, finds his string, and laughing again, dangles the string over the table. The door opens softly. Enter* ED TERN, *a brisk little man, rather flashily dressed. He looks quickly about the room, then beckons from the doorway.*)

ED TERN. Come on in, doctor. (*Enter* DR. WEKELAND.) That was Lou, as slipped past us, down the hill. Never saw us. She's lookin' for us, I reckon, though. Mebbe she saw the lights of the car. Good we cum up the side path.

(JOE *gives no sign of noticing that any one has entered.*)

DR. WEKELAND. Never could have found the place without your guidance, Mr. Tern.

ED TERN. Thought you'd need me.

DR. WEKELAND. Is this the boy?

ED TERN. That's Joe. Quick! let's get him out of here. (*Takes* JOE's *arm, flinging the string down on the table.* JOE *laughs.*) Ain't it just as I said? You see how he is, absolutely foolish.

DR. WEKELAND (*takes some papers from his pocket*). Mrs. Cosgrove must sign these papers before we take the boy.

ED TERN. *Mrs.* Cosgrove! Don't call Lou that, doctor. She ain't a *Mrs.* She don't wear no weddin' ring. She's just Lou Cosgrove, that's all, same as she was always called. Come, Joe.

DR. WEKELAND (*observing* JOE). You are correct, Mr. Tern, as to the boy's condition, but as to taking him without his mother's permission,—

(JOE *laughs again.*)

ED TERN. He's got to go, I say. I'll get Lou to sign the papers afterwards. You don't want to be havin' to come over here again, doctor.

Dr. Wekeland. Well, perhaps you are right. (*Beckons at the door.* Joe *breaks from* Ed Tern, *sits by the table, looks for his string.* Enter The Attendant.) We'll take the patient now, Charles.

Attendant. Yes, sir.

(*Steps toward* Joe, *followed by* Dr. Wekeland. Ed *tries to make* Joe *stand.*)

Ed Tern. Oh, come on, Joe. There's a good boy.

(*Enter* Lou, *out of breath. When she sees the men, and comprehends the situation, stops, then nerves herself, and confronts* Dr. Wekeland.)

Lou. What yo' here fer?

Dr. Wekeland (*turns to* Lou). Oh, Mrs. Cosgrove, I presume.

Ed Tern. Yes, that's Lou.

Lou. Why don't yo' answer me? What yer here fer?

Dr. Wekeland. To get the boy, Mrs. Cosgrove, as we wrote you.

Lou. By what right?

Dr. Wekeland. The residents about here, your neighbors, have complained.

Lou (*stands beside* Joe *protectingly*). Yo' mean Ann and Ed Tern, I suppose. Wull, yo're not goin' ter git Joe.

Dr. Wekeland (*soothingly*). Be reasonable, Mrs. Cosgrove. Surely you realize your son will be much better taken care of in an asylum than here.

Lou. Mebbe, an' mebbe not. Anyhow, I don't want Joe in an asylum. I want him here, to hum, with me.

Dr. Wekeland. Perhaps, but your neighbors have rights. Society has learned it must protect itself. Of course, you do not understand these things.

Lou. No, I guess I don't.

(Joe *finds his string, and dangles it again.*)

Ed Tern. And she don't want to, doctor.

Lou. Quit yer talkin', Ed Tern. I know what yer idea is, but this ain't none of yer affairs.

(Ed *steps angrily toward* Lou. Dr. Wekeland *interferes.*)

Dr. Wekeland. Just a moment, Mr. Tern. Let us hear what Mrs. Cosgrove has to say. That is only fair.

Lou. Thank yo', doctor. But all I hev got ter say, is thet I want Joe to hum. (*Her fear of separation wells within her.*) An' now yo' wants ter take him away from me. But I ain't goin' ter let yo'. I ain't goin' ter let Joe go.

Dr. Wekeland. I'm afraid we shall be obliged to take him, Mrs. Cosgrove. And the sooner it is over, the better.

Ed Tern. Right you are, doctor. Give the word. (Dr. Wekeland *signals* The Attendant, *who with* Ed's *assistance, raises* Joe. Lou *has stolen toward the dresser. As* Ed *leads* Joe *toward the door,* Lou *seizes the gun, points it at* Ed, *and pulls the trigger. Because of the wet powder, of course, the gun does not fire.* Lou *looks dumbly at the gun, feels the water, realizes she is foiled.* Ed *springs to* Lou, *wrenches the gun from her hands.*) What the hell! So that's your game, is it? Ann warned me you meant to shoot. You devil!

(DR. WEKELAND *takes the gun from* ED.)

LOU. Yo'd been stretched out now, Ed Tern, ef the gun hadn't a gone back on me.

ED TERN. Lucky for you! Saved you from the law.

(ED *and* THE ATTENDANT *again try to lead* JOE *toward the door. Desperately* LOU *prevents them, standing in the doorway.*)

LOU. Doctor, I know yo' think Joe crazy. But he ain't. He's not jist like other boys, mebbe, but he warn't born thet way. He war the prettiest, smartest baby yo' ever see.

DR. WEKELAND. It isn't what he was, Mrs. Cosgrove, but what he is now. (*Steps toward the door, motioning the men to move forward with* JOE. *Realizing her physical helplessness against the three,* LOU *knows her only hope is in persuasion.*)

LOU. Wait! wait! Don't take him yit. My gun's gone back on me, an' I can't fight the three of yo'. Doctor, listen to what I hev ter say.

DR. WEKELAND. Very well, Mrs. Cosgrove, but hurry, please. It is growing late.

ED TERN. Oh, come on, doctor.

DR. WEKELAND (*motions* ED *to silence*). It is best to humor her, Mr. Tern. Go on, Mrs. Cosgrove.

(ED *stops impatiently, at the door,* JOE *standing between him and* THE ATTENDANT.)

LOU. Doctor, ef I cud show yo' thet Joe knew somethin', cud say somethin', like other chuldren.

DR. WEKELAND. You mean show some signs of intelligence?

LOU. Yes, doctor, ef thet's what yo' call it. Wud yo' feel then, as yo' do now, about takin' him off?

DR. WEKELAND (*in his endeavor to humor* LOU *for a moment.*) No, I don't suppose I would. There would be no pressing necessity.

LOU. Yo' wud leave him here to hum, then, with me?

DR. WEKELAND. I dare say, of course, if that should happen. But it is out of the question.

LOU. Doctor, many an' many a time, when I'm alone with Joe, it seems ter me, his mind is jist on the pint of cumin' back ter him. Mebbe, I can make it cum to-night. Let me try, doctor. Please let me try, afore yo' take him off. I'm sure I cud make him say somethin'. Please.

ED TERN (*laughs derisively*). She thinks she can work a miracle. Gosh! Oh, come on, doctor.

DR. WEKELAND. Mrs. Cosgrove is in a highly nervous state, Mr. Tern.

ED TERN. Yes, and she's got a weak heart. We'd best get out of here as quick as possible.

LOU. Doctor, yo' don't understand. Ef yo' take Joe off, it 'ull kill me.

DR. WEKELAND. We must humor her, Mr. Tern. (*Turns to* LOU.) Very well, Mrs. Cosgrove. I will wait a few moments.

LOU. But not afore Ed, an' the other.

DR. WEKELAND. Wait outside, Mr. Tern, and you, Charles.

(ED TERN *and* THE ATTENDANT *go out.* LOU *leads* JOE *forward to the table, seating him.* ED TERN *returns, stands in the doorway.*)

ED TERN. A miracle! That's what she thinks is goin' to happen. Ha, Ha!

(*Laughs loudly as he goes out again.* DR. WEKELAND *closes the door,* JOE *dangles his string.* LOU *brings the lamp and a book from the dresser. The book is a first primer. She opens the book on the table before* JOE, *and seats herself beside him.* DR. WEKELAND *sits by the door.* LOU *takes the string from* JOE, *points to the page.*)

LOU. Joe boy, what is this a picter of?

(DR. WEKELAND *takes out his watch.*)

. DR. WEKELAND. Take your time, Mrs. Cosgrove. Don't be nervous.

LOU. See, it is spelled out. C-A-T. (JOE *pays no attention, but tries to find his string. He finds it, and picks it up.* LOU *snatches it from him, and raises the book before his eyes.*) Look! see! You know what this is, Joe boy.

(JOE *takes the book in his hands, gnaws it, as he had the bread.* LOU *quickly takes the book from him, realizing that particular experiment has failed. She turns to* DR. WEKELAND, *apologetically.*)

LOU. We ain't none of us about here much on books, doctor, or learnin'. I ain't myself. An' Ann Tern, fer all her pride, can't write her own name.

DR. WEKELAND. I understand that, Mrs. Cosgrove. You natives, as they call you about here, have had few advantages.

(LOU *leans tensely toward* JOE, *knowing that what she is about to do is her last chance.* JOE *is quiet, gazing vacantly before him.*)

LOU. Joe boy, listen. There ain't no curse on yo', 'cause of me an' yer father. Who's got the right to put curses on anybody, anyhow? Sometimes, when I'm cumin' hum from work, up over the hill where the path runs bare to the wind, an' the big rock draws the sky down close, you know the place, Joe boy, where we go on Sundays? There I stop, an' cry "O God, ef I've done wrong, strike me dead!" But God ain't never struck me dead, not God, nor the lightnin', nor the thunder. God ain't never told me I done wrong. It's only the rector, an' yer aunt, an' the rest. (*Lays her hand on her heart.*) An' sometimes somethin' in me here. But thet's on account of folks, not God. He ain't never spoke to me really, not Himself. I ain't never heard no harsh word from Him. (*Takes* JOE'S *hands in hers.*) No, Joe boy, there ain't no curse on yo', I tell yo'. It war jist somethin' thet happened. Mebbe yo' fell down•or somethin', without my knowin'. An' now, Joe, ef you'd only speak ter me, show the doctor yo've got—(*Turns to* DR. WEKELAND.) What's thet word, doctor?

DR. WEKELAND. You mean intelligence?

LOU. Yes, thet's it. (*Turns back to* JOE.) Show the doctor, Joe, yo've got it, what he says, thet yo' know somethin', even ef it war only—(*Casts about within her mind for the right thought.*) Yes, Joe, ef it war only me. (*With sudden hope.*) Me! Thet's it, Joe boy, thet's easy. Show the doctor yo' know me. Call me Ma! Say it! Yo' used ter, long ago.—(JOE *stirs as if something within him were being aroused)* Thet's me! Ma, Joe. Say it! Ma!

DR. WEKELAND *(looks again at his watch.)* It's getting rather late, Mrs. Cosgrove.

LOU. Jist a minute more, doctor. *(Appeals now to* JOE *in desperation.)* Joe, they'll take yo' away from me, ef yo' don't show the doctor. Then both of us 'll die. You can't live without me, an' I can't live without yo'. *(Her voice breaks. Then all her being goes into a last appeal.)* Joe, hear me! Fer the last time I ask yo'. Say it! Ma! *(JOE leans toward LOU. It seems as if he is about to speak. LOU rises triumphantly.)* Joe, Joe boy, yer goin' ter do it! Yo' are goin' ter show the doctor. Yo' are goin' ter say it . . . Ma! *(A moment of tense silence. Then JOE gives his bleating laugh. LOU in the agony of the moment seizes JOE.)* Joe . . . Joe . . . *(Then lifting herself, frenzied from a realization of what her failure means, the something she has always secretly feared.)* The curse! It's cum. *(She sinks into the chair by the table. Suddenly she clasps her hands over her heart with a dull cry.)* Oh. . . .

(She collapses, her arms outstretched upon the table, her head upon them. DR. WEKELAND springs to her side, looks into her face, feels her pulse. A low whistle escapes him. He hurries out, leaving the door open. Dumbly conscious that something is wrong with LOU, the foolish smile leaves JOE's face, and almost with a glimmer of intelligence he seems distressed. He reaches for the cup, which still stands on the far end of the table, and pathetically offers his mother a drink, as he had the chairs, and the gun. He does not sense, of course, that the cup is empty. DR. WEKELAND returns with ED TERN.)

DR. WEKELAND. It must have been as you said. She had a weak heart.

ED TERN. You are sure, doctor?

DR. WEKELAND. Absolutely. She's gone.

ED TERN *(approaches LOU, but afraid to touch the dead.)* There's the Lord's jedgment for you, on a sinner.

(JOE, still offering the cup to LOU, utters his bleating laugh.)

CURTAIN

THE SHUNAMITE

A BIBLICAL PLAY

By YEHOASH

Translated from the Yiddish by Henry T. Schnittkind

CHARACTERS

KING DAVID, *70 years old*
SHABNA, *overseer over King David's palace, 40 years old*
ZEBADIAH, *the king's attendant, 20 years old*
THE SHUNAMITE, *a peasant girl, 16 years old*

THE SHUNAMITE

SCENE: *An inner chamber in the king's palace.* KING DAVID *sits half-reclining on a couch of rugs and cushions, his feet covered with a tiger skin. His tense eyes are directed toward the door. He appears very uneasy.*

ZEBADIAH (*appears at the entrance. Makes an obeisance*). Shabna is waiting in the outer chamber.

DAVID. Let him enter.

(ZEBADIAH *goes out.*)

SHABNA (*at the door, making a low obeisance*). Peace unto the King of Judea!

DAVID (*makes a motion as if to rise, but remains seated*). Have you fulfilled my commands?

SHABNA (*drawing nearer*). The Lord who envelops your throne with His protecting light, has pointed out the way to me.

DAVID (*impatiently*). And?

SHABNA. And has delivered into my hands a new-blown rose whose fragrance will gladden your heart. Sixteen are the years of her life.

DAVID (*with glittering eyes*). Tell me about it!

SHABNA. I have wandered over Judea from border to border—Hundreds of miles have been traversed by my camels, and my practiced eye has searched out and examined every maiden among the hill dwellers of the Land of Israel as well as among the inhabitants of the valleys. . . . You have commanded that she should be young and beautiful and innocent . . . one whose voice is melodious and to whom the music of the harp is pleasing; whose passionate warmth has never yet felt the caress of a man's hand . . . poor and modest and tenderly devoted to her parents . . . one who might bring new youth to you and enkindle fresh sparks of love in your veins. . . . Difficult was my quest, and I almost gave up in despair; but in the small and secluded village of Shunem, inhabited by poor peasant folk, I found her at last. . . . When I first met her she was carrying a pitcher of water from the village well, and the song that flowed from her lips flooded the entire meadow with its sweetness. . . .

DAVID. And you went to her. . . .

SHABNA. I followed her footsteps until she reached her home, and then I revealed your royal wish to her parents. . . . I promised them a vineyard, and ten acres of land and a flock of sheep, too, did I promise. . . .

DAVID. And they were overjoyed? . . .

SHABNA. They consented. . . . She was the oldest. Ten other children

365

were in that hovel, and they were poor and without food. . . . They called the maiden . . . and the little ones stood around; naked were they and half-starved, and they clung to the skirts of their sister. . . . And the maiden said: "I will obey the wish of my father and my mother." . . . And this day at the rising of the sun she arrived in Jerusalem with our caravan. . . .

DAVID (*hastily*). Where is she? . . .

SHABNA.   She is in the shelter of your palace. . . .

DAVID (*showing new life*). How does she look?

SHABNA.   She is as fresh as the dew that falls on the grass of Hermon. Her limbs are tender and pliant as the willows that bend over Shiloh, and her voice rings like the silver bells that make soft music on the ephod of the High Priest. . . .

DAVID.   And her eyes? . . .

SHABNA.   Dark and big, like the eyes of a young gazelle on the fragrant hills. . . . And their light moves and changes all the time, just like a sunbeam on the surface of the water ruffled under the midday breezes. . . .

DAVID.   Do they glow, those eyes? . . .

SHABNA.   Like two volcanoes flaming through a veil of mist. A born queen, yet mild as a turtle-dove and ready to fulfill the wish of her lord.

DAVID.   You shall be rewarded with a heaping measure of gold from my treasure chamber. (*Bows his head as a sign that* SHABNA *is to leave him.*) Have the girl brought to me.

(SHABNA *goes out.*)

DAVID (*left alone. He is pale and speaks with great agitation.*) Great God, how I tremble! I, who once as a mere shepherd won the daughter of a king with a single glance of my eye! Yet I am now terrified at the thought of a poor peasant girl. . . . Will she love me? . . . He tells me she has big lovely eyes. . . . Shall I be able to look into them with that bold assurance that I possessed of old? Shall I be able to conquer those eyes with that self-same magic that was mine in the days of my youth? . . . Their gaze will fall upon my shrivelled cheeks, my wrinkled forehead, and my snow-covered head, and they will tell me that it was my gold and my regal power that have brought her to me. . . . I shall see in those eyes the reproachful look of a martyr, and I shall tremble at the sight. . . . She will kiss me and her heart will tell her that with those kisses she is paying for her father's acres of land and for the food that will be given to her brothers and sisters. . . . She will not turn away and she will not struggle in my arms. She will press her mouth against my cold lips whenever I shall command her, she will rest her head on my bosom whenever I shall desire it, she will smile at my bidding, and she will dance whenever my foolish fancy shall direct it. . . . But her eyes? . . . They will look upon me softly, prayerfully. . . . They will not reproach me, they will not defy me, they will only *beseech*. . . . In the name of her youth and her innocence will they beseech me to release her. . . . (*He looks at his face in a silver mirror.*) Will she be able to see the heart of the young poet under the old king's wrinkles?

ZEBADIAH (*enters and makes an obeisance.*) The girl of Shunem is here.

DAVID (*overjoyed*). Bring her in! . . . (*Changes his mind.*) No, not yet! Let her wait yet a while and let her be brought in later. (*Rises, throwing the tiger skin away from his feet. Straightens his figure, making an effort to appear young.*) Come, braid my locks, anoint me with myrrh oil and light the pot of incense.

(*The servant lights the pot of incense and busies himself about the king.*)

DAVID. Tell me, Zebadiah, have you a lover?

ZEBADIAH (*confused*). She is in Galilee. . . . It is only seldom that I see her.

DAVID. Is she glad when you visit her? . . . Does she give you many kisses when you come to her?

ZEBADIAH (*abashed*). She loves me very much. . . . We have been betrothed for many years, ever since I was employed as a day-laborer in the vineyards there. . . .

DAVID. And she longs for you, when she does not see you?

ZEBADIAH. She cries when I leave her, and she counts the days till my next furlough.

DAVID (*showing great interest*). Tell me how she received you when you last visited her. . . . To-morrow you shall go to Galilee for a week, and you shall take for your beloved a golden bracelet from me. . . . But tell me how she received you. . . .

ZEBADIAH. She was in the field. . . . It was the time of the reaping, and the entire household was binding the sheaves. . . . She saw me while I was yet at a great distance and she started to run toward me, barefooted over the furrows, between the rows of the gathered sheaves. . . . In her hand she was still holding the withes with which the ears of corn were being bound together, and . . .

DAVID. She fell on your neck?

ZEBADIAH. She playfully wreathed the garland of withes around my temples, saying that I was her crowned . . .

(*Stops suddenly.*)

DAVID (*smiling*). Her crowned king. . . . (*His tone becomes serious.*) Did you ask her to press you closely to her breast? Did you *demand* of her that she should kiss you? . . .

ZEBADIAH (*confused by these questions*). She. . . . We could not utter a word for joy. . . . Both of us. . . .

DAVID (*encourages him*). Tell me. . .

ZEBADIAH. We kissed each other, forgetting everything . . . until her father called to us to come to the field. . . .

DAVID (*with an expression of suppressed sorrow*). Do you bring presents to her when you come? . . .

ZEBADIAH. She wants me to save until we can buy a vineyard and get married. . . .

DAVID (*suddenly assuming a tone of royal dignity*). Bring in the Shunamite!

(ZEBADIAH *goes out. The king becomes deeply agitated. His hands tremble slightly.*)

(THE SHUNAMITE *enters, making an obeisance. Confused*). Peace unto the king!

DAVID (*gazes at her for some time, delighted with her beauty, and becoming still more agitated*). You are beautiful—wondrously beautiful! . . .

THE SHUNAMITE (*as if repeating somebody else's words*). Praised be the Lord that He hath allowed me to find favor in the eyes of the generous monarch.

(*She looks at him timidly, not knowing what to do.*)

DAVID (*tenderly*). Can you sing and play on the harp?

THE SHUNAMITE. In our village we can all sing and play.

DAVID (*takes down a golden harp from the wall, seats* THE SHUNAMITE *on a rug near him, and speaks to her*). Play me a song of love, one of those that they sing in your village of Shunem.

THE SHUNAMITE (*she is still looking at him like a frightened doe. . . . At first she slowly and timidly plucks the strings, until finally her touch becomes more certain and she sings to him, accompanying her words on the instrument.*)

Ten thousand foemen
Lie dead at his feet,
And the victor goes forth
His beloved to meet. . . .

With his sword at his side,
And a smile in his eyes,
He blots out with kisses
Her tears and her sighs. . . .

He gives her his sceptre,
He builds her a tower,
And a palace of cedar
In Lebanon's bower.

She spurns crown and palace,
She clings to her lord,
And prays that his love
Be her own love's reward.

(*During her song the king has kept his face covered. The eyes of* THE SHUNAMITE *are aglow as she looks dreamily before her.*)

DAVID. This song pleases you, I see. . . .

THE SHUNAMITE. It is the most beautiful song that is sung among us by the toilers in the field, and it is my favorite. . . .

DAVID. Who wrote this song?

THE SHUNAMITE (*naïvely*). I do not know. . . . It has been sung among the people for dozens of years. It must have been written way back in those days when our warriors used to go out to battle against the Philistines.

DAVID (*smiling*). When you sing this, you surely think of the man who wrote this song? . . .

THE SHUNAMITE (*in a revery*). He must have been tall and handsome, with red lips and soft black eyes. . . .

DAVID. All the girls in your village would surely have fallen in love with him, if ever he came to Shunem. . . .

THE SHUNAMITE (*in a low voice*). We should have worshiped him as a god! . . .

DAVID (*ironically*). Perhaps he still lives somewhere, and he is old and crippled and his gums are toothless? . . .

THE SHUNAMITE (*frightened*). But how can that be? . . .

DAVID. My child, you know that he could not have remained young forever. . . .

THE SHUNAMITE (*with childish stubbornness*). Among us he is always young. (*Her eyes are lighted up.*) I can see him before my eyes, this handsome singer. . . .

DAVID (*with suppressed bitterness*). Come, describe him to me. . . . I will sit near you and listen. . . .

THE SHUNAMITE (*carried away with enthusiasm*). He is straight as a palm-tree and his eyes shoot forth whole quivers of warm, tender rays of light. . . . His lips look as though stained with the fresh juice of blood-red grapes. . . . His cheeks are softly tinted with the first rosy flush of the rising dawn, and his waving locks curl and flutter like a thick multitude of playful ravens. . . . A silver girdle embraces his tall and slender waist. A jewel-studded helmet glitters on his head, his feet are shod with sandals of white deer skin, and in his hand he carries a golden harp. . . .

DAVID (*his eyes flash once more with youthful fire*). And when he walks upon the street, veiled faces look out through the windows and follow his footsteps with glowing eyes. . . . And hearts beat fast, with longing for the knightly singer. . . .

THE SHUNAMITE (*speaking with increasing ardor, oblivious of the presence of the king*). And when he sings or plays upon his harp, he stirs up a flood of wild desires in all hearts, and each one of us yearns to kiss his lips, to press close to his heart, to caress his locks, to pluck with our lips the golden glowing songs out of his breast and to swoon in his arms and . . .

(DAVID *strokes her neck with his hand.* THE SHUNAMITE *trembles and becomes silent.*)

DAVID (*passionately*). Shunamite, lay your head on my breast. . . .

(THE SHUNAMITE *shudders as though a cold wind were passing through her frame. She obeys mechanically.*)

DAVID.   Tell me, my beautiful child, would you still love that warrior, if you should see him now?

THE SHUNAMITE (*speaking cautiously*).   My love belongs to the king. . . .

DAVID (*with a sad smile*).   No, only your body. . . . You are too young to utter a falsehood, and you have nothing to gain thereby. . . . Tell me, would you love him very much?

THE SHUNAMITE (*looks at the king with mistrust for a moment, and then she nods her head.*)   Yes.

DAVID.   Even though he should be old, and look altogether different from the way you described him? . . .

THE SHUNAMITE.   But his songs, his sweet songs! . . .

DAVID.   And you would give him your youth and your love because of his sweet songs?

THE SHUNAMITE (*in a low voice*).   Yes! . . .

DAVID (*draws her to him suddenly with passionate ardor*).   Kiss me. . . . Pour your young and fruitful soul into my veins. . . .

(THE SHUNAMITE *puts her arms around him and kisses him slowly.*)

DAVID.   You are too cold. . . . Your hands are frosty, your lips are ice, and you are pale. . . . Fill me with that secret fire that flames within your breast. . . .

(THE SHUNAMITE *presses closely to him, struggling against her aversion.*)

DAVID.   Remember that you have promised to love. . . .

THE SHUNAMITE (*lifelessly*).   I have promised to do whatever the king may desire.

DAVID.   No, not that. . . . You have promised to love the singer of that song. . . .

(THE SHUNAMITE *looks at him confused.*)

DAVID.   I am that singer. . . .

THE SHUNAMITE (*staring at him*).   You? . . .

(*She measures him from head to foot, as if looking for the black locks, the broad shoulders and the mighty figure.*)

DAVID (*in answer to her searching look*).   Then, indeed, I was just as you have described me. . . .

(THE SHUNAMITE *shudders.*)

DAVID.   But the songs, the beautiful songs? . . .

THE SHUNAMITE (*coldly, with forced tenderness*).   I will do whatever the king may desire. . . .

CURTAIN FALLS SLOWLY

NOTES

AUSTRALIA

ABIGAIL MARSHALL was born in Melbourne, Australia. She started life as a pianiste and singer, but was soon diverted to the stage, appearing with George Rignold in "Henry V." She came to America, toured in many attractions, and created the rôle of *Alluna* in Rex Beach's "The Barrier" at the New Amsterdam Theater, and was leading woman for the late James O'Neill.

Her one-act play, "Dad and Mother," was presented by Thomas Wise, and several other one-act plays have toured in vaudeville, one lately appearing at the Euston Theater in London.

AUSTRIA

ARTHUR SCHNITZLER (1862——) was the son of Johann Schnitzler. He was born in Vienna May 15, 1862. He studied medicine and took his degree in his native city in 1885. There also he was on the staff of the Imperial General Hospital, from 1886 to 1888, and practiced medicine privately. Turning to literature he published "Anatol" in 1893, seven one-act dramas presenting a graceful and accurate though erotic picture of Viennese life. This was followed by a long list of plays and narratives, some of which went through many editions. His plays which have been translated into English are:

"Anatol" (1911) (played in the United States in 1912)
"Professor Bernhardi" (1913)
"The Green Cockatoo and Other Plays" (1913)
"Playing With Love" (1914)
"The Lonely Way" (1915)
"Intermezzo" (1915)
"Countess Mizzi" (1915)
"Comedies of Words" (1915)

Schnitzler's field is the one-act play, the short story and the sketch. He is distinctly Viennese and smartly modern. Although he possesses the technical skill of a genuine dramatist yet nowhere does he reach the depth of a great artist. Perhaps his best dramatic work is seen in "Peremseme," "Weg" and "Der Grüne Kakadu."

NOTE.—Consult J. G. Huneker's "Ivory Apes and Peacocks" (N. Y. 1915) or Ludwig Lewisohn's "The Modern Drama" (1915).

BELGIUM

MAURICE MAETERLINCK, the Belgian poet and playwright, was born in Gand in 1862. While very young he brought out a little volume of poems called *Les Serres Chaudes* in 1889.

His principal plays are:

    "La Princesse Maleine" (1889)
    "L'Intruse" (The Intruder) (1891)
    "Les Aveugles" (The Blind) (1891)
    "Les Sept Princesses" (1891)
    "Pelléas et Mélisande" (1892)
    "Alladine et Palomides" (1892)
    "Intérieur" (Interior) (1894)
    "La Mort de Tintagiles" (1894)
    "Aglavaine et Aelysette" (1896)

LATER

    "Sœur Beatrice" (Sister Beatrice)
    "L'Oiseau Bleu" (The Blue Bird)
    "Ardiane et Barbe Bleue" (Blue Beard)
    "Monna Vanna" (The Betrothal)

"L'Intruse" was presented at the "Théâtre d'Art" in 1891, and a little later "Les Aveugles" was produced in the same theater, followed by "Les Sept Princesses." In 1893 the Bouffes-Parisien company produced "Pelléas et Mélisande." In 1894 the Théâtre de L'Oeuvre produced "Intérieur."

Maeterlinck excelled in the expression of the obscure, the vague, the fearful, in the subconscious life of the soul. The last books that he has written are entitled, *The Treasure of the Humble* (1896), *Wisdom and Destiny* (1898) and *The Life of the Bee*. These three volumes are the work of an ingenious writer, of a sensitive and serious moralist, and also of a poet.

BENGAL

CHINTAMANI. This drama is mystical and symbolic, some of the meanings being entirely Hindu, *i.e.*, the snake for the rope. The figure has been used many times in the Upanishads, Gita and the other scriptures. Here it implies, "Love is blind when it is guided by passion." As to the word, "Unknowable" which the Pundit flings at Billwamangal, this "Unknowable" is used in the Upanishads in many senses—one being, God is unknowlable to the senses but not to the soul. In this case the author also makes fun of Herbert Spencer's chapter on the Unknowable in his *Synthetic Philosophy*. D. G. M.

GIRISH C. GHOSE from whose drama this adaptation was made died at Calcutta in 1913, at the age of sixty-two, leaving in print ninety-five plays and playlets. He was the father of the Hindu stage and was known as the "Hindu Shakespeare."

DHAN GOPAL MUKERJI was born in Calcutta of pure Brahmin stock. He matriculated at the University and remained there until the great exodus of students to the University of Tokio, where he studied textile engineering. He remained there for one year and then came to the decision that he did not care for the life of an engineer. He came to America and entered the University of California. Later he took his Bachelor of Arts degree at Leland Stanford University. He has since been on the lecture platform. His books of verse are *Sandhya, Rajani,* and *Maylaylanajnu.* He has published a volume of children's stories entitled *Kari, the Elephant,* and *Caste and Outcast,* an autobiographic work; *My Brother's Face,* etc.

BOHEMIA

JAROSLAV VRCHLICKY (Emil Frida) was born in Louny, February 17, 1853. At the age of ten he was sent to the Gymnasium of the Piarists in Prague, and later to the Gymnasium in Klatov. At the age of nineteen he graduated and entered a theological seminary, where he remained but for a few months. Entering the University of Prague, he selected as his major subjects literature, philology and history. In 1901 he and Anton Dvorak received from the Emperor an appointment to the Imperial Council, and were granted an order. He died in Domazlice, September 9, 1912, at the age of 59.

Vrchlicky's work totaled sixty-six volumes. He wrote 4,200 poems, three of which, "Bar Kochba," "Hilarion," and "Twardowski" have over 10,000 printed pages and ran through 130 editions. His translated plays are "At the Chasm," "The Vengeance Catullus," and "The Witness."

BURMA

"PYENTSA" exemplifies the popular tone of the Burman drama. The Ramadzat (Ramhahyana) and other ancient fabulous histories, form the ground-work of nearly all the favorite plays, the outline of the story being merely preserved, while the language of the play depends as much on the fancy of the performer as the taste of the audience. The director who presides over the company of performers drills his actors in their tasks from rough notes which contain only the songs and the substance of the parts assigned to each. In every play, without perhaps a single exception, the following characters are represented—a King, a Queen, a Princess, a Minister of State, a Huntsman, and some kind of Monster. The female characters are usually personated by men, it being considered indecorous in a woman to appear as an actress.

The original, from which this is translated, was written from the mouth of an actor.

CANADA

MERRILL DENISON has been hailed as the first playwright to have contributed an essentially Canadian play to the theater. The son of a noted radical and pioneer, Flora MacD. Denison, his education and training were distinguished by a breadth and freedom which helped to develop the accuracy of observation reflected in his plays. His mastery of the art of writing human and illuminating dialogue, coupled with a pungent sense of humor, mark his lighter comedies as the work of a keen satirist which, with the uncompromising realism of "Marsh Hay," shows his versatility as a playwright. "Brothers in Arms" is from his book "The Unheroic North."

CHINA

"THE THRICE-PROMISED BRIDE" is a Chinese folk-play written by Mr. Chen-Chin Hsiung of Nangchang, China, in the Course in Dramatic Composition and Production at the University of North Carolina for production by The Carolina Playmakers. It was published originally in *The Theatre Arts Magazine* for October, 1923.

The Playmakers, although interested primarily in the writing and producing of Folk-Plays of North Carolina, welcome such graduate students from other sections as may be interested in writing Folk-Plays of their own locality.

Mr. Hsiung came to America in 1918. He took the A.B. degree at the University of Wisconsin, and the A.M. at Cornell University. He came to Carolina primarily for advanced courses in the Department of English. He expects to return to China next fall to carry the Folk-Play idea back to his own people.

The author of "The Thrice-Promised Bride" informs us that this play is based on a folk-tale of old China, told in various versions, to Chinese children to teach them the lesson of filial piety and fidelity, and to impress them with the justice of their superiors. In the incident as it actually occurred the first candidate for the maiden's hand was faithful, and consequently won a beautiful and virtuous wife. He has been engaged to the girl, the daughter of his father's friend, before either of the children had been born—a form of marriage contract not uncommon in China. All the three candidates were insignificant, unromantic, common folks, who were brought to the Magistrate's court because of their rioting in the streets at the time of the interrupted wedding of "the thrice-promised bride." The excuse of long separation by war, flood, or examination is a device in the plot of many a Chinese drama.

Mr. Hsiung suggests that he has assigned the victory to the true lover, who, as in most Chinese plays or entertainments, usually wins out in spite of the customary adversities. He has drawn the characters from his own experience. Those of the Magistrate and the mother are in ironical contrast; at the first what seems benignant in the mother is really cruel, and what seems cruel in the Magistrate is really benignant in the end.

Another Chinese play which Mr. Hsiung wrote for The Carolina Play-makers, "The Marvellous Romance of Wen Chen Chin," will be published in an early issue of *Poet Lore*. Mr. Hsiung has a charming sense of humor, and writes with a naïveté of imagination and a freshness of phrase which our young American playwrights may well emulate. We predict that he will play an important part in the making of a new Chinese drama.

DENMARK

ALBERT THEODOR GNUDTZMANN was born, June 3, 1865, at Humble on the isle of Langeland in Denmark, and died in Copenhagen, October 23, 1912. The son of a clergyman, he began his literary career by writing for the stage. His first drama, "The Heirs of Peter Steen," was produced at the People's Theatre in Copenhagen in 1894. His next play was the one-act play "In Blindness" which was produced at the Royal Theatre in the Danish Capital in 1903 and is conceded by critics to be the finest thing Gnudtzmann has written. In its English version it has been named "Eyes That Cannot See." Then followed a comedy, "Feltmann's Collections" (1905), and several other plays in the lighter vein, all produced at leading theaters in Copenhagen, among them "The Baron," produced at the Dagmar Theatre in 1908.

In addition to his writings for the stage, he has published about a dozen novels, and as literary critic for the *Nationaltidende* in Copenhagen he contributed many criticisms of literary merit to the columns of this newspaper. He was also for many years the editor of a publication devoted to the theater.

FRANCE

"PIERRE PATELIN," "La Farce de Maître Patelin," is a 15th Century farce. They have not been able to discover the author, and it is without definite proofs that it has been attributed to Antoine de la Salle; to Pierre Blanchet and even to Villon. By the natural arrangement of the situations, by the careful drawing of the characters, the gayety of the dialogue and the vigor and vivacity of the style, "La Farce de Maître Patelin"—the only work of its period, is a real comedy. It has been adapted twice for the modern stage, in 1706 (by de Brueys and Palaprot) and in 1872 (by E. Fournier). Several modernizations of de Bruey's version are extant.

HOLLAND

HERMAN HEIJERMANS, one of the leading European dramatists, whose plays have been produced by the Moscow Art Theatre, Antoine's "Théâtre Libre," and other theaters almost equally significant, is practically unknown on this side of the water. His sea drama, "The Good Hope" (Op Hoop van Legen) played by Ellen Terry and published in *The Drama,* being the only one of his longer works which the English speaking public has had the opportunity to know, if we except a poor translation, or rather adaptation of "The Ghetto."

Among the forty or fifty dramas he has written are to be found ten or a dozen one act plays, as strong and gripping as his more important efforts.

A year ago the nine hundredth performance of "The Good Hope" was celebrated in Amsterdam. It was discovered that the evening was also the thirtieth anniversary of the production of his first play, "Dora Kramer."

Heijermans is now about fifty years old, writing vigorously, with an eye upon all the questions of the day.

HUNGARY

Lajos Biro was born in Vienna in 1880, brought up in a little Hungarian village, and later studied for the bar in Budapest. He left the law and tried banking for two years, and finally turned to journalism and literature. For a short time he helped to edit a small radical publication but soon left for the Sorbonne and the Latin Quarter. When he returned he became the editor of a daily newspaper and began to publish many short stories in *feuilleton* form. The best of these were brought out later in book form under the title "Iconoclasts." After serving in the army for a time, he became a correspondent of a large Budapest daily in Berlin, and while there wrote his first play "Familienherd." It was successfully produced at the Freie Bühne in Berlin and elsewhere. A year later his longer play "The Yellow Lily" was produced. "The Bridegroom" was one of a series forming an evening's entertainment under the title "The Home Circle." They were produced at the "Freie Bühne" in Berlin and were well received. "The Bridegroom" in which family hypocrisy is the accepted virtue—an old theme treated from a new angle; "The Grandmother" in which an old scandal is brought to light; and the third, "The Choice of a Profession," which is too true and too bold for puritan ears.

IRELAND

Douglas Hyde (An Craoibhin Aoibhinn) was born at Frenchpark, County Roscommon, Ireland. He was educated at Trinity College, Dublin. President of the Irish National Literary Society and President of the Gaelic League since its foundation in 1893. His plays written in Gaelic have been translated by Lady Gregory.

ITALY

Roberto Bracco was born in Naples in 1861. He has had novels and poetry published, and several notable and very successful comedies. "A Snowy Night" was first presented to an American audience by the late Washington Square Players.

JAPAN

Until very recently there still lingered in Japan the old aristocratic scorn of the common theater, but the theaters which were dedicated to the performance of the Noh plays have never had such stigma attached to them. These plays are wholly supported by the aristocratic and educated classes; they are, indeed, not unlike the old Greek plays in that they are semireligious. They really constitute the classical theater of Japan.

The Nohs, as they are now preserved, date principally from the fourteenth and early fifteenth centuries. They were given distinctive and definite form by Kiyotsugu (1355-1406) who compounded them from much older elements— pantomime dances with words written by Buddhist monks' ritual ceremonies, classical poetry and folk-tales.

Note on production:

The scenery should be suggestive rather than realistic and very subdued in color. The costumes, on the other hand, should be as rich and full of color as possible. The actors may or may not wear masks. The acting should at all times be formal so that every movement in the play suggests a Japanese print or a pattern on a willow-plate. Before the curtain rises a deep gong is struck and the Chorus, robed in blue or blue-gray enters through the audience; he moves to the extreme right of the stage, turns, and facing the audience, squats on his heels with his legs folded straight under him. In front of him he lays his fan, which remains closed throughout the whole play but is raised upright, with one end touching the floor, while he is chanting. The fan is laid down again the moment his words are finished.

Colin Campbell Clements for some reason or other refuses to tell his age or place of birth. He was until a few years ago a worker with the American Relief Committee of the Near East. While there he collaborated with Queen Marie, of Roumania, on several plays. Until last year he was connected with Professor George Pierce Baker at the "47 Workshop." He is the author of *Plays for a Folding Theater* and *Plays for Pagans*.

MEXICO

The Señora Doña Teresa Farias de Isassi is one of the most significant of the literary women of Mexico.

Educated in Mexico, her broad intelligence and progressive views have been developed and stimulated by contact with the centers of culture in Europe and North America but the essence of her thought remains distinctively Mexican and her writings reflect always the viewpoint of her country.

She is an indefatigable writer and, though still a young woman, has to her credit several novels, published in Mexico and Spain and numerous plays, most of which have been produced on both sides of the water.

Two of her plays, "Como las Aves," and "Cerebro y Corazón" were prize-winners in drama competitions instituted by the Direccion de las Bellas Artes. Others, equally well known, are "Religion de Amor" and "Sombra y Luz."

Her most important novels are *Nupcial* and *Ondina*.

Aside from her literary labors Señora de Isassi has many other active interests. She is the founder and director of the "Sociedad Protectora del Niño," a home for orphan boys, to which she devotes a great part of her time and much enthusiasm.

NORWAY

ALVILDE PRYDZ was born 5 August, 1848, on Tosteröd, the estate of her father near Fredrikshald in Norway, and by parentage of German and Danish descent. She died in September, 1922.

Beginning to write already at the age of fourteen, it was not until 1880 that she made her literary début, with a novel showing strong influence of Björnson. In her later work she gained in individuality. She took a lively interest in politics, particularly in the question of woman suffrage, one of the early champions of which she became.

By Ibsen and Björnson considered the foremost woman writer of their time in Scandinavia, her best known works are the novels *The Promised Land* (1903), translated into English by Hester Coddington; *Children of Hero* (1906); *While It Was Summer;* and *Thorbjörn Vik* (1913). The latter one has generally been accepted as her most important work. She also wrote several long plays, "Ainö" (first produced at the National Theatre at Christiania in 1900) and "Undine," and two one act plays "He Is Coming" and "In Confidence." Many of her works have been translated into foreign languages.

RUSSIA

ANTON CHEKOV (1860-1904) (Pavlovitch) is a famous Russian writer of the younger school, which includes Gorky, Andreev, and Artsybaskev. He was born at Taganrog (southern Russia) and although his parents, who were liberated serfs, were uneducated themselves, he himself received a good education. In 1884 he completed the medical course at the Moscow University, but soon decided to follow a literary career. His early work dating from 1879 consisted chiefly of humorous sketches appearing in the more popular periodicals under the pseudonym "Chekhonte." Encouraged by the suggestion that we are capable of worthier things, Chekhov approached his work more seriously and soon was hailed as the greatest figure in Russian literature since the days of Turgenev,—a distinction which, in a measure, is still his. He died, of tuberculosis, at 44, but into his short life he crowded the writing of over 150 short stories, a number of plays, and at least one full novel.

Most of his writings have been translated into English, German and French.

His plays which are available in English are

"The Sea Gull" (1905)
"The Cherry Orchard" (1908)
"The Swan Song" (1912)
"Uncle Vanya"
"Ivanoff"

His distinguishing characteristics are extreme compression, realism, complete aloofness, an unusual mastery of words and a sense of humor.

"ON THE HIGHWAY." The history of this play is this: "On the Highway" was written as early as 1884, but was forbidden by the Russian censorship and almost lost. When Chekov's literary executors were gathering material for a posthumous volume published in 1914, the censor's copy of the play was discovered by mere chance, its existence not having been suspected even by the author's most intimate literary friends. The manuscript still bore the official disapprobation—'Found unfit for presentation. September 20th, 1885." This translation has been made from the posthumous volume aforementioned (edited by Chekhov's wife and published in Moscow). D. A. M.

SPAIN

JOSE ECHEGARAY was born in Madrid in 1832. At an early age he showed marked propensities for mathematics and the exact sciences, but although he never lost interest in these studies, he became interested in literature, and the theater, and in later years made an extensive study of the drama. He was graduated in 1853 from the Escuela de Caminos, with high honors, and not long afterward, he was appointed to the professorship in mathematics in the same school.

At the age of thirty-two he wrote a play, but laid it aside, deeming it unworthy; but his interest in the theater was rapidly increasing. In 1873 he was proscribed, forced to leave the country, and go to France, where he wrote his first play to be produced, "El Libro Talonario." On his return to Spain in 1874, it was presented, but did not attract widespread attention. His first success was "En el Puño de La Espada" (1875), which was followed by a long series of comedies, tragedies and thesis plays. Echegaray died in 1916.

His translated plays are:

"Folly or Saintliness";
"Madman or Saint";
"The Great Galeoto";
"The Son of Don Juan";

"Marianna";
"The Man in Black";
"The Madman Divine";
"Always Ridiculous."

SWEDEN

HANS ALIN is one of the younger generation of writers of Sweden following in the path of Strindberg, who took a kindly interest in him and who was mainly instrumental in getting his first play produced at the Swedish Theatre at Stockholm. Alin, now just past his twenties, was then only sixteen. He is perhaps the most promising of the younger playwrights of Sweden to-day, and several of his plays have already been acted outside of his own country. His plays number about a dozen, almost all in the serious vein. His best known play is "Mother and Son," which has been acted in Sweden periodically since its original presentation there in 1918. This play, dealing with the subject of capital punishment, has been ascribed as one of the causes for the removal of this form of punishment from the penal statutes of Sweden. Other plays by this author are: "Charles XII," a historical drama in four acts; "Robespierre," a play of the French Revolution, in five acts; "Benja," a play of Gypsy life; and a number of short plays.

Having finished his studies in Sweden, he spent some years in Berlin and Paris as correspondent for Swedish newspapers and periodicals. He is now gathering impressions of the theater and the music life in America, serving as critic on the leading Swedish newspaper in New York. On his return to Sweden he will there publish his impressions in book form.

TURKEY

IZZET-MELYH, like all the young Turkish writers of the present day, wrote in the French language, considering it superior in richness, as a medium for literary expression.

It is only in very recent years, scarcely half a century, that there has been any dramatic literature in Turkey, owing to political and social conditions which are opposed to the development of the arts in general and the theater in particular.

One reason for this retarded development is the severity of the censorship which at any moment may forbid all intellectual production. Another is the decided preference of the Turkish people for such sports as fighting, horse racing, and javelin throwing. But the third and most important reason for the late development of the theater arts, is the harem, since it forbids women to show themselves in public, hence on the stage.

It is with this important social problem, its merits and demerits, and the influence on the morals of Turkish women, that Izzet-Melyh deals, in his play "Léïla."

UNITED STATES

DRANSFIELD (JANE) was born in Rochester, New York, and was educated in the city schools. She later attended Vassar College and has since then lived in New York City. She is known as a poet as well as a playwright. Her best known plays and most popular in production are "The Lost Pleiad," a poetic fantasy, and "Joe, a Hudson Valley Play."

(1)

DRAMATIC ANTHOLOGIES

FIFTY CONTEMPORARY ONE-ACT PLAYS

Selected and Edited by Frank Shay and Pierre Loving

Chosen from the dramatic works of contemporary writers all over the world by two men who have been connected for many years with Little Theatres in the United States. $5.00.

25 SHORT PLAYS INTERNATIONAL

Edited by Frank Shay

A collection of the shorter masterpieces of the World's theatre. Here are the stage successes of the Moscow Art Theatre, the Royal Theatres of Madrid and Copenhagen, the Washington Square Players, the Provincetown Theatre, plays by Heijermans, Bracco, Chekov, Chin-Cheng Hsuing, Echegaray and others. $4.00

TWENTY CONTEMPORARY ONE-ACT PLAYS (AMERICAN)

Edited by Frank Shay

A selection of the best one-act plays written by Americans and produced by little theatres in America in 1921. A companion volume to **Fifty Contemporary One-Act Plays**. $3.75.

THE PROVINCETOWN PLAYS

Edited by
George Cram Cook and Frank Shay
Introduction by Hutchins Hapgood

The Provincetown Players are, save perhaps the Theatre Guild, the most progressive Little Theatre group in America. The ten plays in this volume are a record of the Players' achievements. They were selected, it is well to remark, before "The Emperor Jones," their most successful production, had been played. $2.50.

ONE THOUSAND AND ONE PLAYS FOR THE LITTLE THEATRE

Selected and Compiled by Frank Shay

An exhaustive list of short plays suitable for use by amateurs and little theatres. $1.00.

D. APPLETON AND COMPANY   **PUBLISHERS**

Fifty Contemporary One-Act Plays

Edited by
FRANK SHAY and PIERRE LOVING

THIS volume contains FIFTY REPRESENTATIVE ONE-ACT PLAYS of the MODERN THEATER, chosen from the dramatic works of contemporary writers all over the world and is the second volume in *The Appleton Dramatic Anthologies*, the first being European Theories of the Drama, by Barrett H. Clark, which has been so enthusiastically received.

The editors have scrupulously sifted countless plays and have selected the best available in English. One-half the plays have never before been published in book form; thirty-one are no longer available in any other edition.

The work satisfies a long-felt want for a handy collection of the choicest plays produced by the art theaters all over the world. It is a complete repertory for a little theater, a volume for the study of the modern drama, a representative collection of the world's best short plays.

CONTENTS

Large 8vo, 585 pages. Net, $5.00
Special India Paper Edition, less than one-half inch thick.
Limp Cloth, net, $6.00; Limp Leather, net, $7.50.